Henry Morley, John Milton

English Prose Writings

Henry Morley, John Milton

English Prose Writings

ISBN/EAN: 9783744685481

Printed in Europe, USA, Canada, Australia, Japan

Cover: Foto ©Thomas Meinert / pixelio.de

More available books at **www.hansebooks.com**

THE
CARISBROOKE LIBRARY
V.

THE

CARISBROOKE LIBRARY.

THE UNIVERSAL LIBRARY, now completed in sixty-three cheap shilling volumes, has included English versions of the "Iliad," of all extant plays of the Greek tragedians, and of some plays of Aristophanes, of Sanskrit fables, and of Virgil's "Æneid." It has followed the course of time with English versions of the most famous works of Dante, Boccaccio, Machiavelli, Rabelais, Cervantes, Molière, as recast by English dramatists, of Goethe's "Faust" and of Schiller's Poems. It has given currency also to a series of the works of English writers, representative, as far as limits would allow, of our own literature, from Richard of Bury's "Philobiblon" to Sheridan's Plays and Emerson's Essays. In the sequence of publication variety was aimed at, but in the choice of books to be published there was always the unity of purpose that now allows the volumes to be arranged in historical order, illustrating some of the chief epochs of European literature, and especially of English literature, in the long course of time.

THE CARISBROOKE LIBRARY, now begun, will continue the work of its predecessor, with some changes of form and method. It will include books for which the volumes of the former series did not allow sufficient room. Sometimes in the "Universal Library" a large book—Hobbes's "Leviathan," for example—was packed into small type. In the "Carisbrooke Library" there will be no small type.

The volumes will be larger; each of about four hundred and fifty pages. They will be handsome library volumes, printed with clear type upon good paper, at the price of half-a-crown, and they will be published in alternate months. In the "Universal Library" the editor's introduction to each volume was restricted to four pages, and there was no annotation. In the "Carisbrooke Library," with larger leisure and a two months' interval between the volumes, it will be possible for the editor to give more help towards the enjoyment of each book. There will be fuller introductions, and there will be notes.

In the "Carisbrooke Library," as in the predecessor of which it is an extension, there will be order in disorder. Variety will be still aimed at in sequence of the volumes, while the choice of books to be issued will be still guided by the desire to bring home to Englishmen, without unfair exclusion of any form of earnest thought, as far as may be, some living knowledge of their literature along its whole extent, and of its relations with the wisdom and the wit of the surrounding world.

HENRY MORLEY.

THE CARISBROOKE LIBRARY.

VOLUME I. THE TALE OF A TUB, AND OTHER WORKS, BY JONATHAN SWIFT.
  " II. TALES OF THE SEVEN DEADLY SINS, BEING THE "CONFESSIO AMANTIS" OF JOHN GOWER.
  " III. THE EARLIER LIFE, AND THE CHIEF EARLIER WORKS OF DANIEL DEFOE.
  " IV. EARLY PROSE ROMANCES.
  " V. ENGLISH PROSE WRITINGS OF JOHN MILTON.
  " VI. (*In November*) PARODIES AND OTHER PIECES OF BURLESQUE.

ENGLISH PROSE WRITINGS OF MILTON.

ENGLISH PROSE WRITINGS

OF

JOHN MILTON

EDITED BY

HENRY MORLEY, LL.D.

LONDON
GEORGE ROUTLEDGE AND SONS
BROADWAY, LUDGATE HILL
GLASGOW, MANCHESTER, AND NEW YORK
1889

CONTENTS.

	PAGES
INTRODUCTION	11–48

GOD AND MAN—
  Of Reformation Touching Church Discipline in England, and the Causes that hitherto have hindered it. In Two Books. Written to a Friend 49–108
  The Reason of Church Government urged against Prelacy. In Two Books 109–182

MAN AND WIFE—
  The Doctrine and Discipline of Divorce. In Two Books. To the Parliament of England, with the Assembly 183–294

MAN AND CHILD—
  Of Education. A Letter to Samuel Hartlib . . 295–308

MAN AND MAN—
  Areopagitica: a Speech for the Liberty of Unlicensed Printing. To the Parliament of England 309–352
  The Tenure of Kings and Magistrates . . . 353–392

FREEDOM IN CHURCH AND STATE—
  A Treatise of Civil Power in Ecclesiastical Causes . 393–422
  The Ready and Easy Way to Establish a Free Commonwealth, and the Excellence thereof, compared with the Inconveniences and Dangers of readmitting Kingship in this Nation. First published in 1660 423–446

MILTON.

Milton, thou should'st be living at this hour;
England hath need of thee; . . .
 . . . .
    . . . We are selfish men;
Oh, raise us up, return to us again;
And give us manners, virtue, freedom, power.
Thy soul was like a star, and dwelt apart:
Thou hadst a voice whose sound was like the sea
Pure as the naked heavens, majestic, free,
So didst thou travel on life's common way,
In cheerful godliness; and yet thy heart
The lowliest duties on herself did lay.
       —WORDSWORTH.

INTRODUCTION.

THIS volume contains all those Prose Writings of Milton in which he set forth, as he himself thought best, his views on all that is most vital to the body politic. The people make the state, and their well-being is dependent chiefly upon their religious life, their home life, the right training of their children and a civil government adapted to their highest needs. I have grouped Milton's papers under headings which show that they cover all this ground, and deal only with these essentials of citizenship.

There are omitted from this volume all the writings in which Milton replied to the opponents of his views. The controversies of 250 years ago travelled by many paths in which we care no longer to assert a right of way. At all times, the Reformer who is answering opponents has his course of argument determined by the reason or the unreason of other men. Forms of reply dependent upon accidents of the attack are only to be read with measured judgment by those who have read the attack also; and often when we have read both, we have heard a sound of battle in the air that has appealed to our imaginations and disturbed our judgment. The battle of opinion rolls forward to new ground from century to century. The great truths are immutable, the applications of them vary with the change of time.

But when a writer who looks to the highest aims of life and is concerned only with its highest interests has resolved to set forth opinions to the world, and having, as Milton says, summoned up all his reason and deliberation to assist him, searched, meditated, been industrious, and likely consulted and conferred with his judicious friends, he arranges the expression of his thought as he best can, he meets as he goes the objections that are likely to arise from men of differing opinion, ranging all to the utmost of his own capacity into one clear enforcement of what he thinks is for the public good. Of course, also, he applies as he goes his principles,—immutable, if they be true,—to mutable condition of the time for which he writes.

In that way Milton wrote the pieces that are here collected. Of every argument that seemed to strike too boldly against custom and tradition he had to continue the defence against hot controversialists at a time when controversy was a graceless work. And even now it is of little grace. We have not learnt yet how much that most necessary factor in the progress of the world would gain in reason by the loss of passion, how much force there is in fairness, and that only poverty of spirit turns debate to quarrel. Milton's "Eikonoklastes" is an answer to "Eikon Basilike," following that work section by section. The famous Latin works in defence of the People of England were replies to attacks. But the defence in each case is of principles which Milton had set forth in his own way, and upon his own motion, in his treatise on "The Tenure of Kings and Magistrates." Only that treatise falls, therefore, within the plan of this collection of Milton's reasonings upon the principles that should control the settlement of Church and State. To bring the whole collection within the compass of one volume it has been necessary that the suggestion of a plan for the establishment of a Free Commonwealth should be given at the close of the book in smaller type, and that whatever may be said by way of annotation should be confined to the Introduction. Inasmuch as the purpose of this volume is to enable many readers to know clearly for themselves what Milton really taught in his prose writings, and inasmuch as he wrote with an emphasis that made his meaning upon each point in the argument entirely clear, there may, after all, be some advantage in the enforced absence of notes. Notes might possibly divert too much attention from the main course of the argument, by establishing a side interest in many scholarly allusions to books now seldom read and facts known but to few. Thus we lose the fuller sense of wit and knowledge used for illustration and enforcement of each thought; but this is partly, perhaps, compensated by the gain of a less broken attention to the substance and the continuity of reasoning.

All the great books in the world deal with essentials. Those written in former time are of the past and of the present, as those written now are of the present and the future. The true reader of the true old book looks to the soul of it, and while hearing that speak to the day for which it lived and worked, adapts its voice also to the changed conditions of the later day in which it may be still living and working. Custom and tradition have confined too much the reading of Milton's reasonings on Church and State within a narrow circle. Much that he battled for has been already won. The Church of England now leaves conscience free. Our Monarchy has lost its despotism: were Milton living now how would he shape to these our days his exhortation to look upward and be free? Still, if we read them with clear eyes, there is a life beyond life in the prose writings of John Milton.

Of Milton himself, as he was when he published them, let us recall first the memory; then, looking at the time for which he wrote, fix our attention on the purport of his teaching, as it concerned those times and these. We shall not be less loyal subjects or worse Churchmen, but we shall be stronger men to-day for taking Milton into council.

John Milton was born in the reign of James the First, at his father's house in Bread Street, Cheapside, on the 9th of December 1608. That was between seven and eight years before the death of Shakespeare. The Milton family was of Oxfordshire, and in early times may have been named from the Oxfordshire village of Great Milton, about eight miles from Oxford near Halton and Thame. There are some eighteen Miltons in different parts of England, groups of homesteads that first took this name from the wind or water mill conspicuous among them. The poet's grandfather was probably a Richard Milton of Stanton St. Johns, about half a mile from Forest Hill, near the royal forest of Shotover (*Chateau vert*). He is also said to have been a John Milton, living at Holton, which is two miles from Stanton St. Johns, and to have been underranger of Shotover Forest. He is known to have remained a Roman Catholic after the Reformation; and there is record that Richard Milton of Stanton St. Johns was as late as 1601 in the roll of recusants. Twenty pounds a month being the price of his opinions, he was fined £60 for absence from his parish church during three months dated from the 6th of December 1600, and another £60 for three months from the 13th of July 1601, as he had "neither made submission nor promised to be conformable, pursuant to the act." Milton's father, John Milton, whose birth-date may have been very near to that of Shakespeare, was sent to Oxford for study at Christ Church, but he accepted the teaching of the Church Reformers, conformed to the Church as established by Elizabeth, and was then cast off by his father. At a date near to the time when Shakespeare came to London, John Milton the elder came to London, learned the business of a scrivener, and practised it very successfully in Bread Street. He married, probably, about the year 1600; and he had six children, of whom three died in infancy. The three who lived were Anne, a few years older than her brother John; John, born on the 9th of December 1608; and Christopher, who was seven years younger. Between John and Christopher two daughters were born who died, so that until the age of seven John Milton was the only son. Bread Street, when Milton's father settled there, was a street which Stow described as wholly inhabited by rich merchants, and with divers fair inns for good receipt of carriers and other travellers. It is clear that, through family connections now not to be traced, Milton's father had some money of his own when he was cast out from home. He could not have traded as a money scrivener without a little capital from which to make his loans. Milton the poet also had, in his father's lifetime, when he went to Cambridge, money of his own.

John Milton the father was, then, a religious man, not without university training. He had suffered for his fidelity to conscience. His religious character would influence his choice of friends; but among his friends also were some of the chief musicians of the day, for the bent of his own genius was towards music. Seven years before the birth of his poet son he had contributed one (the eighteenth) to a collection of twenty-five madrigals in praise of Queen Elizabeth—"The Triumphs of Oriana." To this work the chief living musicians were contributors, and its editor was Thomas Morley. When his son was a child of six, John Milton, the father, joined again a company of chief musicians of the day, by contributing the music to three pieces in a volume of "Teares and Lamentations of a Sorrowfull Soule." When his son was a boy of thirteen, John Milton, the father, again joined with chief musicians of the day as one of the contributors of harmonised tunes for the whole Book of Psalms from the church psalmody of Europe. The tunes known as Norwich and York are those which the elder Milton harmonised, and Sir John Hawkins said in his "History of Music" that within memory half the nurses in England were used to sing the tenor part of York tune by way of lullaby, and that the chimes of many country churches had played it for many years six or eight times in four and twenty hours.

So Milton grew up as a child, with his father's earnest life breathing its harmonies about him; in care of a mother of whom we hear only that her health was delicate and that she was most known for her charities, and with his sister Anne for a small guide and senior companion. When he was five years old there was another sister born, Tabitha, who lived to be two years and a half, and died five or six months after the birth of Christopher. He had also as teacher before he was sent to a public school, a graduate of St. Andrews and licentiate of the Scottish Kirk, Thomas Young of Loncardy, who had afterwards as a Puritan divine a living in Suffolk, and was made Master of Jesus College, Cambridge. The relation with this early tutor became affectionate, and Milton, writing to him afterwards from college, addressed him as almost a second father.

Milton was ten years old when there came to London a young Dutch painter, Cornelius Jansen, who settled in Blackfriars and took portraits at five broad pieces a head. Milton the father, proud of his elder son, had young John Milton's portrait painted by Cornelius Jansen, and it still remains.

About two years after the painting of the portrait, Milton was sent in his twelfth year to St. Paul's School, where the headmaster was Dr. Alexander Gill the elder, who had a son of his, Alexander Gill the younger, to assist him. Young Alexander Gill had a rough temper, as incidents of his own life show, and those were days of much severity in teaching. But here again there sprang up an affectionate relation between Milton and his teacher. The boy wrote verses; he has allowed us to see no more than a few attempts at versifying psalms, and wisely destroyed all other of his schoolboy rhymes. Alexander Gill the younger was, possibly, the best writer of Latin and Greek verse in his time. Here was a ground of fellowship; and we afterwards find Milton at college asked his opinion of verses sent to him by his old teacher at St. Paul's.

The austerity of Milton is a vulgar error. Such errors rise in clouds from the dry dust of traditional opinion, are much blown to and fro, and get into our eyes and partly blind us, till we wipe them out. In Milton's case it was party feeling that obscured the truth in the first instance, and with other men that is a frequent cause of great misunderstanding. It is not easy to know the truth even about a living man whose life is involved in controversies that excite strong feeling. Milton was not austere. In the height of the excitement caused by the chief controversy of the Commonwealth, when Milton had addressed to Europe his Latin Defence of the English People, and a Dutch scholar wanted to know something about a man whose name was new to him, the information gathered put in the forefront of Milton's character that he was "mitis, comes"—gentle, companionable. Those were the only qualities expressly named; the rest of his merits were contained in an etcetera, "multisque aliis præditus virtutibus"— endowed with many other virtues. So wrote Isaac Voss to

Nicholas Heinsius, upon information sought and obtained from Francis Junius, then living in England and cultivating John Milton's familiar acquaintance. When, many years after Milton's death, it was desired to find the relative truthfulness of several portraits by appeal to the memory of his surviving daughter, at the sight of one portrait, we are told, she broke into tears and said, "That is my father; that is my dear father. He was the life of every company he was in." In his later years, Milton's sense of the need of fellowship to man's true life was shown in his custom of giving two hours of the evening of every day to intercourse with friends, when he was visited or paid visits, and shared easy talk over his pipe.

A boy apt for friendship is likely to find in a large school some companion who has that likeness in essentials and diversity in accidents on which a lifelong friendship can be based. Milton at school found such a friend in Charles Diodati, son of Dr. Theodore Diodati, an Italian Protestant, practising with much success as a physician in London. Giovanni Diodati, who settled as a divine at Geneva—where he was Professor of Hebrew and translated the Bible into Italian—was Theodore's younger brother; Charles Diodati's uncle. When Milton went to Cambridge, his friend Diodati had already gone to Oxford. This friendship remained close and unbroken.

Milton was admitted to Christ's College, Cambridge, on the 12th of February 1625, returned then to London, was at home when James the First died on the 27th of March, and began his actual work at the University by matriculating on the 9th of April. He was in his seventeenth year when he became a Cambridge student, in the first days of the reign of Charles the First. The age of the new king was five-and-twenty. The last family event in Milton's home before he passed from school to college had been the marriage of his sister Anne to Mr. Edward Phillips, who had a good place in the Crown Office. A daughter was born to her in the winter of 1625–26; the infant caught a winter chill and died. The earliest original verse of Milton's that comes down to us is a piece "On a fair infant dying of a cough," devoted to the consolation of his sister. It was so entirely private that Milton did not include it among his poems when he made the first collection of them in 1645, but in the second edition, published by him twenty-eight years later, in the year before that of his death, calm recollections of the past caused this piece to be for the first time included.

On the 26th of March 1629 Milton took his B.A. degree. On the Christmas day of that year, when his age was one-and-twenty, he began his Hymn on the Morning of Christ's Nativity. His epigrams, Latin verses, written as memorials of dead worthies upon whose palls such offerings were laid, still represent the young poet's verse inspired by love to God and love to man. In 1631 the unexpected death of the young Marchioness of Winchester, lamented by Ben Jonson and other poets, drew also from young Milton lines of sympathy. In July 1632 he proceeded at Cambridge to his M.A. degree, and in that year his first printed verses appeared. They were lines of reverence to Shakespeare, printed before the second folio of his plays, then published.

A year before, when the University life was drawing to a close, and he was twenty-three years old, Milton had written on his birthday a sonnet of self-dedication. He did not count himself to have attained, and found in his late spring few signs of ripened power; yet he said—

> "Be it less or more, or soon or slow,
> It shall be still in strictest measure even
> To that same lot, however mean or high,
> Towards which Time leads me, and the will of Heaven.
> All is, if I have grace to use it so,
> As ever in my great Task Master's eye."

Afterwards, to his friend Charles Diodati, who asked what he was doing, Milton answered, "Let me whisper in your ear, lest I blush at the reply. I dream, so help me Heaven, of immortality, but my Muse rises as yet on very slender pinions; let us be humbly wise."

When the time came for leaving college, Milton felt himself to be shut out from the service of the Church, which his father had desired that he should enter, by conditions that appeared to tie his conscience. He tells himself at the close of that earnest review of his own past which forms the Introduction to the second part of his "Reason of Church Government" (page 155 of this volume), that to the service of the Church he was destined from childhood by his parents and friends and by his own resolutions: "'Till coming to some maturity of years, and perceiving what tyranny had invaded the Church, that he who would take orders must subscribe slave, and take an oath withal, which, unless he took with a conscience that could retch, he must either straight perjure or split his faith; I thought it better to prefer a blameless silence before the sacred office of speaking, bought and begun with servitude and forswearing." Having been thus, as he says, "Church outed" by the prelates, he has the better right to meddle with restraints of which he had himself been made to feel the hurt.

Milton's University course was complete when he took his M.A. degree in July 1632. What had been, meanwhile, the course of public events that so influenced his mind as to make him feel that he could not take orders in a Church of which Archbishop Laud had the direction?

William Laud was born at Reading in 1573, a clothier's son. He was educated at the Reading Grammar School, and went on to Oxford. There he became a Fellow of St. John's. From the first, at Oxford, he was eager and zealous in controversy on religious questions of the day, eager to check deviations from Church rule. His bias was towards authority, and he used with an absolute sincerity his great intellectual energy against the Puritans. Under James the First he obtained Church livings at Stanford in Northamptonshire, at North Kilworth in Leicestershire, at Cuckstone in Kent. In 1611 he was elected President of his College; then he became Chaplain to the King; and in 1616—year of the death of Shakespeare—Dr. Laud, who was then forty-three years old, and had taken the degree of D.D. eight years before, was made Dean of Gloucester. In 1617 he went with King

James to Scotland, and advised the King to endeavour to bring the Scotch clergy into conformity with the ritual of the English Church.

William Laud, fifty-two years old, was Bishop of St. David's when Charles the First came to the throne and Milton became a student at Cambridge. Laud officiated as Dean of Westminster at Charles's coronation. Soon afterwards he was translated to the Bishopric of Bath and Wells. Two years later, in 1628, he became Bishop of London. In the August of that year the Duke of Buckingham was stabbed by Felton. Laud then succeeded to his influence over the counsels of the King. Milton had taken his degree of Bachelor of Arts and had written his Hymn on the Morning of the Nativity when Dr. Laud, Bishop of London, became (in 1630) Chancellor of the University of Oxford. To that University, and to St. John's College especially, Laud was a most liberal benefactor. He built the inner quadrangle of his College; built the Convocation House and the Library above it; and presented to the University thirteen hundred valuable MSS. in Hebrew, Syriac, Chaldee, and other languages.

In 1632, when the battle for uniformity, with Dr. Laud as its chief leader, brought such pressure on the consciences of preachers that Milton could not take orders, Laud had not yet been made Archbishop of Canterbury. That office did not become vacant until the death of Dr. George Abbot on the 4th of August 1633, when Dr. William Laud was at once appointed to succeed him.

Of his labours in the Church, Laud himself said frankly and truly in his trial in 1643, "Of all diseases, I have ever hated a palsy in religion, well knowing that too often a dead palsy ends that disease in the fearful forgetfulness of God and His judgments. Ever since I came in place, I laboured nothing more than that the external public worship of God, too much slighted in most parts of the kingdom, might be preserved, and that with as much decency and uniformity as might be; being still of opinion that Unity cannot long continue in the Church when Uniformity is shut out at the church door. And I evidently saw that the public neglect of God's service in the outward face of it, and the nasty lying of many places dedicated to that service, had almost cast a damp upon the true and inward worship of God; which, while we live in the body, needs external helps, and all little enough to keep it in any vigour." This was the battle for securing Unity of Worship by the maintenance of one uniform Ceremonial, in which, Milton saw only "the ghost of a linen decency." In this battle Laud, eager—too eager—for attack, was a most honest and unflinching leader.

Let me say here, what cannot be said too often, or felt too strongly, when great controversies stir the minds and hearts of men. Diversities of mind are like diversities of face; races and families have their prevailing characters, but each man, whatever the sway of heredity or of the accidents of life, has a distinct character of his own. God made us to differ, and our currents of opinions, with their storms and eddies, are as much a part of the divine purpose in Nature as the currents of the air and sea. A little slope of the axis upon which this earth turns daily in its yearly course about the sun, gives us the alternation of the seasons, seed-time and harvest, fills the year with its varieties of charm. A little variation of the direction of slope, so to speak, in the plane surface of the mind establishes the countless differences in the bias,—inclination,—that determines the direction in which thought will run. A round shot on the middle of a sheet of paper held horizontally has as many ways of running to the edge, determined by slight variations of the slope, as we can imagine lines drawn from it. While accidents of life indefinitely multiply distinctions of character among us, every man's character is, in a way, governed by the action of that bias which Nature has established. He acts by it as part of the one divine thought which all Nature expresses. He lives and works by it in the evolution of man as a part of Nature. He is, through it, man taking the image of God by exercise of that one spiritual energy which alone of all things human lifts us to a sense of the divine. In the spiritual as in the physical world, there can be no health in unexercised powers. Man grows by struggle from the lower to the higher life; and for this evolution there is, I believe, divine provision made in those balanced variations of the ways of thought which give rise to our controversies in the search for truth. There may be some man with a mind wholly unbiassed, and, as the shot would stay wherever it is placed upon a level sheet of paper, so on his mind a thought might move in no direction. If there be men subject to this accident of birth, it is to be hoped that they are all well cared for in asylums for the imbeciles and idiots.

A stagnant mind is as a stagnant pool. For the social and spiritual growth of man, our conflicts of opinion provide means as sure as any that help on to the material advancement of our power. We might conceive the minds of men classified into natural orders, genera, and species, and all that produce blossom and fruit ranged under two great families like those of plants which the botanists call exogens and endogens. The exogens grow, like the oak, by additions on their outside; endogens, like the palm, grow by additions within. They differ altogether in that matter of the way of growth, yet they are both right trees. The characteristic difference that would establish two such families for all the thousand thousand forms of thought would lie, I believe, in the degree of bias towards or from Authority.

We agree in thinking that we owe our whole present civilisation to the wisdom of all generations of the past, against which we have now to set only the wisdom and the yet unwinnowed follies of that one generation to which we belong. We all agree also that progress has been due to changes made in each generation for adaptation to the growth of new conditions. We differ only in the degree of stress laid by each one of us on either half of this whole truth.

To some of us Nature has given the stronger bias towards Authority. We hold by the old ways until those eager for change can make their reason for it clear, and overcome our logical—sometimes, while civilisation is yet low, our forcible—resistance. With this bias is associated strong fidelity not only to the Authority of the Past, as an abstraction, but to individual authority established in the Church and in the State, with loyal maintenance of all existing institutions. In all relations of life this bias shows itself—in the home, the place of business, the Church, the State. Our name in the State is rightly chosen from a word of Burke's, that represents our necessary healthy part in the great argument of life—we are Conservative.

To some of us Nature has given the stronger bias towards search for some direction in which to make that beneficial change which is contributed by each generation to the advancement of mankind. We are so many men with so many opinions, each of us most believing in his own ideas, but not all of us urging ideas that would benefit the world. We make our suggestions for the re-shaping of old institutions that have become more or less unsuited to the new conditions of life, and it is well for us that we have to bring all our opinions out into the open ground and meet the serried ranks of men who require proof, and much proof. Only that project of reform which conquers opposition is allowed to pass from theory to practice. If our suggestion prove right in the trial, it is added to the institutions of the country, which the whole body of those who had been our opponents will now join us in preserving. With this bias we associate a strong fidelity to the spirit of individual freedom, and our tendency being towards the questioning and testing of authority, we are apt to consider, as well of the positions of single men as of established institutions, whether, and if so where and how, they can be advantageously reformed. In all relations of life this bias shows itself. In our homes we are given to the readjustment of tables and chairs which conservative wives, brothers, or sisters are anxious to put back in their established places. We often thrive by it in business, and often ruin ourselves by it. We are active for the reformation of the Church and of the State, and in the State we call ourselves, from the spirit of liberty that we cherish, Liberals. But the word liberal has in its common use another sense equally applicable to the right-minded men of all forms of opinion. The correlative word to Conservative would be Reformer.

Lord Brougham, an ardent Reformer, thought it matter of lament that it takes about thirty years to get a reform of any kind accepted and established in this country. I think that matter of rejoicing. Thirty years are but one generation in the story of collective man, and if all the good ideas started at the beginning of one generation could be reasoned out, carefully winnowed from the bad, established and accepted, by the time that generation passed, we should come perhaps too soon into the New Jerusalem.

If these things be so, then it is very clear that the rate of advance in any nation will be in proportion to the freedom given to the working of this great machinery of Nature in the minds of men. If England has made more progress than her neighbours, it may be chiefly because in this country we have taken, when it has not been allowed to us; we have battled for throughout, as for a cardinal principle; the free right of saying what we think. We have given freer play than any other people to those forces of our nature through which alone collective man can go on with slow growth towards the ideal of what Tennyson has called "the crowning race"

> " Of those that, eye to eye, shall look
>   On knowledge; under whose command
>   Is Earth and Earth's, and in their hand
> Is Nature like an open book.
>
> No longer half akin to brute,
>   For all we thought and loved and did,
>   And hoped and suffered, is but seed
> Of what in them is flower and fruit."

It was the sense that this right of free speech, for the full and thorough scrutiny of all forms of opinion, the complete deliberation that should precede all action, is the cardinal principle in our whole social system, the very eye by which we see, or say, the air we need to breathe, that caused Milton to put his utmost energy into the writing of his "Areopagitica, or Defence of the Liberty of Unlicensed Printing."

But if we are to see God's work in the diversity of minds and thank God for our conflicts of opinions; if we are only to see Nature working in the storms and eddies of our thought; shall we fight our battles still as heretofore? Not quite as heretofore, for infirmities of passion will be less liable to make our reasonings infirm. But Nature will not work in us the less for our knowing the fact. Hearts do not cease to beat in men who study their anatomy. Each of us who is worth anything to his neighbour would labour still for what he holds to be the highest right. The difference would all be in the better temper. Men would not then be drawn aside by passion from a clear view of the case they had to meet; reason would try fair issues with reason. Each side would work steadily at the shaking of the sieve that parts wheat from the chaff, and we might get a controversy settled in ten years instead of thirty. There is large scope for feeling, within bounds of reason. Logic has double force when its quick wit is warm with healthy generous emotion. But envy, hatred, malice are diseases of the mind; they cannot help to set a man's life or the world, or any part, however small, of the world's work to rights.

We see Milton in his prose writings an absolute type of the Reformer. He finds man enslaved to Custom and determines to think for himself. He will test all other authority by Scripture and Reason. In the Church he demands Liberty of Conscience, and by direct reference to Scripture and Reason he strives for the reform of the Reformation. In the Home he boldly faces custom in his pleading for higher regard to the spiritual end of marriage, and a consequent reform of marriage laws. For the School he boldly sketches a plan of reform regardless of tradition. In the State he argues for the development and the protection of the individual; and this volume closes with his outline of a plan of his own for the reconstitution of the Commonwealth. Everywhere he respects individual opinion that does not seek to force itself on others. He is intolerant only of intolerance.

Milton aimed at highest truth and highest purity through the conditions in Church and State by which he thought there would be nearest approach to these among the people. He set forth his views with the enthusiasm of a poet and a zealous patriotism. Laud was a type of the other bias of opinion as to the best way of attaining highest truth and highest purity, the aim of both. Instead of claiming for each man a right to form his own opinions from the reading of the Bible, Laud limited the right to points on which the Church had left opinion free. He saw in a claim for complete individual freedom the danger of confusion in the Church, indefinite encouragement to heresy and schism. He looked, as Churchmen had been looking through centuries, for Christian unity in uniformity of doctrine and of ceremonial, although he was ready to allow a wider range for freedom of opinion than had been allowed by Rome or by Geneva. Laud saw in the scrupulous regard for ceremonial, that Milton disdained, a visible sign of respect for public worship which would help the thoughtless into at least decent habits of religion, that would make the people bow as with one act of worship, breathe its prayers as from one soul before the throne of God. To secure this end Authority must be maintained; men, for their own good, must be compelled to worship with their fellow-men in the great congregation, and this good could not be obtained without strictness in enforcing general obedience. So came, especially with Laud, that stricter rule over the Church which interfered, as Milton thought, with liberty of conscience, and made it impossible for him, after he had taken his M.A. degree, to carry out his own former intention and that of his friends for him by taking orders in the Church of England.

When Charles the First became King and Milton went to college, negotiations for the marriage of Charles with the Spanish Infanta had come to an end, and he was pledged to marry Henrietta Maria, then a girl of fifteen, sister to the King of France. There went with the arrangement a secret writing, signed by King James and his son, promising relief to the Catholics in England, although an opposite promise had been made to the English Parliament. The reign began with the bringing home of the bride, with great preparations for war with Spain, and with vague appeal to the first Parliament of the reign for more money than the King and Buckingham, his chief friend and adviser, chose to name. Money also was asked without any distinct information as to what was to be done with it. Parliament was sitting in London during plague-time; it offered at most two subsidies, when the King's unexpressed wish was for ten, and it was dismissed that the members might escape danger of plague. Sir John Eliot had spoken in that Parliament for continued action against the Roman Catholics as disturbers of the essential unity within the Church, yet Eliot agreed with Milton in his way of harmonising unity with liberty of conscience. He sought, as Laud sought also in his different way, what is now almost attained—"Unity of spirit in the bond of peace;" but he agreed then with all Protestant England, and with Milton, in withholding toleration from the Roman Catholics. It was withheld because their principles then seemed to bind them to contend by all means in their power against opinions not sanctioned by their Church. Milton felt in this with Eliot, Pym, and all other Reformers of his day, but I think he was not unconscious of a touch of infidelity to his own principles, for he is careful to guard himself against showing any desire to interfere with Roman Catholic opinions, except as they produced intolerance of the opinions of others. To Charles's Parliament in June 1625 Sir Thomas Wentworth, who was then twenty-nine years old and had an estate of six thousand a year, was elected as Member for Yorkshire. This was the future Earl of Strafford. On the first day of the reassembling of Parliament— at Oxford, to escape the danger of the plague raging in London— complaint was made of pardon to a Jesuit. On the second day Sir Edward Coke complained that permission was given to every particular man to put out books of all sorts, and he wished that "none concerning religion might be printed but such as were allowed by Convocation." Soon afterwards three Bishops, of whom Laud was one, reasoned that the place of the Pope in the English Church, as final appeal in matters of division among the clergy, was with the King and the Bishops in a National Synod or Convocation, the King first giving leave under his broad seal to handle the points in difference. After a session of twelve days, in which the Parliament showed its distrust of Buckingham, though he sought favour by throwing over the cause of the Catholics and risking the displeasure of the King of France, that first Parliament of Charles the First was suddenly dismissed, and the divisions, of which the seed had been planted by King James the First, began to put out more vigorous shoots.

In the summer of 1626 Charles made Buckingham, at a time when he was under impeachment, Chancellor of Milton's University of Cambridge. After Buckingham's assassination in 1628, the King sought to be himself the ruler, and in Laud he found a supporter who believed sincerely that the only cure for the dissensions in the land was to uphold as strongly as he could the King's single authority. The theory of Monarchy was being reasoned out from many points of view, and Laud was among those who held the view that was expressed afterwards by Hobbes in his "Leviathan." The King was the centre of Unity, the mind of the body politic; and as the body natural could not safely obey separate promptings of two or three separate brains, so to the body of a state the king's should be a single, absolute authority. That is what Milton meant by a "single ruler" when he pleaded, at the breaking up of the Commonwealth, for any readjustment except that, provided also liberty of conscience was maintained.

Laud sought, as he himself said, to make truth and peace kiss each other. He moved, he said to a correspondent, every stone to avoid discussion of knotty and perplexed questions before the people, "lest we should violate charity under the appearance of truth. I have always counselled moderation, lest everything should be thrown into confusion by fervid minds, to which the care of religion is not the first object." The much-vexed questions of predestination and election, Laud, as far as he was able, kept from argument before the people. As Bishop of London, he refused to license a book by the Master of Trinity College, Cambridge, though assured that it would crush the Puritans. His desire was to stay controversy upon those knotty questions about which, he said, that there was something "unmasterable in this life." He did what he could to suppress alike controversial books and controversial preaching upon such questions, that so he might abate the causes of disunion. His prohibition of books was under a Star Chamber decree of Elizabeth's reign, which prohibited printing of books without the license of one of the Archbishops or of the Bishop of London. His prohibiting of controversial preaching took in December 1629 the form of instructions sent by the King to the Bishops, enforcing his Declaration against the introduction of controversial topics in the morning sermons and forbidding afternoon sermons. These were to be replaced by the catechising of children. As there were in many churches lecturers appointed by the laity, who were paid only to preach, and preachers so appointed were usually devout expounders of the Word, inclined to the Puritan view of Church duties, Laud caused the King to require that nobody should preach, even in the morning, until he had first read divine service according to the Liturgy printed by authority, and read it in a surplice. The Bishops were required also to observe the behaviour of the preachers, and "take order for any abuse accordingly."

It was in April of the next year, 1630, that Laud became Chancellor of the University of Oxford. He had then recently read Alexander Leighton's argument for the extirpation of Bishops in "An Appeal to Parliament, or, Sion's Plea against Prelacy." He had caused the arrest of the author and lodged him, Leighton said, in "a nasty dog-hole full of rats and mice." Leighton was brought before the Star Chamber, where Laud was among his judges and spoke for two hours in defence of Episcopacy. Leighton was sentenced to pay a fine of £10,000, to be set in the pillory of Westminster, to be there whipped, to have one of his ears cut off and his nose slit, and to be branded in the face with S.S. as a Sower of Sedition. At some later time he was to be pilloried and whipped at Cheapside, and then to be imprisoned for life, unless it should please his Majesty to enlarge him. The sentence against Leighton was carried out at Westminster. The second pillorying was remitted.

It was in April 1630 that John Winthrop sailed for Massachusetts, and within no long time a thousand souls were added to those who endeavoured to establish in New England such rule of God upon earth as Calvin had endeavoured to establish in Geneva. But the Presbyterian Church rule in New England was as strict as the Episcopal rule of Laud in its enforcements of conformity; and when, a few years afterwards, in England the Presbyterians had power in their hands, Milton expressed his sense of the continual forcing of conscience in the assertion that

"New Presbyter is but old Priest writ large."

Laud was enforcing his view of a strict observance of all rules and ordinances of the Church; he had given occasion for new bitterness of controversy over bowings in direction of the altar, while he sought to stay discussion upon what many regarded as essentials of Christian faith; and we may partly learn what it was to be ordained to the service of the Church of England in the year 1632, when Milton felt himself to be excluded from ordination by the action of the prelates, from a letter sent to Laud in that year by the Vicar of Braintree. "If," he said, "I had suddenly and hastily fallen upon the strict practice of conformity, I had undone myself and broken the town to pieces. For upon the first notice of alteration many were resolving to go to New England, others to remove elsewhere, by whose departure the burden of the poor and charges of the town had grown insupportable to those who should have stayed behind. By my moderate and slow proceeding I have made stay of some, and do hope to settle their judgment and abode with us, when the rest that are inexorable are shipped and gone."

Milton, then, in July 1632, in his twenty-fourth year, completed his college studies, became Master of Arts, and was prevented by the policy of those who ruled the Church from carrying out his design of taking orders in it. The world was before him, and a fresh choice must be made of his vocation. There was open to him only one profession worth his following.

He could not enter upon a new course of training for the law or medicine, and would have had no aptitude for either calling. But the mind quickened by culture could diffuse its light, when the day came for independent labour. If he was shut out of the Church, the School was open; he could be a teacher, and so earn his bread by a right service to the Commonwealth.

But there was one other consideration. The gift of the poet's faculty assigned to him another service for which he was answerable to God. It was not a duty by which he could win daily bread, but there was a duty not the less, a talent to be put to highest use. Milton set an ideal before him towards which he could only strive on by long labour. The work of preparation for the full use of whatever gifts God had bestowed upon his mind yet needed years of quiet thought and study. He might have gone abroad when he left college, as others did for whom, as for Milton, home supplies were prompt in aid of a full training. To Milton as to others the time of foreign travel came; but later. It came after his mother died. I think that his mother's weak health caused him to delay it. He could not put mountains and seas between himself and her when her life perhaps might be ebbing away without the consolation of his presence and his daily care. We may safely infer such a feeling from Milton's expression of grief at having been in Italy when his school friend Charles Diodati died.

Milton's father had retired from business, and was living in the rural village of Horton, within easy walk of Datchet Mead, Eton, and Windsor. The house he occupied was near the church. It was pulled down at the end of the last century. Milton went home to Horton after taking his degree. A Latin poem of loving thanks to his father for the liberal education given to him closed this period of training, and the poem includes reference to questions that must have been between them when he wished to give some further time to quiet cultivation of his faculty of verse—a wish to which few fathers could assent without some hesitation. The son's argument would have been based upon the Parable of the Talents, but pleasant blandishment went with it; witness these lines in the Latin poem of thanks, which I quote as they were translated by Cowper:—

> "Nor thou persist, I pray thee, still to slight
> The sacred Nine, and to imagine vain
> And useless powers, by whom inspired? Thyself
> Art skilful to associate verse with airs
> Harmonious, and to give the human voice
> A thousand modulations; heir by right
> Indisputable of Arion's fame:
> Now say, what wonder is it if a son
> Of thine delight in verse, if so conjoined
> In close affinity, we sympathise
> In social arts and kindred studies sweet?
> Such distribution of himself to us
> Was Phœbus' choice: thou hast thy gift, and I
> Mine also, and between us we receive,
> Father and son, the whole inspiring God."

There followed now in Milton's life another seven years of preparation for its highest work. They were five years and about nine months of life at Horton,—from July 1632 to April 1638,—followed by about one year and three months of foreign travel,—from April 1638 to June or July 1639. From Horton, Milton paid visits to London, for purchase of books and for aid in his studies, especially of music and mathematics. He occasionally took a London lodging, and had thought at one time of obtaining, for such uses, a chamber in one of the Inns of Court. If there were plays worth seeing, Milton also when in London visited the theatre.

It was during these years of his training time at Horton that Milton wrote "L'Allegro" and "Il Penseroso," "Arcades," "Comus," "Lycidas;" all in the pastoral form, to which, on the precedent of Virgil, it was thought that poets should confine themselves until their powers were strengthened for a higher flight. "L'Allegro" and "Il Penseroso" paint the gay and the grave side of the same innocent mind. The elder Milton's fellowship among

musicians had no doubt brought Henry Lawes into the round of
the young poet's friends, and the suggestion of Henry Lawes, who
was to write the music, probably caused Milton to be asked for
words to the little domestic entertainment given by younger
members of her family to the old lady at Harefield, the Dowager
Countess of Derby, who was then seventy-four years old, and died
two or three years later. The success of this little aid to the expression of home kindness, and the continued goodwill of Henry
Lawes, their musical adviser, caused some of these younger
members of the family to look again to Milton when another
masque on a far larger scale was wanted.

The Countess of Derby was mother-in-law to the Earl of
Bridgewater, as mother of his wife; and stepmother to him, as
she had been his father's wife. The Earl of Bridgewater was
made Lord President of the West; and when he had established
himself in office at Ludlow Castle, he had to represent the
sovereign with royal hospitality. He joined, therefore, to a state
entertainment a state masque, which was Milton's "Comus,"
acted at Ludlow Castle on Michaelmas night, the 29th of September 1634.

We have not to discuss here Milton's poems, our concern in
this volume is only with his prose; but the year in which Milton's
"Comus" was written suggests a reflection that throws light on
his character.

In 1633, according to the date upon the title-page, but really,
as its author tells us, "about Christide 1632," there was published
a volume of strong Puritan denunciation of plays, masques,
dances. It had this very long title, which saves further description: "Histrio-Mastix. The Players Scourge or Actors Tragædie,
Divided into Two Parts. Wherein it is largely evidenced, by
divers Arguments, by the concurring Authorities and Resolutions
of sundry texts of Scripture; of the whole Primitive Church,
both under the Law and Gospell; of 55 Synodes and Councels;
of 71 Fathers and Christian Writers, before the yeare of our
Lord 1200; of above 150 foraigne and domestique Protestant
and Popish Authors, since; of 40 Heathen Philosophers, His-

torians, Poets; of many Heathen, many Christian Nations, Republiques, Emperors, Princes, Magistrates; of sundry Apostolicall, Canonicall, Imperiall Constitutions; and of our owne English Statutes, Magistrates, Vniversities, Writers, Preachers, That popular Stage-playes (the very Pompes of the Divell which we renounce in Baptisme, if we beleeve the Fathers) are sinfull, heathenish, lewde, ungodly Spectacles, and most pernicious Corruptions; condemned in all ages, as intolerable Mischiefes to Churches, to Republickes, to the manners, mindes and soules of men. And that the Profession of Play-poets, of Stage-players; together with the penning, acting, and frequenting of Stage-playes, are unlawfull, infamous, and misbeseeming Christians. All pretences to the contrary are here likewise fully answered; and the unlawfulness of acting, of beholding Academicall Enterludes, briefly discussed; besides sundry other particulars concerning Dancing, Dicing, Health-drinking, &c., of which the Table will inform you. By William Prynne, an Vtter-Barrester of Lincolnes Inne." There was room still on the title-page for display of Latin quotations from Cyprian, Lactantius, Chrysostom, and Augustine; such long procession of words on a title-page being now to us "very Pompes of the Divell," which we renounce in the baptism of books. Prynne dedicated this volume of more than a thousand pages to the Benchers of Lincoln's Inn, and there were applied in it the worst words in the dictionary to women who took part in masques. Dancing of women was said to be fatal to the soul, and there was little chance of escape from damnation for those who only sat by and looked on. Now masques were a form of private theatricals; none took part in them but the family or friends of the entertainers. At Court it happened that at Christmas, or as the Puritans said Christide, 1632, when Prynne's "Histriomastix" appeared, the Queen was active in production of a pastoral masque at Somerset House in which she danced herself. Enemies of the Puritans at once associated the Queen's masque with Prynne's book, which they took to Court on the next day after the acting of the pastoral, and showed to the King and Queen the coarse name given by the author in his Index to all women-actors. By that name, they said, he had called the Queen. The book had been published six weeks before the Queen's masque was presented, and it could be shown that its license was obtained two years before, and that the printing of it had been three months finished.

Laud, then Bishop of London, employed Dr. Heylin to examine the book and report upon the scandals he could find in it against the King, Queen, State, and Government of the Realm. Heylin digested matters of offence under seven heads, and on the 1st of February 1633 (New Style) Prynne was sent prisoner to the Tower by the Lords of the inner Star Chamber. So he remained a prisoner without trial, in vain seeking release on bail, and without information laid against him till the 21st of June. It was not until the 17th of February 1634 (New Style) that Prynne was condemned by the Star Chamber. He was sentenced to prison during life; to payment of a fine of £5000 to the King; to be disbarred and disabled ever to exercise the profession of a Barrister; to be degraded by the University of Oxford of his degree there taken; and that done, to be set in the Pillory at Westminster with a paper on his head declaring the nature of his offence, and have one of his ears there cut off, and at another time be set in the Pillory in Cheapside, with a paper as aforesaid, and there have his other ear cut off; and a fire was to be made before the said Pillory, that the Hangman, being there ready for the purpose, might publicly in disgraceful manner cast all the said books which could be produced into the fire to be burnt, as unfit to be seen by any hereafter.

Many of the Lords did not believe that such a sentence would be actually carried out, and Prynne says that the Queen herself earnestly interceded with the King for a remission of its execution. But it was carried out in cold blood. Prynne was pilloried and had his ears cut off on the seventh and ninth of May.

Feeling excited by this controversy had made it for a time a point of loyalty to spend money on masques. The Four Inns of Court wishing, as Whitelocke records, "to manifest the difference of their opinion from Mr. Prynne's new learning, and to confute his 'Histriomastix' against Interludes," prepared a masque in which they spent a thousand pounds upon the music only, and ten thousand pounds upon the clothes of the horsemen. It was "The Triumph of Peace," written by James Shirley, with scenery and machinery by Inigo Jones, and was produced on the 3rd of February 1634. But on Shrove Tuesday, the 18th of the same month, there was a masque at Court in which the King danced, which the Master of the Revels thought to be the noblest of his time.

The new impulse given by Prynne's book must have influenced the Lord President of the West when he resolved to spend liberally on the production of a masque at Ludlow; and there is signicance in the fact that the commission to write such a masque must have been accepted by Milton in the midheat of Puritan attack upon such entertainments. As the words when written had yet to be set to music, scenery and machinery invented and prepared, masks designed and made, parts learnt by children, songs and dances practised, the writing could hardly have been undertaken—Ludlow not being London—later than the spring of the same year, possibly in the interval between the sentencing of Prynne on the 17th of February and the unexpected enforcement of the sentence on the 7th of May. What Milton thought of force in the suppression of opinion, this volume shows. But his own way of reasoning against the error of those Puritans who made war against arts adding to the charm of life, innocent in themselves and more than innocent, directly helpful to its higher interests, when rightly used, we find in "Comus." He produced a masque in which Temperance was the theme, which genially fulfilled every requirement of delight, and yet applied action, song, and dance throughout as an incitement to the higher spiritual life.

In 1635 Milton was incorporated as M.A. of Oxford, and in that year his old teacher, Alexander Gill the younger, became by his father's death Head Master of St. Paul's School.

Milton's mother died on the 3rd of April 1637, and was buried in the chancel of the church at Horton.

INTRODUCTION. 37

In 1637 Henry Lawes published "Comus" as a pamphlet of thirty-five pages, with a dedication by himself to John Lord Brackley, who had played the part of the elder brother. Milton's name was not upon its title-page, and Henry Lawes said of it in the dedication, "Although not openly acknowledged by the Author, yet it is a legitimate offspring, so lovely and so much desired that the often copying of it hath tired my pen to give my several friends satisfaction, and brought me to a necessity of producing it to the public view." Milton revised the copy for the press, but in the place upon the title-page where his name would have stood had he given it, is a sigh in a few words from Virgil's second Eclogue—"Ah me, what have I wished? A dry wind spoils my flowers." The dry south wind that Milton felt as withering his spring was in the griefs and contests of the time. The veteran Ben Jonson died in that year, 1637, fallen, as he felt, on evil times. The very writing of the masque of "Comus" was connected with thoughts of oppression and cruelty, with resentment of wrongs done to Prynne that must have made a part of his unwillingness to sign his name at that time to a masque, and be supposed in any way the adversary of a victim to Star Chamber tyranny. *Eheu! quid volui misero mihi?* I would have sung, and discord clashes to the soul of my best music. I would have consecrated all my powers to the pure service of God; the dry wind blighted then what blossom I was ready to put forth: and now what little rill of song within me can expand into the light of heavenly love and beauty before it is dried up by the sirocco of dissension and ill-will that parches all this land? It was no sigh of despair; in time of greatest seeming reason for despair, the last use to which Milton put his genius as a poet was for an outpouring of the music of a patient trust in God. But he has not known life who has never sighed over the little that could be attained, and has not thought of old hopes while they lay dead or asleep, and has not felt as Milton felt in 1637, *Eheu, quid volui.*

That was the year in which he whispered to his friend Diodati of his dream of immortality, of wings too tender for a lofty flight, and said, Let us be humbly wise. In the same letter to his bosom friend there was also this passage:—"As to other points, what God may have determined for me I know not; but this I know, that if he ever instilled an intense love of moral beauty into the breast of any man, he has instilled it into mine: Ceres in the fable pursued not her daughter with a greater keenness of enquiry than I, day and night, the idea of perfection. Hence, wherever I find a man despising the false estimates of the vulgar, and daring to aspire in sentiment, language, and conduct, to what the highest wisdom through every age has taught us as most excellent, to him I unite myself by a sort of necessary attachment; and if I am so influenced by nature or destiny, that by no exertion or labours of my own I may exalt myself to this summit of worth and honour, yet no powers of heaven or earth will hinder me from looking with reverence and affection upon those who have thoroughly attained this glory, or appear engaged in the successful pursuit of it."

This was written on the 23rd of September 1637. About the same time, or soon afterwards, it was agreed at home that Milton should leave England for a year or two and visit Greece and Italy; then, coming back, he would establish himself in what would be his business of life, the better poet and the better teacher for that closing time of rest in Italy and Greece. The two years abroad would yield new pastures to his mind. He would write no more verse until those fresh influences should have breathed into him health and strength. The journey could not be begun with winter at the door. It was resolved, therefore, that he should set out for Italy in the next following spring, the spring of 1638.

But in October 1637 there came to him a request from Cambridge that he would join in the forming of a little volume of memorial verses by members of the University. They were to be in memory of a young friend at Christ's College, Edward King, who had been drowned by the wreck of the vessel in which he was going home to Ireland for the long vacation. Edward King's father was Sir John King, a Privy Councillor for Ireland, whose character and credit at court had obtained for his son a fellowship at Christ's which, perhaps, might otherwise have fallen to Milton. Milton was friend and fellow-worker with him. King took his M.A. degree in 1633, only a year later than Milton. He was about to enter the ministry of the Church when his sudden death led to the request that Milton among others would, according to a good and kindly custom, contribute to the memorial volume of "Obsequies to the Memorie of Mr. Edward King." He at once responded and sent "Lycidas," which is dated in November 1637. In the opening lines Milton referred to his withdrawal from the use of verse while waiting for the day of riper power, a silence broken by the touch of human sympathy, and the piece closed with a glance towards the coming days of travel,—" To-morrow to fresh woods and pastures new." The only part of "Lycidas" that here concerns us is the passage in which Milton draws from his friend's fitness for the service of the Church a comment upon the unfitness of many in it who neglected faithful preaching, and cared only for the incomes they could make. These were the pastors—blind mouths—whose hungry sheep—whose congregations—looked up and were not fed,—

> But swoln with wind and the rank mist they draw,
> Rot inwardly, and foul contagion spread :
> Besides what the grim wolf with privy paw
> Daily devours apace, and nothing said :
> Yet that two-handed engine at the door
> Stands ready to smite once and smite no more.

That two-handed engine is St. Paul's "Sword of the Spirit, which is the Word of God :" "For the Word of God," said Paul, "is quick and powerful, and sharper than any two-edged sword." We wield it by a double grip, on the Old Testament and on the New. The Bible chained to its desk, for use of any who might turn in out of the street to read a chapter and to breathe a prayer, was a familiar object at the old church doors. Milton's complaint is that the spirit of evil laid hold upon men in the congregations of unfaithful preachers, by whom there was *nothing said*. The Bible was at the church door, open to all, but they made no use against evil of the only weapon that could be a sword of victory.

In 1637 Milton must have flinched the more from immediate association of his name with Comus, because in that year William Prynne was again made the victim of a cruel sentence. He had issued in 1636 a pamphlet setting forth judgments against sabbath-breakers who had been multiplied and encouraged by the King's Declaration of Sports. In another pamphlet he charged the Bishops with suppression of preaching, that they might prepare the way for popery. The Rev. Henry Burton preached two sermons in November 1636, which he published as "For God and the King," wherein he attacked the ceremonies on which Laud insisted, the removal of communion tables from the centre of the church where they had commonly stood, and hats had been often placed on them, to the east end where they were railed in, the bowing towards them, and the setting up of crosses, as wrongdoing of Bishops for which the remedy was abolition of Prelacy. Dr. Bastwick, physician, already under sentence of the High Commission Court, published "the Litany of John Bastwick," in which one clause was, "From plague, pestilence and famine, from bishops, priests and deacons, good Lord deliver us." They were all three, Prynne, Burton and Bastwick, brought before the Star Chamber, sentenced to fine, pillory, and loss of ears; Prynne was found to have had ear enough left for a second cropping. Prynne was also again to be branded. The sentence was executed against all three on the last day of June 1637, and the victims had the people on their side. Their path to the pillory was strewn with herbs and flowers.

There had been no parliament called for eight years. In 1637 the King issued his third writ for ship-money. A widespread feeling against personal rule gathered new strength, and blended with rebellion in the Church against Laud's honest and impartial endeavours to build up spiritual life by compelling strict conformity in the observance of all legally appointed forms. In 1635 three thousand persons had crossed the Atlantic to join the New England colony. Young Henry Vane, then twenty-three years old, landed at Boston in that year, and in 1636 he was made Governor of the colony. His opposition to a desire of the religious commonwealth to refuse admission to men holding opinions that would conflict with theirs—Vane arguing for full liberty of judgment, Winthrop for the policy of protection against discord—caused John Winthrop to be elected Governor at the end of Vane's first year of office, and in 1637 Vane returned to England.

The new Service Book sent into Scotland at the beginning of 1637 was to be brought into use there at Easter, but the strength of opposition caused the first day of reading it to be put off to Sunday, the 23rd of July. In St. Giles's Kirk at Edinburgh the people met the opening of the Service Book and the attempt to read from it with uproar, and when the Bishop of Edinburgh came forward to allay the tumult there was a joint stool thrown at his head. Committees were established to maintain the people's cause, and on the 1st of March 1638 there was fervent prayer in St. Giles's Kirk, after which nobles, clergy, burgesses lifted their hands and swore fidelity to the National Covenant, by which they undertook to maintain at all hazards their old form of worship and their old Confession of Faith. This news was fresh in England, and still the Covenant was being signed, when Milton, in the middle of April 1638, left England for Italy and Greece. He was then three or four months older than nine-and-twenty.

Milton left home with one servant, who would be the more necessary because in those days much travel was on horseback. He had letters of recommendation to Lord Scudamore, the English ambassador in Paris, by whom he was introduced to Hugo Grotius, exiled from his own country by the intolerance of an ecclesiastical synod, and then in Paris as ambassador from the Queen of Sweden. From Lord Scudamore he took letters of introduction to English merchants whom he would find upon his way, and travelled to Nice. He sailed from Nice to Genoa, visited Leghorn, Pisa, and Florence, staying two months at Florence, and making friends among the men of letters there. Milton at Horton had become a good Italian scholar, and in Italy he wrote Italian verse that pleased Italian poets. From Florence he went to Siena, thence to Rome. At Rome he stayed during another two months, and made more friends. From Rome he went southward to Naples, and obtained there the friendship of Count Manso, friend and biographer of Tasso. Then the way on would be to Sicily and Greece, but, Milton wrote, in his "Second Defence of the People of England," "When I was preparing to pass over into Sicily and Greece, the melancholy intelligence which I received of the civil commotions in England made me alter my purpose, for I thought it base to be travelling for amusement abroad while my fellow-citizens were fighting for liberty at home." That is to say, the place of a citizen in any state, be his powers great or small, is in the ranks of his countrymen at any time of danger to his country. It did not mean that Milton should go home to handle sword, or pike, or gun, which to him were arguments "of human weakness rather than of strength." While an incomplete civilisation makes it still inevitable that brute force shall oppose brute force in battles of opinion, the conditions of the time must be accepted. But sword and gun achieve only the triumph of a day, if reason be against the cause they battle for. Milton's duty to his country in a time of danger from the clashing of opinions, was to reason against opinions that imperilled liberty, to be a spiritual soldier in the wars of truth. Captain, or colonel, or man-at-arms, every Englishman is, in that way, soldier for his country, and must be at his post when the alarm is sounded.

The English news that reached Milton in Italy told of the King's temporising with the Scots while gathering force to subdue them. The Covenanters were preparing for the danger. Already in July 1638, three months after Milton left England, they had a magazine of pikes, halberts, and muskets. Early in December a ship in which a merchant of Edinburgh was bringing six thousand muskets out of Holland was stopped by the government of the United Provinces, but set free by aid of the King of France, and sent on to Leith. Laud lamented on the 7th of December that "the jealousies of giving the Covenanters umbrage too soon had made preparation so late." At the beginning of the year 1639 the King was appointing officers, ordering the muster of trained bands, and endeavouring to get six thousand foreign troops. The Scots did not wait for attack. Leslie, their General, in March surprised and took Edinburgh Castle, other castles were surrendered to the Covenanters. On the 30th of May the armies of the King and of the Covenanters were encamped within sight of each other. Milton had given up his journey into Greece, where letters would seldom reach him, and turned homeward, again making long stays in Rome and Florence, always within hearing of news from England. He stayed a month at Venice, whence he shipped home books and music, then he came back through Verona, Milan, and Geneva. Imminent risk of the beginning of a civil war was averted by the pacification of Berwick.

When Milton came home, in the summer of 1639, he presently took a lodging in St. Bride's Churchyard, at the house of a tailor named Russel, while looking for a place fit for his purpose of establishing a school. He took charge at once of the education of his nephews, Edward and John Phillips, children born to his sister Anne at the close of her seven years' marriage with Edward Phillips of the Crown Office. She had been left a widow with those boys, one of a year old, named after her husband Edward, the other perhaps unborn when her husband died, named after her brother, John. Her first husband having died in 1631, she had married again. Her second husband was a Mr. Agar, who succeeded also to her former husband's work in the Crown Office. Her boys, now about ten and nine years old, were put under their uncle's care. Milton found for his school what his nephew called "a pretty garden house in Aldersgate Street at the end of an entry." Aldersgate Street then having gardens about its houses, a passage between garden walls of houses fronting to the road led to the gate of a garden in the rear, with a house in it more distant from the line of traffic. Into his garden house, well chosen for such a purpose, Milton gathered his books and his boys. The boys he taught seem to have come from families of merchants and others, prosperous and intellectual. Cyriac Skinner, to whom he wrote afterwards two sonnets, was one of his old boys; two others, of whom we chance to learn, were a son of Robert Boyle's sister, Lady Ranelagh, and her nephew, the Earl of Barrimore.

During Milton's travel in Italy, his friend Charles Diodati died, and the lament for him in Latin verse, "Epitaphium Damonis," written by Milton after his return, expresses a tenderness of feeling which may be illustrated by this passage from it, in Cowper's translation:

> Ah, blest indifference of the playful herd
> None by his fellow chosen or preferred!
> The sparrow meanest of the feathered race
> His fit companion finds in every place,
> With whom he picks the grain that suits him best,
> Flirts here and there, and late returns to rest;
> And whom if chance the falcon make his prey,
> Or hedger with his well aimed arrow slay,
> For no such loss the gay survivor grieves,
> New love he seeks, and new delight receives.
> We only, an obdurate kind, rejoice,
> Scorning all others, in a single choice;
> We scarce in thousands meet one kindred mind,
> And if the long-sought good at last we find,
> When least we fear it, Death our treasure steals,
> And gives our heart a wound that nothing heals.
>
> Go, go, my lambs, unpastured as ye are,
> My thoughts are all now due to other care.
> Ah, what delusion lured me from my flocks,
> To traverse Alpine snows and rugged rocks!
> What need so great had I to visit Rome,
> Now sunk in ruins and herself a tomb?
> Or, had she flourished still as when, of old,
> For her sake Tityrus forsook his fold,
> What need so great had I to incur a pause
> Of thy sweet intercourse for such a cause,
> For such a cause to place the roaring sea,
> Rocks, mountains, woods, between my friend and me?

> Else had I grasped thy feeble hand, composed
> Thy decent limbs, thy drooping eyelids closed,
> And, at the last, had said—" Farewell—ascend—
> Nor even in the skies forget thy friend!"

That is the John Milton who in the year 1640, in the thirty-second year of his life, began to keep school at the garden house in Aldersgate Street. Milton was proposing then to use his leisure in the shaping of an Epic based like Virgil's upon the mythical tale of the founder of his country. His mind was on his two callings of teacher and poet, when the clouds gathered again, and there broke forth in 1641 a storm of public feeling against prelacy.

In August 1640 the Scots had crossed the border and routed in the first conflict five thousand horse and foot at Newburn. While the Scots held Newcastle the King was at last obliged, against his will, to call a Parliament—known now as the Long Parliament—which was to meet at Westminster on the 3rd of November 1640. At the end of January 1641 Bishop Hall published in defence of the Liturgy and Episcopal Government, his "Humble Remonstrance to the High Court of Parliament." Towards the close of March there appeared an answer to this by five divines—one of them Milton's old teacher, Thomas Young—who joined their initials to make one author's name, Smectymnuus (Stephen Marshall, Edmund Calamy, Thomas Young, Matthew Newcomen, and William Sparstow). Usher, Archbishop of Armagh, argued, towards the end of May, out of Antiquity the confirmation of Episcopacy. Laud had been impeached in February, and in March committed to the Tower. On the 27th of May the House of Commons passed the second reading of a bill "for the utter abolishing and taking away of all Archbishops, Bishops, &c.," while there was also awaiting decision a bill for the exclusion of Bishops from the House of Lords.

It was then that Milton joined his voice to the argument by publishing his two books "Of Reformation touching Church Discipline," which was followed quickly by a shorter pamphlet on Prelatical Episcopacy replying to Usher, and a defence of

Smectymnuus against attack. In January 1642 there was the King's arrest of the Five Members on the 14th of February, the King gave his assent to the bill excluding Bishops from the House of Lords, and the second piece of Milton's given in this volume "The Reason of Church Government urged against Prelaty," was published at that time. On the 22nd of the following August the King set up his standard at Nottingham, and Civil War began.

Milton's arguments concerning Prelacy may be left to speak for themselves. His aspiration clearly is for a pure, spiritual Church, and he appeals only to Scripture and reason. It is equally clear that the experience of his time, and of history before his time, gave Milton little hope of such a change as we see now. Whatsoever ailments may remain for time to heal, the Church of England now welcomes the fellowship of all who join her in the labour to establish peace on earth and goodwill among men.

In June 1643, Milton went into Oxfordshire and married the eldest daughter of a near neighbour to the Oxfordshire Miltons, Richard Powell of Forest Hill. He must have known her since her birth. She was in her eighteenth year, he in his thirty-fifth, and it was eighteen years since Milton went to College, where, when he was a student, Mary Powell's father had given evidence of friendship by borrowing of him five hundred pounds. There is no reason at all why we should think ill of Mary Powell. When Milton brought her—about the end of June 1643—into his house of the worker, there were in the first days little adjustments necessary to enable two lives that had hitherto run different courses to take one course and keep step together. Milton's young wife was not prepared. Milton's nephew, Edward Phillips, says that she felt the change from a great house in which there had been much company. Some of her family came with her and feasted for about a week. Then she was left. After another fortnight she was invited to go home till Michaelmas. She had only been married for about a month when she went home, towards the end of July, and had no wise home counsel in aid of her troubled inexperience. She was kept from her husband; and when Milton sent for her, his servant was sent back by her unwise parents with insult. How unwise the father was his money dealings show. In June 1644 John Hampden had received his death wound in Chalgrove Field, and at the end of the month Fairfax had been defeated by the Earl of Newcastle at Atherton Moor. The prospects of the Parliament were clouded, and Richard Powell might have been ready to throw off a son-in-law upon the losing side. But next year, when the King's cause was lost at Naseby, Milton's wife was bidden to seek reconciliation with him. They who had withheld her now returned her. It is no discredit to a girl of eighteen that her father and mother have great influence over her mind. Milton received her back at once. She became the mother of his children, and remained with him until her death.

When Milton married, it hardly needs to be said that his mind was drawn to the subject of marriage. In July 1643—within the first month of his marriage—a National Synod first met at Westminster, known as the Westminster Assembly, for the purpose of settling the government and form of worship of the Church. There were in the Assembly 121 divines, with ten members of the House of Lords, and twenty of the House of Commons, as lay assessors. The time was then for the suggestion of reform, and Milton was prompted by his own experience to write that treatise of the Doctrine and Discipline of Divorce which follows next in this volume, and was, in fact, written to win acceptance of a more spiritual view of marriage than the Church law recognised.

This treatise was published in 1644, and other pieces followed in reply to its opponents. Meanwhile Milton was busy in his school; and in the same year he wrote, at the request of Samuel Hartlib, the letter which next follows in this volume, sketching his ideal of a reformed system of education. Samuel Hartlib was of a good Polish family, and had come to England in 1640 with money that he spent for the public good. His interest was great in questions of religious liberty, of national education for the rich and for the poor, of the improvement of agriculture; and he soon had Milton among his friends. He had translated in 1642, from the Latin of a Moravian pastor, John Amos Komensky, two treatises on "A Reformation of Schooles." Milton thought that there was much room for improvement in the higher education of an Englishman, and Hartlib asked him to sketch an ideal of his own.

But the chief care of Milton as a writer in 1644 was bestowed upon his "Areopagitica." On the 11th of July 1637 a decree of the Star Chamber had increased strictness of licensing. It had contained formally the limitation of the whole numbers of Master Printers to twenty and of type founders to four, with strict provisions for watching, searching, seizing, and suppressing. The Star Chamber was abolished, but on the 9th of March 1643 an Order of the House of Commons gave to a Committee for Examinations, or to any four of them, like power. Taking as his model a Greek oration,—the Areopagitic discourse in which Isocrates sought to press on the Athenian Areopagus reform in its body—Milton, whose aim was to persuade the English Areopagus to cancel one of its own Orders, gave the name of Areopagitica to his defence of the liberty of unlicensed printing. It was published in November 1644.

Milton took no part in the contest with the King. When it was over, there was question of a people's right to bring a king to trial. He then published what is the next piece in this volume, "The Tenure of Kings and Magistrates" upon the main issue in the constitutional question of a king's responsibility. A subject can be tried for treason to a king; can also a king be tried for treason to his people, and condemned if he be guilty. From 1649 to 1689 the problem of the limit of authority was at the heart of much of our best literature, and this is Milton's way of answering it.

Here we might end, but the last section of this volume serves to show that, ten years later, Milton's argument for Civil and Religious Liberty stood firm among the ruins of the Commonwealth.
H. M.

CARISBROOKE, *September*, 1889.

GOD AND MAN.

Henceforth I learn that to obey is best,
And love with fear the only God ; to walk
As in His Presence ; ever to observe
His Providence, and on Him sole depend,
Merciful over all His Works, with Good
Still overcoming Evil, and by small
Accomplishing great things, by things deemed weak
Subverting worldly strong, and worldly wise
By simply meek ; that Suffering for Truth's sake
Is Fortitude to highest Victory,
And to the faithful Death the gate of Life.
.   .   .   .
.   .   .   .   .   Only add
Deeds to thy Knowledge answerable : add Faith,
Add Virtue, Patience, Temperance ; add Love,
By name to come called Charity, the Soul
Of all the rest.

—Paradise Lost.   Book xii.

OF
REFORMATION TOUCHING CHURCH DISCIPLINE IN ENGLAND,

AND THE

CAUSES THAT HITHERTO HAVE HINDERED IT.

IN TWO BOOKS.

WRITTEN TO A FRIEND.

THE FIRST BOOK.

SIR,—Amidst those deep and retired thoughts which with every man Christianly instructed ought to be most frequent, of God and of his miraculous ways and works amongst men, and of our Religion and works to be performed to him; after the story of our Saviour Christ, suffering to the lowest bent of weakness in the flesh, and presently triumphing to the highest pitch of glory in the spirit, which drew up his body also, till we in both be united to him in the revelation of his kingdom, I do not know of anything more worthy to take up the whole passion of pity on the one side, and joy on the other, than to consider first the foul and sudden corruption, and then, after many a tedious age, the long deferred but much more wonderful and happy Reformation of the Church in these latter days. Sad it is to think how that doctrine of the Gospel, planted by teachers divinely inspired, and by them winnowed and sifted from the chaff of overdated ceremonies, and refined to such a spiritual height and temper of purity and knowledge of the Creator, that the body and all the circumstances of time and place were purified by the affections of the regenerate soul, and nothing left impure but sin;—faith needing not the weak and fallible office of the senses to be either the ushers or interpreters of heavenly mysteries, save where our Lord himself in his sacraments ordained;—that such a doctrine should, through the grossness and blindness of her professors, and the fraud of deceivable traditions, drag so downwards as to backslide one way into the Jewish beggary of old cast rudiments, and stumble forward another way into the new-vomited paganism of sensual idolatry, attributing purity or impurity to things indifferent, that they might bring the inward acts of the spirit to the outward and customary eye-service of the body, as if they could make God earthly and fleshly, because they could not make themselves heavenly and spiritual. They began to draw down all the divine intercourse betwixt God and the soul, yea, the very shape of God himself, into an exterior and bodily form. Urgently pretending a necessity and obligement of joining the body in a formal reverence and worship circumscribed, they hallowed it, they fumed it, they sprinkled it, they bedecked it, not in robes of pure innocency, but of pure linen, with other deformed and fantastic dresses, in palls and mitres, gold and gewgaws fetched from Aaron's old wardrobe, or the flamen's vestry. Then was the priest set to con his motions and his postures, his liturgies and his lurries, till the soul by this means of overbodying herself, given up justly to fleshly delights, bated her wing apace downward, and finding the ease she had from her visible and sensuous colleague, the body, in performance of religious duties, her pinions now broken and flagging, shifted off from herself the labour of high soaring any more, forgot her heavenly flight, and left the dull and droiling carcass to plod on in the old road and drudging trade of outward conformity. And here, out of question, from her perverse conceiting of God and holy things, she had fallen to believe no God at all, had not custom and the worm of conscience nipped her incredulity. Hence to all the duties of evangelical grace, instead of the adoptive and cheerful boldness which our new alliance with God requires, came servile and thrall-like fear. For in very deed, the superstitious man by his good will is an atheist; but being scared from thence by the pangs and gripes of a boiling conscience, all in a pudder shuffles up to himself such a God and such a worship as is most agreeable to remedy his fear; which fear of his, as also is his hope, fixed only upon the flesh, renders likewise the whole faculty of his apprehension carnal; and all the inward acts of worship, issuing from the native strength of the soul, run out lavishly to the upper skin, and there harden into a crust of formality. Hence men came to scan the Scriptures by the letter, and in the Covenant of our Redemption, magnified the external signs more than the quickening power of the Spirit; and yet,—looking on them through their own guiltiness with a servile fear, and finding as little comfort, or rather terror from them again,—they knew not how to hide their slavish approach to God's behests, by them not understood nor worthily received, but by cloaking their servile crouching to all religious presentments, sometimes lawful sometimes idolatrous, under the name of Humility, and terming the piebald frippery and ostentation of ceremonies, Decency.

Then was Baptism changed into a kind of exorcism, and water sanctified by Christ's institute thought little enough to wash off the original spot, without the scratch or cross impression of a priest's forefinger. And that Feast of free grace and adoption to which Christ invited his disciples to sit as brethren and coheirs of the happy covenant which at that table was to be sealed to them, even that Feast of love and heavenly-admitted fellowship, the seal of filial grace, became the subject of horror, and glouting adoration, pageanted about like a dreadful idol; which sometimes deceives well-meaning men, and beguiles them of their reward by their voluntary humility, which indeed is fleshly pride, preferring a foolish sacrifice, and the rudiments of the world, as St. Paul to the Colossians explaineth, before a savoury obedience to Christ's example. Such was Peter's unseasonable humility, as then his knowledge was small, when Christ came to wash his feet; who at an impertinent time would needs strain courtesy with his master, and falling troublesomely upon the lowly, all-wise, and unexaminable intention of Christ in what he went with resolution to do, so provoked by his interruption the meek Lord, that he threatened to exclude him from his heavenly portion unless he could be content to be less arrogant and stiffnecked in his humility.

But to dwell no longer in characterizing the depravities of the Church, and how they sprung, and how they took increase; when I recall to mind at last, after so many dark ages, wherein the huge overshadowing train of error had almost swept all the stars out of the firmament of the Church, how the bright and blissful Reformation, by divine power, struck through the black and settled night of ignorance and antichristian tyranny, methinks a sovereign and reviving joy must needs rush into the bosom of him that reads or hears, and the sweet odour of the returning Gospel imbathe his soul with the fragrancy of Heaven. Then was the sacred Bible sought out of the dusty corners where profane falsehood and neglect had thrown it; the schools were opened, divine and human learning raked out of the embers of forgotten tongues; the princes and cities trooping apace to the new-erected banner of salvation, the martyrs, with the unresistible might of weakness, shaking the powers of darkness and scorning the fiery rage of the old red dragon.

The pleasing pursuit of these thoughts hath ofttimes led me into a serious question and debatement with myself, how it should come to pass that England—having had this grace and honour from God, to be the first that should set up a standard for the recovery of lost truth, and blow the first evangelic trumpet to the nations, holding up, as from a hill, the new lamp of saving light to all Christendom—should now be last and most unsettled in the enjoyment of that peace whereof she taught the way to others. Although indeed our Wyclif's preaching, at which all the succeeding Reformers more effectually lighted their tapers, was to his countrymen but a short blaze, soon damped and stifled by the pope and prelates, for six or seven kings' reigns; yet methinks the precedency which God gave this island, to be first restorer of buried truth, should have been followed with more happy success, and sooner attained perfection, in which as yet we are amongst the last. For, albeit in purity of Doctrine we agree with our brethren, yet in Discipline, which is the execution and applying of doctrine home, and laying the salve to the very orifice of the wound, yea, tenting and searching to the core, without which pulpit preaching is but shooting at rovers, in this we are no better than a schism from all the Reformation, and a sore scandal to them. For while we hold ordination to belong only to bishops, as our prelates do, we must of necessity hold also their ministers to be no ministers, and shortly after their Church to be no Church: not to speak of those senseless ceremonies which we only retain as a dangerous earnest of sliding back to Rome, and serving merely, either as a mist to cover nakedness where true grace is extinguished, or as an interlude to set out the pomp of prelatism. Certainly it would be worth the while therefore and the pains, to inquire more particularly what and how many the chief Causes have been, that have still hindered our uniform consent to the rest of the Churches abroad, at this time especially when the kingdom is in a good propensity thereto, and all men in prayers, in hopes, or in disputes, either for or against it.

Yet I will not insist on that which may seem to be the cause on God's part; as his judgment on our sins, the trial of his own, the unmasking of hypocrites. Nor shall I stay to speak of the continual eagerness and extreme diligence of the pope and papists to stop the furtherance of Reformation, which know they have no hold or hope of England, their lost darling, longer than the government of bishops bolsters them out, and therefore plot all they can to uphold them: as may be seen by the book of Santa Clara, the popish priest, in defence of bishops, which came out piping hot much about the time that one of our own prelates, out of an ominous fear, had writ on the same argument; as if they had joined their forces, like good confederates, to support one falling Babel.

But I shall chiefly endeavour to declare those Causes that

hinder the forwarding of true Discipline which are among ourselves. Orderly proceeding will divide our inquiry into our forefathers' days, and into our times.

Henry VIII. was the first that rent this kingdom from the pope's subjection totally; but his quarrel being more about Supremacy than other faultiness in Religion that he regarded, it is no marvel if he stuck where he did. The next default was in the bishops, who though they had renounced the pope, they still hugged the popedom and shared the authority among themselves, by their six bloody articles, persecuting the Protestants no slacker than the pope would have done. And doubtless, whenever the pope shall fall, if his ruin be not like the sudden downcome of a tower, the bishops, when they see him tottering, will leave him, and fall to scrambling, catch who may, he a patriarchdom, and another what comes next hand; as the French cardinal of late and the see of Canterbury hath plainly affected.

In Edward the Sixth's days, why a complete Reformation was not effected, to any considerate man may appear. First, he no sooner entered into his kingdom, but into a war with Scotland; from whence the Protector returning with victory had but newly put his hand to repeal the six articles and throw the images out of churches, but rebellions on all sides, stirred up by obdurate papists, and other tumults, with a plain war in Norfolk, holding tack against two of the king's generals, made them of force content themselves with what they had already done. Hereupon followed ambitious contentions among the peers, which ceased not but with the Protector's death, who was the most zealous in this point. And then Northumberland was he that could do most in England, who little minding Religion, as his apostasy well showed at his death, bent all his wit how to bring the right of the crown into his own line. And for the bishops, they were so far from any such worthy attempts, as that they suffered themselves to be the common stales to countenance with their prostituted gravities every politic fetch that was then on foot, as oft as the potent statists pleased to employ them. Never do we read that they made use of their authority and high place of access to bring the jarring nobility to Christian peace, or to withstand their disloyal projects: but if a toleration for mass were to be begged of the king for his sister Mary, lest Charles the Fifth should be angry, who but the grave prelates, Cranmer and Ridley, must be sent to extort it from the young king? But out of the mouth of that godly and royal child, Christ himself returned such an awful repulse to those halting and time-serving prelates, that after much bold importunity they went their way not without shame and tears.

Nor was this the first time that they discovered to be followers of this world; for when the protector's brother, Lord Sudley, the admiral, through private malice and mal-engine was to lose his life, no man could be found fitter than Bishop Latimer (like another Dr. Shaw) to divulge in his sermon the forged accusations laid to his charge, thereby to defame him with the People, who else, it was thought, would take ill the innocent man's death, unless the reverend bishop could warrant them there was no foul play. What could be more impious than to debar the children of the king from their right to the crown? to comply with the ambitious usurpation of a traitor, and to make void the last will of Henry VIII., to which the breakers had sworn observance? Yet Bishop Cranmer, one of the executors, and the other bishops, none refusing (lest they should resist the Duke of Northumberland), could find in their consciences to set their hands to the disenabling and defeating not only the Princess Mary the papist, but of Elizabeth the protestant, and (by the bishops' judgment) the lawful issue of King Henry.

Who then can think, though these prelates had sought a further Reformation, that the least wry face of a politician would not have hushed them? But it will be said, these men were Martyrs. What then? Though every true Christian will be a martyr when he is called to it, not presently does it follow that every one suffering for religion is, without exception. St. Paul writes, that "a man may give his body to be burnt (meaning for religion), and yet not have charity:" he is not therefore above all possibility of erring, because he burns for some points of truth.

Witness the Arians and Pelagians which were slain by the heathen for Christ's sake, yet we take both these for no true friends of Christ. If the Martyrs, saith Cyprian in his 30th epistle, decree one thing, and the Gospel another, either the Martyrs must lose their crown by not observing the Gospel for which they are martyrs, or the majesty of the Gospel must be broken and lie flat, if it can be overtopped by the novelty of any other decree.

And here withal I invoke the Immortal Deity, revealer and judge of secrets, that wherever I have in this book plainly and roundly, though worthily and truly, laid open the faults and blemishes of Fathers, Martyrs, or Christian Emperors, or have otherwise inveighed against error and superstition with vehement expressions, I have done it neither out of malice, nor list to speak evil, nor any vain glory: but of mere necessity to vindicate the spotless truth from an ignominious bondage, whose native worth is now become of such a low esteem, that she is like to find small credit with us for what she can say unless she can bring a ticket from Cranmer, Latimer, and Ridley; or prove herself a retainer to Constantine, and wear his badge. More tolerable it were for the church of God that all these names were utterly abolished, like the brazen serpent, than that men's fond opinion should thus idolize them, and the heavenly truth be thus captivated.

Now to proceed, whatsoever the bishops were, it seems they themselves were unsatisfied in matters of Religion as they then stood, by that Commission granted to eight bishops, eight other divines, eight civilians, eight common lawyers, to frame ecclesiastical constitutions; which no wonder if it came to nothing, for (as Hayward relates) both their professions and their ends were different. Lastly, we all know by example, that exact Reformation is not perfected at the first push, and those unwieldy times of Edward VI. may hold some plea by this excuse. Now let any reasonable man judge whether that king's reign be a fit time from whence to pattern out the constitution of a church discipline, much less that it should yield occasion from whence to foster and establish the continuance of imperfection, with the commendatory subscriptions of Confessors and Martyrs, to entitle and engage a glorious name to a gross corruption. It was not episcopacy that wrought in them the heavenly fortitude of martyrdom, as little is it that martyrdom can make good episcopacy; but it was episcopacy that led the good and holy men, through the temptation of the enemy and the snare of this present world, to many blameworthy and opprobrious actions. And it is still episcopacy that before all our eyes worsens and slugs the most learned and seeming religious of our ministers, who no sooner advanced to it but, like a seething pot set to cool, sensibly exhale and reek out the greatest part of that zeal and those gifts which were formerly in them, settling in a skinny congealment of ease and sloth at the top. And if they keep their learning by some potent sway of nature, it is a rare chance; but their devotion most commonly comes to that queasy temper of lukewarmness, that gives a vomit to God himself.

But what do we suffer misshapen and enormous prelatism, as we do, thus to blanch and varnish her deformities with the fair colours, as before of martyrdom, so now of episcopacy? They are not bishops, God and all good men know they are not, that have filled this land with late confusion and violence; but a tyrannical crew and corporation of impostors that have blinded and abused the world so long under that name. He that, enabled with gifts from God and the lawful and primitive choice of the Church assembled in convenient number, faithfully from that time forward feeds his parochial flock, has his coequal and compresbyterial power to ordain ministers and deacons by public prayer and vote of Christ's congregation, in like sort as he himself was ordained, and is a true apostolic bishop. But when he steps up into the chair of pontifical pride, and changes a moderate and exemplary house for a misgoverned and haughty palace, spiritual dignity for carnal precedence, and secular high office and employment for the high negotiations of his heavenly embassage, then he degrades, then he unbishops himself. He that makes him bishop, makes him no bishop. No marvel therefore if St. Martin complained to Sulpitius Severus, that since he was bishop he felt inwardly a sensible decay of those virtues and graces that God had given him in great measure before; although the same Sulpitius wrote that he was nothing tainted or altered in his habit, diet, or personal demeanour from that simple plainness to which he first betook himself. It was not, therefore, that thing alone which God took displeasure at in the bishops of those times, but rather an universal rottenness and gangrene in the whole function.

From hence then I pass to Queen Elizabeth, the next Protestant prince, in whose days why Religion attained not a perfect reducement in the beginning of her reign, I suppose the hindering causes will be found to be common with some formerly alleged for King Edward VI.: the greenness of the times, the weak estate which Queen Mary left the realm in, the great places and offices executed by papists,—the judges, the lawyers, the justices of peace for the most part popish, the bishops firm to Rome; from whence was to be expected the furious flashing of excommunications, and absolving the people from their obedience. Next, her private counsellors, whoever they were, persuaded her (as Camden writes) that the altering of Ecclesiastical Policy would move sedition. Then was the Liturgy given to a number of moderate divines, and Sir Thomas Smith, a statesman, to be purged and physicked. And surely they were moderate divines indeed, neither hot nor cold; and Grindal, the best of them, afterwards Archbishop of Canterbury, lost favour in the court, and I think was discharged the government of his see, for favouring the ministers, though Camden seem willing to find another cause. Therefore about her second year, in a parliament of men and minds some scarce well grounded others belching the sour crudities of yesterday's popery, those constitutions of Edward VI.,—which, as you heard before, no way satisfied the men that made them,—are now established for best and not to be mended. From that time followed nothing but imprisonments, troubles, disgraces, on all those that found fault with the decrees of the Convocation, and straight were they branded with the name of Puritans. As for the Queen herself, she was made believe that by putting down bishops her prerogative would be infringed, of which shall be spoken anon as the course of method brings it in. And why the prelates laboured it should be so thought, ask not them, but ask their bellies. They had found a good tabernacle, they sat under a spreading vine, their lot was fallen in a fair inheritance. And these perhaps were the chief impeachments of a more sound rectifying the church in the queen's time.

From this period I count to begin Our Times, which because they concern us more nearly, and our own eyes and ears can give us the ampler scope to judge, will require a more exact search. And to effect this the speedier, I shall distinguish such as I esteem to be the Hinderers of Reformation into three sorts:—Antiquitarians (for so I had rather call them than antiquaries, whose labours are useful and laudable). 2. Libertines. 3. Politicians.

To the votarists of Antiquity I shall think to have fully answered, if I shall be able to prove out of antiquity, First, that if they will conform our bishops to the purer times, they must mew their feathers, and their pounces, and make but curtailed bishops of them; and we know they hate to be docked and clipped, as much as to be put down outright. Secondly, that those purer times were corrupt, and their books corrupted soon after. Thirdly, that the best of those that then wrote disclaim that any man should repose on them, and send all to the Scriptures.

First therefore, if those that over-affect antiquity will follow the square thereof, their bishops must be elected by the hands of the whole Church. The ancientest of the extant fathers, Ignatius, writing to the Philadelphians, saith "that it belongs to them as to the Church of God to choose a bishop." Let no man cavil, but take the Church of God as meaning the whole consistence of orders and members, as St. Paul's epistles express, and this likewise being read over: besides this, it is there to be marked, that those Philadelphians are exhorted to choose a bishop of Antioch. Whence it seems by the way that there was not that wary limitation of diocese in those times, which is confirmed even by a fast ffiend of episcopacy, Camden, who cannot but love bishops as well as old coins, and his much lamented monasteries, for antiquity's sake. He writes in his description of Scotland, that "over all the world bishops had no certain diocese till pope Dionysius about the year 268 did cut them out; and that the bishops of Scotland executed their function in what place soever they came indifferently and without distinction, till King Malcolm the Third, about the year 1070." Whence may be guessed what their function was. Was it to go about circled with a band of rooking officials with cloakbags full of citations, and processes to be served by a corporality of griffonlike promoters and apparitors? Did he go about to pitch down his court, as an empiric does his bank, to inveigle in all the money of the country? No, certainly, it would not have been permitted him to exercise any such function indifferently wherever he came. And verily some such matter it was as want of a fat diocese that kept our Britain bishops so poor in the primitive times, that being called to the Council of Rimini in the year 359, they had not wherewithal to defray the charges of their journey, but were fed and lodged upon the emperor's cost; which must needs be no accidental but usual poverty in them: for the author, Sulpitius Severus, in his 2nd book of Church History, praises them, and avouches it praiseworthy in a bishop to be so poor as to have nothing of his own. But to return to the ancient election of bishops: that it could not lawfully be without the consent of the people is so express in Cyprian, and so often to be met with, that to cite each place at large were to translate a good part of the volume; therefore touching the chief passages, I refer the rest to whom so list peruse the author himself. In the 24th epistle, "If a bishop," saith he, "be once made and allowed by the testimony and judgment of his colleagues and the people, no other can be made." In the 55th, "When a bishop is made by the suffrage of all the people in peace." In the 68th, mark but what he says: "The people chiefly hath power either of choosing worthy ones, or refusing unworthy." This he there proves by authorities out of the Old and New Testament, and with solid reasons: these were his antiquities.

This voice of the people, to be had ever in episcopal elections, was so well known before Cyprian's time, even to those that were without the church, that the emperor Alexander Severus desired to have his governors of provinces chosen in the same manner, as Lampridius can tell; so little thought he it offensive to monarchy. And if single authorities persuade not, hearken what the whole General Council of Nicæa, the first and famousest of all the rest, determines, writing a synodical epistle to the African churches, to warn them of Arianism. It exhorts them to choose orthodox bishops in the place of the dead, so they be worthy and the people choose them; whereby they seem to make the people's assent so necessary, that merit without their free choice were not sufficient to make a bishop. What would ye say now, grave fathers, if you should wake and see unworthy bishops, or rather no bishops but Egyptian taskmasters of ceremonies, thrust purposely upon the groaning Church, to the affliction and vexation of God's people? It was not of old that a conspiracy of bishops could frustrate and fob off the right of the people; for we may read how St. Martin, soon after Constantine, was made bishop of Tours in France, by the people's consent from all places thereabout, maugré all the opposition that the bishops could make. Thus went matters of the church almost 400 years after Christ, and very probably far lower: for Nicephorus Phocas, the Greek emperor, whose reign fell near the 1000th year of our Lord, having done many things tyrannically, is said by Cedrenus to have done nothing more grievous and displeasing to the people, than to have enacted that no bishop should be chosen without his will; so long did this right remain to the people in the midst of other palpable corruptions. Now for episcopal dignity,—what it was, see out of Ignatius, who, in his epistle to those of Trallis, confesseth, that "the presbyters are his fellow-counsellors and fellow-benchers." And Cyprian in many places, as in the 6th, 41st, 52nd epistles, speaking of presbyters, calls them his compresbyters, as if he deemed himself no other, whenas by the same place it appears he was a bishop. He calls them brethren, but that will be thought his meekness; yea, but the presbyters and deacons writing to him think they do him honour enough, when they phrase him no higher than brother Cyprian, and dear Cyprian, in the 26th epistle. For their authority,—it is evident not to have been single, but depending on the counsel of the presbyters, as from Ignatius was erewhile alleged; and the same Cyprian acknowledges as much in the 6th epistle, and adds thereto, that he had determined, from his entrance into the office of bishop, to do nothing without the consent of his people; and so in the 31st epistle, for it were tedious to course through all his writings, which are so full of the like assertions, insomuch that even in the womb and centre of apostasy, Rome itself, there yet remains a glimpse of this truth. For the pope himself, as a learned English writer notes well, performeth all ecclesiastical jurisdiction as in consistory among his cardinals, which were originally but the parish priests of Rome. Thus then did the spirit of unity and meekness inspire and animate every joint and sinew of the mystical body. But now the gravest and worthiest minister, a true bishop of his fold, shall be reviled and ruffled by an insulting and only canon-wise prelate, as if he were some slight paltry companion; and the people of God, redeemed and washed with Christ's blood, and dignified with so many glorious titles of saints and sons in the Gospel, are now no better reputed than impure ethnics and lay dogs. Stones, and pillars, and crucifixes have now the honour and the alms due to Christ's living members. The table of Communion, now become a table of separation, stands like an exalted platform upon the brow of the quire, fortified with bulwark and barricado to keep off the profane touch of the laics, whilst the obscene and surfeited priest scruples not to paw and mammock the sacramental bread as familiarly as his tavern biscuit. And thus the people, vilified and rejected by them, give over the earnest study of virtue and godliness, as a thing of greater purity than* they need, and the search of divine knowledge as a mystery too high for their capacities, and only for churchmen to meddle with: which is what the prelates desire, that when they have brought us back to popish blindness, we might commit to their dispose the whole managing of our salvation; for they think it was never fair world with them since that time. But he that will mould a Modern bishop into a Primitive, must yield him to be elected by the popular voice, undiocesed, unrevenued, unlorded, and leave him nothing but brotherly equality, matchless temperance, frequent fasting, incessant prayer and preaching, continual watchings and labours in his ministry; which what a rich booty it would be, what a plump endowment to the many-benefice-gaping-mouth of a prelate, what a relish it would give to his canary-sucking and swan-eating palate, let old bishop Mountain judge for me.

How little therefore those ancient times make for modern bishops hath been plainly discoursed; but let them make for them as much as they will, yet why we ought not to stand to their arbitrement, shall now appear by a threefold corruption which will be found upon them. 1. The best times were spreadingly infected: 2. The best men of those times, foully tainted: 3. The best writings of those men, dangerously adulterated. These positions are to be made good out of those times witnessing of themselves. First Ignatius in his early days testifies to the churches of Asia, that even then heresies were sprung up, and rife everywhere, as Eusebius relates in his 3rd book, 35 chap., after the Greek number. And Hegesippus, a grave church writer of prime antiquity, affirms in the same book of Eusebius, c. 32, "that while the apostles were on earth, the depravers of doctrine did but lurk; but they once gone, with open forehead they durst preach down the truth with falsities." Yea, those that are reckoned for orthodox began to make sad and shameful rents in the Church about the trivial celebration of feasts, not agreeing when to keep Easter-day; which controversy grew so hot, that Victor, the bishop of Rome, excommunicated all the Churches of Asia for no other cause, and was worthily thereof reproved by Irenæus. For can any sound theologer think, that these great fathers understood what was Gospel, or what was excommunication? Doubtless that which led the good men into fraud and error was, that they attended more to the near tradition of what they heard the apostles sometimes did, than to what they had left written, not considering that many things which they did were by the apostles themselves professed to be done only for the present, and of mere indulgence to some scrupulous converts of the circumcision, but what they writ was of firm decree to all future ages. Look but a century lower in the 1st cap. of Eusebius's 8th book. What a universal tetter of impurity had envenomed every part, order, and degree of the church! To omit the lay herd, which will be little regarded, "Those that seem to be our pastors," saith he, "overturning the law of God's worship, burnt in contentions one towards another, and increasing in hatred and bitterness, outrageously sought to uphold lordship and command as it were a tyranny." Stay but a little, magnanimous bishops; suppress your aspiring thoughts, for there is nothing wanting but Constantine to reign, and then tyranny herself shall give up all her citadels into your hands, and count ye thenceforward her trustiest agents. Such were these that must be called the ancientest and most virgin times between Christ and Constantine. Nor was this general contagion in their actions, and not in their writings. Who is ignorant of the foul errors, the ridiculous wresting of Scripture, the heresies, the vanities thick sown through the volumes of Justin Martyr, Clemens, Origen, Tertullian, and others of eldest time? Who would think him fit to write an apology for Christian faith to the Roman senate, that would tell them "how of the angels," which he must needs mean those in Genesis, called the sons of God, "mixing with women were begotten the devils," as good Justin Martyr in his Apology told them? But more indignation would it move to any Christian that shall read Tertullian terming St. Paul a novice and raw in grace, for reproving St. Peter at Antioch, worthy to be blamed, if we believe the epistle to the Galatians. Perhaps from this hint the blasphemous Jesuits presumed in Italy to give their judgment of St. Paul as of a hotheaded person, as Sandys in his relations tells us.

Now besides all this, who knows not how many superstitious works are ingraffed into the legitimate writings of the fathers? And of those books that pass for authentic, who knows what hath been tampered withal, what hath been razed out, what hath been inserted? Besides the late legerdemain of the papists, that which Sulpitius writes concerning Origen's books gives us cause vehemently to suspect there hath been packing of old. In the third chapter of his 1st Dialogue we may read what wrangling the bishops and monks had about the reading or not reading of Origen; some objecting that he was corrupted by heretics; others answering that all such books had been so dealt with. How then shall I trust these times to lead me, that testify so ill of leading themselves? Certainly of their defects their own witness may be best received; but of the rectitude and sincerity of their life and doctrine, to judge rightly, we must judge by that which was to be their rule.

But it will be objected, that this was an unsettled state of the church, wanting the temporal magistrate to suppress the licence of false brethren, and the extravagancy of still new opinions; a time not imitable for Church government, where the temporal and spiritual power did not close in one belief, as under Constantine. I am not of opinion to think the Church a vine in this respect, because, as they take it, she cannot subsist without clasping about the elm of worldly strength and felicity, as if the heavenly city could not support itself without the props and buttresses of secular authority. They extol Constantine because he extolled them; as our homebred monks in their histories blanch the kings their benefactors, and brand those that went about to be their correctors. If he had curbed the growing pride, avarice, and luxury of the clergy, then every page of his story should have swelled with his faults, and that which Zosimus the heathen writes of him should have come in to boot. We should have heard then in every declamation how he slew his nephew Commodus, a worthy man, his noble and eldest son Crispus, his wife Fausta, besides numbers of his friends: then his cruel exactions, his unsoundness in religion, favouring the Arians that had been condemned in a council, of which himself sat as it were president; his hard measure and banishment of the faithful and invincible Athanasius; his living unbaptized almost to his dying day: these blurs are too apparent in his life. But since he must needs be the lode-star of

Reformation, as some men clatter, it will be good to see further his knowledge of Religion what it was, and by that we may likewise guess at the sincerity of his times in those that were not heretical, it being likely that he would converse with the famousest prelates (for so he had made them) that were to be found for learning.

Of his Arianism we heard, and for the rest a pretty scantling of his knowledge may be taken by his deferring to be baptized so many years, a thing not usual, and repugnant to the tenor of scripture; Philip knowing nothing that should hinder the eunuch to be baptized after profession of his belief. Next, by the excessive devotion, that I may not say superstition, both of him and his mother Helena, to find out the cross on which Christ suffered, that had long lain under the rubbish of old ruins—a thing which the disciples and kindred of our Saviour might with more ease have done, if they had thought it a pious duty;—some of the nails whereof he put into his helmet, to bear off blows in battle; others he fastened among the studs of his bridle, to fulfil, as he thought, or his court bishops persuaded him, the prophecy of Zechariah: "And it shall be that which is in the bridle shall be holy to the Lord." Part of the cross, in which he thought such virtue to reside as would prove a kind of palladium to save the city wherever it remained, he caused to be laid up in a pillar of porphyry by his statue. How he or his teachers could trifle thus with half an eye open upon St. Paul's principles, I know not how to imagine.

How should then the dim taper of this emperor's age, that had such need of snuffing, extend any beam to our times, wherewith we might hope to be better lighted than by those luminaries that God hath set up to shine to us far nearer hand? And what Reformation he wrought for his own time, it will not be amiss to consider. He appointed certain times for fasts and feasts, built stately churches, gave large immunities to the clergy, great riches and promotions to bishops; gave and ministered occasion to bring in a deluge of ceremonies, thereby either to draw in the heathen by a resemblance of their rites, or to set a gloss upon the simplicity and plainness of Christianity, which to the gorgeous solemnities of paganism, and the sense of the world's children, seemed but a homely and yeomanly religion: for the beauty of inward sanctity was not within their prospect.

So that in this manner the prelates, both then and ever since, coming from a mean and plebeian life on a sudden to be lords of stately palaces, rich furniture, delicious fare and princely attendance, thought the plain and homespun verity of Christ's gospel unfit any longer to hold their lordships' acquaintance unless the poor threadbare matron were put into better clothes: her chaste and modest veil, surrounded with celestial beams, they overlaid with wanton tresses, and in a flaring tire bespeckled her with all the gaudy allurements of a whore.

Thus flourished the Church with Constantine's wealth, and thereafter were the effects that followed. His son Constantius proved a flat Arian, and his nephew Julian an apostate, and there his race ended. The Church that before by insensible degrees welked and impaired, now with large steps went down hill decaying. At this time Antichrist began first to put forth his horn, and that saying was common, that former times had wooden chalices and golden priests, but they, golden chalices and wooden priests.

"Formerly," saith Sulpitius, "martyrdom by glorious death was sought more greedily than now bishoprics by vile ambition are hunted after," speaking of those times. And in another place, "They gape after possessions, they tend lands and livings, they cower over their gold, they buy and sell: and if there be any that neither possess nor traffic, that which is worse they sit still and expect gifts, and prostitute every endowment of grace, every holy thing, to sale." And in the end of his history thus he concludes: "All things went to wrack by the faction, wilfulness, and avarice of the bishops; and by this means God's people, and every good man, was had in scorn and derision." Which St. Martin found truly to be said by his friend Sulpitius; for, being held in admiration of all men, he had only the bishops his enemies, found God less favourable to him after he was bishop than before, and for his last sixteen years would come at no bishop's meeting.

Thus you see, Sir, what Constantine's doings in the Church brought forth, either in his own or in his son's reign.

Now, lest it should be thought that something else might ail this author, thus to hamper the bishops of those days, I will bring you the opinion of three the famousest men for wit and learning that Italy at this day glories of, whereby it may be concluded for a received opinion, even among men professing the Romish faith, that Constantine marred all in the church. Dante, in his 19th Canto of Inferno, hath thus, as I will render it you in English blank verse:

> "Ah Constantine! of how much ill was cause,
> Not thy conversion, but those rich domains
> That the first wealthy pope received of thee!"

So, in his 20th Canto of Paradise, he makes the like complaint; and Petrarch seconds him in the same mind in his 108th sonnet, which is wiped out by the inquisitor in some editions; speaking of the Roman Antichrist as merely bred up by Constantine:—

> "Founded in chaste and humble poverty,
> 'Gainst them that raised thee dost thou lift thy horn.
> Impudent whore, where hast thou placed thy hope?
> In thy adulterers, or thy ill-got wealth?
> Another Constantine comes not in haste."

Ariosto of Ferrara, after both these in time, but equal in fame, following the scope of his poem in a difficult knot how to restore Orlando, his chief hero, to his lost senses, brings Astolfo, the English knight, up into the moon, where St. John, as he feigns, met him. Cant. 34:

> "And, to be short, at last his guide him brings
> Into a goodly valley, where he sees
> A mighty mass of things strangely confused,
> Things that on earth were lost, or were abused."

And amongst these so abused things, listen what he met withal, under the conduct of the Evangelist:—

> "Then pass'd he to a flowery mountain green,
> Which once smelt sweet, now stinks as odiously:
> This was that gift (if you the truth will have)
> That Constantine to good Silvestro gave."

And this was a truth well known in England before this poet was born, as our Chaucer's Ploughman shall tell you by and by upon another occasion. By all these circumstances laid together, I do not see how it can be disputed what good this emperor Constantine wrought to the Church; but rather whether ever any, though perhaps not wittingly, set open a door to more mischief in Christendom. There is just cause therefore, that when the prelates cry out, Let the Church be reformed according to Constantine, it should sound to a judicious ear no otherwise than if they should say, Make us rich, make us lofty, make us lawless; for if any under him were not so, thanks to those ancient remains of integrity which were not yet quite worn out, and not to his government.

Thus finally it appears, that those purer times were not such as they are cried up, and not to be followed without suspicion, doubt, and danger. The last point wherein the Antiquary is to be dealt with at his own weapon, is, to make it manifest that the ancientest and best of the Fathers have disclaimed all sufficiency in themselves that men should rely on, and sent all comers to the Scriptures, as all-sufficient. That this is true, will not be unduly gathered, by showing what esteem they had of Antiquity themselves, and what validity they thought in it to prove doctrine or discipline. I must of necessity begin from the second rank of Fathers, because till then Antiquity could have no plea. Cyprian in his 63rd epistle: "If any," saith he, "of our ancestors, either ignorantly or out of simplicity, hath not observed that which the Lord taught us by his example," speaking of the Lord's Supper, "his simplicity God may pardon of his mercy; but we cannot be excused for following him, being instructed by the Lord." And have not we the same instructions? and will not this holy man, with all the whole consistory of saints and martyrs that lived of old, rise up and stop our mouths in judgment, when we shall go about to father our errors and opinions upon their authority? In the 73d epistle he adds, "In vain do they oppose custom to us, if they be overcome by reason; as if custom were greater than truth, or that in spiritual things that were not to be followed which is revealed for the better by the Holy Ghost." In the 74th: "Neither ought custom to hinder that truth should not prevail; for custom without truth is but agedness of error."

Next Lactantius, he that was preferred to have the bringing up of Constantine's children, in his second book of Institutions, chap. 7 and 8, disputes against the vain trust in Antiquity, as being the chiefest argument of the heathen against the Christians: "They do not consider," saith he, "what Religion is, but they are confident it is true, because the ancients delivered it; they count it a trespass to examine it." And in the eighth: "Not because they went before us in time, therefore in wisdom; which being given alike to all ages, cannot be prepossessed by the ancients: wherefore, seeing that to seek the truth is inbred to all, they bereave themselves of wisdom, the gift of God, who without judgment follow the ancients, and are led by others like brute beasts." St. Austin writes to Fortunatian, that "he counts it lawful, in the books of whomsoever, to reject that which he finds otherwise than true; and so he would have others deal by him." He neither accounted, as it seems, those Fathers that went before, nor himself, nor others of his rank, for men of more than ordinary spirit, that might equally deceive and be deceived: and ofttimes setting our servile humours aside, yea, God so ordering, we may find truth with one man, as soon as in a Council, as Cyprian agrees, 71st epistle: "Many things," saith he, "are better revealed to single persons." At Nicæa, in the first and best-reputed Council of all the world, there had gone out a canon to divorce married priests, had not one old man, Paphnutius, stood up and reasoned against it.

Now remains it to shew clearly that the Fathers refer all decision of controversy to the Scriptures, as all-sufficient to direct, to resolve, and to determine. Ignatius, taking his last leave of the Asian Churches as he went to martyrdom, exhorted them to adhere close to the written doctrine of the Apostles, necessarily written for posterity, so far was he from unwritten traditions, as may be read in the 36th chap. of Eusebius, 3rd book. In the 74th epistle of Cyprian against Stefan, Bishop of Rome, imposing upon him a tradition; "Whence," quoth he, "is this tradition? Is it fetched from the authority of Christ in the Gospel, or of the Apostles in their Epistles? for God testifies that those things are to be done which are written." And then thus, "What obstinacy, what presumption is this, to prefer human tradition before divine ordinance?" And in the same epistle: "If we shall return to the head and beginning of divine tradition" (which we all know he means the Bible), "human error ceases; and the reason of heavenly mysteries unfolded, whatsoever was obscure becomes clear." And in the 14th distinct. of the same epistle, directly against our modern fantasies of a still visible church, he teaches, "that successsion of truth may fail; to renew which, we must have recourse to the fountains;" using this excellent similitude, "If a channel, or conduit-pipe which brought in water plentifully before, suddenly fail, do we not go to the fountain to know the cause; whether the spring affords no more, or whether the vein be stopped, or turned aside in the midcourse? Thus ought we to do, keeping God's precepts, that if in aught the truth shall be changed, we may repair to the Gospel and to the Apostles, that thence may arise the reason of our doings, from whence our order and beginning arose." In the 75th he inveighs bitterly against Pope Stephanus, "for that he could boast his succession from Peter, and yet foist in traditions that were not apostolical." And in his book of the Unity of the Church, he compares those that, neglecting God's word, follow the doctrines of men, to Corah, Dathan, and Abiram. The very first page of Athanasius against the Gentiles avers the Scriptures to be sufficient of themselves for the declaration of truth; and that if his friend Macarius read other religious writers, as it was but φιλοκάλος, "come un vertuoso" (as the Italians say), as a lover of elegance: and in his second tome, the 39th page, after he hath reckoned up the canonical books, "In these only," saith he, "is the doctrine of godliness taught; let no man add to these, or take from these." And in his Synopsis, having again set down all the writers of the Old and New Testament, "These," saith he, "be the anchors and props of our faith." Besides these, millions of other books have been written by great and wise men according to rule, and agreement with these, of which I will not now speak, as being of infinite number, and mere dependence on the canonical books. Basil, in his 2nd tome, writing of true faith, tells his auditors, he is bound to teach them that which he hath learned out of the Bible. And in the same treatise he saith, "that seeing the commandments of the Lord are faithful and sure for ever, it is a plain falling from the faith, and a high pride, either to make void anything therein, or to introduce anything not there to be found:" and he gives the reason: "For Christ saith, My sheep hear my voice: they will not follow another, but fly from him because they know not his voice." But not to be endless in quotations, it may chance to be objected, that there be many opinions in the Fathers which have no ground in Scripture. So much the less, may I say, should we follow them, for their own words shall condemn them, and acquit us that lean not on them; otherwise these their words will acquit them, and condemn us. But it will be replied, The Scriptures are difficult to be understood, and therefore require the explanation of the Fathers. It is true, there be some books, and especially some places in these books, that remain clouded. Yet ever that which is most necessary to be known is most easy; and that which is most difficult, so far expounds itself ever, as to tell us how little it imports our saving knowledge. Hence, to infer a general obscurity over all the text is a mere suggestion of the devil to dissuade men from reading it, and casts an aspersion of dishonour both upon the mercy, truth, and wisdom of God. We count it no gentleness or fair dealing in a man of power amongst us, to require strict and punctual obedience and yet give out all his commands ambiguous and obscure: we should think he had a plot upon us; certainly such commands were no commands, but snares. The very essence of truth is plainness and brightness; the darkness and crookedness is our own. The wisdom of God created understanding fit and proportionable to truth the object and end of it, as the eye to the thing visible. If our understanding have a film of ignorance over it, or be blear with gazing on other false glisterings, what is that to truth? If we will but purge with sovereign eyesalve that intellectual ray which God hath planted in us, then we would believe the Scriptures protesting their own plainness and perspicuity; calling to them to be instructed, not only the wise and learned, but the simple, the poor, the babes; foretelling an extraordinary effusion of God's Spirit upon every age and sex; attributing to all men, and requiring from them the ability of searching, trying, examining all things, and by the Spirit discerning that which is good. And as the Scriptures themselves pronounce their own plainness, so do the Fathers testify of them.

I will not run into a paroxysm of citations again in this point, only instance Athanasius in his forementioned first page: "The knowledge of truth," saith he, "wants no human lore, as being evident in itself, and by the preaching of Christ now opens brighter than the sun." If these doctors, who had scarce half the light that we enjoy, who all, except two or three, were ignorant of the Hebrew tongue, and many of the Greek, blundering upon the dangerous and suspectful translations of the apostate Aquila, the heretical Theodotion, the judaized Symmachus, the erroneous Origen; if these could yet find the Bible so easy, why should we doubt, that have all the helps of learning and faithful industry that man in this life can look for, and the assistance of God as near now to us as ever? But let the Scriptures be hard; are they more hard, more crabbed, more abstruse than the Fathers? He that cannot understand the sober, plain, and unaffected style of the Scriptures, will be ten times more puzzled with the knotty Africanisms, the pampered metaphors, the intricate and involved sentences of the Fathers, besides the fantastic and declamatory flashes, the cross-jingling periods which cannot but disturb and come thwart a settled devotion, worse than the din of bells and rattles.

Now, Sir, for the love of holy Reformation, what can be said more against these importunate clients of Antiquity than she herself their patroness had said? Whether, think ye, would she approve still to dote upon immeasurable, innumerable, and therefore unnecessary and unmerciful volumes, choosing rather to err with the specious name of the Fathers, or to take a sound truth at the hand of a plain upright man that all his days had been diligently reading the Holy Scriptures, and thereto imploring God's grace, while the admirers of antiquity have been beating their brains about their ambones, their dyptichs, and meniaias? Now, he that cannot tell of stations and indictions, nor has wasted his precious hours in the endless conferring of councils and conclaves that demolish one another—although I know many of those that pretend to be great rabbis in these studies, have scarce saluted them from the strings, and the title-page; or, to give them more, have been but the ferrets and mousehunts of an index—yet what pastor or minister, how learned, religious, or discreet soever, does not now bring both his cheeks full blown with œcumenical and synodical, shall be counted a lank, shallow, insufficient man, yea, a dunce, and not worthy to speak about Reformation of Church Discipline. But I trust they for whom God hath reserved the honour of reforming this Church, will easily perceive their adversaries' drift in thus calling for antiquity. They fear the plain field of the Scriptures. The chase is too hot; they seek the dark, the bushy, the tangled forest; they would imbosk. They feel themselves struck, in the transparent streams of divine truth: they would plunge, and tumble, and think to lie hid in the foul weeds and muddy waters where no plummet can reach the bottom. But let them beat themselves like whales, and spend their oil till they be dragged ashore. Though wherefore should the ministers give them so much line for shifts and delays? Wherefore should they not urge only the Gospel, and hold it ever in their faces like a mirror of diamond, till it dazzle and pierce their misty eyeballs, maintaining the honour of its absolute sufficiency and supremacy inviolable? For if the Scripture be for Reformation and Antiquity to boot, it is but an advantage to the dozen, it is no winning cast. And though Antiquity be against it, while the Scriptures be for it, the cause is as good as ought to be wished, Antiquity itself sitting judge.

But to draw to an end: the second sort of those that may be

justly numbered among the hinderers of Reformation, are Libertines. These suggest that the Discipline sought would be intolerable: for one bishop now in a diocese, we should then have a pope in every parish. It will not be requisite to answer these men, but only to discover them; for reason they have none but lust and licentiousness, and therefore answer can have none. It is not any discipline that they could live under, it is the corruption and remissness of discipline that they seek. Episcopacy duly executed, yea, the Turkish and Jewish rigour against whoring and drinking, the dear and tender discipline of a father, the sociable and loving reproof of a brother, the bosom admonition of a friend, is a presbytery and a consistory to them. It is only the merry friar in Chaucer can disple them.

> "Full sweetly heardé he confessión,
> And pleasant was his absolutión,
> He was an easy man to give penánce."

And so I leave them; and refer the Political Discourse of Episcopacy to a second book.

THE SECOND BOOK.

SIR,—It is a work good and prudent to be able to guide one man; of larger extended virtue to order well one house: but to govern a nation piously and justly, which only is to say happily, is for a spirit of the greatest size and divinest mettle. And certainly of no less a mind, nor of less excellence in another way, were they who by writing laid the solid and true foundations of this science; which being of greatest importance to the life of man, yet there is no art that hath been more cankered in her principles, more soiled and slubbered with aphorising pedantry, than the Art of Policy; and that most, where a man would think should least be, in Christian Commonwealths. They teach not, that to govern well is to train up a nation in true wisdom and virtue, and that which springs from thence, magnanimity (take heed of that); and that which is our beginning, regeneration, and happiest end, likeness to God, which in one word we call Godliness; and that this is the true flourishing of a land. Other things follow as the shadow does the substance: to teach thus were mere pulpitry to them. This is the masterpiece of a modern politician:—how to qualify and mould the sufferance and subjection of the people to the length of that foot that is to tread on their necks; how rapine may serve itself with the fair and honourable pretences of public good; how the puny law may be brought under the wardship and control of lust and will: in which attempt if they fall short, then must a superficial colour of reputation by all means, direct or indirect, be gotten to wash over the unsightly bruise of honour. To make men governable in this manner, their precepts mainly tend to break a national spirit and courage by countenancing open riot, luxury, and ignorance; till having thus disfigured and made men beneath men, as Juno in the fable of Io, they deliver up the poor transformed heifer of the commonwealth to be stung and vexed with the breese and goad of oppression, under the custody of some Argus with a hundred eyes of jealousy. To be plainer, Sir, how to solder, how to stop a leak, how to keep up the floating carcass of a crazy and diseased Monarchy or State, betwixt wind and water, swimming still upon her own dead lees, that now is the deep design of a politician. Alas, Sir: a Commonwealth ought to be but as one huge Christian personage, one mighty growth and stature of an honest man, as big and compact in virtue as in body. For look what the grounds and causes are of single happiness to one man, the same ye shall find them to a whole state, as Aristotle, both in his Ethics and Politics, from the principles of reason, lays down. By consequence, therefore, that which is good and agreeable to Monarchy, will appear soonest to be so, by being good and agreeable to the true welfare of every Christian; and that which can be justly proved hurtful and offensive to every true Christian, will be evinced to be alike hurtful to Monarchy: for God forbid that we should separate and distinguish the end and good of a Monarch, from the end and good of the Monarchy, or of that, from Christianity. How then this third and last sort that hinder Reformation will justify that it stands not with reason of state, I much muse; for certain I am, the Bible is shut against them; as certain that neither Plato nor Aristotle is for their turns. What they can bring us now from the schools of Loyola with his Jesuits, or their Malvezzi that can cut Tacitus into slivers and steaks, we shall presently hear. They allege, 1. That the Church Government must be conformable to the Civil Polity; next, That no form of Church Government is agreeable to monarchy, but that of bishops. Must Church Government that is appointed in the Gospel, and has chief respect to the soul, be conformable and pliant to civil, that is arbitrary, and chiefly conversant about the visible and external part of man? This is the very maxim that moulded the calves of Bethel and of Dan. This was the quintessence of Jeroboam's policy, he made religion conform to his politic interests; and this was the sin that watched over the Israelites till their final captivity. If this state principle come from the prelates, as they affect to be counted statists, let them look back to Eleutherius bishop of Rome, and see what he thought of the policy of England. Being required by Lucius, the first Christian king of this island, to give his counsel for the founding of religious laws, little thought he of this sage caution, but bids him betake himself to the Old and New Testament, and receive direction from them how to administer both Church and Commonwealth; that he was God's vicar, and therefore to rule by God's laws; that the edicts of Cæsar we may at all times disallow, but the statutes of God for no reason we may reject. Now certain, if Church Government be taught in the Gospel, as the bishops dare not deny, we may well conclude of what late standing this position is, newly calculated for the altitude of bishop-elevation, and lettuce for their lips. But by what example can they shew, that the form of Church Discipline must be minted and modelled out to secular pretences? The ancient republic of the Jews is evident to have run through all the changes of civil estate, if we survey the story from the giving of the Law to the Herods; yet did one manner of priestly government serve without inconvenience to all these temporal mutations. It served the mild aristocracy of elective dukes, and heads of tribes joined with them; the dictatorship of the judges, the easy or hard-handed monarchies, the domestic or foreign tyrannies: lastly, the Roman senate from without, the Jewish senate at home, with the Galilean tetrarch. Yet the Levites had some right to deal in civil affairs: but seeing the evangelical precept forbids churchmen to intermeddle with worldly employments, what interweavings or interworkings can knit the minister and the magistrate in their several functions, to the regard of any precise correspondency! Seeing that the churchman's office is only to teach men the Christian faith, to exhort all, to encourage the good, to admonish the bad, privately the less offender, publicly the scandalous and stubborn; to censure and separate from the communion of Christ's flock the contagious and incorrigible; to receive with joy and fatherly compassion the penitent: all this must be done, and more than this is beyond any Church authority. What is all this either here or there to the temporal regiment of weal public, whether it be popular, princely, or monarchical? Where doth it entrench upon the temporal governor? where does it come in his walk? where doth it make inroad upon his jurisdiction? Indeed if the minister's part be rightly discharged, it renders him the people more conscionable, quiet, and easy to be governed; if otherwise, his life and doctrine will declare him. If, therefore, the Constitution of the Church be already set down by divine prescript, as all sides confess, then can she not be a handmaid to wait on civil commodities and respects; and if the nature and limits of Church Discipline be such, as are either helpful to all political estates indifferently, or have no particular relation to any, then is there no necessity, nor indeed possibility, of linking the one with the other in a special conformation.

Now for their second conclusion, "That no form of Church Government is agreeable to Monarchy, but that of bishops," although it fall to pieces of itself by that which hath been said; yet to give them play, front and rear, it shall be my task to prove that episcopacy, with that authority which it challenges in England, is not only not agreeable, but tending to the destruction of Monarchy. While the primitive pastors of the Church of God laboured faithfully in their ministry, tending only their sheep, and not seeking but avoiding all worldly matters as clogs and indeed derogations and debasements to their high calling, little needed the princes and potentates of the earth, which way soever the Gospel was spread, to study ways how to make a coherence between the Church's Polity and theirs. Therefore, when Pilate heard once our Saviour Christ professing that "his kingdom was not of this world," he thought the man could not stand much in Cæsar's light nor much endamage the Roman empire; for if the life of Christ be hid to this world, much more is his sceptre inoperative but in spiritual things. And thus lived, for two or three ages, the successors of the Apostles. But when, through Constantine's lavish superstition, they forsook their first love, and set themselves up two gods instead, Mammon and their Belly; then taking advantage of the spiritual power which they had on men's consciences, they began to cast a longing eye to get the body also and bodily things into their command. Upon which their carnal desires, the spirit daily quenching and dying in them, knew no way to keep themselves up from falling to nothing, but by bolstering and supporting their inward rottenness by a carnal and outward strength. For a while they rather privily sought opportunity than hastily disclosed their project; but when Constantine was dead, and three or four emperors more, their drift became notorious and offensive to the whole world: for while Theodosius the younger reigned, thus writes Socrates the historian, in his 7th book, chap. 11. "Now began an ill name to stick upon the bishops of Rome and Alexandria, who beyond their priestly bounds now long ago had stepped into principality:" and this was scarce eighty years since their raising from the meanest worldly condition. Of courtesy now let any man tell me, if they draw to themselves a temporal strength and power out of Cæsar's dominion, is not Cæsar's empire thereby diminished? But this was a stolen bit, hitherto he was but a caterpillar secretly gnawing at Monarchy; the next time you shall see him a wolf, a lion, lifting his paw against his raiser, as

Petrarch expressed it, and finally an open enemy and subverter of the Greek empire.

Philippicus and Leo, with divers other emperors after them, not without the advice of their patriarchs, and at length of a whole eastern Council of three hundred and thirty-eight bishops, threw the images out of churches as being decreed idolatrous. Upon this goodly occasion, the bishop of Rome not only seizes the city, and all the territory about, into his own hands, and makes himself lord thereof, which till then was governed by a Greek magistrate, but absolves all Italy of their tribute and obedience due to the emperor, because he obeyed God's commandment in abolishing idolatry.

Mark, Sir, here, how the pope came by St. Peter's patrimony, as he feigns it; not the donation of Constantine, but idolatry and rebellion got it him. Ye need but read Sigonius, one of his own sect, to know the story at large. And now to shroud himself against a storm from the Greek continent, and provide a champion to bear him out of these practices, he takes upon him by papal sentence to unthrone Chilpericus, the rightful king of France, and gives the kingdom to Pepin, for no other cause but that he seemed to him the more active man. If he were a friend herein to monarchy, I know not; but to the monarch I need not ask what he was.

Having thus made Pepin his fast friend, he calls him into Italy against Aistulphus the Lombard, that warred upon him for his late usurpation of Rome, as belonging to Ravenna, which he had newly won. Pepin, not unobedient to the pope's call, passing into Italy, frees him out of danger, and wins for him the whole exarchate of Ravenna; which though it had been almost immediately before the hereditary possession of that monarchy which was his chief patron and benefactor, yet he takes and keeps it to himself as lawful prize, and given to St. Peter. What a dangerous fallacy is this, when a spiritual man may snatch to himself any temporal dignity or dominion, under pretence of receiving it for the Church's use? Thus he claims Naples, Sicily, England, and what not? To be short, under show of his zeal against the errors of the Greek Church, he never ceased baiting and goring the successors of his best lord Constantine, what by his barking curses and excommunications, what by his hindering the western princes from aiding them against the Saracens and Turks, unless when they humoured him; so that it may be truly affirmed, he was the subversion and fall of that Monarchy which was the hoisting of him. This, besides Petrarch, whom I have cited, our Chaucer also hath observed, and gives from hence a caution to England, to beware of her bishops in time, for that their ends and aims are no more friendly to Monarchy than the pope's.

This he begins in the Ploughman speaking, part ii. stanza 28:

> "The emperor yafe the pope sometime
> So high lordship him about,
> That at last the silly kime,
> The proud pope put him out;
> So of this realm is no doubt,
> But lords beware and them defend;
> For now these folks be wonders stout,
> The king and lords now this amend."

And in the next stanza, which begins the third part of the tale, he argues that they ought not to be lords:

> "Moses law forbode it tho
> That priests should no lordship welde,
> Christ's gospel biddeth also
> That they should no lordships held:
> Ne Christ's apostles were never so bold
> No such lordships to hem embrace,
> But smeren her sheep and keep her fold."

And so forward. Whether the bishops of England have deserved thus to be feared by men so wise as our Chaucer is esteemed; and how agreeable to our Monarchy and Monarchs their demeanour has been, he that is but meanly read in our chronicles needs not be instructed. Have they not been as the Canaanites and Philistines to this kingdom? What treasons, what revolts to the pope, what rebellions, and those the basest and most pretenceless, have they not been chief in? What could Monarchy think, when Becket durst challenge the custody of Rochester

Castle, and the Tower of London, as appertaining to his signory? to omit his other insolencies and affronts to regal majesty, until the lashes inflicted on the anointed body of the king washed off the holy unction with his blood drawn by the polluted hands of bishops, abbots, and monks.

What good upholders of royalty were the bishops, when, by their rebellious opposition against king John, Normandy was lost, he himself deposed, and this kingdom made over to the pope? When the bishop of Winchester durst tell the nobles, the pillars of the realm, that there were no peers in England, as in France, but that the king might do what he pleased, what could tyranny say more? It would be pretty now if I should insist upon the rendering up of Tournay by Wolsey's treason, the excommunications, cursings, and interdicts upon the whole land; for haply I shall be cut off short by a reply, that these were the faults of men and their popish errors, not of Episcopacy, that hath now renounced the Pope, and is a Protestant. Yes, sure; as wise and famous men have suspected and feared the Protestant Episcopacy in England, as those that have feared the Papal.

You know, sir, what was the judgment of Padre Paolo, the great Venetian antagonist of the pope, for it is extant in the hands of many men, whereby he declares his fear, that when the hierarchy of England shall light into the hands of busy and audacious men, or shall meet with princes tractable to the prelacy, then much mischief is like to ensue. And can it be nearer hand than when bishops shall openly affirm that, "No Bishop no King"? A trim paradox, and that ye may know where they have been a begging for it, I will fetch you the twin brother to it out of the Jesuits' cell: they feeling the axe of God's Reformation, hewing at the old and hollow trunk of papacy, and finding the Spaniard their surest friend and safest refuge, to soothe him up in his dream of a fifth monarchy, and withal to uphold the decrepit papalty, have invented this superpolitic aphorism, as one terms it, "One pope and one king."

Surely there is not any prince in Christendom, who, hearing this rare sophistry, can choose but smile; and if we be not blind at home, we may as well perceive that this worthy motto, "No Bishop no King," is of the same batch, and infanted out of the same fears, a mere ague-cake, coagulated of a certain fever they have, presaging their time to be but short. And now, like those that are sinking, they catch round of that which is likeliest to hold them up; and would persuade regal power that if they dive, he must after. But what greater debasement can there be to royal dignity, whose towering and steadfast height rests upon the unmovable foundations of justice and heroic virtue, than to, chain it in a dependence of subsisting or ruining to the painted battlements and gaudy rottenness of prelatry, which want but one puff of the King's to blow them down like a pasteboard house built of court-cards? Sir, the little ado which methinks I find in untacking these pleasant sophisms, puts me into the mood to tell you a tale ere I proceed further; and Menenius Agrippa speed us.

Upon a time the Body summoned all the members to meet in the guild, for the common good (as Æsop's chronicles aver many stranger accidents): the head by right takes the first seat, and next to it a huge and monstrous wen, little less than the head itself, growing to it by a narrower excrescency. The members, amazed, began to ask one another what he was that took place next their chief? None could resolve. Whereat the wen, though unwieldy, with much ado gets up, and bespeaks the assembly to this purpose: "That as in place he was second to the head, so by due of merit; that he was to it an ornament, and strength, and of special near relation; and that if the head should fail, none were fitter than himself to step into his place: therefore he thought it for the honour of the body, that such dignities and rich endowments should be decreed him, as did adorn and set out the noblest members." To this was answered that it should be consulted. Then was a wise and learned philosopher sent for, that knew all the charters, laws, and tenures of the Body. On him it is imposed by all, as chief committee, to examine, and discuss the claim and petition of right put in by the wen; who soon perceiving the matter, and wondering at the boldness of such a swoln tumour, "Wilt thou," quoth he, "that art but a bottle of vicious and hardened excrements, contend with the lawful and freeborn members, whose certain number is set by ancient and unrepealable statute? Head thou art none, though thou receive this huge substance from it. What office bearest thou? what good can'st thou shew by thee done to the commonweal?" The wen, not easily dashed, replies that his office was his glory; for so oft as the soul would retire out of the head from over the steaming vapours of the lower parts to divine contemplation, with him she found the purest and quietest retreat, as being most remote from soil and disturbance. "Lourdan," quoth the philosopher, "thy folly is as great as thy filth: know that all the faculties of the soul are confined of old to their several vessels and ventricles, from which they cannot part without dissolution of the whole body; and that thou containest no good thing in thee, but a heap of hard and loathsome uncleanness, and art to the head a foul disfigurement and burden. When I have cut thee off, and opened thee, as by the help of these implements I will do, all men shall see."

But to return whence was digressed: seeing that the throne of a King, as the wise King Solomon often remembers us, "is established in justice," which is the universal justice that Aristotle so much praises, containing in it all other virtues, it may assure us that the fall of prelacy, whose actions are so far distant from justice, cannot shake the least fringe that borders the royal canopy. But that their standing doth continually oppose and lay battery to regal safety, shall by that which follows easily appear. Amongst many secondary and accessory causes that support Monarchy, these are not of least reckoning, though common to all other states; the love of the subjects, the multitude and valour of the people, and store of treasure. In all these things hath the kingdom been of late sore weakened, and chiefly by the prelates. First, let any man consider, that if any prince shall suffer under him a commission of authority to be exercised, till all the land groan and cry out as against a whip of scorpions, whether this be not likely to lessen and keel the affections of the subject.

Next, what numbers of faithful and freeborn Englishmen, and good Christians, have been constrained to forsake their dearest home, their friends and kindred, whom nothing but the wide ocean, and the savage deserts of America, could hide and shelter from the fury of the bishops? Oh, Sir, if we could but see the shape of our dear mother England, as poets are wont to give a personal form to what they please, how would she appear, think ye, but in a mourning weed, with ashes upon her head, and tears abundantly flowing from her eyes, to behold so many of her children exposed at once, and thrust from things of dearest necessity, because their conscience could not assent to things which the bishops thought indifferent? What more binding than conscience? What more free than indifferency? Cruel then must that indifferency needs be, that shall violate the strict necessity of conscience; merciless and inhuman that free choice and liberty that shall break asunder the bonds of Religion! Let the astrologer be dismayed at the portentous blaze of comets, and impressions in the air, as foretelling troubles and changes to states: I shall believe there cannot be a more ill-boding sign to a nation (God turn the omen from us!) than when the inhabitants, to avoid insufferable grievances at home, are enforced by heaps to forsake their native country. Now, whereas the only remedy and amends against the depopulation and thinness of a land within, is the borrowed strength of firm alliance from without, these priestly policies of theirs having thus exhausted our domestic forces, have gone the way also to leave us as naked of our firmest and faithfullest neighbours abroad, by disparaging and alienating from us all protestant princes and commonwealths; who are not ignorant that our prelates, and as many as they can infect, account them no better than a sort of sacrilegious and puritanical rebels, preferring the Spaniard, our deadly enemy, before them, and set all orthodox writers at nought in comparison of the Jesuits, who are indeed the only corrupters of youth and good learning; and I have heard many wise and learned men in Italy say as much. It cannot be that the strongest knot of confederacy should not daily slacken, when Religion, which is the chief engagement of our league, shall be turned to their reproach. Hence it is that the prosperous and prudent states of the United Provinces—whom we ought to love, if not for themselves, yet for our own good work in them, they having been in a manner planted and erected by us, and having been since to us the faithful watchmen and discoverers of many a popish and Austrian complotted treason, and with us the partners of many a bloody and victorious battle,—whom the similitude of manners and language, the commodity of traffic, which founded the old Burgundian league betwixt us, but chiefly Religion, should bind to us immortally; even such friends as these, out of some principles installed into us by the prelates, have been often dismissed with distasteful answers, and sometimes unfriendly actions. Nor is it to be considered to the breach of confederate nations whose mutual interest is of such high consequence though their merchants bicker in the East Indies; neither is it safe, or wary, or indeed Christianly, that the French king, of a different faith, should afford our nearest allies as good protection as we. Sir, I persuade myself, if our zeal to true Religion, and the brotherly usage of our truest friends, were as notorious to the world as our prelatical schism, and captivity to rochet apophthegms, we had ere this seen our old conquerors, and afterwards liegemen, the Normans, together with the Britains, our proper colony, and all the Gascoins, that are the rightful dowry of our ancient kings, come with cap and knee, desiring the shadow of the English sceptre to defend them from the hot persecutions and taxes of the French. But when they come hither, and see a tympany of Spaniolized bishops swaggering in the foretop of the state, and meddling to turn and dandle the royal ball with unskilful and pedantic palms, no marvel though they think it as unsafe to commit religion and liberty to their arbitrating as to a synagogue of Jesuits.

But what do I stand reckoning upon advantages and gains lost by the misrule and turbulency of the prelates? What do I pick up so thriftily their scatterings and diminishings of the meaner subject, whilst they by their seditious practices have endangered to lose the king one third of his main stock? What have they not done to banish him from his own native country? But to speak of this as it ought, would ask a volume by itself.

Thus as they have unpeopled the kingdom by expulsion of so many thousands, as they have endeavoured to lay the skirts of it bare by disheartening and dishonouring our loyalest confederates abroad, so have they hamstrung the valour of the subject by seeking to effeminate us all at home. Well knows every wise nation, that their liberty consists in manly and honest labours, in sobriety and rigorous honour to the marriage-bed, which in both sexes should be bred up from chaste hopes to loyal enjoyments: and when the people slacken, and fall to looseness and riot, then do they as much as if they laid down their necks for some wild tyrant to get up and ride. Thus learnt Cyrus to tame the Lydians, whom by arms he could not whilst they kept themselves from luxury; with one easy proclamation to set up stews, dancing, feasting, and dicing, he made them soon his slaves. I know not what drift the prelates had, whose brokers they were, to prepare and supple as either for a foreign invasion or domestic oppression: but this I am sure, they took the ready way to despoil us both of manhood and grace at once, and that in the shamefullest and ungodliest manner. Upon that day which God's law, and even our own reason hath consecrated, that we might have one day at least of seven set apart wherein to examine and increase our knowledge of God, to meditate and commune of our faith, our hope, our eternal city in heaven, and to quicken withal the study and exercise of charity; at such a time that men should be plucked from their soberest and saddest thoughts, and by bishops, the pretended fathers of the Church, instigated, by public edict and with earnest endeavour pushed forward to gaming, jigging, wassailing, and mixed dancing, is a horror to think! Thus did the reprobate hireling priest Balaam seek to subdue the Israelites to Moab, if not by force, then by this devilish policy, to draw them from the sanctuary of God to the luxurious and ribald feasts of Baal-peor. Thus have they trespassed not only against the Monarchy of England, but of Heaven also, as others, I doubt not, can prosecute against them.

I proceed within my own bounds to shew you next what good agents they are about the revenues and riches of the kingdom, which declare of what moment they are to Monarchy, or what avail. Two leeches they have that still suck and suck the kingdom —their Ceremonies and their Courts. If any man will contend that Ceremonies be lawful under the Gospel, he may be answered otherwhere. This, doubtless, that they ought to be many and overcostly, no true Protestant will affirm. Now I appeal to all wise men, what an excessive waste of treasure hath been within these few years in this land, not in the expedient but in the idolatrous erection of temples beautified exquisitely to outvie the papists, the costly and dear-bought scandals and snares of images, pictures, rich copes, gorgeous altar-cloths: and by the courses they took, and the opinions they held, it was not likely any stay would be, or any end of their madness, where a pious pretext is so ready at hand to cover their insatiate desires. What can we suppose this will come to? What other materials than these have built up the spiritual Babel to the height of her abominations? Believe it, Sir, right truly it may be said, that Antichrist is Mammon's son. The sour leaven of human traditions, mixed in one putrefied mass with the poisonous dregs of hypocrisy in the hearts of prelates that lie basking in the sunny warmth of wealth and promotion, is the serpent's egg that will hatch an Antichrist wheresoever, and engender the same monster as big, or little, as the lump is which breeds him. If the splendour of gold and silver begin to lord it once again in the church of England, we shall see Antichrist shortly wallow here, though his chief kennel be at Rome. If they had one thought upon God's glory, and the advancement of Christian faith, they would be a means that with these expenses, thus profusely thrown away in trash, rather churches and schools might be built where they cry out for want, and more added where too few are; a moderate maintenance distributed to every painful minister, that now scarce sustains his family with bread while the prelates revel like Belshazzar with their full carouses in goblets and vessels of gold snatched from God's temple; which I hope the worthy men of our land will consider. Now then for their Courts. What a mass of money is drawn from the veins into the ulcers of the kingdom this way, their extortions, their open corruptions, the multitude of hungry and ravenous harpies that swarm about their offices, declare sufficiently. And what though all this go not over sea? It were better it did: better a penurious kingdom, than where excessive wealth flows into the graceless and injurious hands of common sponges, to the impoverishing of good and loyal men, and that by such execrable, such irreligious courses.

If the sacred and dreadful works of holy discipline, censure, penance, excommunication, and absolution,—where no profane thing ought to have access, nothing to be assistant but sage and Christianly admonition, brotherly love, flaming charity and zeal; and then, according to the effects, paternal sorrow, or paternal joy, mild severity, melting compassion,—if such divine ministries as these, wherein the Angel of the Church represents the person of Christ Jesus, must lie prostitute to sordid fees, and not pass to and fro between our Saviour, that of free grace redeemed us, and the submissive penitent, without the truckage of perishing coin, and the butcherly execution of tormentors, rooks, and rakeshames sold to lucre: then have the Babylonish merchants of souls just excuse. Hitherto, Sir, you have heard how the prelates have weakened and withdrawn the external accomplishments of kingly prosperity, the love of the people, their multitude, their valour, their wealth; mining and sapping the outworks and redoubts of Monarchy. Now hear how they strike at the very heart and vitals.

We know that Monarchy is made up of two parts, the liberty of the subject, and the supremacy of the king. I begin at the root. See what gentle and benign fathers they have been to our liberty! Their trade being, by the same alchemy that the pope uses, to extract heaps of gold and silver out of the drossy bullion of the people's sins; and justly fearing that the quick-sighted Protestant's eye, cleared in great part from the mist of superstition, may at one time or another look with a good judgment into these their deceitful pedleries; to gain as many associates of guiltiness as they can, and to infect the temporal magistrate with the like lawless, though not sacrilegious extortion, see awhile what they do! they engage themselves to preach and persuade an assertion for truth the most false, and to this Monarchy the most pernicious and destructive that could be chosen. What more baneful to Monarchy than a popular commotion? For the dissolution of monarchy slides aptest into a democracy; and what stirs the Englishmen, as our wisest writers have observed, sooner to rebellion, than violent and heavy hands upon their goods and purses? Yet these devout prelates, spite of our Great Charter, and the souls of our progenitors that wrested their liberties out of the Norman gripe with their dearest blood and highest prowess, for these many years have not ceased in their pulpits wrenching and spraining the text, to set at nought and trample under foot all the most sacred and lifeblood laws, statutes, and acts of parliament, that are the holy covenant of union and marriage between the king and his realm, by proscribing and confiscating from us all the right we have to our own bodies, goods, and liberties. What is this but to blow a trumpet, and proclaim a firecross to an hereditary and perpetual civil war? Thus much against the subjects' liberty hath been assaulted by them. Now how they have spared supremacy, or are likely hereafter to submit to it, remains lastly to be considered.

The emulation that under the Old Law was in the king towards the priest, is now so come about in the Gospel, that all the danger is to be feared from the priest to the king. Whilst the priest's office in the Law was set out with an exterior lustre of pomp and glory, kings were ambitious to be priests; now priests, not perceiving the heavenly brightness and inward splendour of their more glorious evangelic ministry, with as great ambition affect to be kings, as in all their courses is easy to be observed. Their eyes ever eminent upon worldly matters, their desires ever thirsting after worldly employments, instead of diligent and fervent study in the Bible, they covet to be expert in canons and decretals, which may enable them to judge and interpose in temporal causes, however pretended ecclesiastical. Do they not hoard up pelf, seek to be potent in secular strength, in state affairs, in lands, lordships, and domains, to sway and carry all before them in high courts and privy-councils, to bring into their grasp the high and principal offices of the kingdom? Have they not been bold of late to check the common law, to slight and brave the indiminishable majesty of our highest court, the law-giving and sacred parliament? Do they not plainly labour to exempt churchmen from the magistrate? Yea, so presumptuously as to question and menace officers that represent the king's person for using their authority against drunken priests? The cause of protecting murderous clergymen was the first heart-burning that swelled up the audacious Becket to the pestilent and odious vexation of Henry the Second. Nay, more: have not some of their devoted scholars begun, I need not say to nibble, but openly to argue against the king's supremacy? Is not the chief of them accused out of his own book, and his late canons, to affect a certain unquestionable patriarchate, independent, and unsubordinate to the crown? From whence having first brought us to a servile state of religion and manhood, and having predisposed his conditions with the pope, that lays claim to this land, or some Pepin of his own creating, it were all as likely for him to aspire to the monarchy among us, as that the pope could find means so on the sudden both to bereave the emperor of the Roman territory with the favour of Italy, and by an unexpected friend out of France, while he was in danger to lose his new-got purchase, beyond hope to leap into the fair exarchate of Ravenna.

A good while the pope subtly acted the lamb, writing to the emperor, "my lord Tiberius," "my lord Mauritius;" but no sooner did this his lord pluck at the images and idols, but he threw off his sheep's clothing, and started up a wolf, laying his paws upon the emperor's right, as forfeited to Peter. Why may not we as well, having been forewarned at home by our renowned Chaucer, and from abroad by the great and learned Padre Paolo, from the like beginnings, as we see they are, fear the like events? Certainly a wise and provident king ought to suspect a hierarchy in his realm—being ever attended, as it is, with two such greedy purveyors, ambition and usurpation,—I say, he ought to suspect a hierarchy to be as dangerous and derogatory from his crown as a tetrarchy or a heptarchy. Yet now that the prelates had almost attained to what their insolent and unbridled minds had hurried them; to thrust the laity under the despotical rule of the Monarch, that they themselves might confine the Monarch to a kind of pupilage under their hierarchy, observe but how their own principles combat one another, and supplant each one his fellow.

Having fitted us only for peace, and that a servile peace, by lessening our numbers, draining our estates, enfeebling our bodies, cowing our free spirits by those ways as you have heard, their impotent actions cannot sustain themselves the least moment unless they would rouse us up to a war fit for Cain to be the leader of, an abhorred, a cursed, a fraternal war. England and Scotland, dearest brothers both in nature and in Christ, must be set to wade in one another's blood; and Ireland, our free denizen, upon the back of us both, as occasion should serve: a piece of service that the pope and all his factors have been compassing to do ever since the Reformation.

But ever blessed be He, and ever glorified, that from his high watchtower in the heavens, discerning the crooked ways of perverse and cruel men, hath hitherto maimed and infatuated all their damnable inventions, and deluded their great wizards with a delusion fit for fools and children. Had God been so minded, he could have sent a spirit of mutiny amongst us, as he did between Abimelech and the Sechemites, to have made our funerals, and slain heaps more in number than the miserable surviving remnant; but he, when we least deserved, sent out a gentle gale and message of peace from the wings of those his cherubims that fan his mercy-seat. Nor shall the wisdom, the moderation, the Christian piety, the constancy of our Nobility and Commons of England, be ever forgotten, whose calm and temperate connivance could sit still and smile out the stormy bluster of men more audacious and precipitant than of solid and deep reach, until their own fury had run itself out of breath, assailing by rash and heady approaches the impregnable situation of our liberty and safety, that laughed such weak enginery to scorn, such poor drifts to make a national war of a surplice brabble, a tippet scuffle, and engage the untainted honour of English knighthood to unfurl the streaming red cross, or to rear the horrid standard of those fatal guly dragons, for so unworthy a purpose as to force upon their fellow-subjects that which themselves are weary of, the skeleton of a mass-book. Nor must the patience, the fortitude, the firm obedience of the Nobles and People of Scotland, striving against manifold provocations; nor must their sincere and moderate proceedings hitherto, be unremembered, to the shameful conviction of all their detractors.

Go on, both hand in hand, O nations never to be disunited! Be the praise and the heroic song of all posterity! Merit this, but seek only virtue, not to extend your limits—for what needs to win a fading triumphant laurel out of the tears of wretched men?—but to settle the pure worship of God in his Church, and justice in the State: then shall the hardest difficulties smooth out themselves before ye; envy shall sing to hell, craft and malice be confounded, whether it be homebred mischief or outlandish cunning: yea, other nations will then covet to serve ye, for lordship and victory are but the pages of justice and virtue. Commit securely to true wisdom the vanquishing and uncasing of craft and subtlety, which are but her two runagates: join your invincible might to do worthy and godlike deeds; and then he that seeks to break your union, a cleaving curse be his inheritance to all generations.

Sir, you have now at length this question for the time, and as my memory would best serve me in such a copious and vast theme, fully handled, and you yourself may judge whether Prelacy be the only Church-government agreeable to Monarchy. Seeing therefore the perilous and confused state into which we are fallen, and that, to the certain knowledge of all men, through the irreligious pride and hateful tyranny of prelates, as the innumerable and grievous complaints of every shire cry out, if we will now resolve to settle affairs either according to pure religion or sound policy, we must first of all begin roundly to cashier and cut away from the public body the noisome and diseased tumour of prelacy, and come from schism to Unity with our neighbour Reformed Sister Churches, which with the blessing of peace and pure doctrine have now long time flourished; and doubtless with all hearty joy and gratulation will meet and welcome our Christian union with them, as they have been all this while grieved at our strangeness, and little better than separation from them. And for the Discipline propounded, seeing that it hath been inevitably proved, that the natural and fundamental causes of political happiness in all governments are the same, and that this Church Discipline is taught in the Word of God, and, as we see, agrees according to wish with all such states as have received it; we may infallibly assure ourselves that it will as well agree with Monarchy, though all the tribe of Aphorismers and Politicasters would persuade us there be secret and mysterious reasons against it. For upon the settling hereof mark what nourishing and cordial restorements to the State will follow, the Ministers of the Gospel attending only to the work of salvation, every one within his limited charge; besides the diffusive blessings of God upon all our actions, the king shall sit without an old disturber, a daily encroacher and intruder: shall rid his kingdom of a strong sequestered and collateral power; a confronting mitre, whose potent wealth and wakeful ambition he had just cause to hold in jealousy: not to repeat the other present evils which only their removal will remove. And because things simply pure are inconsistent in the mass of nature, nor are the elements or humours in a man's body exactly homogeneal, hence the best-founded commonwealths and least barbarous have aimed at a certain mixture and temperament, partaking the several virtues of each other state, that each part drawing to itself may keep up a steady and even uprightness in common.

There is no civil government that hath been known, no not the Spartan, not the Roman, though both for this respect so much praised by the wise Polybius, more divinely and harmoniously tuned, more equally balanced as it were by the hand and scale of justice, than is the Commonwealth of England; where, under a free and untutored Monarch, the noblest, worthiest, and most prudent men, with full approbation and suffrage of the People, have in their power the supreme and final determination of highest affairs. Now if conformity of Church Discipline to the civil be so desired, there can be nothing more parallel, more uniform, than when under the sovereign prince, Christ's vicegerent, using the sceptre of David, according to God's law, the godliest, the wisest, the learnedest ministers in their several charges have the instructing and disciplining of God's people, by whose full and free election they are consecrated to that holy and equal aristocracy. And why should not the piety and conscience of Englishmen, as members of the Church, be trusted in the election of pastors to functions that nothing concern a Monarch, as well as their worldly wisdoms are privileged as members of the state in suffraging their knights and burgesses to matters that concern him nearly? And if in weighing these several offices, their difference in time and quality be cast in, I know they will not turn the beam of equal judgment the moiety of a scruple. We therefore having already a kind of apostolical and ancient church election in our State, what a perverseness would it be in us of all others to retain forcibly a kind of imperious and stately election in our Church! And what a blindness to think that what is already evangelical, as it were by a happy chance, in our polity, should be repugnant to that which is the same by divine command in the ministry! Thus then we see that our ecclesiastical and political choices may consent and sort as well together without any rupture in the State, as Christians and freeholders. But as for honour, that ought indeed to be different and distinct, as either office looks a several way. The Minister whose calling and end is spiritual, ought to be honoured as a father and physician to the soul (if he be found to be so), with a sonlike and disciplelike reverence, which is indeed the dearest and most affectionate honour, most to be desired by a wise man, and such as will easily command a free and plentiful provision of outward necessaries, without his further care of this world.

The Magistrate, whose charge is to see to our persons and

estates, is to be honoured with a more elaborate and personal courtship, with large salaries and stipends, that he himself may abound in those things whereof his legal justice and watchful care give us the quiet enjoyment. And this distinction of honour will bring forth a seemly and graceful uniformity over all the kingdom.

Then shall the Nobles possess all the dignities and offices of temporal honour to themselves, sole lords without the improper mixture of scholastic and pusillanimous upstarts; the Parliament shall void her Upper House of the same annoyances; the common and civil laws shall be both set free, the former from the control, the other from the mere vassalage and copyhold of the clergy.

And whereas temporal laws rather punish men when they have transgressed, than form them to be such as should transgress seldomest, we may conceive great hopes, through the showers of divine benediction watering the unmolested and watchful pains of the ministry, that the whole inheritance of God will grow up so straight and blameless, that the civil magistrate may with far less toil and difficulty, and far more ease and delight, steer the tall and goodly vessel of the Commonwealth through all the gusts and tides of the world's mutability.

Here I might have ended, but that some objections, which I have heard commonly flying about, press me to the endeavour of an answer. We must not run, they say, into sudden extremes. This is a fallacious rule, unless understood only of the actions of virtue about things indifferent. For if it be found that those two extremes be vice and virtue, falsehood and truth, the greater extremity of virtue and superlative truth we run into, the more virtuous and the more wise we become; and he that, flying from degenerate and traditional corruption, fears to shoot himself too far into the meeting embraces of a divinely warranted Reformation, had better not have run at all. And for the suddenness, it cannot be feared. Who should oppose it? The papists? They dare not. The protestants otherwise affected? They were mad. There is nothing will be removed but what to them is professedly indifferent. The long affection which the people have borne to it, what for itself, what for the odiousness of prelates, is evident: from the first year of queen Elizabeth it hath still been more and more propounded, desired, and beseeched, yea, sometimes favourably forwarded by the parliaments themselves. Yet if it were sudden and swift, provided still it be from worse to better, certainly we ought to hie us from evil like a torrent, and rid ourselves of corrupt discipline, as we would shake fire out of our bosoms.

Speedy and vehement were the reformations of all the good kings of Judah, though the people had been muzzled in idolatry ever so long before; they feared not the bugbear danger, nor the lion in the way that the sluggish and timorous politician thinks he sees; no more did our brethren of the Reformed Churches abroad, they ventured, God being their guide, out of rigid popery, into that which we in mockery call precise puritanism, and yet we see no inconvenience befell them.

Let us not dally with God when he offers us a full blessing, to take as much of it as we think will serve our ends, and turn him back the rest upon his hands; lest in his anger he snatch all from us again. Next, they allege the antiquity of episcopacy through all ages. What it was in the Apostles' time, that questionless it must be still; and therein I trust the ministers will be able to satisfy the parliament. But if episcopacy be taken for prelacy, all the ages they can deduce it through, will make it no more venerable than papacy.

Most certain it is, as all our stories bear witness, that ever since their coming to the see of Canterbury, for near twelve hundred years, to speak of them in general, they have been in England to our souls a sad and doleful succession of illiterate and blind guides; to our purses and goods a wasteful band of robbers, a perpetual havock and rapine; to our State a continual hydra of mischief and molestation, the forge of discord and rebellion: this is the trophy of their antiquity, and boasted succession through so many ages. And for those prelate-martyrs they glory of, they are to be judged what they were by the Gospel, and not the Gospel to be tried by them.

And it is to be noted, that if they were for bishoprics and ceremonies, it was in their prosperity and fulness of bread; but in their persecution, which purified them, and near their death, which was their garland, they plainly disliked and condemned the ceremonies, and threw away those episcopal ornaments where- in they were installed, as foolish and detestable; for so the words of Ridley at his degradement, and his letter to Hooper, expressly shew. Neither doth the author of our Church History spare to record sadly the fall, for so he terms it, and infirmities of these martyrs, though we would deify them. And why should their martyrdom more countenance corrupt doctrine or discipline, than their subscriptions justify their treason to the royal blood of this realm, by diverting and entailing the right of the crown from the true heirs to the houses of Northumberland and Suffolk? which had it took effect, this present king had, in all likelihood, never sat on this throne, and the happy union of this island had been frustrated.

Lastly, whereas they add that some the learnedest of the reformed abroad admire our episcopacy; it had been more for the strength of the argument to tell us that some of the wisest statesmen admire it, for thereby we might guess them weary of the present Discipline, as offensive to their State, which is the bug we fear: but being they are churchmen, we may rather suspect them for some prelatizing spirits that admire our bishoprics, not episcopacy.

The next objection vanishes of itself, propounding a doubt whether a greater inconvenience would not grow from the corruption of any other Discipline than from that of episcopacy. This seems an unseasonable foresight, and out of order, to defer and put off the most needful constitution of one right Discipline, while we stand balancing the discommodities of two corrupt ones. First constitute that which is right, and of itself it will discover and rectify that which swerves, and easily remedy the pretended fear of having a pope in every parish, unless we call the zealous and meek censure of the church a popedom, which whoso does, let him advise how he can reject the pastorly rod and sheephook of Christ, and those cords of love, and not fear to fall under the iron sceptre of his anger, that will dash him to pieces like a potsherd.

At another doubt of theirs I wonder,—whether this Discipline which we desire be such as can be put in practice within this kingdom. They say it cannot stand with the common law nor with the king's safety, the government of episcopacy is now so weaved into the common law. In God's name let it weave out again; let not human quillets keep back divine authority. It is not the common law, nor the civil, but piety and justice that are our foundresses. They stoop not, neither change colour for aristocracy, democracy, or monarchy, nor yet at all interrupt their just courses; but far above the taking notice of these inferior niceties, with perfect sympathy, wherever they meet, kiss each other. Lastly, they are fearful that the Discipline which will succeed cannot stand with the king's safety. Wherefore? It is but episcopacy reduced to what it should be. Were it not that the tyranny of prelates under the name of bishops had made our ears tender and startling, we might call every good minister a bishop, as every bishop, yea, the apostles themselves, are called ministers, and the angels ministering spirits, and the ministers again angels. But wherein is this propounded government so shrewd? Because the government of Assemblies will succeed. Did not the Apostles govern the Church by Assemblies? How should it else be catholic? How should it have communion? We count it sacrilege to take from the rich prelates their lands and revenues, which is sacrilege in them to keep, using them as they do; and can we think it safe to defraud the living church of God of that right which God has given her in Assemblies? Oh, but the consequence! Assemblies draw to them the supremacy of ecclesiastical jurisdiction. No, surely, they draw no supremacy, but that authority which Christ, and St. Paul in his name, confers upon them. The king may still retain the same supremacy in the Assemblies, as in the Parliament; here he can do nothing alone against the Common Law, and there neither alone, nor with consent, against the Scriptures. But is this all? No: this ecclesiastical supremacy draws to it the power to excommunicate kings; and then follows the worst that can be imagined. Do they hope to avoid this, by keeping prelates that have so often done it? Not to exemplify the malapert insolence of our own bishops in this kind towards our kings, I shall turn back to the primitive and pure times, which the objectors would have the rule of Reformation to us.

Not an Assembly, but one bishop alone, St. Ambrose of Milan, held Theodosius, the most Christian emperor, under excommunication above eight months together, drove him from the church in the presence of his nobles; which the good emperor bore with heroic humility, and never ceased by prayers and tears, till he was absolved; for which coming to the bishop with supplication into the salutory, some outporch of the church, he was charged by him with tyrannical madness against God, for coming into holy ground. At last, upon conditions absolved, and after great humiliation approaching to the altar to offer as those thrice pure times then thought meet, he had scarce withdrawn his hand, and stood awhile, when a bold archdeacon comes in the bishop's name, and chases him from within the rails, telling him peremptorily, that the place wherein he stood was for none but the priests to enter, or to touch: and this is another piece of pure primitive divinity! Think ye, then, our bishops will forego the power of excommunication on whomsoever? No, certainly, unless to compass sinister ends, and then revoke when they see their time. And yet this most mild, though withal dreadful and inviolable prerogative of Christ's diadem, excommunication, serves for nothing with them, but to prog and pander for fees, or to display their pride and sharpen their revenge, debarring men the protection of the law; and I remember not whether in some cases it bereave not men all right to their worldly goods and inheritances, besides the denial of Christian burial. But in the evangelical and reformed use of this sacred censure, no such prostitution, no such Iscariotical drifts are to be doubted, as that spiritual doom and sentence should invade worldly possession, which is the rightful lot and portion even of the wickedest men, as frankly bestowed upon them by the all-dispensing bounty as rain and sunshine. No, no, it seeks not to bereave or destroy the body: it seeks to save the soul by humbling the body, not by imprisonment, or pecuniary mulct, much less by stripes, or bonds, or disinheritance, but by fatherly admonishment and Christian rebuke to cast it into godly sorrow, whose end is joy, and ingenuous bashfulness to sin. If that cannot be wrought, then as a tender mother takes her child and holds it over the pit with scaring words, that it may learn to fear where danger is; so doth excommunication as dearly and as freely, without money, use her wholesome and saving terrors. She is instant, she beseeches, by all the dear and sweet promises of salvation she entices and woos; by all the threatenings and thunders of the law, and rejected gospel, she charges and adjures: this is all her armoury, her munition, her artillery; then she awaits with longsufferance, and yet ardent zeal. In brief, there is no act in all the errand of God's ministers to mankind wherein passes more loverlike contestation between Christ and the Soul of a regenerate man lapsing, than before, and in, and after the sentence of excommunication. As for the fogging proctorage of money, with such an eye as struck Gehazi with leprosy and Simon Magus with a curse, so does she look and so threaten her fiery whip against that banking den of thieves that dare thus baffle and buy and sell the awful and majestic wrinkles of her brow. He that is rightly and apostolically sped with her invisible arrow, if he can be at peace in his soul, and not smell within him the brimstone of hell, may have fair leave to tell all his bags over undiminished of the least farthing, may eat his dainties, drink his wine, use his delights, enjoy his lands and liberties, not the least skin rased, not the least hair misplaced, for all that excommunication has done. Much more may a king enjoy his rights and prerogatives undeflowered, untouched, and be as absolute and complete a king, as all his royalties and revenues can make him. And therefore little did Theodosius fear a plot upon his empire, when he stood excommunicate by Saint Ambrose, though it were done either with much haughty pride, or ignorant zeal. But let us rather look upon the Reformed Churches beyond the seas, the Grisons, the Swisses, the Hollanders, the French, that have a supremacy to live under, as well as we : where do the Churches in all these places strive for supremacy? Where do they clash and justle supremacies with the civil magistrate? In France, a more severe Monarchy than ours, the Protestants under this church government carry the name of the best subjects the king has : and yet Presbytery, if it must be so called, does there all that it desires to do. How easy were it, if there be such great suspicion, to give no more scope to it in England! But let us not, for fear of a scarecrow, or else through hatred to be reformed, stand hankering and politizing, when God with spread hands testifies to us and points us out the way to our peace.

Let us not be so over-credulous, unless God hath blinded us, as to trust our dear souls into the hands of men that beg so devoutly for the pride and gluttony of their own backs and bellies, that sue and solicit so eagerly, not for the saving of souls, the consideration of which can have here no place at all, but for their bishoprics, deaneries, prebends, and canonries. How can these men not be corrupt, whose very cause is the bribe of their own pleading, whose mouths cannot open without the strong breath and loud stench of avarice, simony, and sacrilege, embezzling the treasury of the Church on painted and gilded walls of temples, wherein God hath testified to have no delight; warming their palace kitchens, and from thence their unctuous and epicurean paunches, with the alms of the blind, the lame, the impotent, the aged, the orphan, the widow? For with these the treasury of Christ ought to be, here must be his jewels bestowed, his rich cabinet must be emptied here; as the constant martyr St. Lawrence taught the Roman prætor. Sir, would you know what the remonstrance of these men would have, what their petition implies? They entreat us that we would not be weary of those insupportable grievances that our shoulders have hitherto cracked under; they beseech us that we would think them fit to be our justices of peace, our lords, our highest officers of state, though they come furnished with no more experience than they

learnt between the cook and the manciple, or more profoundly
at the college audit or the regent house, or to come to their
deepest insight, at their patron's table. They would request us to
endure still the rustling of their silken cassocks, and that we
would burst our midriffs rather than laugh to see them under
sail in all their lawn and sarcenet, their shrouds and tackle, with
a geometrical rhomboides upon their heads. They would bear us
in hand that we must of duty still appear before them once a
year in Jerusalem, like good circumcised males and females, to
be taxed by the poll, to be sconced our head-money, our two-
pences, in their chandlerly shopbook of Easter. They pray us
that it would please us to let them still hale us and worry us
with their bandogs and pursuivants; and that it would please
the Parliament that they may yet have the whipping, fleecing,
and flaying of us in their diabolical courts, to tear the flesh from
our bones, and into our wide wounds instead of balm, to pour
in the oil of tartar, vitriol, and mercury: surely, a right reasonable, innocent, and soft-hearted petition. Oh, the relenting bowels
of the fathers! Can this be granted them, unless God have
smitten us with frenzy from above, and with a dazzling giddiness
at noonday? Should not those men rather be heard that come
to plead against their own preferments, their worldly advantages,
their own abundance, for honour and obedience to God's word,
the conversion of souls, the Christian peace of the land, and
union of the Reformed Catholic Church, the unappropriating and
unmonopolizing the rewards of learning and industry from the
greasy clutch of ignorance and high feeding? We have tried
already, and miserably felt what ambition, worldly glory, and
immoderate wealth, can do; what the boisterous and contra-
dictional hand of a temporal, earthly, and corporeal spirituality
can avail to the edifying of Christ's holy Church. Were it such a
desperate hazard to put to the venture the universal votes of
Christ's congregation, and fellowly and friendly yoke of a teaching and laborious ministry, the pastorlike and apostolic imitation of meek and unlordly discipline, the gentle and benevolent
mediocrity of church-maintenance, without the ignoble hucksterage

of piddling tithes? Were it such an incurable mischief to make a little trial, what all this would do to the flourishing and growing up of Christ's mystical body, as rather to use every poor shift, and if that serve not, to threaten uproar and combustion, and shake the brand of civil discord?

Oh, Sir, I do now feel myself inwrapped on the sudden into those mazes and labyrinths of dreadful and hideous thoughts, that which way to get out, or which way to end, I know not, unless I turn mine eyes, and with your help lift up my hands to that eternal and propitious throne, where nothing is readier than grace and refuge to the distresses of mortal suppliants : and it were a shame to leave these serious thoughts less piously than the heathen were wont to conclude their graver discourses.

Thou, therefore, that sittest in light and glory unapproachable, Parent of angels and men; next, thee I implore, omnipotent King, Redeemer of that lost remnant whose nature thou didst assume, ineffable and everlasting Love; and thou, the third subsistence of divine infinitude, illumining Spirit, the joy and solace of created things: one Tripersonal Godhead! look upon this thy poor and almost spent and expiring church, leave her not thus a prey to these importunate wolves, that wait and think long till they devour thy tender flock; these wild boars that have broke into thy vineyard, and left the print of their polluting hoofs on the souls of thy servants. Oh, let them not bring about their damned designs, that stand now at the entrance of the bottomless pit, expecting the watchword to open and let out those dreadful locusts and scorpions, to reinvolve us in that pitchy cloud of infernal darkness where we shall never more see the sun of thy truth again, never hope for the cheerful dawn, never more hear the bird of morning sing. Be moved with pity at the afflicted state of this our shaken monarchy, that now lies labouring under her throes, and struggling against the grudges of more dreaded calamities!

O Thou, that, after the impetuous rage of five bloody inundations, and the succeeding sword of intestine war, soaking the land in her own gore, didst pity the sad and ceaseless revolution of our swift and thick-coming sorrows; when we were quite breathless, of thy free grace didst motion peace, and terms of covenant with us; and having first well nigh freed us from antichristian thraldom, didst build up this Britannic empire to a glorious and enviable height, with all her daughter-islands about her; stay us in this felicity, let not the obstinacy of our half-obedience and will-worship bring forth that viper of sedition, that for these fourscore years hath been breeding to eat through the entrails of our peace! But let her cast her abortive spawn without the danger of this travailing and throbbing kingdom: that we may still remember in our solemn thanksgivings, how for us, the northern ocean even to the frozen Thule was scattered with the proud shipwrecks of the Spanish armada, and the very maw of hell ransacked, and made to give up her concealed destruction, ere she could vent it in that horrible and damned blast.

Oh, how much more glorious will those former deliverances appear, when we shall know them not only to have saved us from greatest miseries past, but to have reserved us for greatest happiness to come! Hitherto Thou hast but freed us, and that not fully, from the unjust and tyrannous claim of thy foes; now unite us entirely, and appropriate us to thyself, tie us everlastingly in willing homage to the prerogative of thy eternal throne.

And now we know, O Thou our most certain hope and defence, that thine enemies have been consulting all the sorceries of the great whore, and have joined their plots with that sad intelligencing tyrant that mischiefs the world with his mines of Ophir, and lies thirsting to revenge his naval ruins that have larded our seas: but let them all take counsel together, and let it come to nought; let them decree, and do thou cancel it; let them gather themselves, and be scattered; let them embattle themselves, and be broken; let them embattle, and be broken, for Thou art with us.

Then, amidst the hymns and hallelujahs of saints, some one may perhaps be heard offering at high strains in new and lofty measure to sing and celebrate thy divine mercies and marvellous judgments in this land throughout all ages; whereby this great and warlike nation, instructed and inured to the fervent and continual practice of truth and righteousness, and casting far from her the rags of her whole vices, may press on hard to that high and happy emulation to be found the soberest, wisest, and most Christian people, at that day when Thou, the eternal and shortly expected King, shalt open the clouds to judge the several kingdoms of the world, and distributing national honours and rewards to religious and just commonwealths, shalt put an end to all earthly tyrannies, proclaiming thy universal and mild monarchy through heaven and earth; where they undoubtedly that by their labours counsels and prayers have been earnest for the common good of religion and their country, shall receive above the inferior orders of the blessed, the regal addition of principalities, legions, and thrones into their glorious titles, and in supereminence of beatific vision, progressing the dateless and irrevoluble circle of eternity, shall clasp inseparable hands with joy and bliss in overmeasure for ever.

But they, contrary, that by the impairing and diminution of the true faith, the distresses and servitude of their country, aspire to high dignity, rule, and promotion here, after a shameful end in this life (which God grant them), shall be thrown down eternally into the darkest and deepest gulf of hell, where, under the despiteful control, the trample and spurn of all the other damned, that in the anguish of their torture shall have no other case than to exercise a raving and bestial tyranny over them as their slaves and negroes, they shall remain in that plight for ever, the basest, the lowermost, the most dejected, most underfoot, and downtrodden vassals of perdition.

THE
REASON OF CHURCH GOVERNMENT URGED AGAINST PRELACY.

IN TWO BOOKS.

THE FIRST BOOK.

THE PREFACE.

IN the publishing of human laws, which for the most part aim not beyond the good of civil society, to set them barely forth to the people without reason or preface, like a physical prescript, or only with threatenings, as it were a lordly command, in the judgment of Plato was thought to be done neither generously nor wisely. His advice was, seeing that persuasion certainly is a more winning and more manlike way to keep men in obedience than fear, that to such laws as were of principal moment, there should be used as an induction some well-tempered discourse, shewing how good, how gainful, how happy it must needs be to live according to honesty and justice; which being uttered with those native colours and graces of speech, as true eloquence, the daughter of virtue, can best bestow upon her mother's praises, would so incite, and in a manner charm, the multitude into the love of that which is really good, as to embrace it ever after, not of custom and awe, which most men do, but of choice and purpose, with true and constant delight. But this practice we may learn from a better and more ancient authority than any heathen writer hath to give us; and indeed being a point of so high wisdom and worth, how could it be but we should find it in that book, within sacred context all wisdom is unfolded? Moses, there only lawgiver that we can believe to have been visibly taught of God, knowing how vain it was to write laws to men whose hearts were not first seasoned with the knowledge of God and of his works, began from the book of Genesis, as a prologue to his laws; which Josephus right well hath noted: that the nation of the Jews, reading therein the universal goodness of God to all creatures in the creation, and his peculiar favour to them in his election of Abraham, their ancestor, from whom they could derive so many blessings upon themselves, might be moved to obey sincerely, by knowing so good a reason of their obedience. If then, in the administration of civil justice, and under the obscurity of ceremonial rites, such care was had by the wisest of the heathen, and by Moses among the Jews, to instruct them at least in a general reason of that Government to which their subjection was required; how much more ought the members of the Church, under the Gospel, seek to inform their understanding in the reason of that Government which the Church claims to have over them. Especially for that Church hath in her immediate cure those inner parts and affections of the mind where the seat of reason is, having power to examine our spiritual knowledge and to demand from us, in God's behalf, a service entirely reasonable.

But because about the manner and order of this Government, whether it ought to be presbyterial or prelatical, such endless question, or rather uproar, is arisen in this land as may be justly termed what the fever is to the physicians, the eternal reproach of our divines; whilst other profound clerks of late, greatly, as they conceive, to the advancement of prelaty, are so earnestly meting out the Lydian proconsular Asia, to make good the prime metropolis of Ephesus, as if some of our prelates in all haste meant to change their soil, and become neighbours to the English bishop of Chalcedon; and whilst good Brerewood as busily bestirs himself in our vulgar tongue, to divide precisely the three patriarchates of Rome, Alexandria, and Antioch, and whether to any of these England doth belong: I shall in the hile not cease to hope through the mercy and grace of the head and husband of his Church, that England shortly is to belong, neither to see patriarchal nor see prelatical, but to the faithful feeding and disciplining of that ministerial order, which the blessed Apostles constituted throughout the Churches; and this, I shall essay to prove, can be no other than that of presbyters and deacons. And if any man incline to think I undertake a task too difficult for my years, I trust through the supreme enlightening assistance far otherwise; for my years, be they few or many, what imports it? So they bring reason, let that be looked on. And for the task, from hence, that the question in hand is so needful to be known at this time, chiefly by every meaner capacity, and contains in it the explication of many admirable and heavenly privileges reached out to us by the Gospel, I conclude the task must be easy: God having to this end ordained his Gospel to be the revelation of his power and wisdom in Christ Jesus. And this is one depth of his wisdom, that he could so plainly reveal so great a measure of it to the gross distorted apprehension of decayed mankind. Let others, therefore, dread and shun the Scriptures for their darkness; I shall wish I may deserve to be reckoned among those who admire and dwell upon them for their clearness. And this seems to be the cause why in those places of Holy Writ wherein is treated of Church Government the reasons thereof are not formally and professedly set down, because to him that heeds attentively the drift and scope of Christian profession they easily imply themselves; which thing further to explain, having now prefaced enough, I shall no longer defer.

CHAPTER I.

That Church Government is prescribed in the Gospel; and that to say otherwise is unsound.

THE first and greatest Reason of Church Government we may securely, with the assent of many on the adverse part, affirm to be, because we find it so ordained and set out to us by the appointment of God in the Scriptures; but whether this be presbyterial, or prelatical, it cannot be brought to the scanning until I have said what is meet to some who do not think it for the ease of their inconsequent opinions to grant that Church Discipline is platformed in the Bible, but that it is left to the discretion of men. To this conceit of theirs I answer, that it is both unsound and untrue; for there is not that thing in the world of more grave and urgent importance throughout the whole life of man, than is Discipline. What need I instance? He that hath read with judgment, of nations and commonwealths, of cities and camps, of peace and war, sea and land, will readily agree that the flourishing and decaying of all civil societies, all the moments and turnings of human occasions, are moved to and fro as upon the axle of Discipline. So that whatsoever power or sway in mortal things weaker men have attributed to Fortune, I durst with more confidence (the honour of Divine Providence ever saved) ascribe either to the vigour or the slackness of Discipline. Nor is there any sociable perfection in this life, civil or sacred, that can be above Discipline, but she is that which with her musical cords preserves and holds all the parts thereof together. Hence in those perfect armies of Cyrus in Xenophon, and Scipio in the Roman stories, the excellence of military skill was esteemed, not by the not needing, but by the readiest submitting to the edicts of their commander. And certainly Discipline is not only the removal of disorder but, if any visible shape can be given to divine things, the very visible shape and image of Virtue, whereby she is not only seen in the regular gestures and motions of her heavenly paces as she walks, but also makes the harmony of her voice audible to mortal ears. Yea, the angels themselves, in whom no disorder is feared, as the Apostle that saw them in his rapture describes, are distinguished and quaternioned into their celestial princedoms and satrapies, according as God himself has writ his imperial decrees through the great provinces of heaven. The state also of the blessed in Paradise, though never so perfect, is not therefore left without Discipline, whose golden surveying reed marks out and measures every quarter and circuit of New Jerusalem. Yet is it not to be conceived, that those eternal effluences of sanctity and love in the glorified saints should by this means be confined and cloyed with repetition of that which is prescribed, but that our happiness may orb itself into a thousand vagancies of glory and delight, and with a kind of eccentrical equation be, as it were, an invariable planet of joy and felicity; how much less can we believe that God would leave his frail and feeble, though not less beloved Church here below, to the perpetual stumble of conjecture and disturbance in this our dark voyage, without the card and compass of Discipline? Which is so hard to be of man's making, that we may see even in the guidance of a civil state to worldly happiness, it is not for every learned or every wise man, though many of them consult in common, to invent or frame a Discipline. But if it be at all the work of man, it must be of such a one as is a true knower of himself, and in whom contemplation and practice, wit, prudence, fortitude, and eloquence, must be rarely met, both to comprehend the hidden causes of things and span in his thoughts all the various effects that passion or complexion can work in man's nature. And hereto must his hand be at defiance with gain, and his heart in all virtues heroic; so far is it from the ken of these wretched projectors of ours that bescrawl their pamphlets every day with new forms of government for our Church. And therefore all the ancient lawgivers were either truly inspired, as Moses, or were such men as with authority enough might give it out to be so, as Minos, Lycurgus, Numa, because they wisely forethought that men would never quietly submit to such a Discipline as had not more of God's hand in it than man's. To come within the narrowness of household government, observation will shew us many deep counsellors of state and judges to demean themselves incorruptly in the settled course of affairs, and many worthy preachers upright in their lives, powerful in their audience: but look upon either of these men where they are left to their own disciplining at home, and you shall soon perceive, for all their single knowledge and uprightness, how deficient they are in the regulating of their own family; not only in what may concern the virtuous and decent composure of their minds in their several places, but, that which is of a lower and easier performance, the right possessing of the outward vessel, their body, in health or sickness, rest or labour, diet or abstinence, whereby to render it more pliant to the soul, and useful to the commonwealth: which if men were but as good to discipline themselves, as some are to tutor their horses and hawks, it could not be so gross in most households. If then it appear so hard, and so little known, how to govern a house well, which is thought of so easy discharge and for every man's undertaking, what skill of man, what wisdom, what parts can be sufficient to give laws and ordinances to the elect household of God? If we could imagine that He had left it at random without his provident and gracious ordering, who is he so arrogant, so presumptuous, that durst dispose and guide the living ark of the Holy Ghost, though he should find it wandering in the field of Bethshemesh, without the conscious warrant of some high calling? But no profane insolence can parallel that which our prelates dare avouch, to drive outrageously, and shatter the holy ark of the Church, not borne upon their shoulders with pains and labour in the Word, but drawn with rude oxen, their officials, and their own brute inventions. Let them make shows of reforming while they will, so long as the Church is mounted upon the prelatical cart, and not, as it ought, between the hands of the ministers, it will but shake and totter: and he that sets to his hand, though with a good intent to hinder the shogging of it, in this unlawful waggonry wherein it rides, let him beware it be not fatal to him, as it was to Uzza. Certainly if God be the Father of his family the Church, wherein could he express that name more, than in training it up under his own all-wise and dear economy, not turning it loose to the havoc of strangers and wolves that would ask no better plea than this, to do in the church of Christ whatever humour, faction, policy, or licentious will would prompt them to? Again, if Christ be the church's Husband, expecting her to be presented before him a pure unspotted virgin; in what could he shew his tender love to her more than in prescribing his own ways, which he best knew would be to the improvement of her health and beauty, with much greater care doubtless than the Persian king could appoint for his queen Esther those maiden dietings and set prescriptions of baths and odours, which may render her at last more amiable to his eye? For of any age or sex, most unfitly may a virgin be left to an uncertain and arbitrary education. Yea, though she be well instructed, yet is she still under a more strait tuition, especially if betrothed. In like manner the Church bearing the same resemblance, it were not reason to think she should be left destitute of that care which is as necessary and proper to her as instruction. For public preaching indeed is the gift of the Spirit, working as best seems to his secret will; but Discipline is the practic work of preaching directed and applied, as is most requisite, to particular duty; without which it were all one to the benefit of souls, as it would be to the cure of bodies, if all the physicians in London should get into the several pulpits of the city, and assembling all the diseased in every parish, should begin a learned lecture of pleurisies, palsies, lethargies, to which perhaps none there present were inclined; and so, without so much as feeling one pulse, or giving the least order to any skilful apothecary, should dismiss them from time to time, some groaning, some languishing, some expiring, with this only charge, to look well to themselves, and do as they hear. Of what excellence and necessity then Church Discipline is, how beyond the faculty of man to frame, and how dangerous to be left to man's invention, who would be every foot turning it to sinister ends; how properly also it is the work of God as Father and of Christ as Husband of the Church, we have by thus much heard.

CHAPTER II.

That Church Government is set down in Holy Scripture; and that to say otherwise is untrue.

As therefore it is unsound to say, that God hath not appointed any set Government in his Church, so it is untrue. Of the time of the Law there can be no doubt; for to let pass the first institution of priests and Levites, which is too clear to be insisted upon, when the temple came to be built, which in plain judgment could breed no essential change, either in religion or in the priestly government; yet God, to shew how little he could endure that men should be tampering and contriving in his worship, though in things of less regard, gave to David for Solomon not only a pattern and model of the temple, but a direction for the courses of the priests and Levites, and for all the work of their service. At the return from the captivity, things were only restored after the ordinance of Moses and David; or if the least alteration be to be found, they had with them inspired men, prophets; and it were not sober to say they did aught of moment without divine intimation. In the prophecy of Ezekiel, from the fortieth chapter onward, after the destruction of the temple, God, by his prophet, seeking to wean the hearts of the Jews from their Old Law, to expect a new and more perfect reformation under Christ, sets out before their eyes the stately fabric and constitution of his Church, with all the ecclesiastical functions appertaining: indeed the description is as sorted best to the apprehension of those times, typical and shadowy, but in such manner as never yet came to pass, nor ever must literally, unless we mean to annihilate the Gospel. But so exquisite and lively the description is in portraying the new state of the Church, and especially in those points where government seems to be most active, that both Jews and Gentiles might have good cause to be assured, that God, whenever he meant to reform the Church, never intended to leave the government thereof, delineated here in such curious architecture, to be patched afterwards and varnished over with the devices and embellishings of man's imagination. Did God take such delight in measuring out the pillars, arches, and doors of a material temple? Was he so punctual and circumspect in lavers, altars, and sacrifices soon after to be abrogated, lest any of these should have been made contrary to his mind? Is not a far more perfect work, more agreeable to his perfections, in the most perfect state of the Church Militant, the new alliance of God to Man?

Should not he rather now by his own prescribed Discipline have cast his line and level upon the Soul of Man, which is his rational temple, and, by the divine square and compass thereof, form and regenerate in us the lovely shapes of virtues and graces, the sooner to edify and accomplish that immortal stature of Christ's Body, which is his Church, in all her glorious lineaments and proportions? And that this indeed God hath done for us in the Gospel we shall see with open eyes not under a veil. We may pass over the history of the Acts and other places, turning only to those epistles of St. Paul to Timothy and Titus, where the spiritual eye may discern, more goodly and gracefully erected than all the magnificence of temple or tabernacle, such a heavenly structure of Evangelical Discipline, so diffusive of knowledge and charity to the prosperous increase and growth of the Church, that it cannot be wondered if that elegant and artful symmetry of the promised new temple in Ezekiel, and all those sumptuous things under the law, were made to signify the inward beauty and splendour of the Christian Church thus governed. And whether this be commanded, let it now be judged. St. Paul, after his preface to the first of Timothy, which he concludes in the 17th verse with Amen, enters upon the subject of this epistle, which is to establish the Church Government, with a command: "This charge I commit to thee, son Timothy; according to the prophecies which went before on thee, that thou by them mightest war a good warfare." Which is plain enough thus expounded: This charge I commit to thee, wherein I now go about to instruct thee how thou shalt set up Church Discipline, that thou mightest war a good warfare, bearing thyself constantly and faithfully in the ministry, which, in the first to the Corinthians, is also called a warfare. And so, after a kind of parenthesis concerning Hymenæus, he returns to his command, though under the mild word of exhorting, chap. ii. ver. 1, "I exhort therefore;" as if he had interrupted his former command by the occasional mention of Hymenæus. More beneath in the 14th verse of the third chapter, when he had delivered the duties of bishops or presbyters, and deacons, not once naming any other order in the church, he thus adds:

"These things write I unto thee, hoping to come unto thee shortly;—such necessity it seems there was;—but if I tarry long, that thou mayest know how thou oughtest to behave thyself in the House of God." From this place it may be justly asked, Whether Timothy, by this here written, might know what was to be known concerning the orders of Church Governors or no? If he might,—then, in such a clear text as this, may we know too without further jangle. If he might not,—then did St. Paul write insufficiently, and moreover said not true, for he saith here he might know; and I persuade myself he did know ere this was written, but that the apostle had more regard to the instruction of us than to the informing of him. In the fifth chapter, after some other Church-precepts concerning Discipline, mark what a dreadful command follows, ver. 21: "I charge thee before God and the Lord Jesus Christ, and the elect angels, that thou observe these things." And as if all were not yet sure enough, he closes up the epistle with an adjuring charge thus: "I give thee charge in the sight of God, who quickeneth all things, and before Christ Jesus, that thou keep this commandment:" that is, the old commandment concerning Discipline, being the main purpose of the epistle: although Hooker would fain have this denouncement referred to the particular precept going before, because the word commandment is in the singular number, not remembering that even in the first chapter of this epistle the word commandment is used in a plural sense, ver. 5: "Now the end of the commandment is charity;" and what more frequent than in like manner to say the law of Moses? So that either to restrain the significance too much, or too much to enlarge it, would make the adjuration either not so weighty or not so pertinent. And thus we find here that the rules of Church Discipline are not only commanded, but hedged about with such a terrible impalement of commands, as he that will break through wilfully to violate the least of them must hazard the wounding of his conscience even unto death. Yet all this notwithstanding, we shall find them broken well-nigh all by the fair pretenders of the next ages; no less to the contempt of him whom they feign to be the archfounder of prelaty, St. Peter, who, by what he writes in the fifth chapter of his first epistle, should seem to be far another man than tradition reports him. There he commits to the presbyters only full authority both of feeding the flock and episcopating, and commands that obedience be given to them as to the mighty hand of God, which is his mighty ordinance. Yet all this was as nothing to repel the venturous boldness of innovation that ensued, changing the decrees of God that are immutable, as if they had been breathed by man. Nevertheless, when Christ, by these visions of St. John, foreshews the Reformation of his Church, he bids him take his reed and mete it out again after the first pattern, for he prescribes no other. "Arise," said the angel, "and measure the temple of God, and the altar, and them that worship therein." What is there in the world can measure men but Discipline? Our word ruling imports no less. Doctrine indeed is the measure, or at least the reason of the measure, it is true; but unless the measure be applied to that which it is to measure, how can it actually do its proper work? Whether therefore Discipline be all one with Doctrine, or the particular application thereof to this or that person, we all agree that Doctrine must be such only as is commanded; or whether it be something really differing from Doctrine, yet was it only of God's appointment, as being the most adequate measure of the Church and her children, which is here the office of a great evangelist, and the reed given him from heaven. But that part of the temple which is not thus measured, so far is it from being in God's tuition or delight, that in the following verse he rejects it; however in show and visibility it may seem a part of His Church, yet inasmuch as it lies thus unmeasured, he leaves it to be trampled by the Gentiles, that is, to be polluted with idolatrous and gentilish rites and ceremonies. And that the principal Reformation here foretold is already come to pass, as well in Discipline as in Doctrine, the state of our neighbour Churches affords us to behold. Thus, through all the periods and changes of the Church, it hath been proved, that God hath still reserved to himself the right of enacting Church Government.

CHAPTER III.

That it is dangerous and unworthy the Gospel, to hold that Church Government is to be patterned by the Law, as Bishop Andrewes and the Primate of Armagh maintain.

We may return now from this interposing difficulty thus removed to affirm, that since Church Government is so strictly commanded in God's word, the first and greatest Reason why we should submit thereto is, because God hath so commanded. But whether of these two, prelaty or presbytery, can prove itself to be supported by this first and greatest Reason, must be the next dispute; wherein this position is to be first laid down as granted, that I may not follow a chase rather than an argument, that one of these two, and none other, is of God's ordaining; and if it be, that ordinance must be evident in the Gospel. For the imperfect and obscure institution of the Law, which the Apostles themselves doubt not ofttimes to vilify, cannot give rules to the complete and glorious ministration of the Gospel, which looks on the Law as on a child, not as on a tutor. And that the prelates have no sure foundation in the Gospel, their own guiltiness doth manifest; they would not else run questing up as high as Adam to fetch their original, as it is said one of them lately did in public. To which assertion, had I heard it, because I see they are so insatiable of antiquity, I should have gladly assented, and confessed them yet more ancient: for Lucifer, before Adam, was the first prelate angel; and both he, as is commonly thought, and our forefather Adam, as we all know, for aspiring above their orders, were miserably degraded. But others, better advised, are content to receive their beginning from Aaron and his sons, among whom bishop Andrewes of late years, and in these times the primate of Armagh, for their learning are reputed the best able to say what may be said in this opinion. The primate, in his discourse about the original of episcopacy newly revised, begins thus: "The ground of episcopacy is fetched partly from the pattern prescribed by God in the Old Testament, and partly from the imitation thereof brought in by the Apostles." Herein I must entreat to be excused of the desire I have to be satisfied, how, for example, the ground of episcopacy is fetched partly from the example of the Old Testament, by whom next, and by whose authority. Secondly, how the Church Government under the Gospel can be rightly called an imitation of that in the Old Testament; for that the Gospel is the end and fulfilling of the Law, our liberty also from the bondage of the Law, I plainly read. How then the ripe age of the Gospel should be put to school again, and learn to govern herself from the infancy of the Law,—the stronger to imitate the weaker, the freeman to follow the captive, the learned to be lessoned by the rude,—will be a hard undertaking to evince from any of those principles which either art or inspiration hath written. If anything done by the Apostles may be drawn howsoever to a likeness of something Mosaical, if it cannot be proved that it was done of purpose in imitation, as having the right thereof grounded in nature and not in ceremony or type, it will little avail the matter. The whole Judaic Law is either political—and to take pattern by that, no Christian nation ever thought itself obliged in conscience—or moral, which contains in it the observation of whatsoever is substantially and perpetually true and good, either in religion or course of life. That which is thus moral, besides what we fetch from those unwritten laws and ideas which nature hath engraven in us, the Gospel, as stands with her dignity most, lectures to her from her own authentic handwriting and command, not copies out from the borrowed manuscript of a subservient scroll, by way of imitating: as well might she be said, in her sacrament of water, to imitate the baptism of John. What though she retain excommunication used in the synagogue, retain the morality of the sabbath. She does not therefore imitate the Law, her underling, but perfect her. All that was morally delivered from the Law to the Gospel, in the office of the priests and Levites, was, that there should be a ministry set apart to teach and discipline the Church; both which duties the Apostles thought good to commit to the presbyters. And if any distinction of honour were to be made among them, they directed it should be to those not that only rule well, but especially to those that labour in the word and doctrine. By which we are told that laborious teaching is the most honourable prelaty that one minister can have above another in the gospel. If, therefore, the superiority of bishopship be grounded on the priesthood as a part of the moral law, it cannot be said to be an imitation; for it were ridiculous that morality should imitate morality, which ever was the same thing. This very word of patterning or imitating excludes episcopacy from the solid and grave ethical law, and betrays it to be a mere child of ceremony, or likelier some misbegotten thing that, having plucked the gay feathers of her obsolete bravery to hide her own deformed barrenness, now vaunts and glories in her stolen plumes. In the meanwhile, what danger there is against the very life of the Gospel, to make in anything the typical Law her pattern, and how impossible in that which touches the priestly government, I shall use such light as I have received to lay open. It cannot be unknown by what expressions the holy Apostle St. Paul spares not to explain to us the nature and condition of the Law, calling those ordinances which were the chief and essential offices of the priests, the elements and rudiments of the world, both weak and beggarly. Now to breed and bring up the Children of the Promise, the heirs of liberty and grace, under such a kind of government as is professed to be but an imitation of that ministry which engendered to bondage the sons of Agar, how can this be but a foul injury and derogation, if not a cancelling of that birthright and immunity which Christ hath purchased for us with his blood? For the ministration of the Law, consisting of carnal things, drew to it such a Ministry as consisted of carnal respects, dignity, precedence, and the like. And such a Ministry established in the Gospel, as is founded upon the points and terms of superiority, and nests itself in worldly honours, will draw to it, and we see it doth, such a religion as runs back again to the old pomp and glory of the flesh: for doubtless there is a certain attraction and magnetic force betwixt the religion and the ministerial form thereof. If the Religion be pure, spiritual, simple, and lowly, as the Gospel most truly is, such must the face of the Ministry be. And in like manner, if the form of the Ministry be grounded in the worldly degrees of authority, honour, temporal jurisdiction, we see with our eyes it will turn the inward power and purity of the Gospel into the outward carnality of the Law; evaporating and exhaling the internal worship into empty conformities and gay shews. And what remains then, but that we should run into as dangerous and deadly apostasy as our lamentable neighbours the papists, who, by this very snare and pitfall of imitating the ceremonial Law, fell into that irrecoverable superstition, as must needs make void the covenant of salvation to them that persist in this blindness?

CHAPTER IV.

That it is impossible to make the Priesthood of Aaron a Pattern whereon to ground Episcopacy.

THAT which was promised next is, to declare the impossibility of grounding evangelic government in the imitation of the Jewish priesthood; which will be done by considering both the quality of the persons and the office itself. Aaron and his sons were the princes of their tribe, before they were sanctified to the priesthood: that personal eminence, which they held above the other Levites, they received not only from their office, but partly brought it into their office; and so from that time forward the priests were not chosen out of the whole number of the Levites, as our bishops, but were born inheritors of the dignity. Therefore, unless we shall choose our prelates only out of the nobility, and let them run in a blood, there can be no possible imitation of lording over their brethren, in regard of their persons altogether unlike. As for the office, which was a representation of Christ's own person more immediately in the high-priest, and of his whole priestly office in all the other, to the performance of which the Levites were but as servitors and deacons, it was necessary there should be a distinction of dignity between two functions of so great odds. But there being no such difference among our ministers, unless it be in reference to the deacons, it is impossible to found a prelaty upon the imitation of this priesthood: for wherein, or in what work, is the office of a prelate excellent above that of a pastor? In ordination, you will say; but flatly against Scripture: for there we know Timothy received ordination by the hands of the presbytery, notwithstanding all the vain delusions that are used to evade that testimony and maintain an unwarrantable usurpation. But wherefore should ordination be a cause of setting up a superior degree in the church? Is not that whereby Christ became our Saviour a higher and greater work, than that whereby he did ordain messengers to preach and publish him our Saviour? Every Minister sustains the person of Christ in his highest work of communicating to us the mysteries of our salvation, and hath the power of binding and absolving. How should he need a higher dignity, to represent or execute that which is an inferior work in Christ? Why should the performance of ordination, which is a lower office, exalt a prelate, and not the seldom discharge of a higher and more noble office, which is preaching and administering, much rather depress him? Verily, neither the nature nor the example of ordination doth any way require an imparity between the ordainer and the ordained; for what more natural than every like to produce his like, man to beget man, fire to propagate fire? And in examples of highest opinion the ordainer is inferior to the ordained; for the pope is not made by the precedent pope, but by cardinals, who ordain and consecrate to a higher and greater office than their own.

CHAPTER V.

To the Arguments of Bishop Andrewes and the Primate.

IT follows here to attend to certain objections in a little treatise lately printed among others of like sort at Oxford, and in the title said to be out of the rude draughts of bishop Andrewes. And surely they be rude draughts indeed, insomuch that it is marvel to think what his friends meant, to let come abroad such shallow reasonings with the name of a man so much bruited for learning. In the twelfth and twenty-third pages he seems most notoriously inconstant to himself. For in the former place he tells us he forbears to take any argument of prelaty from Aaron, as being the type of Christ: in the latter he can forbear no longer, but repents him of his rash gratuity, affirming, that to say, Christ being come in the flesh his figure in the high-priest ceaseth, is the shift of an anabaptist; and stiffly argues that Christ being as well king as priest, was as well foreresembled by the kings then as by the high-priest: so that if his coming take away the one type, it must also the other. Marvellous piece of divinity, and well worth that the land should pay six thousand pounds a year for in a bishopric! Although I read of no sophister among the Greeks that was so dear, neither Hippias nor Protagoras, nor any whom the Socratic school famously refuted without hire. Here we have the type of the king sewed to the tippet of the bishop, subtlely to cast a jealousy upon the crown, as if the right of kings, like Meleager in the Metamorphosis, were no longer-lived than the firebrand of prelaty. But more likely the prelates, fearing—for their own guilty carriage protests they do fear—that their fair days cannot long hold, practise by possessing the king with this most false doctrine, to engage his power for them as in his own quarrel, that when they fall they may fall in a general ruin; just as cruel Tiberius would wish:

"When I die let the earth be rolled in flames."

But where, O bishop, doth the purpose of the Law set forth Christ to us as a king? That which never was intended in the Law can never be abolished as part thereof. When the Law was made, there was no king: if before the Law, or under the Law, God by a special type in any king would foresignify the future kingdom of Christ, which is not yet visibly come, what was that to the Law? The whole ceremonial Law (and types can be in no law else) comprehends nothing but the propitiatory office of

Christ's priesthood, which being in substance accomplished, both Law and priesthood fades away of itself, and passes into air like a transitory vision, and the right of kings neither stands by any type nor falls. We acknowledge that the civil magistrate wears an authority of God's giving, and ought to be obeyed as his vicegerent. But to make a king a type, we say, is an abusive and unskilful speech, and of a moral solidity makes it seem a ceremonial shadow: therefore your typical chain of king and priest must unlink. But is not the type of priest taken away by Christ's coming? No, saith this famous Protestant bishop of Winchester, it is not; and he that saith it is, is an Anabaptist. What think ye, readers? Do ye not understand him? What can be gathered hence, but that the prelate would still sacrifice? Conceive him, readers: he would missificate. Their altars, indeed, were in a fair forwardness: and by such arguments as these they were setting up the molten calf of their mass again, and of their great hierarch the pope. For if the type of priest be, and that one can be no less than a pope. And this doubtless was the bent of his career, though never so covertly. Yea, but there was something else in the high-priest besides the figure, as is plain by St. Paul's acknowledging him. It is true that in the seventeenth of Deuteronomy, whence this authority arises to the priest in matters too hard for the secular judges, as must needs be many in the occasions of those times, involved so with ceremonial niceties, no wonder though it be commanded to inquire at the mouth of the priests who, besides the magistrates their colleagues, had the oracle of Urim to consult with. And whether the high-priest Ananias had not encroached beyond the limits of his priestly authority, or whether he used it rightly, was no time then for St. Paul to contest about. But if this instance be able to assert any right of jurisdiction to the clergy, it must impart it in common to all ministers, since it were a great folly to seek for counsel in a hard intricate scruple from a dunce prelate, when there might be found a speedier solution from a grave and

learned minister, whom God hath gifted with the judgment of
Urim, more amply ofttimes than all the prelates together; and
now in the Gospel hath granted the privilege of this oraculous
ephod alike to all his ministers. The reason, therefore, of imparity in the priests, being now, as is aforesaid, really annulled
both in their person and in their representative office, what right
of jurisdiction soever can be from this place Levitically bequeathed must descend upon the ministers of the Gospel equally,
as it finds them in all other points equal. Well, then, he is
finally content to let Aaron go; Eleazar will serve his turn, as
being a superior of superiors, and yet no type of Christ in Aaron's
lifetime. O thou that wouldest wind into any figment or phantasm, to save thy mite! yet all this will not fadge, though it be
cunningly interpolished by some second hand with crooks and
emendations. Hear, then, the type of Christ in some one particular, as of entering yearly into the holy of holies, and such-like,
rested upon the high-priest only as more immediately personating
our Saviour: but to resemble his whole satisfactory office, all the
lineage of Aaron was no more than sufficient. And all or any of
the priests, considered separately without relation to the highest,
are but as a lifeless trunk, and signify nothing. And this shews
the excellence of Christ's sacrifice, who at once and in one
person fulfilled that which many hundreds of priests many times
repeating had enough to foreshew. What other imparity there
was among themselves, we may safely suppose it depended on
the dignity of their birth and family, together with the circumstances of a carnal service, which might afford many priorities.
And this I take to be the sum of what the bishop hath laid
together to make plea for prelaty by imitation of the Law: though,
indeed, if it may stand, it will infer popedom all as well. Many
other courses he tries, enforcing himself with much ostentation
of endless genealogies, as if he were the man that St. Paul fore-
warns us of in Timothy; but so unvigorously, that I do not fear
his winning of many to his cause but such as, doting upon great
names, are either over-weak or over-sudden of faith. I shall not
refuse, therefore, to learn so much prudence as I find in the

Roman soldier that attended the cross, not to stand breaking of legs when the breath is quite out of the body, but pass to that which follows. The primate of Armagh, at the beginning of his tractate, seeks to avail himself of that place in the sixty-sixth of Isaiah, "I will take of them for priests and Levites, saith the Lord," to uphold hereby such a form of superiority among the Ministers of the Gospel, succeeding those in the Law, as the Lord's-day did the sabbath. But certain if this method may be admitted of interpreting those prophetical passages concerning Christian times and punctual correspondence, it may with equal probability be urged upon us, that we are bound to observe some monthly solemnity answerable to the new moons, as well as the Lord's-day which we keep in lieu of the sabbath: for in the 23rd verse the prophet joins them in the same manner together, as before he did the priests and Levites, thus: "And it shall come to pass that from one new moon to another, and from one sabbath to another, shall all flesh come to worship before me, saith the Lord." Undoubtedly, with as good consequence may it be alleged from hence that we are to solemnize some religious monthly meeting different from the sabbath, as from the other any distinct formality of ecclesiastical orders may be inferred. This rather will appear to be the lawful and unconstrained sense of the text, that God, in taking of them for priests and Levites, will not esteem them unworthy, though Gentiles, to undergo any function in the Church, but will make of them a full and perfect ministry, as was that of the priests and Levites in their kind. And bishop Andrewes himself, to end the controversy, sends us a candid exposition of this quoted verse from the twenty-fourth page of his said book, plainly deciding that God, by those legal names there of priests and Levites, means our presbyters and deacons; for which either ingenuous confession, or slip of his pen, we give him thanks, and withal to him that brought these treatises into one volume, who, setting the contradictions of two learned men so near together, did not foresee. What other deducements or analogies are cited out of St. Paul, to prove a likeness between the ministers of the Old and New Testament, having tried their sinews, I judge they may pass without harm-doing to our cause.

We may remember, then, that prelaty neither hath nor can have foundation in the Law, nor yet in the Gospel; which assertion, as being for the plainness thereof a matter of eyesight rather than of disquisition, I voluntarily omit; not forgetting to specify this note again, that the earnest desire which the prelates have to build their hierarchy upon the sandy bottom of the Law, gives us to see abundantly the little assurance which they find to rear up their high roofs by the authority of the Gospel, repulsed as it were from the writings of the Apostles, and driven to take sanctuary among the Jews. Hence that open confession of the primate before mentioned: "Episcopacy is fetched partly from the pattern of the Old Testament, and partly from the New, as an imitation of the Old;" though nothing can be more rotten in divinity than such a position as this, and is all one as to say, Episcopacy is partly of divine institution, and partly of man's own carving. For who gave the authority to fetch more from the pattern of the Law, than what the apostles had already fetched, if they fetched anything at all, as hath been proved they did not? So was Jeroboam's episcopacy partly from the pattern of the Law, and partly from the pattern of his own carnality; a party-coloured and a party-membered episcopacy: and what can this be less than a monstrous? Others therefore among the prelates, perhaps not so well able to brook, or rather to justify, this foul relapsing to the Old Law, have condescended at last to a plain confessing, that both the names and offices of bishops and presbyters at first were the same, and in the Scriptures nowhere distinguished. This grants the Remonstrant in the fifth section of his Defence, and in the preface to his last short Answer. But what need respect be had whether he grant it or grant it not, whenas through all antiquity, and even in the loftiest times of prelaty, we find it granted? Jerome, the learnedest of the fathers, hides not his opinion, that custom only, which the proverb calls a tyrant, was the maker of prelaty. Before his audacious workmanship the churches were ruled in common by the presbyters; and such a

I

certain truth this was esteemed, that it became a decree among the papal canons compiled by Gratian. Anselm also, of Canterbury, who, to uphold the points of his prelatism, made himself a traitor to his country, yet, commenting the epistles to Titus and the Philippians, acknowledges, from the clearness of the text, what Jerome and the Church rubric hath before acknowledged. He little dreamed then that the weeding-hook of Reformation would after two ages pluck up his glorious poppy from insulting over the good corn. Though since, some of our British prelates, seeing themselves pressed to produce Scripture, try all their cunning, if the New Testament will not help them, to frame of their own heads, as it were with wax, a kind of mimic bishop limned out to the life of a dead priesthood: or else they would strain us out a certain figurative prelate, by wringing the collective allegory of those seven angels into seven single rochets. Howsoever, since it thus appears that custom was the creator of prelaty, being less ancient than the government of presbyters, it is an extreme folly to give them the hearing that tell us of bishops through so many ages. And if against their tedious muster of citations, sees, and successions, it be replied that wagers and church antiquities, such as are repugnant to the plain dictate of Scripture, are both alike the arguments of fools, they have their answer. We rather are to cite all those ages to an arraignment before the Word of God, wherefore, and what pretending, how presuming, they durst alter that divine institution of presbyters, which the Apostles, who were no various and inconstant men, surely had set up in the Churches; and why they choose to live by custom and catalogue, or, as St. Paul saith, by sight and visibility, rather than by faith? But, first, I conclude, from their own mouths, that God's command in Scripture, which doubtless ought to be the first and greatest Reason of Church Government, is wanting to prelaty. And certainly we have plenteous warrant in the doctrine of Christ, to determine that the want of this Reason is of itself sufficient to confute all other pretences that may be brought in favour of it.

CHAPTER VI.

That Prelaty was not set up for Prevention of Schism, as is pretended; or if it were, that it performs not what it was first set up for, but quite the contrary.

YET because it hath the outside of a specious reason, and specious things we know are aptest to work with human lightness and frailty even against the solidest truth that sounds not plausibly, let us think it worth the examining, for the love of infirmer Christians, of what importance this their second Reason may be. Tradition they say hath taught them, that, for the Prevention of growing Schism, the bishop was heaved above the presbyter. And must tradition then ever thus to the world's end be the perpetual cankerworm to eat out God's commandments? Are his decrees so inconsiderate and so fickle, that when the statutes of Solon or Lycurgus shall prove durably good to many ages, his, in forty years, shall be found defective, ill-contrived, and for needful causes to be altered? Our Saviour and his Apostles did not only foresee, but foretell and forewarn us to look for Schism. Is it a thing to be imagined of God's wisdom, or at least of apostolic prudence, to set up such a government in the tenderness of the Church, as should incline, or not be more able than any others to oppose itself to Schism? It was well known what a bold lurker Schism was, even in the household of Christ, between his own disciples and those of John the Baptist, about fasting; and early in the Acts of the Apostles the noise of Schism had almost drowned the proclaiming of the Gospel; yet we read not in Scripture that any thought was had of making prelates, no, not in those places where dissension was most rife. If prelaty had been then esteemed a remedy against Schism, where was it more needful than in that great variance among the Corinthians, which St. Paul so laboured to reconcile? and whose eye could have found the fittest remedy sooner than his? And what could have made the remedy more available, than to have it speedily? And, lastly, what could have been more necessary, than to have written it for our instruction? Yet we see he neither commended it to us, nor used it himself.— For the same division remaining there, or else bursting forth again more than twenty years after St. Paul's death, we find in Clement's epistle, of venerable authority, written to the yet factious Corinthians, that they were still governed by presbyters. And the same of other churches out of Hermas, and divers other the scholars of the Apostles, by the late industry of the learned Salmasius appears. Neither yet did this worthy Clement, St. Paul's disciple, though writing to them to lay aside Schism, in the least word advise them to change the presbyterian government into prelaty. And therefore, if God afterward gave or permitted this insurrection of episcopacy, it is to be feared he did it in his wrath, as he gave the Israelites a king. With so good a will doth he use to alter his own chosen government once established? For mark whether this rare device of man's brain, thus preferred before the ordinance of God, had better success than fleshly wisdom, not counselling with God, is wont to have. So far was it from removing Schism, that if Schism parted the congregations before, now it rent and mangled, now it raged. Heresy begat heresy with a certain monstrous haste of pregnancy in her birth, at once born and bringing forth. Contentions, before brotherly, were now hostile. Men went to choose their bishop as they went to a pitched field, and the day of his election was like the sacking of a city, sometimes ended with the blood of thousands. Nor this among heretics only, but men of the same belief, yea, confessors; and that with such odious ambition, that Eusebius, in his eighth book, testifies he abhorred to write. And the reason is not obscure, for the poor dignity, or rather burden, of a parochial presbyter could not engage any great party, nor that to any deadly feud: but prelaty was a power of that extent and sway, that if her election were popular, it was seldom not the cause of some faction or broil in the Church. But if her dignity came by favour of some prince, she was from that time his creature, and obnoxious to comply with his ends in state, were they right or wrong. So that, instead of finding prelaty an impeacher of Schism or faction, the more I search, the more I grow into all persuasion to think rather that faction and she, as with a spousal ring, are wedded together, never to be divorced. But here let every one behold the just and dreadful judgment of God meeting with the audacious pride of man, that durst offer to mend the ordinances of heaven. God, out of the strife of men, brought forth by his Apostles to the Church that beneficent and ever-distributing office of deacons, the stewards and ministers of holy alms. Man, out of the pretended care of peace and unity, being caught in the snare of his impious boldness to correct the will of Christ, brought forth to himself upon the Church that irreconcilable Schism of perdition and apostasy, the Roman Antichrist; for that the exaltation of the pope arose out of the reason of prelaty, it cannot be denied. And as I noted before, that the pattern of the high-priest pleaded for in the gospel,—for take away the head priest, the rest are but a carcass—sets up with better reason a pope than an archbishop; for if prelaty must still rise and rise till it come to a primate, why should it stay there? Whenas the catholic government is not to follow the division of kingdoms, the Temple best representing the universal Church, and the high-priest the universal head: so I observe here, that if to quiet Schism there must be one head of prelaty in a land, or monarchy, rising from a provincial to a national primacy, there may, upon better grounds of repressing Schism, be set up one catholic head over the catholic church. For the peace and good of the Church is not terminated in the schismless estate of one or two kingdoms, but should be provided for by the joint consultation of all Reformed Christendom: that all controversy may end in the final pronounce or canon of one archprimate or Protestant Pope: although by this means, for aught I see, all the diameters of Schism may as well meet and be knit up in the centre of one grand falsehood. Now let all impartial men arbitrate what goodly inference these two main Reasons of the prelates have, that by a natural league of consequence make more for the pope than for themselves; yea, to say more home, are the very womb for a new Subantichrist to breed in, if it be not rather the old force and power of the same Man of Sin counterfeiting Protestant. It was not the Prevention of Schism, but it was Schism itself, and the hateful thirst of lording in the Church, that first bestowed a being upon prelaty; this was the true cause, but the pretence is still the same. The prelates, as they would have it thought, are the only mauls of Schism. Forsooth, if they be put down, a deluge of innumerable sects will follow; we shall be all Brownists, Familists, Anabaptists. For the word Puritan seems to be quashed, and all that heretofore were counted such are now Brownists. And thus do they raise an evil report upon the expected reforming grace that God hath bid us hope for; like those faithless spies, whose carcasses shall perish in the wilderness of their own confused ignorance, and never taste the good of Reformation. Do they keep away Schism? If to bring a numb and chill stupidity of soul, an unactive blindness of mind, upon the people by their leaden doctrine or no doctrine at all; if to persecute all knowing and zealous Christians by the violence of their courts, be to keep away Schism, they keep Schism away indeed: and by this kind of Discipline all Italy and Spain is as purely and politicly kept from Schism as England hath been by them. With as good a plea might the dead-palsy boast to a man, It is I that free you from stitches and pains, and the troublesome feeling of cold and heat, of wounds and strokes: if I were gone, all these would molest you. The winter might as well vaunt itself against the spring, I destroy all noisome and rank weeds, I keep down all pestilent vapours. Yes, and all wholesome herbs, and all fresh dews, by your violent and hide-bound frost: but when the gentle west winds shall open the fruitful bosom of the earth, thus overgirded by your imprisonment, then the flowers put forth and spring, and then the sun shall scatter the mists, and the manuring hand of the tiller shall root up all that burdens the soil without thank to your bondage. But far worse than any frozen captivity is the bondage of prelates: for that other, if it keep down anything which is good within the earth, so doth it likewise that which is ill; but these let out freely the ill, and keep down the good, or else keep down the lesser ill, and let out the greatest.

Be ashamed at last to tell the parliament ye curb Schismatics, whenas they know ye cherish and side with papists, and are now as it were one party with them, and it is said they help to petition for ye. Can we believe that your government strains in good earnest at the petty gnats of Schism, whenas we see it makes nothing to swallow the camel heresy of Rome, but that indeed your throats are of the right pharisaical strain? Where are those schismatics, with whom the prelates hold such hot skirmish? Shew us your acts, those glorious annals which your courts of loathed memory lately deceased have left us? Those Schismatics I doubt me will be found the most of them such as whose only Schism was to have spoken the truth against your high abominations and cruelties in the Church; this is the Schism ye hate most, the removal of your criminous hierarchy. A politic government of yours, and of a pleasant conceit, set up to remove those as a pretended Schism, that would remove you as a palpable heresy in government. If the Schism would pardon ye that, she might go jagged in as many cuts and slashes as she pleased for you. As for the rending of the Church, we have many reasons to think it is not that which ye labour to prevent, so much as the rending of your pontifical sleeves. That Schism would be the sorest Schism to you; that would be Brownism and Anabaptism indeed. If we go down, say you,—as if Hadrian's wall were broken,—a flood of sects will rush in. What sects? What are their opinions? Give us the inventory. It will appear both by your former prosecutions and your present instances, that they are only such, to speak of, as are offended with your lawless government, your ceremonies, your liturgy, an extract of the mass-book translated. But that they should be contemners of public prayer, and churches used without superstition, I trust God will manifest it ere long to be as false a slander as your former slanders against the Scots. Noise it till ye be hoarse, that a rabble of Sects will come in; it will be answered ye, No rabble, Sir Priest; but an unanimous multitude of good Protestants will then join to the Church, which now, because of you, stand separated. This will be the dreadful consequence of your removal. As for those terrible names of sectaries and schismatics, which ye have got together, we know your manner of fight. When the quiver of your arguments, which is ever thin and weakly stored, after the first brunt is quite empty, your course is to betake ye to your other quiver of slander, wherein lies your best archery. And whom you could not move by sophistical arguing, them you think to confute by scandalous misnaming; thereby inciting the blinder sort of people to mislike and deride sound doctrine and good Christianity, under two or three vile and hateful terms. But if we could easily endure and dissolve your doughtiest reasons in argument, we shall more easily bear the worst of your unreasonableness in calumny and false report: especially being foretold by Christ, that if he, our master, were by your predecessors called Samaritan and Beelzebub, we must not think it strange if his best disciples in the Reformation, as at first by those of your tribe they were called Lollards and Hussites, so now by you be termed Puritans and Brownists. But my hope is, that the people of England will not suffer themselves to be juggled thus out of their faith and religion by a mist of names cast before their eyes, but will search wisely by the Scriptures, and look quite through this fraudulent aspersion of a disgraceful name into the things themselves: knowing that the primitive Christians in their times were accounted such as are now called Familists and Adamites, or worse. And many on the prelatic side, like the church of Sardis, have a name to live, and yet are dead; to be Protestants, and are indeed papists in most of their principles. Thus persuaded, this your old fallacy we shall soon unmask, and quickly apprehend how you prevent Schism, and who are your Schismatics. But what if we prevent and hinder all good means of preventing Schism? That way which the Apostles used, was to call a Council: from which, by anything that can be learned from the fifteenth of the Acts, no faithful Christian was debarred to whom knowledge and piety might give entrance. Of such a Council as this every parochial consistory is a right homogeneous and constituting part, being in itself, as it were, a little synod, and towards a General Assembly moving upon her own basis in an even and firm progression, as those smaller squares in battle unite in one great cube, the main phalanx, an emblem of truth and steadfastness. Whereas, on the other side, prelaty ascending by a gradual monarchy from bishop to archbishop, from thence to primate, and from thence—for there can be no reason yielded neither in nature nor in religion, wherefore, if it have lawfully mounted thus high, it should not be a lordly ascendant in the horoscope of the Church—from primate to patriarch, and so to pope : I say, prelaty thus ascending in a continual pyramid upon pretence to perfect the Church's unity, if notwithstanding it be found most needful, yea, the utmost help to darn up the rents of Schism by calling a Council, what does it but teach us that prelaty is of no force to effect this work, which she boasts to be her masterpiece; and that her pyramid aspires and sharpens to ambition, not to perfection or unity? This we know, that as often as any great Schism disparts the Church, and synods be proclaimed, the presbyters have as great right there, and as free vote of old, as the bishops, which the canon law conceals not. So that prelaty, if she will seek to close up divisions in the Church, must be forced to dissolve and unmake her own pyramidal figure, which she affirms to be of such uniting power, whenas indeed it is the most dividing and schismatical form that geometricians know of, and must be fain to inglobe or incube herself among the presbyters. Which she hating to do, sends her haughty prelates from all parts with their forked mitres,—the badge of Schism, or the stamp of his cloven foot whom they serve, I think,—who, according to their hierarchies acuminating still higher and higher in a cone of prelaty, instead of healing up the gashes of the Church, as it happens in such pointed bodies meeting, fall to gore one another with their sharp spires for upper place and precedence, till the Council itself proves the greatest Schism of all. And thus they are so far from hindering dissension, that they have made unprofitable, and even noisome, the chiefest remedy we have to keep Christendom at one, which is by Councils : and these, if we rightly consider apostolic example, are nothing else but general presbyteries. This seemed so far from the Apostles to think much of, as if hereby their dignity were impaired, that, as we may gather by those epistles of Peter and John which are likely to be latest written when the Church grew to a settling, like those heroic patricians of Rome (if we may use such comparison) hastening to lay down their dictatorship, they rejoiced to call themselves and to be as fellow-elders among their brethren; knowing that their high office was but as the scaffolding of the Church yet unbuilt, and would be but a troublesome disfigurement, so soon as the building was finished. But the lofty minds of an age or two after, such was their small discerning, thought it a poor indignity, that the high-reared government of the Church should so on a sudden, as it seemed to them, squat into a presbytery.

Next, or rather, before Councils, the timeliest Prevention of Schism is to preach the Gospel abundantly and powerfully throughout all the land, to instruct the youth religiously, to endeavour how the Scriptures may be easiest understood by all men; to all which the proceedings of these men have been on set purpose contrary. But how, O prelates, should you remove Schism, and how should you not remove and oppose all the means of removing Schism, when prelaty is a Schism itself from the most reformed and most flourishing of our neighbour Churches abroad, and a sad subject of discord and offence to the whole nation at home. The remedy which you allege is the very disease we groan under, and never can be to us a remedy but by removing itself. Your predecessors were believed to assume this pre-eminence above their brethren, only that they might appease dissension. Now God and the Church call upon you, for the same reason, to lay it down, as being to thousands of good men offensive, burdensome, intolerable. Surrender that pledge, which, unless you foully usurped it, the Church gave you, and now claims it again, for the reason she first lent it. Discharge the trust committed to you, prevent Schism; and that ye can never do, but by discharging yourselves. That government which ye hold, we confess, prevents much, hinders much, removes much. But what? The schisms and grievances of the Church? No, but all the peace and unity, all the welfare not of the Church alone, but of the whole kingdom, and if it be still permitted ye to hold, will cause the most sad, I know not whether separation be enough to say, but such a wide gulf of distraction in this land, as will never close her dismal gap until ye be forced,—for of yourselves you will never do as that Roman, Curtius, nobly did,—for the Church's peace and your country's, to leap into the midst, and be no more seen. By this we shall know whether yours be that ancient prelaty, which you say was first constituted for the reducement of quiet and unanimity into the Church, for then you will not delay to prefer that above your own preferment. If otherwise, we must be confident that your prelaty is nothing else but your ambition, an insolent preferring of yourselves above your brethren; and all your learned scraping in antiquity, even to disturb the bones of old Aaron and his sons in their graves, is but to maintain and set upon our necks a stately and severe dignity, which you call sacred, and is nothing in very deed but a grave and reverend gluttony, a sanctimonious avarice; in comparison of which, all the duties and dearnesses which ye owe to God or to His Church, to law, custom, or nature, ye have resolved to set at nought. I could put you in mind what counsel Clement, a fellow-labourer with the Apostles, gave to the presbyters of Corinth, whom the people, though unjustly, sought to remove. "Who among you," saith he, "is noble-minded, who is pitiful, who is charitable? let him say thus, If for me this sedition, this enmity, these differences be, I willingly depart, I go my ways; only let the flock of Christ be at peace with the presbyters that are set over it. He that shall do this," saith he, "shall get him great honour in the Lord, and all places will receive him." This was Clement's counsel to good and holy men, that they should depart rather from their just office, than by their stay to ravel out the seamless garment of concord in the Church.

But I have better counsel to give the prelates, and far more acceptable to their ears; this advice in my opinion is fitter for them: Cling fast to your pontifical sees, bate not, quit yourselves like barons, stand to the utmost for your haughty courts and votes in parliament. Still tell us, that you prevent Schism, though Schism and combustion be the very issue of your bodies, your first-born; and set your country a-bleeding in a prelatical mutiny, to fight for your pomp, and that ill-favoured weed of temporal honour that sits dishonourably upon your laic shoulders; that ye may be fat and fleshy, swoln with high thoughts and big with mischievous designs, when God comes to visit upon you all this fourscore years' vexation of His Church under your Egyptian tyranny. For certainly of all those blessed souls which you have persecuted, and those miserable ones which you have lost, the just vengeance does not sleep.

CHAPTER VII.

That those many Sects and Schisms by some supposed to be among us, and that Rebellion in Ireland, ought not to be a Hindrance, but a Hastening of Reformation.

As for those many sects and divisions rumoured abroad to be amongst us, it is not hard to perceive, that they are partly the mere fictions and false alarms of the prelates, thereby to cast amazements and panic terrors into the hearts of weaker Christians, that they should not venture to change the present deformity of the Church, for fear of I know not what worse inconveniencies. With the same objected fears and suspicions, we know that subtle prelate Gardiner sought to divert the Reformation. It may suffice us to be taught by St. Paul, that there must be sects for the manifesting of those that are sound-hearted. These are but winds and flaws to try the floating vessel of our faith, whether it be staunch and sail well, whether our ballast be just, our anchorage and cable strong. By this is seen who lives by faith and certain knowledge, and who by credulity and the prevailing opinion of the age; whose virtue is of an unchangeable grain, and whose of a slight wash. If God come to try our constancy, we ought not to shrink or stand the less firmly for that, but pass on with more steadfast resolution to establish the truth, though it were through a lane of sects and heresies on each side. Other things men do to the glory of God : but sects and errors, it seems, God suffers to be for the glory of good men, that the world may know and reverence their true fortitude and undaunted constancy in the truth.

Let us not therefore make these things an incumbrance, or an excuse of our delay in reforming, which God sends us as an incitement to proceed with more honour and alacrity. For if there were no opposition, where were the trial of an unfeigned goodness and magnanimity? Virtue that wavers is not virtue, but vice revolted from itself, and after a while returning. The actions of just and pious men do not darken in their middle course ; but Solomon tells us, they are as the shining light, that shineth more and more unto the perfect day. But if we shall suffer the trifling doubts and jealousies of future sects to overcloud the fair beginnings of purposed Reformation, let us rather fear that another proverb of the same wise man be not upbraided to us, that "the way of the wicked is as darkness ; they stumble at they know not what." If sects and schisms be turbulent in the unsettled estate of a Church, while it lies under the amending hand, it best beseems our Christian courage to think they are but as the throes and pangs that go before the birth of Reformation, and that the work itself is now in doing. For if we look but on the nature of elemental and mixed things, we know they cannot suffer any change of one kind or quality into another, without the struggle of contrarieties. And in things artificial, seldom any elegance is wrought without a superfluous waste and refuse in the transaction. No marble statue can be politely carved, no fair edifice built, without almost as much rubbish and sweeping. Insomuch that even in the spiritual conflict of St. Paul's conversion, there fell scales from his eyes, that were not perceived before. No wonder then, in the Reforming of a Church, which is never brought to effect without the fierce encounter of truth and falsehood together, if, as it were the splinters and shards of so violent a jousting, there fall from between the shock many fond errors and fanatic opinions, which, when truth has the upper hand and the Reformation shall be perfected, will easily be rid out of the way or kept so low as that they shall be only the exercise of our knowledge, not the disturbance or interruption of our faith. As for that which Barclay, in his "Image of Minds," writes concerning the horrible and barbarous conceits of Englishmen in their Religion, I deem it spoken like what he was, a fugitive papist traducing the island whence he sprung. It may be more judiciously gathered from hence, that the Englishman, of many other nations, is least atheistical, and bears a natural disposition of much reverence and awe towards the Deity. But in his weakness and want of better instruction, which among us too frequently is neglected, especially by the meaner sort, turning the bent of his own wits with a scrupulous and ceaseless care what he might do to inform himself aright of God and His Worship, he may fall not unlikely sometimes, as any other landman, into an uncouth opinion. And verily if we look at his native towardliness in the roughcast without breeding, some nation or other may haply be better composed to a natural civility and right judgment than he; but if he get the benefit once of a wise and well-rectified nurture, which must first come in general from the godly vigilance of the Church, I suppose that wherever mention is made of countries, manners, or men, the English People, among the first that shall be praised, may deserve to be accounted a right pious, right honest, and right hardy nation. But thus while some stand dallying and deferring to reform for fear of that which should mainly hasten them forward, lest Schism and error should increase, we may now thank ourselves and our delays if instead of Schism a bloody and inhuman Rebellion be struck in between our slow movings. Indeed against violent and powerful opposition there can be no just blame of a lingering dispatch. But this I urge against those that discourse it for a maxim, as if the swift opportunities of establishing or reforming religion were to attend upon the phlegm of state-business. In state many things at first are crude and hard to digest, which only time and deliberation can supple and concoct. But in religion, wherein is no immaturity, nothing out of season, it goes far otherwise. The door of grace turns upon smooth hinges, wide opening to send out but soon shutting to recall the precious offers of mercy to a nation: which, unless watchfulness and zeal, two quick-sighted and ready-handed virgins, be there in our behalf to receive, we lose: and still the oftener we lose, the straiter the door opens, and the less is offered. This is all we get by demurring in God's service. It is not Rebellion that ought to be the hindrance of Reformation, but it is the want of this which is the cause of that. The prelates which boast themselves the only bridlers of Schism, God knows, have been so cold and backward both there and with us to repress heresy and idolatry, that, either through their carelessness or their craft, all this mischief is befallen. What can the Irish subjects do less in God's just displeasure against us, than revenge upon English bodies the little care that our prelates have had of their souls? Nor hath their negligence been new in that island, but ever notorious in Queen Elizabeth's days, as Camden, their known friend, forbears not to complain. Yet so little are they touched with remorse of these their cruelties—for these cruelties are theirs, the bloody revenge of those souls which they have famished,—that whenas against our brethren the Scots, who, by their upright and loyal deeds, have now brought themselves an honourable name to posterity, whatsoever malice slander could invent, rage in hostility attempt, they greedily attempted, toward these murderous Irish, the enemies of God and mankind, a cursed offspring of their own connivance, no man takes notice but that they seem to be very calmly and indifferently affected. Where then should we begin to extinguish a Rebellion that hath its cause from the misgovernment of the Church? where, but at the Church's Reformation, and the removal of that government which pursues and wars with all good Christians under the name of schismatics, but maintains and fosters all papists and idolaters as tolerable Christians? And if the sacred Bible may be our light, we are neither without example. nor the witness of God himself, that the corrupted estate of the Church is both the cause of tumult and civil wars, and that to stint them, the peace of the Church must first be settled. "Now, for a long season," saith Azariah to King Asa, "Israel hath been without the true God, and without a teaching priest, and without law: and in those times there was no peace to him that went out, nor to him that came in, but great vexations were upon all the inhabitants of the countries. And nation was destroyed of nation, and city of city, for God did vex them with all adversity. Be ye strong therefore," saith he to the Reformers of that age, "and let not your hands be weak, for your work shall be rewarded." And in those prophets that lived in the times of Reformation after the Captivity, often doth God stir up the people to consider, that while establishment of Church matters was neglected and put off, there "was no peace to him that went out or came in; for I," saith God, "had set all men every one against his neighbour." But from the very day forward that they went seriously and effectually about the welfare of the Church, he tells them, that they themselves might perceive the sudden change of things into a prosperous and peaceful condition. But it will here be said, that the Reformation is a long work, and the miseries of Ireland are urgent of a speedy redress. They be indeed; and how speedy we are, the poor afflicted remnant of our martyred countrymen that sit there on the sea-shore, counting the hours of our delay with their sighs and the minutes with their falling tears, perhaps with the distilling of their bloody wounds, if they have not quite by this time cast off and almost cursed the vain hope of our foundered ships and aids, can best judge how speedy we are to their relief. But let their succours be hasted, as all need and reason is; and let not therefore the Reformation, which is the chiefest cause of success and victory, be still procrastinated. They of the Captivity in their greatest extremities could find both counsel and hands enough at once to build, and to expect the enemy's assault. And we, for our parts, a populous and mighty nation, must needs be fallen into a strange plight either of effeminacy or confusion, if Ireland, that was once the conquest of one single earl with his private forces and the small assistance of a petty Kernish prince, should now take up all the wisdom and prowess of this potent monarchy to quell a barbarous crew of rebels, whom if we take but the right course to subdue, that is, beginning at the Reformation of our Church, their own horrid murders and rapes will so fight against them, that the very sutlers and horse-boys of the camp will be able to rout and chase them, without the staining of any noble sword. To proceed by other method in this enterprise, be our captains and commanders never so expert, will be as great an error in the art of war, as any novice in soldiership ever committed. And thus I leave it as a declared truth, that neither the fear of sects, no, nor rebellion, can be a fit plea to stay Reformation, but rather to push it forward with all possible diligence and speed.

THE SECOND BOOK.

How happy were it for this frail, and as it may be called mortal life of man, since all earthly things which have the name of good and convenient in our daily use, are withal so cumbersome and full of trouble, if knowledge, yet which is the best and lightsomest possession of the mind, were, as the common saying is, no burden; and that what it wanted of being a load to any part of the body, it did not with a heavy advantage overlay upon the spirit. For not to speak of that knowledge that rests in the contemplation of natural causes and dimensions, which must needs be a lower wisdom, as the object is low, certain it is, that he who hath obtained in more than the scantiest measure to know anything distinctly of God, and of his true worship, and what is infallibly good and happy in the state of man's life, what in itself evil and miserable, though vulgarly not so esteemed, he that hath obtained to know this, the only high valuable wisdom indeed, remembering also that God, even to a strictness, requires the improvement of these his entrusted gifts, cannot but sustain a sorer burden of mind, and more pressing, than any supportable toil or weight which the body can labour under, how and in what manner he shall dispose and employ those sums of knowledge and illumination which God hath sent him into this world to trade with. And that which aggravates the burden more is, that, having received amongst his allotted parcels certain precious truths, of such an orient lustre as no diamond can equal, which nevertheless he has in charge to put off at any cheap rate, yea, for nothing to them that will; the great merchants of this world, fearing that this course would soon discover and disgrace the false glitter of their deceitful wares, wherewith they abuse the people, like poor Indians with beads and glasses, practise by all means how they may suppress the vending of such rarities and at such a cheapness as would undo them, and turn their trash upon their hands. Therefore by gratifying the corrupt desires of men in fleshly doctrines, they stir them up to persecute with hatred and contempt all those that seek to bear themselves uprightly in this their spiritual factory. Which they foreseeing, though they cannot but testify of truth, and the excellency of that heavenly traffic which they bring against what opposition or danger soever, yet needs must it sit heavily upon their spirits, that being, in God's prime intention and their own, selected heralds of peace and dispensers of treasure inestimable, without price, to them that have no peace, they find in the discharge of their commission, that they are made the greatest variance and offence, a very sword and fire both in house and city over the whole earth. This is that which the sad prophet Jeremiah laments: "Wo is me, my mother, that thou hast borne me, a man of strife and contention!" And although divine inspiration must certainly have been sweet to those ancient prophets, yet the irksomeness of that truth which they brought was so unpleasant unto them, that everywhere they call it a burden. Yea, that mysterious book of Revelation, which the great evangelist was bid to eat, as it had been some eye-brightening electuary of knowledge and foresight, though it were sweet in his mouth and in the learning, it was bitter in his belly, bitter in the denouncing. Nor was this hid from the wise poet Sophocles, who in that place of his tragedy where Tiresias is called to resolve king Œdipus in a matter which he knew would be grievous, brings him in bemoaning his lot, that he knew more than other men. For surely to every good and peaceable man, it must in nature needs be a hateful thing to be the displeaser and molester of thousands; much better would it like him doubtless to be the messenger of gladness and contentment, which is his chief intended business to all mankind, but that they resist and oppose their own true happiness. But when God commands to take the trumpet, and blow a dolorous or a jarring blast, it lies not in man's will what he shall say, or what he shall conceal. If he shall think to be silent, as Jeremiah did, because of the reproach and derision he met with daily, "And all his familiar friends watched for his halting," to be revenged on him for speaking the truth, he would be forced to confess as he confessed: "His word was in my heart as a burning fire shut up in my bones; I was weary with forbearing, and could not stay." Which might teach these times not suddenly to condemn all things that are sharply spoken or vehemently written as proceeding out of stomach, virulence, and ill-nature; but to consider rather, that if the prelates have leave to say the worst that can be said, or do the worst that can be done, while they strive to keep to themselves, to their great pleasure and commodity, those things which they ought to render up, no man can be justly offended with him that shall endeavour to impart and bestow, without any gain to himself, those sharp but saving words which would be a terror and a torment in him to keep back.

For me, I have determined to lay up as the best treasure and solace of a good old age, if God vouchsafe it me, the honest liberty of free speech from my youth, where I shall think it available in so dear a concernment as the Church's good. For if I be, either by disposition or what other cause, too inquisitive or suspicious of myself and mine own doings, who can help it? But this I foresee, that should the Church be brought under heavy oppression, and God have given me ability the while to reason against that man that should be the author of so foul a deed; or should she, by blessing from above on the industry and courage of faithful men, change this her distracted estate into better days, without the least furtherance or contribution of those few talents, which God at that present had lent me: I foresee what stories I should hear within myself, all my life after, of discourage and reproach. Timorous and ungrateful, the Church of God is now again at the foot of her insulting enemies, and thou bewailest. What matters it for thee, or thy bewailing? When time was, thou couldst not find a syllable of all that thou hast read, or studied, to utter in her behalf. Yet ease and leisure was given thee for thy retired thoughts, out of the sweat of other men. Thou hast the diligence, the parts, the language of a man, if a vain subject were to be adorned or beautified; but when the cause of God and His Church was to be pleaded, for which purpose that tongue was given thee which thou hast, God listened if he could hear thy voice among his zealous servants, but thou wert dumb as a beast: from henceforward be that which thine own brutish silence hath made thee. Or else I should have heard on the other ear: Slothful, and ever to be set light by, the Church hath now overcome her late distresses after the unwearied labours of many her true servants that stood up in her defence; thou also wouldst take upon thee to share amongst them of their joy: but wherefore thou? Where canst thou shew any word or deed of thine which might have hastened her peace? Whatever thou dost now talk, or write, or look, is the alms of other men's active prudence and zeal. Dare not now to say or do anything better than thy former sloth and infancy; or if thou darest, thou dost impudently to make a thrifty purchase of boldness to thyself, out of the painful merits of other men; what before was thy sin is now thy duty, to be abject and worthless. These, and suchlike lessons as these, I know would have been my matins duly, and my even-song. But now by this little diligence, mark what a privilege I have gained with good men and saints, to claim my right of lamenting the tribulations of the Church, if she should suffer, when others, that have ventured nothing for her sake, have not the honour to be admitted mourners. But if she lift up her drooping head and prosper, among those that have something more than wished her welfare, I have my charter and freehold of rejoicing to me and my heirs. Concerning therefore this wayward subject against prelaty, the touching whereof is so distasteful and disquietous to a number of men, as by what hath been said I may deserve of charitable readers to be credited, that neither envy nor gall hath entered me upon this controversy, but the enforcement of conscience only, and a preventive fear lest the omitting of this duty should be against me, when I would store up to myself the good provision of peaceful hours. So, lest it should be still imputed to me, as I have found it hath been, that some self-pleasing humour of vain-glory hath incited me to contest with men of high estimation, now while green years are upon my head, from this needless surmisal I shall hope to dissuade the intelligent and equal auditor, if I can but say successfully that which in this exigent behoves me; although I would be heard only, if it might be, by the elegant and learned reader, to whom principally for a while I shall beg leave I may address myself. To him it will be no new thing, though I tell him that if I hunted after praise, by the ostentation of wit and learning, I should not write thus out of mine own season when I have neither yet completed to my mind the full circle of my private studies, although I complain not of any insufficiency to the matter in hand, or were I ready to my wishes, it were a folly to commit anything elaborately composed to the careless and interrupted listening of these tumultuous times. Next, if I were wise only to my own ends, I would certainly take such a subject as of itself might catch applause, whereas this hath all the disadvantages on the contrary; and such a subject as the publishing whereof might be delayed at pleasure, and time enough to pencil it over with all the curious touches of art, even to the perfection of a faultless picture: whenas in this argument the not deferring is of great moment to the good speeding, that if solidity have leisure to do her office, art cannot have much. Lastly, I should not choose this manner of writing, wherein knowing myself inferior to myself, led by the genial power of nature to another task, I have the use, as I may account, but of my left hand. And though I shall be foolish in saying more to this purpose, yet since it will be such a folly as wisest men go about to commit, having only confessed and so committed, I may trust with more reason, because with more folly, to have courteous pardon. For although a poet, soaring in the high reason of his fancies, with his garland and singing robes about him, might, without apology, speak more of himself than I mean to do; yet for me sitting here below in the cool element of prose, a mortal thing among many readers of no empyreal conceit, to venture and divulge unusual things of myself, I shall petition to the gentler sort, it may not be envy to me. I must say, therefore, that after I had for my first years, by the ceaseless diligence and care of my father—whom God recompense!—been exercised to the tongues, and some sciences, as my age would suffer, by sundry masters and teachers both at home and at the schools, it was found that whether aught was imposed me by them that had the overlooking, or betaken to of mine own choice in English or other tongue, prosing or versing, but chiefly by this latter, the style, by certain vital signs it had, was likely to live. But much latelier in the private academies of Italy, whither I was favoured to resort, perceiving that some trifles which I had in memory, composed at under twenty or thereabout—for the manner is, that every one must give some proof of his wit and reading there,— met with acceptance above what was looked for; and other things, which I had shifted in scarcity of books and conveniences to patch up amongst them, were received with written encomiums, which the Italian is not forward to bestow on men of this side the Alps; I began thus far to assent both to them and divers of my friends here at home, and not less to an inward prompting which now grew daily upon me, that by labour and intense study, which I take to be my portion in this life, joined with the strong propensity of nature, I might perhaps leave something so written to aftertimes, as they should not willingly let it die. These thoughts at once possessed me, and these other; that if I were certain to write as men buy leases, for three lives and downward, there ought no regard be sooner had than to God's glory, by the honour and instruction of my country. For which cause, and not only for that I knew it would be hard to arrive at the second rank among the Latins, I applied myself to that resolution, which Ariosto followed against the persuasions of Bembo, to fix all the industry and art I could unite to the adorning of my native tongue; not to make verbal curiosities the end—that were a toilsome vanity,—but to be an interpreter and relater of the best and sagest things among mine own citizens throughout this island in the mother dialect. That what the greatest and choicest wits of Athens, Rome, or modern Italy, and those Hebrews of old did for their country, I, in my proportion, with this over and above, of being a Christian, might do for mine; not caring to be once named abroad, though perhaps I could attain to that, but content with these British islands as my world; whose fortune hath hitherto been, that if the Athenians, as some say, made their small deeds great and renowned by their eloquent writers, England hath had her noble achievements made small by the unskilful handling of monks and mechanics.

Time serves not now, and perhaps I might seem too profuse, to give any certain account of what the mind at home, in the spacious circuits of her musing, hath liberty to propose to herself, though of highest hope and hardest attempting; whether that epic form whereof the two poems of Homer, and those other two of Virgil and Tasso, are a diffuse, and the book of Job a brief model: or whether the rules of Aristotle herein are strictly to be kept, or nature to be followed, which in them that know art and use judgment is no transgression but an enriching of art: and lastly, what king or knight before the Conquest might be chosen, in whom to lay the pattern of a Christian hero. And as Tasso gave to a prince of Italy his choice whether he would command him to write of Godfrey's expedition against the Infidels, or Belisarius against the Goths, or Charlemain against the Lombards; if to the instinct of nature and the emboldening of art aught may be trusted, and that there be nothing adverse in our climate or the fate of this age, it haply would be no rashness, from an equal dilligence and inclination, to present the like offer in our own ancient stories; or whether those dramatic constitutions wherein Sophocles and Euripides reign shall be found more doctrinal and exemplary to a nation. The Scripture also affords us a divine pastoral drama in the Song of Solomon, consisting of two persons and a double chorus, as Origen rightly judges. And the Apocalypse of St. John is the majestic image of a high and stately tragedy, shutting up and intermingling her solemn scenes and acts with a sevenfold chorus of hallelujahs and harping symphonies: and this my opinion the grave authority of Pareus, commenting that book, is sufficient to confirm. Or if occasion shall lead, to imitate those magnific odes and hymns, wherein Pindarus and Callimachus are in most things worthy, some others in their frame judicious, in their matter most an end faulty. But those frequent songs throughout the Law and Prophets beyond all these, not in their divine argument alone, but in the very critical art of composition, may be easily made appear over all the kinds of lyric poesy to be incomparable. These abilities, wheresoever they be found, are the inspired gift of God, rarely bestowed, but yet to some—though most abuse—in every nation; and are of power, beside the office of a pulpit, to imbreed and cherish in a great people the seeds of virtue and public civility, to allay the perturbations of the mind, and set the affections in right tune; to celebrate in glorious and lofty hymns the throne and equipage of God's Almightiness, and what He works, and what He suffers to be wrought with high providence in His Church: to sing victorious agonies of martyrs and saints, the deeds and triumphs of just and pious nations, doing valiantly through faith against the enemies of Christ; to deplore the general relapses of kingdoms and states from justice and God's true worship. Lastly, whatsoever in religion is holy and sublime, in virtue amiable or grave, whatsoever hath passion or admiration in all the changes of that which is called fortune from without, or the wily subtleties and refluxes of man's thoughts from within; all these things with a solid and treatable smoothness to paint out and describe. Teaching over the whole book of sanctity and virtue, through all the instances of example, with such delight to those especially of soft and delicious temper, who will not so much as look upon Truth herself, unless they see her elegantly dressed; that whereas the paths of honesty and good life appear now rugged and difficult, though they be indeed easy and pleasant, they will appear to all men both easy and pleasant, though they were rugged and difficult indeed. And what a benefit this would be to our youth and gentry, may be soon guessed by what we know of the corruption and bane which they suck in daily from the writings and interludes of libidinous and ignorant poetasters, who having scarce ever heard of that which is the main consistence of a true poem, the choice of such persons as they ought to introduce, and what is moral and decent to each one, do for the most part lay up vicious principles in sweet pills to be swallowed down, and make the taste of virtuous documents harsh and sour. But because the spirit of man cannot demean itself lively in this body without some recreating intermission of labour and serious things, it were happy for the commonwealth, if our magistrates, as in those famous governments of old, would take into their care, not only the deciding of our contentious law-cases and brawls, but the managing of our public sports and festival pastimes; that they might be, not such as were authorized a while since, the provocations of drunkenness and lust, but such as may inure and harden our bodies by martial exercises to all warlike skill and performance; and may civilize, adorn, and make discreet our minds by the learned and affable meeting of frequent academies, and the procurement of wise and artful recitations, sweetened with eloquent and graceful enticements to the love and practice of justice, temperance, and fortitude, instructing and bettering the nation, at all opportunities, that the call of wisdom and virtue may be heard everywhere, as Solomon saith: "She crieth without, she uttereth her voice in the streets, in the top of high places, in the chief concourse, and in the openings of the gates." Whether this may not be, not only in pulpits, but after another persuasive method, at set and solemn paneguries, in theatres, porches, or what other place or way may win most upon the people to receive at once both recreation and instruction, let them in authority consult. The thing which I had to say, and those intentions which have lived within me ever since I could conceive myself anything worth to my country, I return to crave excuse that urgent reason hath plucked from me, by an abortive and foredated discovery. And the accomplishment of them lies not but in a power above man's to promise. But that none hath by more studious ways endeavoured, and with more unwearied spirit that none shall, that I dare almost aver of myself, as far as life and free leisure will extend; and that the land had once enfranchised herself from this impertinent yoke of prelaty, under whose inquisitorious and tyrannical duncery, no free and splendid wit can flourish. Neither do I think it shame to covenant with any knowing reader, that for some few years yet I may go on trust with him toward the payment of what I am now indebted, as being a work not to be raised from the heat of youth, or the vapours of wine; like that which flows at waste from the pen of some vulgar amourist, or the trencher fury of a rhyming parasite; nor to be obtained by the invocation of dame Memory and her siren daughters, but by devout prayer to that eternal Spirit, who can enrich with all utterance and knowledge, and sends out his seraphim, with the hallowed fire of his altar, to touch and purify the lips of whom he pleases. To this must be added industrious and select reading, steady observation, insight into all seemly and generous arts and affairs; till which in some measure be compassed, at mine own peril and cost, I refuse not to sustain this expectation from as many as are not loth to hazard so much credulity upon the best pledges that I can give them. Although it nothing content me to have disclosed thus much beforehand, but that I trust hereby to make it manifest with what small willingness I endure to interrupt the pursuit of no less hopes than these, and leave a calm and pleasing solitariness fed with cheerful and confident thoughts, to embark in a troubled sea of noises and hoarse disputes; put from beholding the bright countenance of Truth in the quiet and still air of delightful studies, to come into the dim reflection of hollow antiquities sold by the seeming bulk, and there be fain to club quotations with men whose learning and belief lies in marginal stuffings, who, when they have, like good sumpters, laid ye down their horse-loads of citations and fathers at your door, with a rhapsody of who and who were bishops here or there, ye may take off their packsaddles, their day's work is done, and episcopacy, as they think, stoutly vindicated. Let any gentle apprehension, that can distinguish learned pains from unlearned drudgery, imagine what pleasure or profoundness can be in this, or what honour to deal against such adversaries. But were it the meanest under-service, if God by His secretary Conscience enjoin it, it were sad for me if I should draw back; for me especially, now when all men offer their aid to help, ease, and lighten the difficult labours of the Church, to whose service, by the intentions of my parents and friends, I was destined of a child, and in mine own resolutions : till coming to some maturity of years, and perceiving what tyranny had invaded the Church, that he who would take orders must subscribe slave, and take an oath withal, which, unless he took with a conscience that would retch, he must either straight perjure, or split his faith; I thought it better to prefer a blameless silence before the sacred office of speaking, bought and begun with servitude and forswearing. Howsoever, thus church-outed by the prelates, hence may appear the right I have to meddle in these matters, as before the necessity and constraint appeared.

CHAPTER I.

That Prelaty opposeth the Reason and End of the Gospel three Ways; and first, in her outward Form.

AFTER this digression, it would remain that I should single out some other reason, which might undertake for prelaty to be a fit and lawful Church Government; but finding none of like validity with these that have already sped according to their fortune, I shall add one reason why it is not to be thought a Church Government at all, but a church tyranny, and is at hostile terms with the end and reason of Christ's evangelic ministry. Albeit I must confess to be half in doubt whether I should bring it forth or no, it being so contrary to the eye of the world, and the world so potent in most men's hearts, that I shall endanger either not to be regarded or not to be understood. For who is there almost that measures wisdom by simplicity, strength by suffering, dignity by lowliness? Who is there that counts it first to be last, something to be nothing, and reckons himself of great command in that he is a servant? Yet God, when he meant to subdue the world and hell at once, part of that to salvation, and this wholly to perdition, made choice of no other weapons or auxiliaries than these, whether to save or to destroy. It had been a small mastery for him to have drawn out his legions into array, and flanked them with his thunder; therefore he sent foolishness to confute wisdom, weakness to bind strength, despisedness to vanquish pride. And this is the great mystery of the Gospel made good in Christ himself, who, as he testifies, came not to be ministered to, but to minister; and must be fulfilled in all his ministers till his second coming. To go against these principles St. Paul so feared, that if he should but affect the wisdom of words in his preaching he thought it would be laid to his charge that he had made the cross of Christ to be of none effect. Whether, then, prelaty do not make of none effect the cross of Christ by the principles it hath so contrary to these, nullifying the power and end of the Gospel, it shall not want due proof, if it want not due belief. Neither shall I stand to trifle with one that would tell me of quiddities and formalities, whether prelaty or prelateity, in abstract notion, be this or that; it suffices me that I find it in his skin, so I find it inseparable, or not oftener otherwise than a phœnix hath been seen; although I persuade me, that whatever faultiness was but superficial to prelaty at the beginning, is now, by the just judgment of God, long since branded and inworn into the very essence thereof. First, therefore, if to do the work of the Gospel, Christ our Lord took upon him the form of a servant, how can his servant in this ministry take upon him the form of a lord? I know Bilson hath deciphered us all the gallantries of signore and monsignore, and monsieur, as circumstantially as any punctualist of Castile, Naples, or Fontainebleau could have done: but this must not so compliment us out of our right minds, as to be to learn that the form of a servant was a mean, laborious, and vulgar life, aptest to teach; which form Christ thought fittest, that he might bring about his will according to his own principles, choosing the meaner things of this world that he might put under the high. Now, whether the pompous garb, the lordly life, the wealth, the haughty distance of prelaty, be those meaner things of the world whereby God in them would manage the mystery of his Gospel, be it the verdict of common sense. For Christ saith, in St. John, "The servant is not greater than his lord, nor he that is sent greater than he that sent him;" and adds, "If ye know these things, happy are ye if ye do them." Then let the prelates well advise, if they neither know nor do these things, or if they know and yet do them not, wherein their happiness consists. And thus is the Gospel frustrated by the Lordly Form of prelaty.

CHAPTER II.

That the ceremonious Doctrine of Prelaty opposeth the Reason and End of the Gospel.

THAT which next declares the heavenly power and reveals the deep mystery of the Gospel, is the pure simplicity of doctrine, accounted the foolishness of this world, yet crossing and confounding the pride and wisdom of the flesh. And wherein consists this fleshly wisdom and pride? In being altogether ignorant of God and His worship? No, surely; for men are naturally ashamed of that. Where then? It consists in a bold presumption of ordering the worship and service of God after man's own will in traditions and ceremonies. Now if the pride and wisdom of the flesh were to be defeated and confounded, no doubt but in that very point wherein it was proudest and thought itself wisest, that so the victory of the Gospel might be the more illustrious. But our prelates, instead of expressing the spiritual power of their ministry by warring against this chief bulwark and stronghold of the flesh, have entered into fast league with the principal enemy against whom they were sent, and turned the strength of fleshly pride and wisdom against the pure simplicity of saving truth.

First, mistrusting to find the authority of their order in the immediate institution of Christ, or his Apostles by the clear evidence of Scripture, they fly to the carnal supportment of tradition. When we appeal to the Bible, they to the unwieldy volumes of tradition: and do not shame to reject the ordinance of Him that is Eternal, for the perverse iniquity of sixteen hundred years; choosing rather to think truth itself a liar, than that sixteen ages should be taxed with an error; not considering the general apostacy that was foretold, and the Church's flight into the wilderness. Nor is this enough; instead of showing the reason of their lowly condition from divine example and command, they seek to prove their high pre-eminence from human consent and authority. But let them chant while they will of prerogatives, we shall tell them of Scripture; of custom, we of Scripture; of acts and statutes, still of Scripture; till the quick and piercing Word enter to the dividing of their souls, and the mighty weakness of the Gospel throw down the weak mightiness of man's reasoning. Now for their demeanour within the church, how have they disfigured and defaced that more than angelic brightness, the unclouded serenity of Christian religion, with the dark overcasting of superstitious copes and flaminical vestures, wearing on their backs, and, I abhor to think, perhaps in some worse place, the inexpressible image of God the Father? Tell me, ye priests, wherefore this gold, wherefore these robes and surplices over the Gospel? Is our religion guilty of the first trespass, and hath need of clothing to cover her nakedness? What does this else but cast an ignominy upon the perfection of Christ's ministry, by seeking to adorn it with that which was the poor remedy of our shame? Believe it, wondrous doctors, all corporeal resemblances of inward holiness and beauty are now past; he that will clothe the Gospel now, intimates plainly that the Gospel is naked, uncomely, that I may not say reproachful. Do not, ye church maskers, while Christ is clothing upon our barrenness with his righteous garment to make us acceptable in his Father's sight, do not, as ye do, cover and hide his righteous verity with the polluted clothing of your ceremonies, to make it seem more decent in your own eyes. "How beautiful," saith Isaiah, "are the feet of him that bringeth good tidings, that publisheth salvation!" Are the feet so beautiful, and is the very bringing of these tidings so decent of itself? What new decency can then be added to this by your spinstry? Ye think by these gaudy glisterings to stir up the devotion of the rude multitude; ye think so, because ye forsake the heavenly teaching of St. Paul for the hellish sophistry of papism. If the multitude be rude, the lips of the preacher must give knowledge, and not ceremonies. And although some Christians be new-born babes comparatively to some that are stronger, yet in respect of ceremony, which is but a rudiment of the law, the weakest Christian hath thrown off the robes of his minority, and is a perfect man, as to legal rites. What children's food there is in the Gospel we know to be no other than the "sincerity of the Word, that they may grow thereby." But is here the utmost of your outbraving the service of God? No. Ye have been bold, not to set your threshold by his threshold, or your posts by his posts; but your sacrament, your sign, call it what you will, by his sacrament, baptizing the Christian infant with a solemn sprinkle, and unbaptizing for your own part with a profane and impious forefinger; as if when ye had laid the purifying element upon his forehead, ye meant to cancel and cross it out again with a character not of God's bidding. Oh but the innocence of these ceremonies! Oh rather the sottish absurdity of this excuse. What could be more innocent than the washing of a cup, a glass, or hands, before meat, and that under the Law, when so many washings were commanded, and by long tradition? Yet our Saviour detested their customs, though never so seeming harmless, and charges them severely, that they had transgressed the commandments of God by their traditions, and worshipped him in vain. How much more then must these, and much grosser ceremonies now in force, delude the end of Christ's coming in the flesh against the flesh, and stifle the sincerity of our new covenant which hath bound us to forsake all carnal pride and wisdom, especially in matters of religion? Thus we see again how prelaty, failing in opposition to the main end and power of the Gospel, doth not join in that mysterious work of Christ, by lowliness to confound height; by simplicity of doctrine, the wisdom of the world; but contrariwise hath made itself high in the world and the flesh, to vanquish things by the world accounted low, and make itself wise in Tradition and fleshly Ceremony, to confound the purity of doctrine which is the wisdom of God.

CHAPTER III.

That prelatical Jurisdiction opposeth the Reason and end of the Gospel and of State.

THE third and last consideration remains, whether the prelates in their function do work according to the Gospel, practising to subdue the mighty things of this world by things weak, which St. Paul hath set forth to be the power and excellence of the Gospel; or whether in more likelihood they band themselves with the prevalent things of this world, to overrun the weak things which Christ hath made choice to work by: and this will soonest be discerned by the course of their Jurisdiction. But here again I find my thoughts almost in suspense betwixt yea and no, and am nigh turning mine eye which way I may best retire, and not proceed in this subject, blaming the ardency of my mind that fixed me too attentively to come thus far. For Truth, I know not how, hath this unhappiness fatal to her, ere she can come to the trial and inspection of the Understanding; being to pass through many little wards and limits of the several Affections and Desires, she cannot shift it, but must put on such colours and attire as those pathetic handmaids of the Soul please to lead her in to their queen: and if she find so much favour with them, they let her pass in her own likeness; if not, they bring her into the presence habited and coloured like a notorious Falsehood. And contrary, when any Falsehood comes that way, if they like the errand she brings, they are so artful to counterfeit the very shape

and visage of Truth, that the Understanding not being able to
discern the fucus which these enchantresses with such cunning
have laid upon the feature sometimes of Truth, sometimes of
Falsehood interchangeably, sentences for the most part one for the
other at the first blush, according to the subtle imposture of these
sensual mistresses, that keep the ports and passages between her
and the object. So that were it not for leaving imperfect that
which is already said, I should go near to relinquish that which
is to follow. And because I see that most men, as it happens
in this world, either weakly or falsely principled, what through
ignorance, and what through custom of licence, both in discourse
and writing, by what hath been of late written in vulgar, have not
seemed to attain the decision of this point: I shall likewise assay
those wily arbitresses who in most men have, as was heard, the
sole ushering of Truth and Falsehood between the Sense and the
Soul, with what loyalty they will use me in convoying this Truth
to my Understanding; the rather for that, by as much acquaintance as I can obtain with them, I do not find them engaged
either one way or other. Concerning therefore Ecclesiastical
Jurisdiction, I find still more controversy, who should administer
it than diligent inquiry made to learn what it is. For had the
pains been taken to search out that, it had been long ago enrolled
to be nothing else but a pure tyrannical forgery of the prelates;
and that jurisdictive power in the Church there ought to be none
at all. It cannot be conceived that what men now call jurisdiction in the Church, should be other thing than a Christian
censorship; and therefore it is most commonly and truly named
ecclesiastical censure. Now if the Roman censor, a civil function,
to that severe assize of surveying and controlling the privatest
and slyest manners of all men and all degrees, had no jurisdiction, no courts of plea or indictment, no punitive force annexed;
whether it were that to this manner of correction the entanglement of suits was improper, or that the notice of those upright
inquisitors extended to such the most covert and spirituous vices
as would slip easily between the wider and more material grasp of
the law, or that it stood more with the majesty of that office to

have no other sergeants or maces about them but those invisible ones of terror and shame; or, lastly, were it their fear, lest the greatness of this authority and honour, armed with jurisdiction, might step with ease into a tyranny: in all these respects, with much more reason undoubtedly ought the censure of the Church be quite divested and disentailed of all jurisdiction whatsoever.

For if the course of judicature to a political censorship seem either too tedious, or too contentious, much more may it to the discipline of the Church, whose definitive decrees are to be speedy, but the execution of rigour slow, contrary to what in legal proceedings is most usual; and by how much the less contentious it is, by so much will it be the more Christian. And if the Censor, in his moral episcopy being to judge most in matters not answerable by writ or action, could not use an instrument so gross and bodily as jurisdiction is, how can the Minister of the Gospel manage the corpulent and secular trial of bill and process in things merely spiritual? Or could that Roman office, without this juridical sword or saw, strike such a reverence of itself into the most undaunted hearts, as with one single dash of ignominy to put all the Senate and Knighthood of Rome into a tremble, surely much rather might the heavenly ministry of the evangel bind herself about with far more piercing beams of majesty and awe, by wanting the beggarly help of halings and amercements in the use of her powerful keys. For when the Church without temporal support is able to do her great works upon the unforced obedience of men, it argues a divinity about her. But when she thinks to credit and better her spiritual efficacy, and to win herself respect and dread by strutting in the false vizard of worldly authority, it is evident that God is not there, but that her apostolic virtue is departed from her, and hath left her key cold. Which she perceiving, as in a decayed nature seeks to the outward fomentations and chafings of worldly help, and external flourishes, to fetch, if it be possible, some motion into her extreme parts, or to hatch a counterfeit life with the crafty and artificial heat of jurisdiction. But it is observable, that so long as the Church, in true imitation of Christ, can be content to ride upon an ass carrying herself and her government along in a mean and simple guise, she may be, as he is, a lion of the tribe of Judah; and in her humility all men with loud hosannas will confess her greatness. But when, despising the mighty operation of the Spirit by the weak things of this world, she thinks to make herself bigger and more considerable, by using the way of civil force and jurisdiction, as she sits upon this lion she changes into an ass, and instead of hosannas every man pelts her with stones and dirt. Lastly, if the wisdom of the Romans feared to commit jurisdiction to an office of so high esteem and dread as was the Censor's, we may see what a solecism in the art of policy it hath been all this while through Christendom to give jurisdiction to ecclesiastical censure. For that strength, joined with religion abused and pretended to ambitious ends, must of necessity breed the heaviest and most quelling tyranny not only upon the necks but even to the souls of men: which if Christian Rome had been so cautelous to prevent in her Church, as pagan Rome was in her State, we had not such a lamentable experience thereof as now we have from thence upon all Christendom. For although I said before, that the Church coveting to ride upon the lionly form of jurisdiction, makes a transformation of herself into an ass and becomes despicable, that is to those whom God hath enlightened with true knowledge; but where they remain yet in the reliques of superstition, this is the extremity of their bondage and blindness that while they think they do obeisance to the lordly vision of a lion, they do it to an ass, that through the just judgment of God is permitted to play the dragon among them because of their wilful stupidity. And let England here well rub her eyes, lest by leaving Jurisdiction and Church Censure to the same persons, now that God hath been so long medicining her eyesight, she do not with her over-politic fetches mar all and bring herself back again to worship this ass bestriding a lion. Having hitherto explained, that to ecclesiastical censure no jurisdictive power can be added without a childish and dangerous oversight in policy and a pernicious contradiction in evangelical discipline, as anon more fully, it will be next to declare wherein the true reason and force of Church Censure consists, which by then it shall be laid open to the root, so little is it that I fear lest any crookedness, any wrinkle or spot should be found in Presbyterian government, that if Bodin, the famous French writer, though a Papist, yet affirms that the commonwealth which maintains this discipline will certainly flourish in virtue and piety, I dare assure myself, that every true Protestant will admire the integrity, the uprightness, the divine and gracious purposes thereof, and even for the reason of it so coherent with the doctrine of the Gospel, beside the evidence of command in Scripture, will confess it to be the only true Church Government; and that, contrary to the whole end and mystery of Christ's coming in the flesh, a false appearance of the same is exercised by prelaty. But because some count it rigorous, and that hereby men shall be liable to a double punishment, I will begin somewhat higher, and speak of punishment; which, as it is an evil, I esteem to be of two sorts, or rather two degrees only, a reprobate conscience in this life, and hell in the other world. Whatever else men call punishment or censure, is not properly an evil, so it be not an illegal violence, but a saving medicine ordained of God both for the public and private good of man; who consisting of two parts, the inward and the outward, was by the eternal Providence left under two sorts of cure, the Church and the Magistrate. The magistrate hath only to deal with the outward part, I mean not of the body alone, but of the mind in all her outward acts, which in Scripture is called the outward man. So that it would be helpful to us if we might borrow such authority as the rhetoricians by patent may give us, with a kind of Promethean skill to shape and fashion this outward man into the similitude of a body, and set him visible before us; imagining the inner man only as the soul. Thus then the civil magistrate looking only upon the outward man—I say as a magistrate, for what he doth further, he doth it as a member of the Church—if he find in his complexion, skin, or outward temperature the signs and marks, or in his doings the effects of injustice, rapine, lust, cruelty, or the like, sometimes he shuts up as in frenetick or infectious diseases; or confines within doors, as in every sickly estate. Sometimes he shaves by penalty or mulct, or else to cool and take down those luxuriant humours which wealth and excess have caused to abound. Otherwhiles he sears, he cauterizes, he scarifies, lets blood; and finally, for utmost remedy, cuts off. The patients, which most an end are brought into his hospital, are such as are far gone, and beside themselves, unless they be falsely accused; so that force is necessary to tame and quiet them in their unruly fits before they can be made capable of a more human cure. His general end is the outward peace and welfare of the commonwealth, and civil happiness in this life. His particular end in every man is, by the infliction of pain, damage, and disgrace, that the senses and common perceivance might carry this message to the soul within, that it is neither easeful, profitable, nor praiseworthy in this life to do evil. Which must needs tend to the good of man, whether he be to live or die; and be undoubtedly the first means to a natural man, especially an offender, which might open his eyes to a higher consideration of good and evil, as it is taught in religion. This is seen in the often penitence of those that suffer, who, had they escaped, had gone on sinning to an immeasurable heap, which is one of the extremest punishments. And this is all that the civil magistrate, as so being, confers to the healing of man's mind, working only by terrifying plasters upon the rind and orifice of the sore; and by all outward appliances, as the logicians say, a posteriori, at the effect, and not from the cause; not once touching the inward bed of corruption, and that hectic disposition to evil, the source of all vice and obliquity against the rule of law. Which how insufficient it is to cure the soul of man, we cannot better guess than by the art of bodily physic.

Therefore God, to the intent of further healing man's depraved mind, to this power of the magistrate, which contents itself with the restraint of evil-doing in the external man, added that which we call Censure, to purge it and remove it clean out of the inmost soul. In the beginning this authority seems to have been placed, as all both civil and religious rites once were, only in each father of a family; afterwards, among the heathen, in the wise men and philosophers of the age; but so as it was a thing voluntary, and no set government. More distinctly among the Jews, as being God's peculiar people, where the Priests, Levites, Prophets, and at last the Scribes and Pharisees, took charge of instructing and overseeing the lives of the people. But in the Gospel, which is the straightest and the dearest covenant can be made between God and Man, we being now his adopted sons, and nothing fitter for us to think on than to be like him, united to him, and, as he pleases to express it, to have fellowship with him; 'it is all necessity that we should expect this blessed efficacy of healing our inward man to be ministered to us in a more familiar and effectual method than ever before. God being now no more a judge after the sentence of the law, nor, as it were, a schoolmaster of perishable rites, but a most indulgent father, governing His Church as a family of sons in their discreet age, and therefore, in the sweetest and mildest manner of paternal discipline, he hath committed this other office of preserving in healthful constitution the inner man, which may be termed the spirit of the soul, to his spiritual deputy the minister of each congregation; who being best acquainted with his own flock, hath best reason to know all the secretest diseases likely to be there. And look by how much the internal man is more excellent and noble than the external, by so much is his cure more exactly, more thoroughly, and more particularly to be performed. For which cause the Holy Ghost by the Apostles, joined to the minister, as assistant in this great office, sometimes a certain number of grave and faithful brethren—for neither doth the physician do all in restoring his patient; he prescribes, another prepares the medicine; some tend, some watch, some visit—much more may a minister partly not see all, partly err as a man. Besides, that nothing can be more for the mutual honour and love of the people to their pastor, and his to them, than when in select numbers and courses they are seen partaking and doing reverence to the holy duties of discipline by their serviceable and solemn presence, and receiving honour again from their employment, not now any more to be separated in the church by veils and partitions, as laics and unclean, but admitted to wait upon the tabernacle as the rightful clergy of Christ, a chosen generation, a royal priesthood, to offer up spiritual sacrifice in that meet place to which God and the congregation shall call and assign them. And this all Christians ought to know, that the title of clergy St. Peter gave to all God's people, till pope Higinus and the succeeding prelates took it from them, appropriating that name to themselves and their priests only. And condemning the rest of God's inheritance to an injurious and alienate condition of laity, they separated from them by local partitions in churches, through their gross ignorance and pride imitating the old temple, and excluding the members of Christ from the property of being members, the bearing of orderly and fit offices in the ecclesiastical body; as if they had meant to sew up that Jewish veil, which Christ by his death on the cross rent in sunder. Although these usurpers could not so presently overmaster the liberties and lawful titles of God's freeborn Church but that Origen, being yet a layman, expounded the Scriptures publicly, and was therein defended by Alexander of Jerusalem, and Theoctistus of Cæsarea, producing in his behalf divers examples, that the privilege of teaching was anciently permitted to many worthy laymen. And Cyprian in his epistles professes he will do nothing without the advice and assent of his assistant laics. Neither did the first Nicene Council, as great and learned as it was, think it any robbery to receive in, and require the help and presence of many learned lay-brethren, as they were then called. Many other authorities to confirm this assertion, both out of Scripture and the writings of next antiquity, Golartius hath collected in his notes upon Cyprian; whereby it will be evident that the laity, not only by apostolic permission, but by consent of many of the ancientest prelates, did participate in church offices as much as is desired any lay elder should now do.

Sometimes also not the elders alone, but the whole body of the Church is interested in the work of discipline, as oft as public satisfaction is given by those that have given public scandal. Not to speak now of her right in elections. But another reason there is in it which though religion did not commend to us yet moral and civil prudence could not but extol. It was thought of old in philosophy, that shame, or to call it better, the reverence of our elders, our brethren, and friends, was the greatest incitement to virtuous deeds and the greater dissuasion from unworthy attempts that might be. Hence we may read in the Iliad, where Hector being wished to retire from the battle, many of his forces being routed, makes answer, that he durst not for shame, lest the Trojan knights and dames should think he did ignobly. And certain it is, that whereas terror is thought such a great stickler in a commonwealth, honourable shame is a far greater, and has more reason: for where shame is, there is fear; but where fear is, there is not presently shame. And if anything may be done to imbreed in us this generous and Christianly reverence one of another, the very nurse and guardian of piety and virtue, it cannot sooner be than by such a discipline in the Church as may use us to have in awe the assemblies of the faithful, and to count it a thing most grievous, next to the grieving of God's Spirit, to offend those whom he hath put in authority as a healing superintendence over our lives and behaviours, both to our own happiness, and that we may not give offence to good men, who, without amends by us made, dare not, against God's command, hold communion with us in holy things. And this will be accompanied with a religious dread of being outcast from the company of saints, and from the fatherly protection of God in his Church, to consort with the devil and his angels. But there is yet a more ingenuous and noble degree of honest shame, or, call it, if you will, an esteem, whereby men bear an inward reverence toward their own persons. And if the love of God, as a fire sent from heaven to be ever kept alive upon the altars of our hearts, be the first principle of all godly and virtuous actions in men, this pious and just honouring of ourselves is the second, and may be thought as the radical moisture and fountain-head whence every laudable and worthy enterprise issues forth. And although I have given it the name of a liquid thing, yet it is not incontinent to bound itself, as humid things are, but hath in it a most restraining and powerful abstinence to start back, and globe itself upward from the mixture of any ungenerous and unbeseeming motion or any soil wherewith it may peril to stain itself.

Something I confess it is, to be ashamed of evildoing in the presence of any; and to reverence the opinion and the countenance of a good man rather than a bad, fearing most in his sight to offend, goes so far as almost to be virtuous. Yet this is but still the fear of infamy, and many such, when they find themselves alone saving their reputation, will compound with other scruples and come to a close treaty with their dearer vices in secret. But he that holds himself in reverence and due esteem, both for the dignity of God's image upon him and for the price of his redemption which he thinks is visibly marked upon his forehead, accounts himself both a fit person to do the noblest and godliest deeds, and much better worth than to deject and defile with such a debasement and such a pollution as sin is himself so highly ransomed and ennobled to a new friendship and filial relation with God. Nor can he fear so much the offence and reproach of others, as he dreads and would blush at the reflection of his own severe and modest eye upon himself, if it should see him doing or imagining that which is sinful, though in the deepest secrecy. How shall a man know to do himself this right, how to perform his honourable duty of estimation and respect towards his own soul and body? Which way will lead him best to this hill-top of sanctity and goodness, above which there is no higher ascent but to the love of God, which from this selfpious regard cannot be asunder? No better way doubtless, than to let him duly understand, that as he is called by the high calling of God to be holy and pure, so is he by the same appointment ordained, and by the Church's call admitted, to such offices of discipline in the Church to which his own spiritual gifts, by the example of apostolic institution, have authorised him. For we have learned that the scornful term of laic, the consecrating of temples, carpets, and tablecloths, the railing in of a repugnant and contradictive mount Sinai in the Gospel, as if the touch of a lay-christian, who is nevertheless God's living temple, could profane dead Judaisms, the exclusion of Christ's people from the offices of holy discipline through the pride of a usurping clergy, causes the rest to have an unworthy and abject opinion of themselves, to approach to holy duties with a slavish fear, and to unholy doings with a familiar boldness. For seeing such a wide and terrible distance between religious things and themselves, and that in respect of a wooden table, and the perimeter of holy ground about it, a flagon pot, and a linen corporal, the priest esteems their layships unhallowed and unclean, they fear Religion with such a fear as loves not, and think the purity of the Gospel too pure for them, and that any uncleanness is more suitable to their unconsecrated estate. But when every good Christian, thoroughly acquainted with all those glorious privileges of sanctification and adoption which render him more sacred than any dedicated altar or element, shall be restored to his right in the Church, and not excluded from such place of spiritual government as his Christian abilities, and his approved good life in the eye and testimony of the Church shall prefer him to, this and nothing sooner will open his eyes to a wise and true valuation of himself —which is so requisite and high a point of Christianity—and will stir him up to walk worthy the honourable and grave employment wherewith God and the Church hath dignified him; not fearing lest he should meet with some outward holy thing in religion, which his lay-touch or presence might profane; but lest something unholy from within his own heart should dishonour and profane in himself that priestly unction and clergy-right whereto Christ hath entitled him. Then would the Congregation of the Lord soon recover the true likeness and visage of what she is indeed, a holy generation, a royal priesthood, a saintly communion, the household and city of God. And this I hold to be another considerable reason why the functions of Church Government ought to be free and open to any Christian man, though never so laic, if his capacity, his faith, and prudent demeanour, commend him. And this the Apostles warrant us to do.

But the prelates object, that this will bring profaneness into the church: to whom may be replied, that none have brought that in more than their own irreligious courses, nor more driven holiness out of living into lifeless things. For whereas God, who hath cleansed every beast and creeping worm, would not suffer St. Peter to call them common or unclean, the prelate bishops, in their printed orders hung up in churches, have proclaimed the best of creatures, mankind, so unpurified and contagious, that for him to lay his hat or his garment upon the chancel table, they have defined it no less than heinous, in express words, than to profane the table of the Lord. And thus have they by their Canaanitish doctrine—for that which was to the Jew but Jewish, is to the Christian no better than Canaanitish,—thus have they made common and unclean, thus have they made profane that nature which God hath not only cleansed, but Christ also hath assumed. And now that the equity and just reason is so perspicuous, why in ecclesiastic censure the assistance should be added of such as whom not the vile odour of gain and fees (forbid it, God, and blow it with a whirlwind out of our land!), but charity, neighbourhood, and duty to church government hath called together, where could a wise man wish a more equal, gratuitous, and meek examination of any offence that he might happen to commit against Christianity, than here? Would he prefer those proud simoniacal courts? Thus therefore the minister assisted, attends his heavenly and spiritual cure : where we shall see him both in the course of his proceedings, and first in the excellency of his end, from the magistrate far different, and not more different than excelling. His end is to recover all that is of man, both soul and body, to an everlasting health ; and yet as for worldly happiness, which is the proper sphere wherein the magistrate cannot but confine his motion without a hideous exorbitancy from law, so little aims the minister as his intended scope to procure the much prosperity of this life, that ofttimes he may have cause to wish much of it away, as a diet puffing up the soul with a slimy fleshiness and weakening her principal organic parts. Two heads of evil he has to cope with, ignorance and malice. Against the former he provides the daily manna of incorruptible doctrine, not at those set meals only in public, but as oft as he shall know that each infirmity or constitution requires.

Against the latter with all the branches thereof, not meddling with that restraining and styptic surgery which the law uses, not indeed against the malady but against the eruptions and outermost effects thereof; he on the contrary, beginning at the prime causes and roots of the disease, sends in those two divine ingredients of most cleansing power to the soul, admonition and reproof; besides which two there is no drug or antidote that can reach to purge the mind, and without which all other experiments are but vain, unless by accident. And he that will not let these pass into him, though he be the greatest king, as Plato affirms, must be thought to remain impure within and unknowing of those things wherein his pureness and his knowledge should most appear. As soon therefore as it may be discerned that the Christian patient, by feeding otherwhere on meats not allowable but of evil juice, hath disordered his diet and spread an ill-humour through his veins immediately disposing to a sickness, the minister, as being much nearer both in eye and duty than the magistrate, speeds him betimes to overtake that diffused malignance with some gentle potion of admonishment; or if aught be obstructed, puts in his opening and discussive confections. This not succeeding after once or twice or oftener, in the presence of two or three his faithful brethren appointed thereto he advises him to be more careful of his dearest health, and what it is that he so rashly hath let down into the divine vessel of his soul, God's temple. If this obtain not, he then, with the counsel of more assistants, who are informed of what diligence hath been already used, with more speedy remedies lays nearer siege to the entrenched causes of his distemper, not sparing such fervent and well-aimed reproofs as may best give him to see the dangerous estate wherein he is. To this also his brethren and friends entreat, exhort, adjure; and all these endeavours, as there is hope left, are more or less repeated. But if neither the regard of himself nor the reverence of his elders and friends prevail with him to leave his vicious appetite, then as the time urges, such engines of terror God hath given into the hand of his minister as to search the tenderest angles of the heart. One while he shakes his stubbornness with racking convulsions nigh despair; otherwhiles with deadly corrosives he gripes the very roots of his faulty liver to bring him to life through the entry of death. Hereto the whole Church beseech him, beg of him, deplore him, pray for him. After all this performed with what patience and attendance is possible, and no relenting on his part, having done the utmost of their cure, in the name of God and of the Church they dissolve their fellowship with him, and holding forth the dreadful sponge of excommunion, pronounce him wiped out of the list of God's inheritance, and in the custody of Satan till he repent. Which horrid sentence, though it touch neither life nor limb nor any worldly possession, yet has it such a penetrating force, that swifter than any chemical sulphur, or that lightning which harms not the skin and rifles the entrails, it scorches the inmost soul. Yet even this terrible denouncement is left to the Church for no other cause but to be as a rough and vehement cleansing medicine where the malady is obdurate, a mortifying to life, a kind of saving by undoing.

And it may be truly said, that as the mercies of wicked men are cruelties, so the cruelties of the Church are mercies. For if repentance sent from Heaven meet this lost wanderer, and draw him out of that steep journey wherein he was hasting towards destruction to come and reconcile to the Church, if he bring with him his bill of health and that he is now clear of infection and of no danger to the other sheep; then with incredible expressions of joy all his brethren receive him, and set before him those perfumed banquets of Christian consolation; with precious ointments bathing and fomenting the old and now to be forgotten stripes which terror and shame had inflicted; and thus with heavenly solaces they cheer up his humble remorse, till he regain his first health and felicity. This is the approved way, which the Gospel prescribes, these are the "spiritual weapons of holy censure, and ministerial warfare, not carnal, but mighty through God to the pulling down of strong holds, casting down imaginations, and every high thing that exalteth itself against the knowledge of God, and bringing into captivity every thought to the obedience of Christ." What could be done more for the healing and reclaiming that divine particle of God's breathing, the soul? And what could be done less? He that would hide his faults from such a wholesome curing as this, and count it a twofold punishment, as some do, is like a man that having foul diseases about him, perishes for shame, and the fear he has of a rigorous incision to come upon his flesh. We shall be able by this time to discern whether prelatical jurisdiction be contrary to the Gospel or no.

First, therefore, the government of the Gospel being economical and paternal, that is, of such a family where there be no servants but all sons, in obedience not in servility, as cannot be denied by him that lives but within the sound of Scripture; how can the prelates justify to have turned the fatherly orders of Christ's household, the blessed meekness of his lowly roof, those ever-open and inviting doors of his dwellinghouse, which delight to be frequented with only filial accesses; how can they justify to have turned these domestic privileges into the bar of a proud judicial court, where fees and clamours keep shop and drive a trade, where bribery and corruption solicits, paltering the free and moneyless power of discipline with a carnal satisfaction by the purse? Contrition, humiliation, confession, the very sighs of a repentant spirit, are there sold by the penny. That undeflowered and unblemishable Simplicity of the Gospel, not she herself, for that could never be, but a false-whited, a lawny resemblance of her, like that airborn Helena in the fables, made by the sorcery of prelates, instead of calling her disciples from the receipt of custom, is now turned publican herself, and gives up her body to a mercenary whoredom under those fornicated Arches, which she calls God's house; and in the sight of those her altars which she hath set up to be adored, makes merchandise of the bodies and souls of men, rejecting purgatory for no other reason, as it seems, than because her greediness cannot defer, but had rather use the utmost extortion of redeemed penances in this life.

But because these matters could not be thus carried without a begged and borrowed Force from worldly authority, therefore prelaty, slighting the deliberate and chosen council of Christ in his spiritual government, whose glory is in the weakness of fleshly things to tread upon the crest of the world's pride and violence by the power of spiritual ordinances, hath on the contrary made these her friends and champions which are Christ's enemies in this his high design, smothering and extinguishing the spiritual force of his bodily weakness in the discipline of his Church with the boisterous and carnal tyranny of an undue, unlawful, and ungospel-like Jurisdiction. And thus prelaty, both in her fleshly supportments, in her carnal doctrine of ceremony and tradition, in her violent and secular power, going quite counter to the prime end of Christ's coming in the flesh, that is, to reveal his truth, his glory, and his might in a clean contrary manner than prelaty seeks to do, thwarting and defeating the great mystery of God, I do not conclude that prelaty is antichristian: for what need I? the things themselves conclude it. Yet if such like practices, and not many worse than these of our prelates in that great darkness of the Roman church, have not exempted both her and her present members from being judged to be antichristian in all orthodoxal esteem; I cannot think but that it is the absolute voice of truth and all her children to pronounce this prelaty, and these her dark deeds in the midst of this great light wherein we live, to be more antichristian than Antichrist himself.

THE CONCLUSION.

The Mischief that Prelaty does in the State.

I ADD one thing more to those great ones that are so fond of prelaty. This is certain, that the Gospel being the hidden might of Christ, as hath been heard, that ever a victorious power joined with it, like him in the Revelation that went forth on the white horse with his bow and his crown, conquering and to conquer. If we let the Angel of the Gospel ride on his own way, he does his proper business, conquering the high thoughts and the proud reasonings of the flesh, and brings them under to give obedience to Christ with the salvation of many souls. But if ye turn him out of his road, and in a manner force him to express his irresistible power by a doctrine of carnal might, as prelaty is, he will use that fleshly strength which ye put into his hands to subdue your spirits by a servile and blind Superstition; and that again shall hold such dominion over your captive minds, as returning with an insatiate greediness and force upon your worldly wealth and power, wherewith to deck and magnify herself and her false worships, he shall spoil and havoc your estates, disturb your ease, diminish your honour, enthral your liberty under the swelling mood of a proud clergy who will not serve or feed your souls with spiritual food; look not for it, they have not wherewithal, or if they had it is not in their purpose. But when they have glutted their ungrateful bodies, at least if it be possible that those open sepulchres should ever be glutted, and when they have stuffed their idolish temples with the wasteful pillage of your estates, will they yet have any compassion upon you and that poor pittance which they have left you? Will they be but so good to you as that ravisher was to his sister, when he had used her at his pleasure: will they but only hate ye, and so turn ye loose? No, they will not, Lords and Commons, they will not favour ye so much. What will they do then, in the name of God and saints, what will these manhaters yet with more despite and mischief do? I will tell ye, or at least remember ye, for most of ye know it already: that they may want nothing to make them true merchants of Babylon, as they have done to your souls, they will sell your bodies, your wives, your children, your liberties, your parliaments, all these things and if there be ought else dearer than these, they will sell at an outcry in their pulpits to the arbitrary and illegal dispose of any one that may hereafter be called a king, whose mind shall serve him to listen to their bargain. And by their corrupt and servile doctrines boring our ears to an everlasting slavery, as they have done hitherto, so will they yet do their best to repeal and erase every line and clause of both our great charters. Nor is this only what they will do, but what they hold as the main reason and mystery of their advancement that they must do; be the prince never so just and equal to his subjects, yet such are their malicious and depraved eyes, that they so look on him and so understand him as if he required no other gratitude or piece of service from them than this. And indeed they stand so opportunely for the disturbing or the destroying of a state, being a knot of creatures whose dignities, means, and preferments have no foundation in the Gospel, as they themselves acknowledge, but only in the prince's favour, and to continue so long to them as by pleasing him they shall deserve. Whence it must needs be they should bend all their intentions and services to no other ends but to his, that if it should happen that a tyrant—God turn such a scourge from us to our enemies!—should come to grasp the sceptre, here were his spearmen and his lances, here were his firelocks ready, he should need no other pretorian band nor pensionary than these, if they could once with their perfidious preachments awe the people. For although the prelates in time of popery were sometimes friendly enough to Magna Charta, it was because they stood upon their own bottom, without their main dependence on the royal nod. But now being well acquainted that the Protestant religion, if she will reform herself rightly by the Scriptures, must undress them of all their gilded vanities and reduce them as they were at first to the lowly and equal order of presbyters, they know it concerns them nearly to study the times more than the text, and to lift up their eyes to the hills of the Court from whence only comes their help. But if their pride grow weary of this crouching and observance, as ere long it would, and that yet their minds climb still to a higher ascent of worldly honour, this only refuge can remain to them, that they must of necessity contrive to bring themselves and us back again to the pope's supremacy; and this we see they had by fair degrees of late been doing. These be the two fair supporters between which the strength of prelaty is borne up, either of inducing tyranny or of reducing popery. Hence also we may judge that prelaty is mere falsehood. For the property of truth is, where she is publicly taught, to unyoke and set free the minds and spirits of a nation first from the thraldom of sin and superstition, after which all honest and legal freedom of civil life cannot be long absent. But prelaty, whom the tyrant custom begot, a natural tyrant in religion and in state the agent and minister of tyranny, seems to have had this fatal gift in her nativity, like another Midas, that whatsoever she should touch or come near either in ecclesial or political government, it should turn, not to gold,—though she for her part could wish it,—but to the dross and scum of slavery, breeding and settling both in the bodies and the souls of all such as do not in time, with the sovereign treacle of sound doctrine, provide to fortify their hearts against her hierarchy. The service of God, who is Truth, her liturgy confesses to be perfect freedom: but her works and her opinions declare, that the service of prelaty is perfect slavery, and by consequence perfect falsehood. Which makes me wonder much that many of the gentry, studious men as I hear, should engage themselves to write and speak publicly in her defence; but that I believe their honest and ingenuous natures coming to the universities to store themselves with good and solid learning, and there unfortunately fed with nothing else but the scragged and thorny lectures of monkish and miserable sophistry, were sent home again with such a scholastic bur in their throats as hath stopped and hindered all true and generous philosophy from entering, cracked their voices for ever with metaphysical gargarisms, and hath made them admire a sort of formal outside men, prelatically addicted, whose unchastened and unwrought minds were never yet initiated or subdued under the true lore of religion or moral virtue, which two are the best and greatest points of learning, but either slightly trained up in a kind of hypocritical and hackney course of literature, to get their living by and dazzle the ignorant, or else fondly over-studied in useless controversies, except those which they use, with all the specious and delusive subtlety they are able, to defend their prelatical Sparta. Having a Gospel and Church Government set before their eyes, as a fair field wherein they might exercise the greatest virtues and the greatest deeds of Christian authority in mean fortunes and little furniture of this world—which even the sage heathen writers, and those old Fabritii and Curii, well knew to be a manner of working than which nothing could liken a mortal man more to God, who delights most to work from within Himself and not by the heavy luggage of corporeal instruments —they understand it not, and think no such matter but admire and dote upon worldly riches and honours with an easy and intemperate life, to the bane of Christianity. Yea, they and their seminaries shame not to profess, to petition, and never leave pealing our ears, that unless we fat them like boars and cram them as they list with wealth, with deaneries and pluralities, with baronies and stately preferments, all learning and religion will go underfoot. Which is such a shameless, such a bestial plea, and of that odious impudence in churchmen who should be to us a pattern of temperance and frugal mediocrity, who should teach us to contemn this world and the gaudy things thereof according to the promise which they themselves require from us in baptism, that should the Scripture stand by and be mute, there is not that sect of philosophers among the heathen so dissolute, no not Epicurus nor Aristippus with all his Cyrenaic rout, but would shut his school-doors against such greasy sophisters; not any college of mountebanks but would think scorn to discover in themselves with such a brazen forehead the outrageous desire of filthy lucre. Which the prelates make so little conscience of, that they are ready to fight, and if it lay in their power, to massacre all good Christians under the names of horrible schismatics, for only finding fault with their temporal dignities, their unconscionable wealth and revenues, their cruel authority over their brethren that labour in the Word while they snore in their luxurious excess; openly proclaiming themselves now in the sight of all men to be those which for a while they sought to cover under sheep's clothing, ravenous and savage wolves, threatening inroads and bloody incursions upon the flock of Christ, which they took upon them to feed but now claim to devour as their prey. More like that huge dragon of Egypt, breathing out waste and desolation to the land unless he were daily fattened with virgin's blood. Him our old patron St. George by his matchless valour slew, as the Prelate of the Garter that reads his collect can tell. And if our princes and knights will imitate the fame of that old champion, as by their order of knighthood solemnly taken they vow, far be it that they should uphold and side with this English dragon; but rather to do as indeed their oaths bind them they should make it their knightly adventure to pursue and vanquish this mighty sail-winged monster that menaces to swallow up the land unless her bottomless gorge may be satisfied with the blood of the king's daughter, the Church; and may, as she was wont, fill her dark and infamous den with the bones of the saints. Nor will any one have reason to think this as too incredible or too tragical to be spoken of prelaty, if he consider well from what a mass of slime and mud, the slothful, the covetous and ambitious hopes of Church-promotions and fat bishoprics she is bred up and muzzled in, like a great Python, from her youth, to prove the general poison both of Doctrine and good Discipline in the land. For certainly such hopes and such principles of earth as these wherein she welters from a young one, are the immediate generation both of a slavish and tyrannous life to follow, and a pestiferous contagion to the whole kingdom, till like that fen-born serpent she be shot to death with the darts of the Sun, the pure and powerful beams of God's Word. And this may serve to describe to us in part what prelaty hath been, and what, if she stand, she is like to be towards the whole body of People in England.

Now that it may appear how she is not such a kind of evil as hath any good or use in it, which many evils have, but a distilled quintessence, a pure elixir of mischief, pestilent alike to all, I shall show briefly, ere I conclude, that the prelates, as they are to the Subjects a calamity, so are they the greatest underminers and betrayers of the Monarch, to whom they seem to be most favourable. I cannot better liken the state and person of a king than to that mighty Nazarite Samson, who being disciplined from his birth in the precepts and the practice of temperance and sobriety, without the strong drink of injurious and excessive desires, grows up to a noble strength and perfection with those his illustrious and sunny locks, the laws, waving and curling about his godlike shoulders. And while he keeps them about him undiminished and unshorn, he may with the jawbone of an ass, that is, with the word of his meanest officer, suppress and put to confusion thousands of those that rise against his just power. But laying down his head among the strumpet flatteries of prelates, while he sleeps and thinks no harm, they wickedly shaving off all those bright and weighty tresses of his law, and just prerogatives, which were his ornament and strength, deliver him over to indirect and violent counsels, which, as those Philistines, put out the fair and far-sighted eyes of his natural discerning, and make him grind in the prisonhouse of their sinister ends and practices upon him: till he, knowing this prelatical razor to have bereft him of his wonted might, nourish again his puissant hair, the golden beams of law and right; and they sternly shook thunder with ruin upon the heads of those his evil counsellors, but not without great affliction to himself. This is the sum of their royal service to kings; yet these are the men that still cry, The king, the king, the Lord's anointed! We grant it; and wonder how they came to light upon anything so true; and wonder more, if kings be the Lord's anointed, how they dare thus oil over and besmear so holy an unction with the corrupt and putrid ointment of their base flatteries, which while they smooth the skin, strike inward and envenom the lifeblood. What fidelity kings can expect from prelates, both examples past and our present experience of their doings at this day, whereon is grounded all that hath been said, may suffice to inform us. And if they be such clippers of regal power and shavers of the laws, how they stand affected to the lawgiving Parliament, yourselves, worthy Peers and Commons, can best testify; the current of whose glorious and immortal actions hath been only opposed by the obscure and pernicious designs of the prelates, until their insolence broke out to such a bold affront as hath justly immured their haughty looks within strong walls. Nor have they done anything of late with more diligence than to hinder or break the happy assembling of parliaments. however needful to repair the shattered and disjointed frame of the commonwealth; or if they cannot do this, to cross, to disenable, and traduce all parliamentary proceedings. And this, if nothing else, plainly accuses them to be no lawful members of the House, if they thus perpetually mutiny against their own body. And though they pretend, like Solomon's harlot, that they have right thereto, by the same judgment that Solomon gave, it cannot belong to them, whenas it is not only their assent but their endeavour continually to divide Parliaments in twain; and not only by dividing, but by all other means to abolish and destroy the free use of them to all posterity. For the which, and for all their former misdeeds, whereof this book and many volumes more cannot contain the moiety, I shall move ye, Lords, in the behalf I dare say of many thousand good Christians, to let your justice and speedy sentence pass against this great malefactor, prelaty. And yet in the midst of rigour I would beseech ye to think of mercy; and such a mercy (I fear I shall overshoot with a desire to save this falling prelaty), such a mercy (if I may venture to say it) as may exceed that which for only ten righteous persons would have saved Sodom. Not that I dare advise ye to contend with God, whether he or you shall be more merciful, but in your wise esteems to balance the offences of those peccant cities with these enormous riots of ungodly misrule that prelaty hath wrought both in the Church of Christ, and in the State of this Kingdom. And if ye think ye may with a pious presumption strive to go beyond God in mercy, I shall not be one now that would dissuade ye. Though God for less than ten just persons would not spare Sodom, yet if you can find, after due search, but only one good thing in prelaty, either to religion or civil government, to king or parliament, to prince or people, to law, liberty, wealth, or learning, spare her, let her live, let her spread among ye, till with her shadow all your dignities and honours and all the glory of the land be darkened and obscured. But on the contrary, if she be found to be malignant, hostile, destructive to all these, as nothing can be surer, then let your severe and impartial doom imitate the divine vengeance. Rain down your punishing force upon this godless and oppressing government, and bring such a Dead Sea of subversion upon her, that she may never in this land rise more to afflict the holy Reformed Church, and the elect people of God.

MAN AND WIFE.

" Hail Wedded Love, mysterious Law, true Source
Of human Offspring, sole propriety
In Paradise of all things common else.
By thee adulterous Lust was driven from Men
Among the bestial herds to range ; by thee,
Founded in Reason, loyal, just, and pure,
Relations dear, and all the Charities
Of Father, Son, and Brother first were known.
.   .   .   .

Here Love his golden shafts employs, here lights
His constant lamp, and waves his purple wings."
—*Paradise Lost.*   Book iv.

THE DOCTRINE AND DISCIPLINE OF DIVORCE;

Restored to the good of both Sexes, from the Bondage of Canon Law, and other Mistakes, to the True Meaning of Scripture in the Law and Gospel compared.

Wherein also are set down the bad consequences of Abolishing, or Condemning as Sin, that which the Law of God allows, and Christ abolished not.

NOW THE SECOND TIME REVISED AND MUCH AUGMENTED.

IN TWO BOOKS.

TO THE PARLIAMENT OF ENGLAND, WITH THE ASSEMBLY.

MATT. xiii. 52: "Every scribe instructed in the kingdom of heaven is like the master of a house, which bringeth out of his treasury things new and old."

PROV. xviii. 13: "He that answereth a matter before he heareth it, it is folly and shame unto him."

To the Parliament of England, with the Assembly.

IF it were seriously asked, and it would be no untimely question, renowned Parliament, select Assembly, who of all teachers and masters that have ever taught, hath drawn the most disciples after him, both in religion and in manners, it might be not untruly answered, Custom. Though virtue be commended for the most persuasive in her theory, and conscience in the plain demonstration of the spirit finds most evincing; yet whether it be the secret of divine will or the original blindness we are born in, so it happens for the most part that Custom still is silently received for the best instructor. Except it be because her method is so glib and easy; in some manner like to that vision of Ezekiel rolling up her sudden book of implicit knowledge for him that will to take and swallow down at pleasure, which proving but of bad nourishment in the concoction as it was heedless in the devouring, puffs up unhealthily a certain big face of pretended learning, mistaken among credulous men for the wholesome habit of soundness and good constitution but is indeed no other than that swoln visage of counterfeit knowledge and literature which not only in private mars our education but also in public is the common climber into every chair where either religion is preached or law reported, filling each estate of life and profession with abject and servile principles, depressing the high and heaven-born spirit of man far beneath the condition wherein either God created him or sin hath sunk him. To pursue the allegory, Custom being but a mere face, as echo is a mere voice, rests not in her unaccomplishment until by secret inclination she accorporate herself with Error, who being a blind and serpentine body without a head, willingly accepts what he wants, and supplies what her incompleteness went seeking. Hence it is, that Error supports Custom, Custom countenances Error; and these two between them would persecute and chase away all Truth and solid Wisdom out of human life, were it not that God, rather than man, once in many ages calls together the prudent and religious counsels of men, deputed to repress the incroachments and to work off the inveterate blots and obscurities wrought upon our minds by the subtle insinuating of Error and Custom, who, with the numerous and vulgar train of their followers, make it their chief design to envy and cry down the industry of free reasoning, under the terms of humour and innovation; as if the womb of teeming Truth were to be closed up if she presume to bring forth aught that sorts not with their unchewed notions and suppositions. Against which notorious injury and abuse of man's free soul, to testify and oppose the utmost that study and true labour can attain, heretofore the incitement of men reputed grave hath led me among others; and now the duty and the right of an instructed Christian calls me, through the chance of good or evil report, to be the sole advocate of a discountenanced truth: a high enterprise, lords and commons, a high enterprise and a hard, and such as every seventh son of a seventh son does not venture on. Nor have I amidst the clamour of so much envy and impertinence whither to appeal, but to the concourse of so much piety and wisdom here assembled, bringing in my hands an ancient and most necessary, most charitable, and yet most injured statute of Moses: not repealed ever by him who only had the authority, but thrown aside with much inconsiderate neglect under the rubbish of canonical ignorance; as once the whole Law was by some such like conveyance in Josiah's time. And he who shall endeavour the amendment of any old neglected grievance in Church or State or in the daily course of life, if he be gifted with abilities of mind that may raise him to so high an undertaking, I grant he hath already much whereof not to repent him; yet let me aread him not to be the foreman of any misjudged opinion, unless his resolutions be firmly seated in a square and constant mind, not conscious to itself of any deserved blame and regardless of ungrounded suspicions. For this let him be sure, he shall be boarded presently by the ruder sort, but not by discreet and well-nurtured men, with a thousand idle descants and surmises. Who when they cannot confute the least joint or sinew of any passage in the book, yet God forbid that Truth should be Truth, because they have a boisterous conceit of some pretences in the writer. But were they not more busy and inquisitive than the apostle commends, they would hear him at least "rejoicing so the Truth be preached, whether of envy or other pretence whatsoever:" for Truth is as impossible to be soiled by any outward touch, as the sunbeam; though this ill hap wait on her nativity, that she never comes into the world but like a bastard, to the ignominy of him that brought her forth, till Time, the midwife rather than the mother of Truth, have washed and salted the infant, declared her legitimate, and churched the father of his young Minerva from the needless causes of his purgation. Yourselves can best witness this, worthy patriots, and better will, no doubt, hereafter: for who among ye of the foremost that have travailed in her behalf to the good of Church or State, hath not been often traduced to be the agent of his own by-ends, under pretext of Reformation? So much the more I shall not be unjust to hope, that however infamy or envy may work in other men to do her fretful will against this discourse, yet that the experience of your own uprightness misinterpreted will put ye in mind to give it free audience and generous construction. What though the brood of Belial, the draff of men, to whom no liberty is pleasing but unbridled and vagabond lust without pale or partition, will laugh broad perhaps to see so great a strength of Scripture mustering up in favour, as they suppose, of their debaucheries; they will know better when they shall hence learn, that honest liberty is the greatest foe to dishonest licence. And what though others, out of a waterish and queasy conscience, because ever crazy and never yet sound, will rail and fancy to themselves that injury and licence is the best of this book? Did not the distemper of their own stomachs affect them with a dizzy megrim, they would soon tie up their tongues and discern themselves, like that Assyrian blasphemer, all this while reproaching not man, but the Almighty, the Holy One of Israel, whom they do not deny to have belawgiven his own sacred people with this very allowance which they now call injury and licence, and dare cry shame on, and will do yet a while, till they get a little cordial sobriety to settle their qualming zeal. But this question concerns not us perhaps. Indeed man's disposition, though prone to search after vain curiosities, yet when points of difficulty are to be discussed appertaining to the removal of unreasonable wrong and burden from the perplexed life of our brother, it is incredible how cold, how dull, and far from all fellow-feeling we are, without the spur of self-concernment. Yet if the wisdom, the justice, the purity of God be to be cleared from foulest imputations, which are not yet avoided; if charity be not to be degraded and trodden down under a civil ordinance; if matrimony be not to be advanced like that exalted perdition written of to the Thessalonians, "above all that is called God," or goodness, nay, against them both; then I dare affirm, there will be found in the contents of this book that which may concern us all. You it concerns chiefly, Worthies in Parliament, on whom, as on our deliverers, all our grievances and cares, by the merit of your eminence and fortitude, are devolved. Me it concerns next, having with much labour and faithful diligence first found out, or at least with a fearless and communicative candour first published, to the manifest good of Christendom, that which, calling to witness everything mortal and immortal, I believe unfeignedly to be true. Let not other men think their conscience bound to search continually after truth, to pray for enlightening from above, to publish what they think they have so obtained, and debar me from conceiving myself tied by the same duties. Ye have now, doubtless, by the favour and appointment of God, ye have now in your hands a great and populous nation to reform. From what corruption, what blindness in religion, ye know well; in what a degenerate and fallen spirit from the apprehension of native liberty, and true manliness, I am sure ye find; with what unbounded licence rushing to whoredoms and adulteries, needs not long inquiry: insomuch that the fears, which men have of too strict a Discipline, perhaps exceed the hopes that can be in others of ever introducing it with any great success. What if I should tell ye now of dispensations and indulgences; to give a little the reins, to let them play and nibble with the bait awhile, a people as hard of heart as that Egyptian colony that went to Canaan. This is the common doctrine that adulterous and injurious divorces were not connived only, but with eye open allowed of old for hardness of heart. But that opinion, I trust, by then this following argument hath been well read, will be left for one of the mysteries of an indulgent Antichrist to farm out incest by and those his other tributary pollutions. What middle way can be taken then, may some interrupt, if we must neither turn to the right, nor to the left, and that the people hate to be reformed?

Mark then, judges and lawgivers, and ye whose office it is to be our teachers, for I will utter now a doctrine, if ever any other, though neglected or not understood, yet of great and powerful importance to the governing of mankind. He who wisely would restrain the reasonable soul of man within due bounds, must first himself know perfectly how far the territory and dominion extends of just and honest liberty. As little must he offer to bind that which God hath loosened, as to loosen that which He hath bound. The ignorance and mistake of this high point hath heaped up one huge half of all the misery that hath been since Adam.

In the Gospel we shall read a supercilious crew of masters, whose holiness, or rather whose evil eye, grieving that God should be so facile to man, was to set straiter limits to obedience than God hath set; to enslave the dignity of man, to put a garrison upon his neck of empty and over-dignified precepts: and we shall read our Saviour never more grieved and troubled than to meet with such a peevish madness among men against their own freedom. How can we expect him to be less offended with us, when much of the same folly shall be found yet remaining where it least ought, to the perishing of thousands? The greatest burden in the world is superstition, not only of ceremonies in the Church, but of imaginary and scarecrow sins at home. What greater weakening, what more subtle stratagem against our Christian warfare, when besides the gross body of real transgressions to encounter, we shall be terrified by a vain and shadowy menacing of faults that are not? When things indifferent shall be set to overfront us under the banners of sin, what wonder if we be routed, and by this art of our adversary, fall into the subjection of worst and deadliest offences? The superstition of the papist is, "Touch not, taste not," when God bids both; and ours is, "Part not, separate not," when God and Charity both permits and commands. "Let all your things be done with Charity," saith St. Paul; and his Master saith, "She is the fulfilling of the law." Yet now a civil, an indifferent, a sometime dissuaded law of marriage, must be forced upon us to fulfil, not only without Charity but against her. No place in heaven or earth, except hell, where Charity may not enter: yet Marriage, the ordinance of our solace and contentment, the remedy of our loneliness, will not admit now either of Charity or Mercy, to come in and mediate, or pacify the fierceness of this gentle ordinance, the unremedied loneliness of this remedy. Advise ye well, supreme Senate, if Charity be thus excluded and expulsed, how ye will defend the untainted honour of your own actions and proceedings.

He who marries, intends as little to conspire his own ruin, as he that swears allegiance: and as a whole people is in proportion to an ill government, so is one man to an ill marriage. If they, against any authority, covenant, or statute, may, by the sovereign edict of Charity, save not only their lives but honest liberties from unworthy bondage, as well may he against any private covenant which he never entered to his mischief, redeem himself from unsupportable disturbances to honest peace and just contentment. And much the rather, for that to resist the highest magistrate though tyrannizing, God never gave us express allowance; only he gave us reason, charity, nature, and good example to bear us out: but in this economical misfortune thus to demean ourselves, besides the warrant of those four great directors, which doth as justly belong hither, we have an express law of God, and such a law as whereof our Saviour with a solemn threat forbade the abrogating. For no effect of tyranny can sit more heavy on the Commonwealth, than this household unhappiness on the Family. And farewell all hope of true reformation in the State, while such an evil as this lies undiscerned or unregarded in the House: on the redress whereof depends not only the spiritful and orderly life of our grown men, but the willing and careful education of our children. Let this therefore be new examined, this tenure and freehold of mankind, this native and domestic charter given us by a greater lord than that Saxon king the Confessor. Let the statutes of God be turned over, be scanned anew and considered not altogether by the narrow intellectuals of quotationists and common places, but, as was the ancient right of Councils, by men of what liberal profession soever, of eminent spirit and breeding joined with a diffuse and various knowledge of divine and human things; able to balance and define good and evil, right and wrong, throughout every state of life; able to shew us the ways of the Lord straight and faithful as they are, not full of cranks and contradictions, and pitfalling dispenses, but with divine insight and benignity measured out to the proportion of each mind and spirit, each temper and disposition, created so different each from other and yet by the skill of wise conducting all to become uniform in virtue. To expedite these knots, were worthy a learned and memorable synod; while our enemies expect to see the expectation of the Church tired out with dependencies and independencies, how they will compound and in what calends. Doubt not, worthy Senators, to vindicate the sacred honour and judgment of Moses your predecessor from the shallow commenting of scholastics and canonists. Doubt not, after him to reach out your steady hands to the misinformed and wearied life of man; to restore this his lost heritage into the household state: wherewith be sure that peace and love, the best subsistance of a Christian family, will return home from whence they are now banished; places of prostitution will be less haunted, the neighbour's bed less attempted, the yoke of prudent and manly discipline will be generally submitted to; sober and well-ordered living will soon spring up in the commonwealth. Ye have an author great beyond exception, Moses; and one yet greater, he who hedged in from abolishing every smallest jot and tittle of precious equity contained in that law, with a more accurate and lasting Masoreth, than either the synagogue of Ezra or the Galilæan school at Tiberias hath left us. Whatever else you can enact will scarce concern a third part of the British name: but the benefit and good of this your magnanimous example will easily spread far beyond the banks of Tweed and the Norman isles. It would not be the first or second time, since our ancient druids, by whom this island was the cathedral of philosophy to France, left off their pagan rites, that England hath had this honour vouchsafed from heaven, to give out Reformation to the World. Who was it but our English Constantine that baptized the Roman empire? Who but the Northumbrian Willibrord, and Winfrith of Devon, with their followers, were the first apostles of Germany? Who but Alcuin and Wyclif our countrymen, opened the eyes of Europe, the one in arts, the other in religion? Let not England forget her precedence of teaching nations how to live.

Know, worthies, and exercise the privilege of your honoured country. A greater title I here bring ye than is either in the power or in the policy of Rome to give her monarchs; this glorious act will style ye the defenders of Charity. Nor is this yet the highest inscription that will adorn so religious and so holy a defence as this; behold here the pure and sacred Law of God, and His yet purer and more sacred name, offering themselves to you, first of all, Christian Reformers, to be acquitted from the long-suffered ungodly attribute of patronizing adultery. Defer not to wipe off instantly these imputative blurs and stains cast by rude fancies upon the throne and beauty itself of inviolable holiness: lest some other people more devout and wise than we bereave us this offered immortal glory, our wonted prerogative, of being the first asserters in every great vindication. For me, as far as my part leads me, I have already my greatest gain, assurance and inward satisfaction to have done in this nothing unworthy of an honest life and studies well employed. With what event, among the wise and right understanding handful of men, I am secure. But how among the drove of custom and prejudice this will be relished, by such whose capacity since their youth, run ahead into the easy creek of a system or a medulla, sails there at will under the blown physiognomy of their unlaboured rudiments; for them, what their taste will be I have also surety sufficient, from the entire league that hath ever been between formal ignorance and grave obstinacy. Yet when I remember the little that our Saviour could prevail about this doctrine of Charity against the crabbed textuists of his time, I make no wonder, but rest confident, that whoso prefers either matrimony or other ordinance before the good of man and the plain exigence of Charity, let him profess papist, or protestant, or what he will, he is no better than a pharisee, and understands not the Gospel. Whom as a misinterpreter of Christ I openly protest against, and provoke him to the trial of this Truth before all the world. And let him bethink him withal how he will sodder up the shifting flaws of his ungirt Permissions, his venial and unvenial Dispenses, wherewith the Law of God, pardoning and unpardoning, hath been shamefully branded, for want of heed in glossing, to have eluded and baffled out all faith and chastity from the marriage-bed of that holy seed with politic and judicial adulteries. I seek not to seduce the simple and illiterate. My errand is to find out the choicest and the learnedest, who have this high gift of wisdom,— to answer solidly or to be convinced. I crave it from the piety, the learning, and the prudence which is housed in this place. It might perhaps more fitly have been written in another tongue: and I had done so, but that the esteem I have of my country's judgment, and the love I bear to my native language to serve it first with what I endeavour, make me speak it thus ere I assay the verdict of outlandish readers. And perhaps also here I might have ended nameless, but that the address of these lines chiefly to the Parliament of England might have seemed ingrateful not to acknowledge by whose religious care, unwearied watchfulness, courageous and heroic resolutions, I enjoy the peace and studious leisure to remain, the Honourer and Attendant of their noble Worth and Virtues,   JOHN MILTON.

THE DOCTRINE AND DISCIPLINE OF DIVORCE.

BOOK I.

THE PREFACE.

That Man is the Occasion of his own Miseries in most of those Evils which he imputes to God's inflicting. The Absurdity of our Canonists in their Decrees about Divorce. The Christian Imperial Laws framed with more Equity. The opinion of Hugo Grotius and Paulus Fagius: And the Purpose in General of this Discourse.

MANY men, whether it be their fate or fond opinion, easily persuade themselves, if God would but be pleased a while to withdraw his just punishments from us, and to restrain what power either the devil or any earthly enemy hath to work us wo, that then man's nature would find immediate rest and releasement from all evils. But verily they who think so, if they be such as have a mind large enough to take into their thoughts a general survey of human things, would soon prove themselves in that opinion far deceived. For though it were granted us by divine indulgence to be exempt from all that can be harmful to us from without, yet the perverseness of our folly is so bent, that we should never cease hammering out of our own hearts, as it were out of a flint, the seeds and sparkles of new misery to ourselves, till all were in a blaze again. And no marvel if out of our own hearts, for they are evil; but even out of those things which God means us, either for a principal good, or a pure contentment, we are still hatching and contriving upon ourselves matter of continual sorrow and perplexity. What greater good to man than that revealed rule, whereby God vouchsafes to shew us how he would be worshipped? And yet that not rightly understood became the cause that once a famous man in Israel could not but oblige his conscience to be the sacrificer, or if not, the gaoler of his innocent and only daughter; and was the cause ofttimes that armies of valiant men have given up their throats to a heathenish enemy on the sabbath day, fondly thinking their defensive resistance to be as then a work unlawful. What thing more instituted to the solace and delight of man than marriage? And yet the misinterpreting of some scripture, directed mainly against the abusers of the law for divorce given by Moses, hath changed the blessing of matrimony not seldom into a familiar and coinhabiting mischief; at least into a drooping and disconsolate household captivity, without refuge or redemption. So ungoverned and so wild a race doth superstition run us, from one extreme of abused liberty into the other of unmerciful restraint. For although God in the first ordaining of marriage taught us to what end he did it, in words expressly implying the apt and cheerful conversation of man with woman, to comfort and refresh him against the evil of solitary life, not mentioning the purpose of generation till afterwards, as being but a secondary end in dignity, though not in necessity: yet now, if any two be but once handed in the church, and have tasted in any sort the nuptial bed, let them find themselves never so mistaken in their dispositions through any error, concealment, or misadventure, that through their different tempers, thoughts, and constitutions, they can neither be to one another a remedy against loneliness, nor live in any union or contentment all their days; yet they shall, so they be but found suitably weaponed to the least possibility of sensual enjoyment, be made, spite of antipathy, to fadge together, and combine as they may to their unspeakable wearisomeness and despair of all sociable delight in the ordinance which God established to that very end. What a calamity is this? and, as the wise man, if he were alive, would sigh out in his own phrase, what a "sore evil is this under the sun!" All which we can refer justly to no other author than the Canon Law and her adherents, not consulting with Charity, the interpreter and guide of our Faith, but resting in the mere element of the text; doubtless by the policy of the devil to make that gracious ordinance become unsupportable, that what with men not daring to venture upon wedlock, and what with men wearied out of it, all inordinate licence might abound. It was for many ages that marriage lay in disgrace with most of the ancient doctors, as a work of the flesh, almost a defilement, wholly denied to priests, and the second time dissuaded to all, as he that reads Tertullian or Jerome may see at large. Afterwards it was thought so sacramental, that no adultery or desertion could dissolve it. And this is the sense of our Canon Courts in England to this day, but in no other reformed church else. Yet there remains in them also a burden on it as heavy as the other two were disgraceful or superstitious, and of as much iniquity, crossing a law not only written by Moses, but charactered in us by nature, of more antiquity and deeper ground than marriage itself; which law is to force nothing against the faultless proprieties of nature. Yet that this may be colourably done, our Saviour's words touching divorce are as it were congealed into a stony rigour, inconsistent both with his doctrine and his office; and that which he preached only to the conscience as by canonical tyranny snatched into the compulsive censure of a judicial court, where laws are imposed even against the venerable and secret power of nature's impression, to love, whatever cause be found to loathe : which is a heinous barbarism both against the honour of marriage, the dignity of man and his soul, the goodness of Christianity, and all the human respects of civility. Notwithstanding that some the wisest and gravest among the Christian Emperors, who had about them, to consult with, those of the Fathers then living who for their learning and holiness of life are still with us in great renown, have made their statutes and edicts concerning this debate far more easy and relenting, in many necessary cases wherein the canon is inflexible. And Hugo Grotius, a man of these times one of the best learned, seems not obscurely to adhere in his persuasion to the equity of those imperial decrees, in his notes upon the Evangelists; much allaying the outward roughness of the text, which hath for the most part been too immoderately expounded, and excites the diligence of others to inquire further into this question, as containing many points that have not yet been explained. Which ever likely to remain intricate and hopeless upon the suppositions commonly stuck to, the authority of Paulus Fagius, one so learned and so eminent in England once, if it might persuade, would straight acquaint us with a solution of these differences no less prudent than compendious. He, in his comment on the Pentateuch, doubted not to maintain that divorces might be as lawfully permitted by the magistrate to Christians, as they were to the Jews. But because he is but brief, and these things of great consequence not to be kept obscure, I shall conceive it nothing above my duty, either for the difficulty or the censure that may pass thereon, to communicate such thoughts as I also have had, and do offer them now in this general labour of Reformation to the candid view both of Church and Magistrate: especially because I see it the hope of good men, that those irregular and unspiritual courts have spun their utmost date in this land, and some better course must now be constituted.

This therefore shall be the task and period of this discourse: to prove, first, that other reasons of divorce besides adultery were by the law of Moses, and are yet, to be allowed by the Christian magistrate as a piece of justice, and that the words of Christ are not hereby contraried. Next, that to prohibit absolutely any divorce whatsoever, except those which Moses excepted, is against the reason of law, as in due place I shall shew out of Fagius, with many additions. He therefore who by adventuring, shall be so happy as with success to light the way of such an expedient liberty and truth as this, shall restore the much-wronged and over-sorrowed state of matrimony, not only to those merciful and life-giving remedies of Moses, but, as much as may be, to that serene and blissful condition it was in at the beginning, and shall deserve of all apprehensive men (considering the troubles and distempers, which, for want of this in sight, have been so oft in kingdoms, in states, and families), shall deserve to be reckoned among the public benefactors of civil and human life, above the inventors of wine and oil; for this is a far dearer, far nobler, and more desirable cherishing to man's life, unworthily exposed to sadness and mistake, which he shall vindicate. Not that licence, and levity, and unconsented breach of faith, should herein be countenanced; but that some conscionable and tender pity might be had of those who have unwarily, in a thing they never practised before, made themselves the bondmen of a luckless and helpless matrimony. In which argument, he whose courage can serve him to give the first onset, must look for two several oppositions. The one from those who, having sworn themselves to long custom and the letter of the text, will not out of the road. The other from those whose gross and vulgar apprehensions conceit but low of matrimonial purposes, and in the work of male and female think they have all. Nevertheless, it shall be here sought by due ways to be made appear, that those words of God in the institution, promising a meet help against loneliness, and those words of Christ, that "his yoke is easy, and his burden light," were not spoken in vain: for if the knot of marriage may in no case be dissolved but for adultery, all the burdens and services of the law are not so intolerable. This only is desired of them who are minded to judge hardly of thus maintaining, that they would be still and hear all out, nor think it equal to answer deliberate reason with sudden heat and noise; remembering this, that many truths now of reverend esteem and credit had their birth and beginning once from singular and private thoughts, while the most of men were otherwise possessed, and had the fate at first to be generally exploded and exclaimed on by many violent opposers. Yet I may err perhaps in soothing myself that this present truth revived will deserve on all hands to be not sinisterly received, in that it undertakes the cure of an inveterate disease crept into the best part of human society, and to do this with no smarting corrosive, but a smooth and pleasing lesson, which received both the virtue to soften and dispel rooted and knotty sorrows, and without enchantment, if that be feared, or spell used, hath regard at once both to serious pity and upright honesty; that tends to the redeeming and restoring of none but such as are the object of compassion, having in an ill hour hampered themselves, to the utter dispatch of all their most beloved comforts and repose for this life's term. But if we shall obstinately dislike this new overture of unexpected ease and recovery, what remains but to deplore the frowardness of our hopeless condition, which neither can endure the estate we are in, nor admit of remedy either sharp or sweet? Sharp we ourselves distaste; and sweet, under whose hands we are, is scrupled and suspected as too luscious. In such a posture Christ found the Jews, who were neither won with the austerity of John the Baptist, and thought it too much licence to follow freely the charming pipe of him who sounded and proclaimed liberty and relief to all distresses. Yet Truth in some age or other will find her witness, and shall be justified at last by her own children.

CHAPTER I.

The Position proved by the Law of Moses. That Law expounded and asserted to a moral and charitable Use, first by Paulus Fagius, next with other Additions.

To remove therefore, if it be possible, this great and sad oppression which, through the strictness of a literal interpreting, hath invaded and disturbed the dearest and most peaceable estate of household society, to the overburdening if not the overwhelming of many Christians better worth than to be so deserted of the Church's considerate care, this position shall be laid down, first proving, then answering what may be objected either from Scripture or light of Reason.

"That indisposition, unfitness, or contrariety of mind, arising from a cause in nature unchangeable, hindering, and ever likely to hinder, the main benefits of conjugal society, which are solace and peace; is a greater reason of divorce than natural frigidity, especially if there be no children and that there be mutual consent."

This I gather from the law in Deut. xxiv. 1: "When a man hath taken a wife and married her, and it come to pass that she find no favour in his eyes because he hath found some uncleanness in her, let him write her a bill of divorcement, and give it in her hand, and send her out of his house," &c. This law, if the words of Christ may be admitted into our belief, shall never, while the world stands, for him be abrogated. First, therefore, I here set down what learned Fagius hath observed on this law: "The law of God," saith he, "permitted divorce for the help of human weakness. For every one that of necessity separates, cannot live single. That Christ denied divorce to his own, hinders not; for what is that to the unregenerate, who hath not attained such perfection? Let not the remedy be despised which was given to weakness. And when Christ saith, who marries the divorced commits adultery, it is to be understood, if he had any plot in the divorce." The rest I reserve until it be disputed how the magistrate is to do herein. From hence we may plainly discern a twofold consideration in this law: first, the end of the lawgiver and the proper act of the law, to command or to allow something just and honest or indifferent. Secondly, his sufferance from some accidental result of evil by this allowance, which the law cannot remedy. For if this law have no other end or act but only the allowance of sin, though never to so good intention, that law is no law, but sin muffled in the robe of law or law disguised in the loose garment of sin. Both which are too foul hypotheses, to save the phenomenon of our Saviour's answer to the Pharisees about this matter. And I trust anon, by the help of an infallible guide, to perfect such Prytinic tables as shall mend the astronomy of our wide expositors.

The cause of divorce mentioned in the law is translated "some uncleanness," but in the Hebrew it sounds "nakedness of aught, or any real nakedness:" which by all the learned interpreters is referred to the mind as well as to the body. And what greater nakedness or unfitness of mind than that which hinders ever the solace and peaceful society of the married couple? And what hinders that more than the unfitness and defectiveness of an unconjugal mind? The cause, therefore, of divorce expressed in the position cannot but agree with that described in the best and equallest sense of Moses's law. Which, being a matter of pure Charity, is plainly moral, and more now in force than ever; therefore surely lawful. For if under the law such was God's gracious indulgence, as not to suffer the ordinance of his goodness and favour through any error to be seared and stigmatized upon his servants to their misery and thraldom; much less will he suffer it now under the covenant of grace, by abrogating his former grant of remedy and relief. But the first institution will be objected to have ordained marriage inseparable. To that a little patience, until this first part have amply discoursed the grave and pious reasons of this divorcive law; and then I doubt not but with one gentle stroking to wipe away ten thousands tears out of the life of man. Yet thus much I shall now insist on, that whatever the institution were, it could not be so enormous, nor so rebellious against both nature and reason, as to exalt itself above the end and person for whom it was instituted.

CHAPTER II.

The first Reason of the Law grounded on the prime Reason of Matrimony. That no Covenant whatsoever obliges against the main End both of itself, and of the parties covenanting.

FOR all sense and equity reclaims that any Law or Covenant, how solemn or strait soever, either between God and Man, or Man and Man, though of God's joining, should bind against a prime and principal scope of its own institution, and of both or either party covenanting. Neither can it be of force to engage a blameless creature, to his own perpetual sorrow mistaken for his expected solace, without suffering charity to step in and do a confessed good work of parting those whom nothing holds together but this God's joining falsely supposed, against the express end of his own ordinance. And what his chief end was of creating woman to be joined with man, his own instituting words declare, and are infallible to inform us what is marriage and what is no marriage; unless we can think them set there to no purpose: "It is not good," saith he, "that man should be alone. I will make him a help meet for him." From which words, so plain, less cannot be concluded, nor is by any learned interpreter, than that in God's intention a meet and happy conversation is the chiefest and the noblest end of marriage. For we find here no expression so necessarily implying carnal knowledge as this prevention of loneliness to the mind and spirit of man. To this, Fagius, Calvin, Pareus, Rivetus, as willingly and largely assent as can be wished. And indeed it is a greater blessing from God, more worthy so excellent a creature as man is, and a higher end to honour and sanctify the league of marriage, whenas the solace and satisfaction of the mind is regarded and provided for before the sensitive pleasing of the body. And with all generous persons married, thus it is, that where the mind and person pleases aptly there some unaccomplishment of the body's delight may be better borne with than when the mind hangs off in an unclosing disproportion, though the body be as it ought; for there all corporal delight will soon become unsavoury and contemptible. And the solitariness of man, which God had mainly and principally ordered to prevent by marriage, hath no remedy, but lies under a worse condition than the loneliest single life. For in single life the absence and remoteness of a helper might inure him to expect his own comforts out of himself, or to seek with hope; but here the continual sight of his deluded thoughts, without cure, must needs be to him, if especially his complexion incline him to melancholy, a daily trouble and pain of loss in some degree like that which reprobates feel. Lest, therefore, so noble a creature as man should be shut up incurably under a worse evil, by an easy mistake in that ordinance which God gave him to remedy a less evil, reaping to himself sorrow while he went to rid away solitariness, it cannot avoid to be concluded, that if the woman be naturally so of disposition as will not help to remove but help to increase that same Godforbidden loneliness, which in time draws on with it a general discomfort and dejection of mind not beseeming either Christian profession or moral conversation, unprofitable and dangerous to the commonwealth when the household estate, out of which must flourish forth the vigour and spirit of all public enterprises, is so ill-contented and procured at home and cannot be supported; such a marriage can be no marriage, whereto the most honest end is wanting. And the aggrieved person shall do more manly to be extraordinary and singular in claiming the due right whereof he is frustrated, than to piece up his lost contentment by visiting the stews, or stepping to his neighbour's bed, which is the common shift in this misfortune; or else by suffering his useful life to waste away and be lost under a secret affliction of an unconscionable size to human strength. Against all which evils the mercy of this Mosaic law was graciously exhibited.

CHAPTER III.

The Ignorance and Iniquity of Canon-law, providing for the Right of the Body in Marriage, but nothing for the Wrongs and Grievances of the Mind. An Objection, that the Mind should be better looked to before contract, answered.

How vain, therefore, is it, and how preposterous in the Canon Law, to have made such careful provision against the impediment of carnal performance, and to have had no care about the unconversing inability of mind so defective to the purest and most sacred end of matrimony; and that the vessel of voluptuous enjoyment must be made good to him that has taken it upon trust, without any caution, whenas the mind, from whence must flow the acts of peace and love, a far more precious mixture than the quintessence of an excrement, though it be found never so deficient and unable to perform the best duty of marriage in a cheerful and agreeable conversation, shall be thought good enough, however flat and melancholious it be, and must serve, though to the eternal disturbance and languishing of him that complains! Yet Wisdom and Charity, weighing God's own institution, would think that the pining of a sad spirit wedded to loneliness should deserve to be freed, as well as the impatience of a sensual desire so providently relieved. It is read to us in the Liturgy, that "we must not marry to satisfy the fleshly appetite, like brute beasts, that have no understanding;" but the Canon so runs as if it dreamed of no other matter than such an appetite to be satisfied; for if it happen that nature hath stopped or extinguished the veins of sensuality, that marriage is annulled. But though all the faculties of the understanding and conversing part, after trial, appear to be so ill and so aversely met through nature's unalterable working as that neither peace nor any sociable contentment can follow, it is as nothing; the contract shall stand as firm as ever, betide what will. What is this but secretly to instruct us, that however many grave reasons are pretended to the married life, yet that nothing indeed is thought worth regard therein but the prescribed satisfaction of an irrational heat? Which cannot be but ignominious to the state of marriage, dishonourable to the undervalued soul of man, and even to Christian doctrine itself: while it seems more moved at the disappointing of an impetuous nerve, than at the ingenuous grievance of a mind unreasonably yoked; and to place more of marriage in the channel of concupiscence, than in the pure influence of peace and love, whereof the soul's lawful contentment is the only fountain.

But some are ready to object, that the disposition ought seriously to be considered before. But let them know again, that for all the wariness can be used, it may yet befall a discreet man to be mistaken in his choice: and we have plenty of examples. The soberest and best governed men are least practised in these affairs; and who knows not that the bashful muteness of a virgin may ofttimes hide all the unliveliness and natural sloth which is really unfit for conversation? Nor is there that freedom of access granted or presumed as may suffice to a perfect discerning, till too late. And where any indisposition is suspected, what more usual than the persuasion of friends, that acquaintance, as it increases, will amend all? And lastly, it is not strange though many who have spent their youth chastely are in some things not so quick-sighted, while they haste too eagerly to light the nuptial torch; nor is it, therefore, that for a modest error a man should forfeit so great a happiness, and no charitable means to release him, since they who have lived most loosely, by reason of their bold accustoming, prove most successful in their matches, because their wild affections unsettling at will have been as so many divorces to teach them experience. Whenas the sober man honouring the appearance of modesty, and hoping well of every social virtue under that veil, may easily chance to meet, if not with a body impenetrable yet often with a mind to all other due conversation inaccessible, and to all the more estimable and superior purposes of matrimony useless and almost lifeless. And what a solace, what a fit help such a consort would be through the whole life of a man, is less pain to conjecture than to have experience.

CHAPTER IV.

The second Reason of this Law, because without it Marriage, as it happens oft, is not a Remedy of that which it promises, as any rational Creature would expect. That Marriage, if we pattern from the Beginning, as our Saviour bids, was not properly the Remedy of Lust, but the fulfilling of conjugal Love and Helpfulness.

AND that we may further see what a violent cruel thing it is to force the continuing of those together whom God and nature in the gentlest end of marriage never joined; divers evils and extremities, that follow upon such a compulsion, shall here be set in view. Of evils, the first and greatest is, that hereby a most absurd and rash imputation is fixed upon God and His holy Laws, of conniving and dispensing with open and common adultery among his chosen people; a thing which the rankest politician would think it shame and disworship that his laws should countenance: how and in what manner that comes to pass I shall reserve till the course of method brings on the unfolding of many scriptures. Next, the Law and Gospel are hereby made liable to more than one contradiction, which I refer also thither. Lastly, the supreme dictate of Charity is hereby many ways neglected and violated; which I shall forthwith address to prove. First, we know St. Paul saith, "It is better to marry than to burn." Marriage, therefore, was given as a remedy of that trouble: but what might this burning mean? Certainly not the mere motion of carnal, not the mere goad of a sensitive desire: God does not principally take care for such cattle. What is it then but that desire which God put into Adam in Paradise, before he knew the sin of incontinence; that desire which God saw it was not good that man should be left alone to burn in; the desire and longing to put off an unkindly solitariness by uniting another body, but not without a fit soul to his, in the cheerful society of wedlock? Which if it were so needful before the fall, when man was much more perfect in himself, how much more is it needful now against all the sorrows and casualties of this life, to have an intimate and speaking help, a ready and reviving associate in marriage? Whereof who misses, by chancing on a mute and spiritless mate, remains more alone than before, and in a burning less to be contained than that which is fleshly, and more to be considered; as being more deeply rooted even in the faultless innocence of nature. As for that other burning, which is but as it were the venom of a lusty and over-abounding concoction, strict life and labour, with the abatement of a full diet, may keep that low and obedient enough; but this pure and more inbred desire of joining to itself in conjugal fellowship a fit conversing soul (which desire is properly called love) "is stronger than death," as the spouse of Christ thought; "many waters cannot quench it, neither can the floods drown it." This is that rational burning that marriage is to remedy, not to be allayed with fasting, nor with any penance to be subdued: which how can he assuage who by mishap hath met the most unmeet and unsuitable mind? Who hath the power to struggle with an intelligible flame, not in Paradise to be resisted, become now more ardent by being failed of what in reason it looked for; and even then most unquenched, when the importunity of a provender burning is well enough appeased and yet the soul hath obtained nothing of what it justly desires. Certainly such a one forbidden to divorce, is in effect forbidden to marry, and compelled to greater difficulties than in a single life; for if there be not a more humane burning, which marriage must satisfy or else may be dissolved, than that of copulation, marriage cannot be honourable for the meet reducing and terminating lust between two; seeing many beasts in voluntary and chosen couples live together as unadulterously, and are as truly married in that respect. But all ingenuous men will see that the dignity and blessing of marriage is placed rather in the mutual enjoyment of that which the wanting Soul needfully seeks, than of that which the plenteous Body would joyfully give away. Hence it is that Plato, in his festival discourse, brings in Socrates relating what he feigned to have learned from the prophetess Diotima, how Love was the son of Penury, begot of Plenty in the garden of Jupiter. Which divinely sorts with that which in effect Moses tell us, that Love was the son of Loneliness, begot in Paradise by that sociable and helpful aptitude which God implanted between man and woman toward each other. The same, also, is that burning mentioned by St. Paul, whereof marriage ought to be the remedy: the flesh hath other mutual and easy curbs which are in the power of any temperate man. When, therefore, this original and sinless penury, or loneliness of the soul, cannot lay itself down by the side of such a meet and acceptable union as God ordained in marriage, at least in some proportion, it cannot conceive and bring forth Love, but remains utterly unmarried under a former wedlock, and still burns in the proper meaning of St. Paul. Then enters Hate; not that hate that sins, but that which only is natural dissatisfaction, and the turning aside from a mistaken object. If that mistake have done injury, it fails not to dismiss with recompense; for to retain still, and not be able to love, is to heap up more injury. Hence this wise and pious law of dismission now defended took beginning: he, therefore, who lacking of his due in the most native and humane end of marriage, thinks it better to part than to live sadly and injuriously to that cheerful covenant (for not to be beloved, and yet retained, is the greatest injury to a gentle spirit), he, I say, who therefore seeks to part, is one who highly honours the married life and would not stain it. And the reasons which now move him to divorce are equal to the best of those that could first warrant him to marry; for, as was plainly shewn, both the hate which now diverts him, and the loneliness which leads him still powerfully to seek a fit help, hath not the least grain of a sin in it, if he be worthy to understand himself.

CHAPTER V.

The third Reason of this Law, because without it, he who has happened where he finds nothing but remediless Offences and Discontents, is in more and greater Temptations than ever before.

THIRDLY, Yet it is next to be feared, if he must be still bound without reason by a deaf rigour, that when he perceives the just expectance of his mind defeated, he will begin even against law to cast about where he may find his satisfaction more complete, unless he be a thing heroically virtuous; and that are not the common lump of men, for whom chiefly the laws ought to be made, though not to their sins, yet to their unsinning weaknesses, it being above their strength to endure the lonely estate which while they shunned they are fallen into. And yet there follows upon this a worse temptation. For if he be such as hath spent his youth unblamedly, and laid up his chiefest earthly comforts in the enjoyments of a contented marriage, nor did neglect that furtherance which was to be obtained therein by constant prayers; when he shall find himself bound fast to an uncomplying discord of nature, or, as it oft happens, to an image of earth and phlegm, with whom he looked to be the copartner of a sweet and glad-

O

some society, and sees withal that his bondage is now inevitable; though he be almost the strongest Christian, he will be ready to despair in virtue, and mutiny against Divine Providence. And this doubtless is the reason of those lapses, and that melancholy despair, which we see in many wedded persons—though they understand it not, or pretend other causes, because they know no remedy—and is of extreme danger. Therefore when human frailty surcharged is at such a loss, Charity ought to venture much and use bold physic, lest an overtossed faith endanger to shipwreck.

CHAPTER VI.

The fourth Reason of this Law, that God regards Love and Peace in the Family more than a compulsive Performance of Marriage, which is more broke by grievous Continuance than by a needful Divorce.

FOURTHLY, Marriage is a covenant, the very being whereof consists not in a forced co-habitation, and counterfeit performance of duties, but in unfeigned love and peace. And of matrimonial love, no doubt but that was chiefly meant which by the ancient sages was thus parabled; that Love, if he be not twin born, yet hath a brother wondrous like him, called Anteros; whom while he seeks all about, his chance is to meet with many false and feigning desires that wander singly up and down in his likeness: by them in their borrowed garb, Love, though not wholly blind, as poets wrong him, yet having but one eye, as being born an archer aiming, and that eye not the quickest in this dark region here below which is not Love's proper sphere, partly out of the simplicity and credulity which is native to him, often deceived, embraces and consorts him with these obvious and suborned striplings, as if they were his mother's own sons; for so he thinks them, while they subtilly keep themselves most on his blind side. But after a while, as his manner is, when soaring up into the high tower of his Apogæum, above the shadow of the earth, he darts out the direct rays of his then most piercing eyesight upon the impostures and trim disguises that were used with him, and discerns that this is not his genuine brother, as he imagined; he has no longer the power to hold fellowship with such a personated mate: for straight his arrows lose their golden heads, and shed their purple feathers, his silken braids untwine, and slip their knots, and that original and fiery virtue given him by Fate all on a sudden goes out, and leaves him undeified and despoiled of all his force: till finding Anteros at last, he kindles and repairs the almost-faded ammunition of his deity by the reflection of a coequal and homogeneal fire. Thus mine author sung it to me: and by the leave of those who would be counted the only grave ones, this is no mere amatorious novel (though to be wise and skilful in these matters, men heretofore of greatest name in virtue have esteemed it one of the highest arcs that human contemplation circling upwards can make from the globy sea whereon she stands); but this is a deep and serious verity, shewing us that love in marriage cannot live nor subsist unless it be mutual; and where love cannot be, there can be left of wedlock nothing but the empty husk of an outside matrimony, as undelightful and unpleasing to God as any other kind of hypocrisy. So far is his command from tying men to the observance of duties which there is no help for but they must be dissembled. If Solomon's advice be not over-frolic, "Live joyfully," saith he, "with the wife whom thou lovest, all thy days, for that is thy portion:" how then, where we find it impossible to rejoice or to love, can we obey this precept? How miserably do we defraud ourselves of that comfortable portion which God gives us, by striving vainly to glue an error together which God and nature will not join, adding but more vexation and violence to that blissful society by our importunate superstition, that will not hearken to St. Paul, 1 Cor. vii., who, speaking of marriage and divorce, determines plain enough in general, that God therein "hath called us to peace, and not to bondage!" Yea, God himself commands in His Law more than once, and by his prophet Malachi, as Calvin and the best translations read, that "he who hates, let him divorce," that is, he who cannot love. Hence it is that the rabbins, and Maimonides, famous among the rest, in a book of his set forth by Buxtorfius, tells us, that "divorce was permitted by Moses to preserve peace in marriage, and quiet in the family." Surely the Jews had their saving peace about them as well as we; yet care was taken that this wholesome provision for household peace should also be allowed them. And must this be denied to Christians? O perverseness! that the Law should be made more provident of peace-making than the Gospel! that the Gospel should be put to beg a most necessary help of mercy from the Law, but must not have it! and that to grind in the mill of an undelighted and servile copulation must be the only forced work of a Christian marriage, ofttimes with such a yokefellow from whom both love and peace, both nature and religion mourns to be separated. I cannot therefore be so diffident as not securely to conclude that he who can receive nothing of the most important helps in marriage, being thereby disenabled to return that duty which is his with a clear and hearty countenance, and thus continues to grieve whom he would not and is no less grieved, that man ought even for love's sake and peace to move divorce, upon good and liberal conditions to the divorced. And it is a less breach of wedlock to part, with wise and quiet consent, betimes, than still to soil and profane that mystery of joy and union with a polluting sadness and perpetual distemper. For it is not the outward continuing of marriage that keeps whole that covenant, but whatsoever does most according to peace and love, whether in marriage or in divorce, he it is that breaks marriage least; it being so often written, that "Love only is the fulfilling of every commandment."

CHAPTER VII.

The fifth Reason, that nothing more hinders and disturbs the whole Life of a Christian, than a Matrimony found to be incurably unfit, and doth the same in effect that an idolatrous Match.

FIFTHLY, As those priests of old were not to be long in sorrow, or if they were, they could not rightly execute their function; so every true Christian in a higher order of priesthood, is a person dedicate to joy and peace, offering himself a lively sacrifice of praise and thanksgiving, and there is no Christian duty that is not to be seasoned and set off with cheerishness. Which in a thousand outward and intermitting crosses may yet be done well, as in this vale of tears: but in such a bosom affliction as this, crushing the very foundation of his inmost nature, when he shall be forced to love against a possibility, and to use a dissimulation against his soul in the perpetual and ceaseless duties of a husband; doubtless his whole duty of serving God must needs be blurred and tainted with a sad unpreparedness and dejection of spirit, wherein God has no delight. Who sees not therefore how much more Christianity it would be to break by divorce that which is more broken by undue and forcible keeping, rather than "to cover the altar of the Lord with continual tears, so that he regardeth not the offering any more," rather than that the whole worship of a Christian man's life should languish and fade away beneath the weight of an immeasurable grief and discouragement? And because some think the children of a second matrimony succeeding a divorce would not be a holy seed, it hindered not the Jews from being so; and why should we not think them more holy than the offspring of a former ill-twisted wedlock, begotten only out of a bestial necessity, without any true love or contentment or joy to their parents? So that in some sense we may call them the "children of wrath" and anguish, which will as little conduce to their sanctifying as if they had been bastards. For nothing more than disturbance of mind suspends us from approaching to God; such a disturbance especially, as both assaults our faith and trust in God's providence, and ends, if there be not a miracle of virtue on either side, not only in bitterness and wrath, the canker of devotion, but in a desperate and vicious carelessness, when he sees himself, without fault of his, trained by a deceitful bait into a snare of misery, betrayed by an alluring ordinance, and then made the thrall of heaviness and discomfort by an undivorcing law of God, as he erroneously thinks, but of man's iniquity, as the truth is. For that God prefers the free and cheerful worship of a Christian, before the grievance and exacted observance of an unhappy marriage, besides that the general maxims of religion assure us, will be more manifest by drawing a parallel argument from the ground of divorcing an idolatress, which was, lest he should alienate his heart from the true worship of God. And, what difference is there, whether she pervert him to superstition by her enticing sorcery, or disenable him in the whole service of God through the disturbance of her unhelpful and unfit society, and so drive him at last, through murmuring and despair, to thoughts of atheism? Neither doth it lessen the cause of separating, in that the one willingly allures him from the faith, the other perhaps unwillingly drives him; for in the account of God it comes all to one, that the wife loses him a servant. And therefore by all the united force of the Decalogue she ought to be disbanded, unless we must set marriage above God and Charity, which is the doctrine of devils, no less than forbidding to marry.

CHAPTER VIII.

That an idolatrous Heretic ought to be divorced, after a convenient Space given to hope of Conversion. That Place of 1 Cor. vii. *restored from a twofold erroneous Exposition; and that the common Expositors flatly contradict the moral Law.*

AND here by the way, to illustrate the whole question of divorce ere this treatise end, I shall not be loath to spend a few lines in hope to give a full resolve of that which is yet so much controverted: whether an idolatrous heretic ought to be divorced. To the resolving whereof we must first know, that the Jews were commanded to divorce an unbelieving Gentile for two causes: First, because all other nations, especially the Canaanites, were to them unclean. Secondly, to avoid seducement. That other nations were to the Jews impure, even to the separating of marriage, will appear out of Exod. xxxiv. 16, Deut. vii. 3, 6, compared with Ezra ix. 2, also chap. x. 10, 11, Neh. xiii. 30. This was the ground of that doubt raised among the Corinthians by some of the circumcision, whether an unbeliever were not still to be counted an unclean thing, so as that they ought to divorce from such a person. This doubt of theirs St. Paul removes by an evangelical reason, having respect to that vision of St. Peter wherein, the distinction of clean and unclean being abolished, all living creatures were sanctified to a pure and Christian use, and mankind especially now invited by a general call to the covenant of grace. Therefore, saith St. Paul, "The unbelieving wife is sanctified by the husband;" that is, made pure and lawful to his use, so that he need not put her away for fear lest her unbelief should defile him; but that if he found her love still towards him he might rather hope to win her. The second reason of that divorce was to avoid seducement, as is proved by comparing those two places of the law to that which Ezra and Nehemiah did by divine warrant in compelling the Jews to forego their wives. And this reason is moral and perpetual in the rule of Christian faith, without evasion; therefore, saith the apostle, 2 Cor. vi., "Misyoke not together with infidels," which is interpreted of marriage in the first place. And although the former legal pollution be now done off, yet there is a spiritual contagion in idolatry as much to be shunned; and though seducement were not to be feared, yet where there is no hope of converting there always ought to be a certain religious aversion and abhorring which can no way sort with marriage: therefore saith St. Paul, "What fellowship hath righteousness with unrighteousness? What communion hath light with darkness? What concord hath Christ with Belial? What part hath he that believeth with an infidel?" And in the next verse but one he moralizes, and makes us liable to that command of Isaiah, "Wherefore come out from among them, and be ye separate, saith the Lord; touch not the unclean thing, and I will receive ye." And this command thus gospelized to us, hath the same force with that whereon Ezra grounded the pious necessity of divorcing. Neither had he other commission for what he did than such a general command in Deuteronomy as this; nay, not so direct, for he is bid there not to marry, but not bid to divorce; and yet we see with what a zeal and confidence he was the author of a general divorce between the faithful and the unfaithful seed. The Gospel is more plainly on his side, according to three of the evangelists, than the words of the Law. For where the case of divorce is handled with such severity, as was fittest to aggravate the fault of unbounded licence, yet still in the same chapter, when it comes into question afterwards whether any civil respect or natural relation, which is dearest, may be our plea to divide or hinder or but delay our duty to religion, we hear it determined that father, and mother, and wife also, is not only to be hated but forsaken, if we mean to inherit the great reward there promised. Nor will it suffice to be put off by saying we must forsake them only by not consenting or not complying with them, for that were to be done and roundly too though, being of the same faith, they should but seek out of a fleshly tenderness to weaken our Christian fortitude with worldly persuasions, or but to unsettle our constancy with timorous and softening suggestions; as we may read with what a vehemence Job, the patientest of men, rejected the desperate counsels of his wife; and Moses, the meekest, being thoroughly offended with the profane speeches of Zippora, sent her back to her father. But if they shall perpetually, at our elbow, seduce us from the true worship of God, or defile and daily scandalize our conscience by their hopeless continuance in misbelief; then even in the due progress of reason, and that ever equal proportion which justice proceeds by, it cannot be imagined that his cited place commands less than a total and final separation from such an adherent; at least that no force should be used to keep them together, while we remember that God commanded Abraham to send away his irreligious wife and her son for the offences which they gave in a pious family. And it may be guessed that David for the like cause disposed of Michal in such a sort as little differed from a dismission. Therefore, against reiterated scandals and seducements, which never cease, much more can no other remedy or retirement be found but absolute departure. For what kind of matrimony can that remain to be, what one duty between such can be performed as it should be from the heart, when their thoughts and spirits fly asunder as far as heaven from hell; especially if the time that hope should send forth her expected blossoms, be past in vain? It will easily be true, that a father or a brother may be hated zealously, and loved civilly or naturally; for those duties may be performed at distance, and do admit of any long absence. But how the peace and perpetual cohabitation of marriage can be kept, how that benevolent and intimate communion of body can be held, with one that must be hated with a most operative hatred, must be forsaken and yet continually dwelt with and accompanied, he who can distinguish, hath the gift of an affection very oddly divided and contrived; while others both just and wise, and Solomon among the rest, if they may not hate and forsake as Moses enjoins, and the Gospel imports, will find it impossible not to love otherwise than will sort with the love of God, whose jealousy brooks no corrival. And whether is more likely that Christ bidding to forsake wife for religion, meant it by divorce as Moses meant it, whose Law grounded on moral reason was both his office and his essence to maintain; or that he should bring a new morality into religion, not only new, but contrary to an unchangeable command, and dangerously derogating from our love and worship of God? As if when Moses had bid divorce absolutely, and Christ had said, hate and forsake, and his apostle had said, no communication with Christ and Belial; yet that Christ after all this could be understood to say, Divorce not; no, not for religion, seduce or seduce not. What mighty and invisible remora is this in matrimony, able to demur and to contemn all the divorcive engines in heaven or earth, both which may now pass away, if this be true; for more than many jots or tittles, a whole moral law is abolished. But if we dare believe it is not, then in the method of religion, and to save the honour and dignity of our faith, we are to retreat and gather up ourselves from the observance of an inferior and civil ordinance, to the strict maintaining of a general and religious command, which is written, "Thou shalt make no covenant with them," Deut. vii. 2, 3 : and that covenant which cannot be lawfully made, we have directions and examples lawfully to dissolve. Also 2 Chron. ii. 19, "Shouldest thou love them that hate the Lord?" No, doubtless ; for there is a certain scale of duties, there is a certain hierarchy of upper and lower commands, which for want of studying in right order, all the world is in confusion.

Upon these principles I answer, that a right believer ought to divorce an idolatrous heretic, unless upon better hopes : however, that it is in the believer's choice to divorce or not.

The former part will be manifest thus first, than an apostate idolater, whether husband or wife seducing, was to die by the decree of God, Deut. xiii. 6, 9; that marriage, therefore, God himself disjoins : for others born idolaters, the moral reason of their dangerous keeping, and the incommunicable antagony that is between Christ and Belial, will be sufficient to enforce the commandment of those two inspired reformers, Ezra and Nehemiah, to put an idolater away as well under the Gospel.

The latter part, that although there be no seducement feared, yet if there be no hope given, the divorce is lawful, will appear by this; that idolatrous marriage is still hateful to God, therefore still it may be divorced by the pattern of that warrant that Ezra had, and by the same everlasting reason : neither can any man give an account wherefore, if those whom God joins no man can separate, it should not follow, that whom he joins not, but hates to join, those men ought to separate. But saith the lawyer, "'That which ought not to have been done, once done, avails." I answer, "This is but a crotchet of the law, but that brought against it is plain scripture." As for what Christ spake concerning divorce, it is confessed by all knowing men, he meant only between them of the same faith. But what shall we say then to St. Paul, who seems to bid us not divorce an infidel willing to stay? We may safely say thus, that wrong collections have been hitherto made out of those words by modern divines. His drift, as was heard before, is plain; not to command our stay in marriage with an infidel, that had been a flat renouncing of the religious and moral law; but to inform the Corinthians that the body of an unbeliever was not defiling, if his desire to live in Christian wedlock shewed any likelihood that his heart was opening to the faith; and therefore advises to forbear departure so long till nothing have been neglected to set forward a conversion: this, I say, he advises, and that with certain cautions, not commands, if we can take up so much credit for him, as to get him believed upon his own word: for what is this else but his counsel in a thing indifferent, "To the rest speak I, not the Lord"? for though it be, true that the Lord never spake it, yet from St. Paul's mouth we should have took it as a command, had not himself forewarned us, and disclaimed; which notwithstanding if we shall still avouch to be a command, he palpably denying it, this is not to expound St. Paul, but to outface him. Neither doth it follow that the apostle may interpose his judgment in a case of Christian liberty, without the guilt of adding to God's word. How do we know marriage or single life to be of choice, by such like words as these, "I speak this by permission, not of commandment; I have no command of the Lord, yet I give my judgment"? Why shall not the like words have leave to signify a freedom in this our present question, though Beza deny? Neither is the Scripture hereby less inspired, because St. Paul confesses to have written therein what he had not of command; for we grant that the Spirit of God led him thus to express himself to Christian prudence, in a matter which God thought best to leave uncommanded. Beza, therefore, must be warily read, when he taxes St. Austin of blasphemy, for holding that St. Paul spake here as of a thing indifferent. But if it must be a command, I shall yet the more evince it to be a command that we should herein be left free; and that out of the Greek word used in the 12th verse, which instructs us plainly there must be a joint assent and good liking on both sides. He that will not deprave the text must thus render it : " If a brother have an unbelieving wife, and she join in consent to dwell with him " (which cannot utter less to us than a mutual agreement), let him not put her away from the mere surmise of Judaical uncleanness : and the reason follows, for the body of an infidel is not polluted, neither to benevolence, nor to procreation. Moreover, this note of mutual complacency forbids all offer of seducement, which to a person of zeal cannot be attempted without great offence : if, therefore, seducement be feared, this place hinders not divorce. Another caution was put in this supposed command, of not bringing the believer into " bondage " hereby, which doubtless might prove extreme, if Christian liberty, and to play with and to vex and wound with a thousand scandals conscience, were left to the humour of a pagan straying at pleasure, and burden above strength to bear. If, therefore, the conceived hope of gaining a soul come to nothing, then charity commands that the believer be not wearied out with endless waiting under many grievances sore to his spirit ; but that respect be had rather to the present suffering of a true Christian, than the uncertain winning of an obdured heretic. The counsel we have from St. Paul to hope, cannot countermand the moral and evangelic charge we have from God to fear seducement, to separate from the misbeliever, the unclean, the obdurate. The Apostle wisheth us to hope ; but does not send us a wool-gathering after vain hope ; he saith, " How knowest thou, O man, whether thou shalt save thy wife ?" that is, till he try all due means, and set some reasonable time to himself, after which he may give over washing an Ethiop, if he will hear the advice of the Gospel. " Cast not pearls before swine," saith Christ himself. " Let him be to thee as a heathen." " Shake the dust off thy feet." If this be not enough, " hate and forsake " what relation soever. And this also that follows must appertain to the precept, " Let every man wherein he is called, therein abide with God," v. 24, that is, so walking in his inferior calling of marriage, as not, by dangerous subjection to that ordinance, to hinder and disturb the higher calling of his Christianity. Last, and never too oft remembered, whether this be a command or an advice, we must look that it be so understood as not to contradict the least point of moral religion that God hath formerly commanded; otherwise what do we but set the Moral Law and the Gospel at civil war together? and who then shall be able to serve these two masters?

CHAPTER IX.

That Adultery is not the greatest Breach of Matrimony: that there may be other Violations as great.

Now, whether idolatry or adultery be the greatest violation of marriage, if any demand let him thus consider; that among Christian writers touching matrimony, there be three chief ends thereof agreed on: godly society; next, civil; and thirdly, that of the marriage bed. Of these the first in name to be the highest and most excellent, no baptized man can deny, nor that idolatry smites directly against this prime end; nor that such as the violated end is, such is the violation. But he who affirms adultery to be the highest breach, affirms the bed to be the highest of marriage, which is in truth a gross and boorish opinion, how common soever; as far from the countenance of Scripture, as from the light of all clean philosophy or civil nature. And out of question the cheerful help that may be in marriage toward sanctity of life, is the purest, and so the noblest end of that contract. But if the particular of each person be considered, then of those three ends which God appointed, that to him is greatest which is most necessary; and marriage is then most broken to him when he utterly wants the fruition of that which he most sought therein, whether it were religious, civil, or corporal society. Of which wants, to do him right by divorce only for the last and meanest is a perverse injury, and the pretended reason of it as frigid as frigidity itself, which the code and canon are only sensible of. Thus much of this controversy. I now return to the former argument. And having shewn that disproportion, contrariety, or numbness of mind may justly be divorced, by proving already the prohibition thereof opposes the express end of God's institution, suffers not marriage to satisfy that intellectual and innocent desire which God himself kindled in man to be the bond of wedlock, but only to remedy a sublunary and bestial burning, which frugal diet, without marriage, would easily chasten. Next, that it drives many to transgress the conjugal bed, while the soul wanders after that satisfaction which it had hope to find at home, but hath missed; or else it sits repining, even to atheism, finding itself hardly dealt with, but misdeeming the cause to be in God's law, which is in man's unrighteous ignorance. I have shewn also how it unties the inward knot of marriage, which is peace and love (if that can be untied which was never knit), while it aims to keep fast the outward formality: how it lets perish the Christian man, to compel impossibly the married man.

CHAPTER X.

The sixth Reason of this Law; that to prohibit Divorce sought for natural Causes, is against Nature.

THE sixth place declares this prohibition to be as respectless of human nature as it is of religion, and therefore is not of God. He teaches, that an unlawful marriage may be lawfully divorced; and that those who having thoroughly discerned each other's disposition, which oft-times cannot be till after matrimony, shall then find a powerful reluctance and recoil of nature on either side, blasting all the content of their mutual society, that such persons are not lawfully married. To use the Apostle's words, "Say I these things as a man; or saith not the law also the same? For it is written, Deut. xxii., 'Thou shalt not sow thy vineyard with different seeds, lest thou defile both. Thou shalt not plough with an ox and an ass together;'" and the like. I follow the pattern of St. Paul's reasoning: Doth God care for asses and oxen, how ill they yoke together? or is it not said altogether for our sakes? For our sakes no doubt this is written. Yea, the Apostle himself, in the forecited 2 Cor. vi. 14, alludes from that place of Deuteronomy to forbid misyoking marriage, as by the Greek word is evident. Though he instance but in one example of mismatching with an infidel, yet next to that, what can be a fouler incongruity, a greater violence to the reverend secret of nature, than to force a mixture of minds that cannot unite, and to sow the sorrow of man's nativity with seed of too incoherent and incombining dispositions? Which act being kindly and voluntary, as it ought, the apostle in the language he wrote called "eunoia," and the Latins "benevolence," intimating the original thereof to be in the understanding and the will. If not, surely there is nothing which might more properly be called a malevolence rather; and is the most injurious and unnatural tribute that can be extorted from a person endued with reason, to be made pay out the best substance of his body, and of his soul too, as some think, when either for just and powerful causes he cannot like, or from unequal causes finds not recompense. And that there is a hidden efficacy of love and hatred in man as well as in other kinds, not moral but natural, which though not always in the choice yet in the success of marriage will ever be most predominant. Besides daily experience, the author of Ecclesiasticus, whose wisdom hath set him next the Bible, acknowledges, xiii. 16, "A man," saith he, "will cleave to his like." But what might be the cause, whether each one's allotted genius or proper star, or whether the supernal influence of schemes and angular aspects, or this elemental crasis here below; whether all these jointly or singly meeting, friendly or unfriendly in either party, I dare not, with the men I am like to clash, appear so much a philosopher as to conjecture. The ancient proverb in Homer, less abstruse, entitles this work of leading each like person to his like, peculiarly to God himself. Which is plain enough also by His naming of a meet or like help in the first espousal instituted; and that every woman is meet for every man, none so absurd as to affirm. Seeing then there is a twofold seminary, or stock in nature, from whence are derived the issues of love and hatred, distinctly flowing through the whole mass of created things, and that God's doing ever is to bring the due likenesses and harmonies of his works together, except when out of two contraries met to their own destruction, he moulds a third existence; and that it is error, or some evil angel which either blindly or maliciously hath drawn together, in two persons ill embarked in wedlock, the sleeping discords and enmities of nature, lulled on purpose with some false bait, that they may wake to agony and strife later than prevention could have wished. If from the bent of just and honest intentions beginning what was begun and so continuing, all that is equal all that is fair and possible hath been tried, and no accommodation likely to succeed, what folly is it still to stand combating and battering against invincible causes and effects, with evil upon evil, till either the best of our days be lingered out or ended with some speeding sorrow! The wise Ecclesiasticus advises rather, xxxvii. 27, "My son, prove thy soul in thy life; see what is evil for it, and give not that unto it." Reason he had to say so; for if the noisomeness or disfigurement of body can soon destroy the sympathy of mind to wedlock duties, much more will the annoyance and trouble of mind infuse itself into all the faculties and acts of the body, to render them invalid, unkindly, and even unholy against the fundamental lawbook of nature, which Moses never thwarts but reverences. Therefore he commands us to force nothing against sympathy or natural order, no, not upon the most abject creatures; to shew that such an indignity cannot be offered to man without an impious crime. And certainly those divine meditating words of finding out a meet and like help to man, have in them a consideration of more than the indefinite likeness of womanhood (nor are they to be made waste paper on, for the dulness of canon divinity): no, nor those other allegoric precepts of beneficence fetched out of the closet of nature, to teach us goodness and compassion in not compelling together unmatchable societies, or if they meet through mischance by all consequence to disjoin them, as God and nature signifies and lectures to us not only by those recited decrees, but even by the first and last of all His visible works; when by His divorcing command the world first rose out of chaos, nor can be renewed again out of confusion but by the separating of unmeet consorts.

CHAPTER XI.

The seventh Reason, that sometimes Continuance in Marriage may be evidently the Shortening or Endangering of Life to either Party: both Law and Divinity concluding, that Life is to be preferred before Marriage, the intended Solace of Life.

SEVENTHLY, The Canon Law and divines consent, that if either party be found contriving against another's life, they may be severed by divorce: for a sin against the life of marriage is greater than a sin against the bed; the one destroys, the other but defiles. The same may be said touching those persons who, being of a pensive nature and course of life, have summed up all their solace in that free and lightsome conversation which God and man intends in marriage; whereof when they see themselves deprived by meeting an unsociable consort, they ofttimes resent one another's mistake so deeply that long it is not ere grief end one of them. When therefore this danger is foreseen, that the life is in peril by living together, what matter is it whether helpless grief or wilful practice be the cause? This is certain, that the preservation of life is more worth than the compulsory keeping of marriage; and it is no less than cruelty to force a man to remain in that state as the solace of his life which he and his friends know will be either the undoing or the disheartening of his life. And what is life without the vigour and spiritual exercise of life? How can it be useful either to private or public employment? Shall it therefore be quite dejected, though never so valuable, and left to moulder away in heaviness, for the superstitious and impossible performance of an ill-driven bargain? Nothing more inviolable than vows made to God; yet we read in Numbers, that if a wife had made such a vow, the mere will and authority of her husband might break it. How much more then may he break the error of his own bonds with an unfit and mistaken wife, to the saving of his welfare, his life, yea, his faith and virtue, from the hazard of overstrong temptations! For if man be lord of the sabbath, to the curing of a fever, can he be less than lord of marriage in such important causes as these?

CHAPTER XII.

The eighth Reason, It is probable, or rather certain, that every one who happens to marry hath not the Calling: and therefore upon Unfitness found and considered, Force ought not to be used.

EIGHTHLY, It is most sure that some even of those who are not plainly defective in body, yet are destitute of all other marriageable gifts, and consequently have not the calling to marry unless nothing be requisite thereto but a mere instrumental body—which to affirm, is to that unanimous covenant a reproach: yet it is as sure that many such, not of their own desire, but by the persuasion of friends, or not knowing themselves, do often enter into wedlock. Where finding the difference at length between the duties of a married life and the gifts of a single life, what unfitness of mind, what wearisomeness, scruples and doubts, to an incredible offence and displeasure, are like to follow between, may be soon imagined; whom thus to shut up, and immure, and shut up together, the one with a mischosen mate, the other in a mistaken calling, is not a course that Christian wisdom and tenderness ought to use. As for the custom that some parents and guardians have of forcing marriages, it will be better to say nothing of such a savage inhumanity, but only thus:—that the law which gives not all freedom of divorce to any creature endued with reason so assassinated, is next in cruelty.

CHAPTER XIII.

The ninth Reason; because Marriage is not a mere carnal Coition, but a human Society: where that cannot reasonably be had, there can be no true Matrimony. Marriage compared with all other Covenants and Vows warrantably broken for the good of Man. Marriage the Papist's Sacrament, and unfit Marriage the Protestant's Idol.

NINTHLY, I suppose it will be allowed us that marriage is a human society, and that all human society must proceed from the Mind rather than the Body, else it would be but a kind of animal or beastish meeting. If the Mind therefore cannot have that due company by marriage that it may reasonably and humanly desire, that marriage can be no human society, but a certain formality or gilding over of little better than a brutish congress, and so in very wisdom and pureness to be dissolved.

But marriage is more than human, "the covenant of God," Prov. ii. 17; therefore man cannot dissolve it. I answer, if it be more than human, so much the more it argues the chief society thereof to be in the Soul rather than in the Body, and the greatest breach thereof to be unfitness of Mind rather than defect of Body: for the Body can have least affinity in a covenant more than human, so that the reason of dissolving holds good the rather. Again, I answer, that the sabbath is a higher institution, a command of the first table, for the breach whereof God hath far more and oftener testified his anger than for divorces, which from Moses to Malachi he never took displeasure at, nor then neither if we mark the text; and yet as oft as the good of man is concerned, he not only permits but commands to break the sabbath. What covenant more contracted with God and less in man's power than the vow which hath once passed his lips? Yet if it be found rash, if offensive, if unfruitful either to God's glory or the good of man, our doctrine forces not error and unwillingness irksomely to keep it, but counsels wisdom and better thoughts boldly to break it. Therefore to enjoy the indissoluble keeping of a marriage found unfit against the good of man both Soul and Body, as hath been evidenced, is to make an idol of marriage, to advance it above the worship of God and the good of man, to make it a transcendant command, above both the second and first table; which is a most prodigious doctrine.

Next, whereas they cite out of the Proverbs, that it is the covenant of God, and therefore more than human, that consequence is manifestly false. For so the covenant which Zedekiah made with the infidel king of Babel is called the covenant of God, Ezek. xvii. 19, which would be strange to hear counted more than a human covenant. So every covenant between man and man, bound by oath, may be called the covenant of God, because God therein is attested. So of marriage he is the author and the witness; yet hence will not follow any divine astriction more than what is subordinate to the glory of God, and the main good of either party. For as the glory of God and their esteemed fitness one for the other was the motive which led them both at first to think without other revelation that God had joined them together; so when it shall be found by their apparent unfitness that their continuing to be man and wife is against the glory of God and their mutual happiness, it may assure them that God never joined them, who hath revealed his gracious will not to set the ordinance above the man for whom it was ordained; not to canonize marriage either as a tyranness or a goddess over the enfranchised life and soul of man. For wherein can God delight, wherein be worshipped, wherein be glorified by the forcible continuing of an improper and ill-yoking couple? He that loved not to see the disparity of several cattle at the plough, cannot be pleased with vast unmeetness in marriage. Where can be the peace and love which must invite God to such a house? May it not be feared that the not divorcing of such a helpless disagreement will be the divorcing of God finally from such a place? But it is a trial of our patience, say they. I grant it. But which of Job's afflictions were sent him with that law that he might not use means to remove any of them if he could? And what if it subvert our patience and our faith too? Who shall answer for the perishing of all those souls, perishing by stubborn expositions of particular and inferior precepts against the general and supreme rule of Charity? They dare not affirm that marriage is either a sacrament or a mystery, though all those sacred things give place to man; and yet they invest it with such an awful sanctity, and give it such adamantine chains to bind with, as if it were to be worshipped like some Indian deity, when it can confer no blessing upon us, but works more and more to our misery. To such teachers the saying of St. Peter at the council of Jerusalem will do well to be applied: "Why tempt ye God to put a yoke upon the necks of" Christian men, which neither the Jews, God's ancient people, " nor we are able to bear;" and nothing but unwary expounding hath brought upon us?

CHAPTER XIV.

Considerations concerning Familism, Antinomianism; and why it may be thought that such Opinions may proceed from the undue Restraint of some just Liberty, than which no greater Cause to contemn Discipline.

To these considerations this also may be added as no improbable conjecture. Seeing that sort of men who follow Anabaptism, Familism, Antinomianism, and other fanatic dreams (if we understand them not amiss), be such most commonly as are by nature addicted to religion, of life also not debauched, and that their opinions having full swing, do end in satisfaction of the flesh; it may be come with reason into the thoughts of a wise man, whether all this proceed not partly, if not chiefly, from the restraint of some lawful liberty, which ought to be given men, and is denied them, as by physic we learn in menstruous bodies, where nature's current hath been stopped, that the suffocation and upward forcing of some lower part affects the head and inward sense with dotage and idle fancies. And on the other hand, whether the rest of vulgar men not so religiously professing, do not give themselves much the more to whoredom and adulteries, loving the corrupt and venial discipline of clergy-courts, but hating to hear of perfect Reformation whenas they forsee that then fornication shall be austerely censured, adultery punished, and marriage, the appointed refuge of nature, though it hap to be never so incongruous and displeasing, must yet of force be worn out when it can be to no other purpose but of strife and hatred, a thing odious to God? This may be worth the study of skilful men in theology and the reason of things. And lastly, to examine whether some undue and ill-grounded strictness upon the blameless nature of man, be not the cause in those places where already Reformation is, that the discipline of the church, so often, and so unavoidably broken, is brought into contempt and derision? And if it be thus, let those who are still bent to hold this obstinate literality, so prepare themselves as to share in the account for all these transgressions, when it shall be demanded at the last day by one who will scan and sift things with more than a literal wisdom of equity. For if these reasons be duly pondered, and that the Gospel is more jealous of laying on excessive burdens than ever the Law was, lest the soul of a Christian, which is inestimable, should be overtempted and cast away; considering also that many properties of nature which the power of regeneration itself never alters may cause dislike of conversing, even between the most sanctified; which continually grating in harsh tone together, may breed some jar and discord, and that end in rancour and strife, a thing so opposite both to marriage and to Christianity, it would perhaps be less scandal to divorce a natural disparity, than to link violently together an unchristian dissension, committing two insnared souls inevitably to kindle one another not with the fire of love but with a hatred irreconcileable; who, were they dissevered, would be straight friends in any other relation. But if an alphabetical servility must be still urged, it may so fall out that the true Church may unwittingly use as much cruelty in forbidding to divorce, as the Church of Antichrist doth wilfully in forbidding to marry.

BOOK II.

CHAPTER I.

The Ordinance of Sabbath and Marriage compared. Hyperbole no unfrequent Figure in the Gospel. Excess cured by contrary Excess. Christ neither did nor could abrogate the Law of Divorce, but only reprieve the Abuse thereof.

HITHERTO the position undertaken has been declared, and proved by a law of God, that law proved to be moral, and unabolishable, for many reasons equal, honest, charitable, just, annexed thereto. It follows now, that those places of Scripture, which have a seeming to revoke the prudence of Moses, or rather that merciful decree of God, be forthwith explained and reconciled. For what are all these reasonings worth, will some reply, whenas the words of Christ are plainly against all divorce, "except in case of fornication"? To whom he whose mind were to answer no more but this, "except also in case of charity," might safely appeal to the more plain words of Christ in defence of so excepting. "Thou shalt do no manner of work," saith the commandment of the Sabbath. Yes, saith Christ, works of Charity. And shall we be more severe in paraphrasing the considerate and tender Gospel, than he was in expounding the rigid and peremptory law? What was ever in all appearance less made for man, and more for God alone, than the Sabbath? Yet when the good of man comes into the scales, we hear that voice of infinite goodness and benignity, that "Sabbath was made for man, not man for Sabbath." What thing ever was more made for man alone, and less for God, than Marriage? And shall we load it with a cruel and senseless bondage utterly against both the good of man, and the glory of God? Let whoso will now listen. I want neither pall nor mitre, I stay neither for ordination nor induction; but in the firm faith of a knowing Christian, which is the best and truest endowment of the keys, I pronounce the man who shall bind so cruelly a good and gracious ordinance of God, hath not in that the spirit of Christ. Yet that every text of Scripture seeming opposite may be attended with a due exposition, this other part ensues, and makes account to find no slender arguments for this assertion out of those very Scriptures which are commonly urged against it.

First therefore let us remember, as a thing not to be denied, that all places of Scripture wherein just reason of doubt arises from the letter are to be expounded by considering upon what occasion everything is set down, and by comparing other texts. The occasion which induced our Saviour to speak of divorce, was either to convince the extravagance of the Pharisees in that point, or to give a sharp and vehement answer to a tempting question. And in such cases, that we are not to repose all upon the literal terms of so many words, many instances will teach us wherein we may plainly discover how Christ meant not to be taken word for word, but like a wise physician, administering one excess against another to reduce us to a permiss. Where they were too remiss, he saw it needful to seem most severe. In one place he censures an unchaste look to be adultery already committed; another time he passes over actual adultery with less reproof than for an unchaste look, not so heavily condemning secret weakness, as open malice. So here he may be justly thought to have given this rigid sentence against divorce, not to cut off all remedy from a good man who finds himself consuming away in a disconsolate and unenjoined matrimony, but to lay a bridle upon the bold abuses of those overweening rabbis; which he could not more effectually do, than by a counter-sway of restraint curbing their wild exorbitance almost in the other extreme, as when we bow things the contrary way, to make them come to their natural straightness. And that this was the only intention of Christ is most evident if we attend out to his own words and protestation made in the same sermon, not many verses before he treats of divorcing, that he came not to abrogate from the law "one jot or tittle," and denounces against them that shall so teach.

But St. Luke, the verse immediately foregoing that of divorce, inserts the same caveat, as if the latter could not be understood without the former, and as a witness to produce against this our wilful mistake of abrogating, which must needs confirm us that whatever else in the political law of more special relation to the Jews might cease to us, yet that of those precepts concerning divorce not one of them was repealed by the doctrine of Christ, unless we have vowed not to believe his own cautious and immediate profession. For if these our Saviour's words inveigh against all divorce, and condemn it as adultery except it be for adultery, and be not rather understood against the abuse of those divorces permitted in the Law, then is that law of Moses, Deut. xxiv. 1, not only repealed and wholly annulled, against the promise of Christ and his known profession not to meddle in matters judicial; but that which is more strange, the very substance and purpose of that law is contradicted, and convinced both of injustice and impurity, as having authorized and maintained legal adultery by statute. Moses also cannot scape to be guilty of unequal and unwise decrees, punishing one act of secret adultery by death, and permitting a whole life of open adultery by law. And albeit lawyers write that some political edicts, though not approved, are yet allowed to the scum of the people and the necessity of the times; these excuses have but a weak pulse. For first, we read, not that the scoundrel people, but the choicest, the wisest, the holiest of that nation, have frequently used these laws, or such as these, in the best and holiest times. Secondly, be it yielded that in matters not very bad or impure a human lawgiver may slacken something of that which is exactly good, to the disposition of the people and the times: but if the perfect, the pure, the righteous Law of God (for so are all his statutes and his judgments), be found to have allowed smoothly, without any certain reprehension, that which Christ afterward declares to be adultery, how can we free this Law from the horrible indictment of being both impure, unjust, and fallacious?

CHAPTER II.

How Divorce was permitted for Hardness of Heart, cannot be understood by the common Exposition. That the Law cannot permit, much less enact a Permission of Sin.

NEITHER will it serve to say this was permitted for the hardness of their hearts, in that sense as it is usually explained; for the law were then but a corrupt and eroneous schoolmaster, teaching us to dash against a vital maxim of religion by doing foul evil in hope of some certain good.

This only text is not to be matched again throughout the whole Scripture, whereby God in his perfect Law should seem to have granted to the hard hearts of his holy people, under his own hand, a civil immunity and free charter to live and die in a long successive adultery, under a Covenant of Works, till the Messiah, and then that indulgent permission to be strictly denied by a Covenant of Grace. Besides, the incoherence of such a doctrine cannot, must not be thus interpreted, to the raising of a paradox never known till then, only hanging by the twined thread of one doubtful scripture, against so many other rules and leading principles of religion, of justice, and purity of life. For what could be granted more either to the fear, or to the lust of any tyrant or politician, than this authority of Moses thus expounded; which opens him a way at will to dam up justice, and not only to admit of any Romish or Austrian dispenses but to enact a statute of that which he dares not seem to approve, even to legitimate vice, to make sin itself, the ever alien and vassal sin, a free citizen of the commonwealth, pretending only these or these plausible reasons? And well he might, all the while that Moses shall be alleged to have done as much without shewing any reason at all. Yet this could not enter into the heart of David, Psalm xciv. 20, how any such authority as endeavours to "fashion wickedness by a law," should derive itself from God. And Isaiah says, "Woe upon them that decree unrighteous decrees," chap.

X. 1. Now which of these two is the better lawgiver, and which deserves most a woe, he that gives out an edict singly unjust, or he that confirms to generations a fixed and unmolested impunity of that which is not only held to be unjust, but also unclean, and both in a high degree ; not only, as they themselves affirm, an injurious expulsion of one wife, but also an unclean freedom by more than a patent to wed another adulterously? How can we therefore with safety thus dangerously confine the free simplicity of our Saviour's meaning to that which merely amounts from so many letters, whenas it can consist neither with its former and cautionary words, nor with other more pure and holy principles, nor finally with a scope of Charity, commanding by his express commission in a higher strain? But all rather of necessity must be understood as only against the abuse of that wise and ingenuous liberty which Moses gave, and to terrify a roving conscience from sinning under that pretext.

CHAPTER III.

That to allow Sin by Law is against the Nature of Law, the End of the Lawgiver, and the Good of the People. Impossible therefore in the Law of God. That it makes God the Author of Sin more than anything objected by the Jesuits or Arminians against Predestination.

BUT let us yet further examine upon what consideration a law of licence could be thus given to a holy people for their hardness of heart. I suppose all will answer that, for some good end or other. But here the contrary shall be proved. First, that many ill effects but no good end of such a sufferance can be shewn ; next, that a thing unlawful can, for no good end whatever, be either done or allowed by a positive law. If there were any good end aimed at, that end was then good either to the law or to the lawgiver licensing or as to the person licensed. That it could not be the end of the law, whether moral or judicial, to license a sin, I prove easily

out of Rom. v. 20: "The Law entered, that the offence might
abound;" that is, that sin might be made abundantly manifest
to be heinous and displeasing to God, that so his offered grace
might be the more esteemed. Now if the Law, instead of aggravating and terrifying sin, shall give out licence, it foils itself and
turns recreant from its own end: it forestalls the pure grace
of Christ, which is through righteousness, with impure indulgences, which are through sin. And instead of discovering sin,
for "by the Law is the knowledge thereof," saith St. Paul, and
that by certain and true light for men to walk in safety, it
holds out false and dazzling fires to stumble men; or, like
those miserable flies, to run into with delight and be burnt. For
how many souls might easily think that to be lawful which the
law and magistrate allowed them? Again, we read, 1 Tim. i. 5,
"The end of the commandment is Charity out of a pure heart,
and of a good conscience, and of faith unfeigned." But never
could that be Charity, to allow a people what they could not use
with a pure heart, but with conscience and faith both deceived
or else despised. The more particular end of the judicial law is
set forth to us clearly, Rom. xiii. That God hath given to that
Law "a sword not in vain, but to be a terror to evil works, a revenge to execute wrath upon him that doth evil." If this terrible
commission should but forbear to punish wickedness, were it
other to be accounted than partial and unjust? But if it begin
to write indulgence to vulgar uncleanness, can it do more to
corrupt and shame the end of its own being? Lastly, if the Law
allow sin, it enters into a kind of covenant with sin; and if it
do, there is not a greater sinner in the world than the Law itself.
The Law, to use an allegory something different from that in Philo-
Judæus concerning Amalek, though haply more significant, the
Law is the Israelite, and hath this absolute charge given it, Deut.
xxv., To blot out the memory of sin, the Amalekite, from under
heaven, not to forget it. Again, the law is the Israelite, and
hath this express repeated command, to make no covenant with
sin, the Canaanite, but to expel him, lest he prove a snare.
And to say truth, it were too rigid and reasonless to proclaim

such an enmity between man and man, were it not the type of a greater enmity between Law and Sin. I speak even now, as if sin were condemned in a perpetual villanage never to be free by law, never to be manumitted: but sure sin can have no tenure by law at all, but is rather an eternal outlaw, and in hostility with law past all atonement: both diagonal contraries, as much allowing one another as day and night together in one hemisphere. Or if it be possible that Sin with his darkness may come to composition, it cannot be without a foul eclipse and twilight to the Law whose brightness ought to surpass the noon. Thus we see how this unclean permittance defeats the sacred and glorious end both of the moral and judicial law.

As little good can the lawgiver propose to equity by such a lavish remissness as this. If to remedy hardness of heart, Paræus and other divines confess it more increases by this liberty than is lessened. And how is it probable that their hearts were more hard in this, that it should be yielded to, than in any other crime? Their hearts were set upon usury, and are to this day, no nation more; yet that which was the endamaging only of their estates was narrowly forbid: this, which is thought the extreme injury and dishonour of their wives and daughters, with the defilement also of themselves, is bounteously allowed. Their hearts were as hard under their best kings to offer in high places, though to the true God: yet that, but a small thing, it strictly forewarned; this, accounted a high offence against one of the greatest moral duties, is calmly permitted and established. How can it be evaded, but that the heavy censure of Christ should fall worse upon this Lawgiver of theirs, than upon all the Scribes and Pharisees? For they did but omit judgment and mercy to trifle in mint and cummin, yet all according to Law; but this their lawgiver, altogether as punctual in such niceties, goes marching on to adulteries, through the violence of divorce by law against law. If it were such a cursed act of Pilate, a subordinate judge to Cæsar, overswayed by those hard hearts, with much ado to suffer one transgression of law but once; what is it then, with less ado, to publish a law of transgression for many ages? Did God for this come down and cover the mount of Sinai with His glory, uttering in thunder those His sacred ordinances out of the bottomless treasures of His Wisdom and infinite Pureness, to patch up an ulcerous and rotten commonwealth with strict and stern injunctions, to wash the skin and garments for every unclean touch; and such easy permission given to pollute the soul with adulteries by public authority, without disgrace or question? No; it had been better that man had never known law or matrimony, than that such foul iniquity should be fastened upon the Holy One of Israel, the Judge of all the earth. And such a piece of folly as Beelzebub would not commit, to divide against himself, and prevent his own ends: or if he, to compass more certain mischief, might yield perhaps to feign some good deed, yet that God should enact a licence of certain evil for uncertain good against His own Glory and Pureness, is abominable to conceive. And as it is destructive to the end of Law, and blasphemous to the honour of the Lawgiver licensing, so is it as pernicious to the person licensed. If a private friend admonish not, the Scripture saith, "He hates his brother, and lets him perish;" but if he soothe him and allow him in his faults, the Proverbs teach us, "He spreads a net for his neighbour's feet, and worketh ruin." If the magistrate or prince forget to administer due justice, and restrain not sin, Eli himself could say, "It made the Lord's people to transgress." But if he countenance them against law by his own example, what havoc it makes both in religion and virtue among the people may be guessed by the anger it brought upon Hophni and Phineas, not to be appeased "with sacrifice nor offering for ever." If the law be silent to declare sin, the people must needs generally go astray, for the Apostle himself saith, he had not known lust but by the law. And surely such a nation seems not to be under the illuminating guidance of God's Law, but under the horrible doom rather of such as despise the Gospel, "He that is filthy, let him be filthy still." But where the Law itself gives a warrant for sin, I know not what condition of misery to imagine miserable enough for such a people, unless that portion of the wicked, or rather of the damned, on whom God threatens, in Psalm xi., to rain snares. But that questionless cannot be by any law, which the Apostle saith is "a ministry ordained of God for our good," and not so many ways and in so high a degree to our destruction, as we have now been graduating. And this is all the good can come to the person licensed in his hardness of heart.

I am next to mention that, which because it is a ground in divinity (Rom. iii.), will save the labour of demonstrating, unless her given axioms be more doubted than in other hearts (although it be no less firm in the precepts of philosophy), that a thing unlawful can for no good whatsoever be done, much less allowed by a positive law. And this is the matter why interpreters upon that passage in Hosea will not consent it to be a true story, that the prophet took a harlot to wife : because God, being a pure spirit, could not command a thing repugnant to his own nature, no, not for so good an end as to exhibit more to the life a wholesome and perhaps a converting parable to many an Israelite. Yet that he commanded the allowance of adulterous and injurious divorces for hardness of heart, a reason obscure and in a wrong sense, they can very favourably persuade themselves ; so tenacious is the leaven of an old conceit. But they shift it : He permitted only. Yet silence in the Law is consent, and consent is accessory : why then is not the Law, being silent, or not active against a crime, accessory to its own conviction, itself judging? For though we should grant that it approves not, yet it will : and the lawyers' maxim is, that "the will compelled is yet the will." And though Aristotle in his Ethics calls this "a mixed action," yet he concludes it to be voluntary and inexcusable, if it be evil. How justly, then, might human law and philosophy rise up against the righteousness of Moses, if this be true which our vulgar divinity fathers upon him, yea, upon God himself; not silently, and only negatively to permit, but in his Law to divulge a written and general privilege to commit and persist in unlawful divorces, with a high hand with security and no ill fame ? For this is more than permitting and contriving, this is maintaining : this is warranting, this is protecting, yea, this is doing evil, and such an evil as that reprobate lawgiver did, whose lasting infamy is engraven upon him like a surname, "he who made Israel to sin." This is the lowest pitch contrary to God that public fraud and injustice can descend.

If it be affirmed, that God, as being Lord, may do what He will, yet we must know, that God hath not two wills, but one will, much less two contrary. If he once willed adultery should be sinful, and to be punished with death, all his omnipotence will not allow him to will the allowance that his holiest people might, as it were, by his own antinomy or counterstatute, live unreproved in the same fact as he himself esteemed it, according to our common explainers. The hidden ways of His Providence we adore and search not, but the Law is his revealed will, his complete, his evident and certain will. Herein he appears to us, as it were, in human shape, enters into covenant with us, swears to keep it, binds himself like a just lawgiver to his own prescriptions, gives himself to be understood by men, judges and is judged, measures and is commensurate to right reason; cannot require less of us in one cantle of his law than in another, his legal justice cannot be so fickle and so variable, sometimes like a devouring fire, and by and by connivant in the embers, or, if I may so say, oscitant and supine. The vigour of His Law could no more remit, than the hallowed fire upon His Altar could be let go out. The lamps that burned before him might need snuffing, but the light of His Law never. Of this also more beneath, in discussing a solution of Rivetus.

The Jesuits, and that sect among us which is named of Arminius, are wont to charge us of making God the author of sin, in two degrees especially, not to speak of his permission: 1. Because we hold, that he hath decreed some to damnation, and consequently to sin, say they; next, Because those means which are of saving knowledge to others, he makes to them an occasion of greater sin. Yet considering the perfection wherein man was created, and might have stood, no degree necessitating his freewill, but subsequent, though not in time yet in order, to causes which were in his own power; they might methinks be persuaded to absolve both God and us. Whenas the doctrine of Plato and

Chrysippus, with their followers, the Academics and the Stoics, who knew not what a consummate and most adorned Pandora was bestowed upon Adam, to be the nurse and guide of his arbitrary happiness and perseverance, I mean, his native innocence and perfection, which might have kept him from being our true Epimetheus; and though they taught of virtue and vice to be both the gift of divine destiny, they could yet give reasons not invalid to justify the counsels of God and fate from the insulsity of mortal tongues, that man's own freewill self-corrupted is the adequate and sufficient cause of his disobedience besides fate; as Homer also wanted not to express, both in his Iliad and Odyssee. And Manilius the poet, although in his fourth book he tells of some "created both to sin and punishment;" yet without murmuring, and with an industrious cheerfulness, he acquits the Deity. They were not ignorant in their heathen lore, that it is most godlike to punish those who of his creatures became his enemies with the greatest punishment; and they could attain also to think that the greatest, when God himself throws a man furthest from him; which then they held he did, when he blinded, hardened and stirred up his offenders, to finish and pile up their desperate work, since they had undertaken it. To banish for ever into a local hell, whether in the air or in the centre or in that uttermost and bottomless gulf of chaos, deeper from holy bliss than the world's diameter multiplied, they thought not a punishing so proper and proportionate for God to inflict, as to punish sin with sin. Thus were the common sort of Gentiles wont to think, without any wry thoughts cast upon divine governance. And therefore Cicero, not in his Tusculan or Campanian retirements among the learned wits of that age, but even in the Senate to a mixed auditory (though he were sparing otherwise to broach his philosophy among statists and lawyers), yet as to this point, both in his Oration against Piso, and in that which is about the answers of the soothsayers against Clodius, he declares it publicly as no paradox to common ears, that God cannot punish man more, nor make him more miserable, than still by making him more sinful. Thus we see how in this controversy the justice of God stood upright even among heathen disputers. But if any one be truly, and not pretendedly, zealous for God's honour, here I call him forth, before men and angels, to use his best and most advised skill, lest God more unavoidably than ever yet, and in the guiltiest manner, be made the author of sin,— if He shall not only deliver over and incite his enemies by rebuke to sin as a punishment, but shall by patent under his own broad seal allow his friends, whom he would sanctify and save, whom he would unite to himself and not disjoin, whom he would correct by wholesome chastening and not punish as he doth the damned by lewd sinning, if he shall allow these in his Law, the perfect rule of his own purest will, and our most edified conscience, the perpetrating of an odious and manifold sin without the least contesting. It is wondered how there can be in God a secret and a revealed will; and yet what wonder, if there be in man two answerable causes. But here there must be two revealed wills grappling in a fraternal war with one another without any reasonable cause apprehended. This cannot be less than to engraft sin into the substance of the Law, which Law is to provoke sin by crossing and forbidding, not by complying with it. Nay, this is, which I tremble in uttering, to incarnate sin into the unpunishing and well-pleased will of God. To avoid these dreadful consequences that tread upon the heels of those allowances to sin, will be a task of far more difficulty than to appease those minds which, perhaps out of a vigilant and wary conscience, except against predestination. Thus finally we may conclude, that a Law wholly giving license cannot upon any good consideration be given to a holy people for hardness of heart in the vulgar sense.

CHAPTER IV.

That if Divorce be no command, no more is Marriage. That Divorce could be no Dispensation, if it were sinful. The Solution of Rivetus, that God dispensed by some unknown Way, ought not to satisfy a Christian Mind.

OTHERS think to evade the matter by not granting any Law of divorce, but only a Dispensation; which is contrary to the words of Christ, who himself calls it a "law," Mark x. 5, or if we speak of a command in the strictest definition, then marriage itself is no more a command than divorce, but only a free permission to him who cannot contain. But as to Dispensation I affirm the same as before of the Law, that it can never be given to the allowance of sin. God cannot give it, neither in respect of himself, nor in respect of man. Not in respect of himself, being a most pure essence, the just avenger of sin; neither can he make that cease to be a sin, which is in itself unjust and impure, as all divorces, they say, were, which were not for adultery. Not in respect of man, for then it must be either to his good, or to his evil. Not to his good; for how can that be imagined any good to a sinner, whom nothing but rebuke and due correction can save, to hear the determinate oracle of divine law louder than any reproof dispensing and providing for the impunity and convenience of sin; to make that doubtful, or rather lawful, which the end of the law was to make most evidently hateful? Nor to the evil of man can a dispense be given; for if "the law were ordained unto life," Rom. vii. 10, how can the same God publish dispenses against that law, which must needs be unto death? Absurd and monstrous would that dispense be, if any judge or law should give it a man to cut his own throat, or to damn himself. Dispense, therefore, presupposes full pardon, or else it is not a dispense, but a most baneful and bloody snare. And why should God enter covenant with a people to be holy, as "the command is holy and just, and good," Rom. vii. 12, and yet suffer an impure and treacherous dispense, to mislead and betray them under the vizard of law to a legitimate practice of uncleanness? God is no covenant-breaker; He cannot do this.

Rivetus, a diligent and learned writer, having well weighed what hath been written by those founders of dispense, and finding the small agreement among them, would fain work himself aloof these rocks and quicksands, and thinks it best to conclude that God certainly did dispense, but by some way to us unknown, and so to leave it. But to this I oppose that a Christian by no means ought to rest himself in such an ignorance; whereby so many absurdities will straight reflect both against the purity, justice, and wisdom of God, the end also both of Law and Gospel, and the comparison of them both together. God indeed in some ways of his Providence is high and secret, past finding out : but in the delivery and execution of his Law, especially in the managing of a duty so daily and so familiar as this is whereof we reason, hath plain enough revealed himself, and requires the observance thereof not otherwise than to the law of nature and equity imprinted in us seems correspondent. And he hath taught us to love and extol his laws, not only as they are his, but as they are just and good to every wise and sober understanding. Therefore Abraham, even to the face of God himself, seemed to doubt of divine justice, if it should swerve from the irradiation wherewith it had enlightened the mind of man and bound itself to observe its own rule ; " Wilt Thou destroy the righteous with the wicked? that be far from thee; shall not the Judge of the Earth do right?" Thereby declaring that God hath created a righteousness in right itself, against which he cannot do. So David, Psalm cxix., "The testimonies which thou hast commanded are righteous and very faithful; thy word is very pure, therefore thy servant loveth it." Not only then for the author's sake, but for its own purity. "He is faithful," saith St. Paul, "He cannot deny himself;" that is, cannot deny his own promises, cannot but be true to his own rules. He often pleads with men the uprightness of his ways by their own principles. How should we imitate him else, to "be perfect as He is perfect," if at pleasure He can dispense with golden poetic ages of such pleasing licence, as in the fabled reign of old Saturn? And this perhaps before the Law might have some covert; but under such an undispensing covenant as Moses made with them, and not to tell us why and wherefore, indulgence cannot give quiet to the breast of an intelligent man? We must be resolved how the Law can be pure and perspicuous, and yet throw a polluted skirt over these Eleusinian mysteries, that no man can utter what they mean: worse in this than the worst obscenities of heathen superstition; for their filthiness was hid but the mystic reason thereof known to their sages. But this Jewish imputed filthiness was daily and open, but the reason of it is not known to our divines. We know of no design the Gospel can have to impose new righteousness upon works, but to remit the old by faith without works, if we mean justifying works. We know no mystery our Saviour could have to lay new bonds upon marriage in the covenant of grace, which himself had loosened to the severity of law. So that Rivetus may pardon us if we cannot be contented with his nonsolution, to remain in such a peck of uncertainties and doubts so dangerous and ghastly to the fundamentals of our faith.

CHAPTER V.

What a Dispensation is.

THEREFORE to get some better satisfaction, we must proceed to inquire as diligently as we can what a Dispensation is, which I find to be either properly so called, or improperly. Improperly so called, is rather a particular and exceptive law, absolving and disobliging from a more general command for some just and reasonable cause. As Numb. ix. they who were unclean, or in a journey, had leave to keep the passover in the second month, but otherwise ever in the first. As for that in Leviticus of marrying the brother's wife, it was a penal statute rather than a dispense; and commands nothing injurious or in itself unclean, only prefers a special reason of charity before an institutive decency, and perhaps is meant for lifetime only, as is expressed beneath in the prohibition of taking two sisters. What other edict of Moses, carrying but the semblance of a law in any other kind, may bear the name of a dispense, I have not readily to instance. But a dispensation most properly is some particular accident rarely happening, and therefore not specified in the law, but left to the decision of Charity even under the bondage of Jewish rites, much more under the liberty of the Gospel. Thus did "David enter into the house of God, and did eat the shewbread, he and his followers, which was" ceremonially "unlawful." Of such dispenses as these it was that Verdune the French divine so gravely disputed in the council of Trent against friar Adrian, who held that the pope might dispense with anything. "It is a fond persuasion," saith Verdune, "that dispensing is a favour; nay, it is as good distributive justice as what is most, and the priest sins if he gives it not, for it is nothing else but a right interpretation of law." Thus far that I can learn touching this matter wholesomely decreed. But that God, who is the giver of every good and perfect gift, James i., should give out a rule and directory to sin by, should enact a dispensation as longlived as a law, whereby to live in privileged adultery for hardness of heart (and this obdurate disease cannot be conceived how it was the more amended by this unclean remedy), is the most deadly and scorpionlike gift that the enemy of mankind could have given to any miserable sinner, and is rather such a dispense as that was which the serpent gave to our first parents. God gave quails in his wrath, and kings in his wrath, yet neither of these things evil in themselves. But that he whose eyes cannot behold impurity, should in the book of his holy covenant, his most unpassionate law, give licence and statute for uncontrolled adultery, although it go for the received opinion, I shall ever dissuade my soul from such a creed, such an indulgence as the shop of Antichrist never forged a baser.

CHAPTER VI.

That the Jew had no more Right to this supposed Dispense than the Christian hath; and rather not so much.

BUT if we must needs dispense, let us for a while so far dispense with truth, as to grant that sin may be dispensed; yet there will be copious reason found to prove, that the Jew had no more right to such a supposed indulgence than the Christian, whether we look at the clear knowledge wherein he lived, or the strict performance of works whereto he was bound. Besides visions and prophecies, they had the law of God, which in the Psalms and Proverbs is chiefly praised for sureness and certainty, both easy and perfect to the enlightening of the simple. How could it be so obscure then, or they so sottishly blind in this plain, moral, and household duty? They had the same precepts about marriage; Christ added nothing to their clearness, for that had argued them imperfect; he opens not the law, but removes the Pharisaic mists raised between the law and the people's eyes. The only sentence which he adds, "What God hath joined let no man put asunder," is as obscure as any clause fetched out of Genesis, and hath increased a yet undecided controversy of clandestine marriages. If we examine over all his sayings, we shall find him not so much interpreting the law with his words, as referring his own words to be interpreted by the law, and oftener obscures his mind in short, and vehement, and compact sentences, to blind and puzzle them the more who would not understand the law. The Jews therefore were as little to be dispensed with for lack of moral knowledge as we.

Next, none I think will deny but that they were as much bound to perform the law as any Christian. That severe and rigorous knife not sparing the tender foreskin of any male infant to carve upon his flesh the mark of that strict and pure covenant whereinto he entered, might give us to understand enough against the fancy of dispensing. St. Paul testifies, that every "circumcised man is a debtor to the whole law," Gal. v., or else "circumcision is in vain," Rom. ii. 25. How vain then, and how preposterous must it needs be to exact a circumcision of the flesh from an infant into an outward sign of purity, and to dispense an uncircumcision in the soul of a grown man to an inward and real impurity! How vain again was that law, to impose tedious expiations for every slight sin of ignorance and error, and to privilege without penance or disturbance an odious crime whether of ignorance or obstinacy! How unjust also inflicting death and extirpation for the mark of circumstantial pureness omitted, and proclaiming all honest and liberal indemnity to the act of a substantial impureness committed, making void the covenant that was made against it! Thus if we consider the tenour of the Law, to be circumcised and to perform all, not pardoning so much as the scapes of error and ignorance, and compare this with the condition of the Gospel, "believe and be baptized," I suppose it cannot be long ere we grant, that the Jew was bound as strictly to the performance of every duty as was possible; and therefore could not be dispensed with more than the Christian, perhaps not so much.

CHAPTER VII.

That the Gospel is apter to dispense than the Law. Paræus answered.

IF then the Law will afford no reason why the Jew should be more gently dealt with than the Christian, then surely the Gospel can afford as little why the Christian should be less gently dealt with than the Jew. The Gospel indeed exhorts to highest perfection, but bears with weakest infirmity more than the Law. Hence those indulgences, "All cannot receive this saying," "Every man hath his proper gift," with express charges not to "lay on yokes, which our fathers could not bear." The nature of man still is as weak, and yet as hard; and that weakness and hardness as unfit and as unteachable to be harshly used as ever. Ay, but, saith Paræus, there is a greater portion of Spirit poured upon the Gospel, which requires from us perfecter obedience. I answer, this does not prove that the Law might give allowance to sin more than the Gospel; and if it were no sin, we know it were the work of the spirit to "mortify our corrupt desires and evil concupiscence," but not to root up our natural affections and disaffections; moving to and fro even in wisest men upon just and necessary reasons, which were the true ground of that Mosaic dispense, and is the utmost extent of our pleading. What is more or less perfect we dispute not, but what is sin or no sin. And in that I still affirm the Law required as perfect obedience as the Gospel: besides that the prime end of the Gospel is not so much to exact our obedience, as to reveal grace, and the satisfaction of our disobedience. What is now exacted from us, it is the accusing Law that does it, even yet under the Gospel; but cannot be more extreme to us now than to the Jews of old; for the Law ever was of works, and the Gospel ever was of grace.

. Either then the Law by harmless and needful dispenses, which the Gospel is now made to deny, must have anticipated and exceeded the grace of the Gospel, or else must be found to have given politic and superficial graces without real pardon, saying in general, "Do this and live," and yet deceiving and damning underhand with unsound and hollow permissions; which is utterly abhorring from the end of all law, as hath been showed. But if those indulgences were safe and sinless, out of tenderness and compassion, as indeed they were, and yet shall be abrogated by the Gospel; then the Law, whose end is by rigour to magnify grace, shall itself give grace, and pluck a fair plume from the Gospel; instead of hastening us thither, alluring us from it. And whereas the terror of the Law was a servant to amplify and illustrate the mildness of grace; now the unmildness of evangelic grace shall turn servant to declare the grace and mildness of the rigorous Law. The Law was harsh to extol the grace of the Gospel, and now the Gospel by a new affected strictness of her own shall extenuate the grace which herself offers. For by exacting a duty which the Law dispensed if we perform it then is grace diminished, by how much performance advances, unless the Apostle argue wrong: if we perform it not, and perish for not performing, then are the conditions of grace harder than those of rigour. If through faith and repentance we perish not, yet grace still remains the less, by requiring that which rigour did not require or at least not so strictly. Thus much therefore to Paræus; that if the Gospel require perfecter obedience than the Law as a duty, it exalts the Law and debases itself, which is dishonourable to the work of our redemption. Seeing therefore that all the causes of any allowance that the Jews might have remain as well to the Christians, this is a certain rule, that so long as the causes remain, the allowance ought. And having thus at length inquired the truth concerning Law and Dispense, their ends, their uses, their limits, and in what manner both Jew and Christian stand liable to the one or capable of the other; we may safely conclude, that to affirm the giving of any law or lawlike dispense to sin for hardness of heart, is a doctrine of that extravagance from the sage principles of piety, that whoso considers thoroughly cannot but admire how this hath been digested all this while.

CHAPTER VIII.

The true Sense how Moses suffered Divorce for Hardness of Heart.

WHAT may we do then to salve this seeming inconsistence? I must not dissemble that I am confident it can be done no other way than this:

Moses, Deut. xxiv. 1, established a grave and prudent law, full of moral equity, full of due consideration towards nature, that cannot be resisted, a law consenting with the laws of wisest men and civilest nations; that when a man hath married a wife, if it come to pass that he cannot love her by reason of some displeasing natural quality or unfitness in her, let him write her a bill of divorce. The intent of which law undoubtedly was this, that if any good and peaceable man should discover some helpless disagreement or dislike either of mind or body, whereby he could not cheerfully perform the duty of a husband without the perpetual dissembling of offence and disturbance to his spirit; rather than to live uncomfortably and unhappily both to himself and to his wife, rather than to continue undertaking duty which he could not possibly discharge, he might dismiss her whom he could not tolerably and so not conscionably retain. And this law the Spirit of God by the mouth of Solomon, Prov. xxx. 21, 23, testifies to be a good and a necessary law, by granting it that "a hated woman" (for so the Hebrew word signifies, rather than "odious," though it come all to one), that "a hated woman, when she is married, is a thing that the earth cannot bear." What follows then, but that the charitable law must remedy what nature cannot undergo? Now that many licentious and hard-hearted men took hold of this law to cloke their bad purposes, is nothing strange to believe. And these were they, not for whom Moses made the law (God forbid!), but whose hardness of heart taking ill-advantage by this law he held it better to suffer as by accident, where it could not be detected, rather than good men should lose their just and lawful privilege of remedy. Christ therefore having to answer these tempting Pharisees, according as his custom was, not meaning to inform their proud ignorance what Moses did in the true intent of the law which they had ill cited, suppressing the true cause for which Moses gave it and extending it to every slight matter, tells them their own, what Moses was forced to suffer by their abuse of his law. Which is yet more plain, if we mark that our Saviour, in Matt. v., cites not the law of Moses but the Pharisaical tradition falsely grounded upon that law. And in those other places, chap. xix. and Mark x., the Pharisees cite the law, but conceal the wise and humane reason there expressed; which our Saviour corrects not in them, whose pride deserved not his instruction, only returns them what is proper to them: "Moses for the hardness of your heart suffered you," that is, such as you, "to put away your wives; and to you he wrote this precept for that cause," which ("to you") must be read with an impression, and understood limitedly of such as covered ill purposes under that law.

For it was seasonable, that they should hear their own unbounded licence rebuked, but not seasonable for them to hear a good man's requisite liberty explained. But as he hath taught better, if we have ears to hear, he himself acknowledged it to be a law, Mark x., and being a law of God, it must have an undoubted "end of charity, which may be used with a pure heart, a good conscience, and faith unfeigned," as was heard: it cannot allow sin, but is purposely to resist sin, as by the same chapter to Timothy appears. There we learn also, "that the law is good, if a man use it lawfully." Out of doubt then there must be a certain good in this law, which Moses willingly allowed, and there might be an unlawful use made thereof by hypocrites; and that was it which was unwillingly suffered, foreseeing it in general, but not able to discern it in particulars. Christ therefore mentions not here what Moses and the law intended; for good men might know that by many other rules; and the scornful Pharisees were not fit to be told, until they could employ that knowledge they had less abusively. Only he acquaints them with what Moses by them was put to suffer.

CHAPTER IX.

The Words of the Institution how to be understood; and of our Saviour's Answer to his Disciples.

AND to entertain a little their overweening arrogance as best befitted, and to amaze them yet further, because they thought it no hard matter to fulfil the Law, he draws them up to that unseparable institution which God ordained in the beginning before the Fall, when man and woman were both perfect, and could have no cause to separate. Just as in the same chapter he stands not to contend with the arrogant young man, who boasted his observance of the whole law, whether he had indeed kept it or not, but screws him up higher to a task of that perfection which no man is bound to imitate. And in like manner, that pattern of the first institution he set before the opinionative Pharisees to dazzle them, and not to bind us. For this is a solid rule, that every command given with a reason, binds our obedience no otherwise than that reason holds. Of this sort was that command in Eden, "Therefore shall a man cleave to his wife, and they shall be one flesh;" which we see is no absolute command, but with an inference "therefore:" the reason then must be first considered, that our obedience be not misobedience. The first is, for it is not single, because the wife is to the husband "flesh of his flesh," as in the verse going before. But this reason cannot be sufficient of itself: for why then should he for his wife leave his father and mother, with whom he is far more "flesh of flesh, and bone of bone," as being made of their substance? And besides, it can be but a sorry and ignoble society of life whose inseparable injunction depends merely upon flesh and bones. Therefore we must look higher, since Christ himself recalls us to the beginning, and we shall find, that the primitive reason of never divorcing was that sacred and not vain promise of God to remedy man's loneliness by "making him a meet help for him," though not now in perfection, as at first, yet still in proportion as things now are. And this is repeated, verse 20, when all other creatures were fitly associated and brought to Adam, as if the Divine Power had been in some care and deep thought, because "there was not yet found any help meet for man." And can we so slightly depress the allwise purpose of a deliberating God, as if his consultation had produced no other good for man but to join him with an accidental companion of propagation, which his sudden word had already made for every beast? Nay, a far less good to man it will be found, if she must at all adventures be fastened upon him individually. And therefore even plain sense and equity, and, which is above them both, the all-interpreting voice of Charity herself cries aloud, that this primitive reason, this consulted promise of God, "to make a meet help," is the only cause that gives authority to this command of not divorcing, to be a command. And it might be further added, that if the true definition of a wife were asked at good earnest, this clause of being "a meet help" would show itself so necessary and so essential in that demonstrative argument, that it might be logically concluded: Therefore she who naturally and perpetually is no "meet help," can be no wife; which clearly takes away the difficulty of dismissing such a one. If this be not thought enough, I answer yet further, that marriage, unless it mean a fit and tolerable marriage, is not inseparable neither by nature nor institution. Not by nature, for then Mosaic divorces had been against nature, if separable and inseparable be contraries, as who doubts they be? And what is against nature is against law, if soundest philosophy abuse us not; by this reckoning Moses should be most unmosaic, that is, most illegal, not to say most unnatural. Nor is it inseparable by the first institution; for then no second institution of the same law for so many causes could dissolve it; it being most unworthy a human (as Plato's judgment is in the fourth book of his Laws), much more a divine lawgiver, to write two several decrees upon the same thing. But what would Plato have deemed, if one of these were good and the other evil to be done?

Lastly, suppose it to be inseparable by institution, yet in competition with higher things, as Religion and Charity in mainest matters, and when the chief end is frustrate for which it was ordained, as hath been shewn, if still it must remain inseparable, it holds a strange and lawless propriety from all other works of God under heaven. From these many considerations we may safely gather that so much of the first institution as our Saviour mentions, for he mentions not all, was but to quell and put to nonplus the tempting Pharisees, and to lay open their ignorance and shallow understanding of the Scriptures. For, saith he, "have ye not read that He which made them at the beginning, made them male and female, and said, For this cause shall a man cleave to his wife?" which the blind usurpers of Moses's chair could not gainsay As if this single respect of male and female were sufficient, against a thousand inconveniences and mischiefs, to clog a rational creature to his endless sorrow unrelinquishably under the guileful superscription of his intended solace and comfort. What if they had thus answered? "Master, if thou mean to make wedlock as inseparable as it was from the beginning, let it be made also a fit society, as God meant it, which we shall soon understand it ought to be, if thou recite the whole reason of the law." Doubtless our Saviour had applauded their just answer. For then they had expounded his command of Paradise, even as Moses himself expounds it by the laws of divorce, that is, with due and wise regard to the premises and reasons of the first command; according to which, without unclean and temporizing permissions, he instructs us in this imperfect state what we may lawfully do about divorce.

But if it be thought that the Disciples, offended at the rigour of Christ's answer, could yet obtain no mitigation of the former sentence pronounced to the Pharisees, it may be fully answered, that our Saviour continues the same reply to his Disciples, as men leavened with the same customary licence which the Pharisees maintained, and displeased at the removing of a traditional abuse whereto they had so long not unwillingly been used. It was no time then to contend with their slow and prejudicial belief in a thing wherein an ordinary measure of light in Scripture, with some attention, might afterwards inform them well enough. And yet ere Christ had finished this argument, they might have picked out of his own concluding words an answer more to their minds, and in effect the same with that which hath been all this while entreating audience: "All men," saith he, "cannot receive this saying, save they to whom it is given; he that is able to receive it, let him receive it." What saying is this which is left to a man's choice to receive or not receive? What but the married life? Was our Saviour so mild and so favourable to the weakness of a single man, and is he turned on the sudden so rigorous and inexorable, to the distresses and extremities of an ill-wedded man? Did he so graciously give leave to change the better single life for the worse married life? Did he open so to us this hazardous and accidental door of marriage, to shut upon us like the gate of death, without retracting or returning, without permitting to change the worst, most insupportable, most unchristian mischance of marriage, for all the mischiefs and sorrows that can ensue; being an ordinance which was especially given as a cordial and exhilarating cup of solace, the better to bear our other crosses and afflictions? Questionless this was a hard-heartedness of divorcing, worse than that in the Jews, which, they say, extorted the allowance from Moses, and is utterly dissonant from all the doctrine of our Saviour. After these considerations, therefore, to take a law out of Paradise given in time of original perfection, and to take it barely without those just and equal inferences and reasons which mainly establish it, nor so much as admitting those needful and safe allowances wherewith Moses himself interprets it to the fallen condition of man; argues nothing in us but rashness and contempt of those means that God left us in his pure and chaste law, without which it will not be possible for us to perform the strict imposition of this command: or if we strive beyond our strength, we shall strive to obey it otherwise than God commands it. And lamented experience daily teaches the bitter and vain fruits of this our presumption, forcing men in a thing wherein we are not able to judge either of their strength or their sufferance, whom neither one voice nor other by natural addiction, but only marriage ruins. Which doubtless is not the fault of that ordinance, for God gave it as a blessing; nor always of man's mischoosing, it being an error above wisdom to prevent, as examples of wisest men so mistaken manifest: it is the fault therefore of a perverse opinion, that will have it continued in despite of nature and reason when indeed it was never so truly joined. All those expositors upon the fifth Matthew confess the law of Moses to be the law of the Lord, wherein no addition or diminution hath place; yet coming to the point of divorce, as if they feared not to be called least in the kingdom of heaven, any slight evasion will content them to reconcile those contradictions which they make between Christ and Moses, between Christ and Christ.

CHAPTER X.

The vain Shift of those who make the Law of Divorce to be only the Premises of a succeeding Law.

SOME will have it no Law, but the granted premises of another Law following, contrary to the words of Christ, Mark x. 5, and all other translations of gravest authority, who render it in form of a law, agreeably to Mal. ii. 16, as it is most anciently and modernly expounded. Besides, the bill of divorce, and the particular occasion therein mentioned, declares it to be orderly and legal. And what avails this to make the matter more righteous, if such an adulterous condition shall be mentioned to build a law upon, without either punishment or so much as forbidding? They pretend it is implicitly reproved in these words, Deut. xxiv. 4, "after she is defiled;" but who sees not that this defilement is only in respect of returning to her former husband after an intermixed marriage? Else why was not the defiling condition first forbidden, which would have saved the labour of this after-law? Nor is it seemly or piously attributed to the justice of God and his known hatred of sin, that such a heinous fault as this through all the law should be only wiped with an implicit and oblique touch—which yet is falsely supposed,—and that his peculiar people should be let wallow in adulterous marriages almost two thousand years, for want of a direct law to prohibit them. It is rather to be confidently assumed that this was granted to apparent necessities, as being of unquestionable right and reason in the law of nature, in that it still passes without inhibition even when the greatest cause is given to us to expect it should be directly forbidden.

CHAPTER XI.

The other Shift of saying Divorce was permitted by Law, but not approved. More of the Institution.

But it was not approved. So much the worse that it was allowed; as if sin had over-mastered the Word of God to conform her steady and straight rule to sin's crookedness, which is impossible. Besides, what needed a positive grant of that which was not approved? It restrained no liberty to him that could but use a little fraud; it had been better silenced, unless it were approved in some case or other. But still it was not approved. Miserable excusers! He who doth evil that good may come thereby, approves not what he doth; and yet the grand rule forbids him, and counts his damnation just if he do it. The sorceress Medea did not approve her own evil doings, yet looked not to be excused for that. And it is the constant opinion of Plato in Protagoras, and other of his dialogues, agreeing with that proverbial sentence among the Greeks, that "no man is wicked willingly." Which also the Peripatetics do rather distinguish than deny. What great thank then if any man, reputed wise and constant, will neither do nor permit others under his charge to do that which he approves not, especially in matter of sin? but for a judge, but for a magistrate, the shepherd of his people, to surrender up his approbation, against law and his own judgment, to the obstinacy of his herd, what more unjudgelike, unmagistratelike, and in war more uncommanderlike? Twice in a short time it was the undoing of the Roman state, first when Pompey, next when Marcus Brutus, had not magnanimity enough but to make so poor a resignation of what they approved to what the boisterous tribunes and soldiers bawled for. Twice it was the saving of two of the greatest Commonwealths in the world, of Athens by Themistocles at the seafight of Salamis, of Rome by Fabius Maximus in the Punic war, for that these two matchless generals had the fortitude at home, against the rashness and the clamours of their own captains and confederates, to withstand the doing or permitting of what they could not approve in their duty of their great command. Thus far of civil prudence. But when we speak of sin, let us look again upon the old reverend Eli, who in his heavy punishment found no difference between the doing and permitting of what he did not approve. If hardness of heart in the people may be an excuse, why then is Pilate branded through all memory? He approved not what he did, he openly protested, he washed his hands and laboured not a little ere he would yield to the hard hearts of a whole people, both princes and plebeians, importuning and tumulting even to the fear of a revolt. Yet is there any will undertake his cause? If therefore Pilate for suffering but one act of cruelty against law, though with much unwillingness testified, at the violent demand of a whole nation, shall stand so black upon record to all posterity; alas for Moses! What shall we say for him, while we are taught to believe he suffered not one act only both of cruelty and uncleanliness in one divorce, but made it a plain and lasting law against law, whereby ten thousand acts accounted both cruel and unclean might be daily committed, and this without the least suit or petition of the people, that we can read of?

And can we conceive without vile thoughts, that the majesty and holiness of God could endure so many ages to gratify a stubborn people in the practice of a foul polluting sin? And could he expect they should abstain, he not signifying his mind in a plain command, at such time especially when he was framing their laws and them to all possible perfection? But they were to look back to the first institution; nay, rather why was not that individual institution brought out of Paradise, as was that of the Sabbath, and repeated in the body of the law, that men might have understood it to be a command? For that any sentence that bears the resemblance of a precept, set there so out of place in another world, at such a distance from the whole law, and not once mentioned there, should be an obliging command to us, is very disputable; and perhaps it might be denied to be a command without further dispute. However, it commands not absolutely as hath been cleared, but only with reference to that precedent promise of God, which is the very ground of his institution. If that appear not in some tolerable sort, how can we affirm such a matrimony to be the same which God instituted? In such an accident it will best behoove our soberness to follow rather what moral Sinai prescribes equal to our strength, than fondly to think within our strength all that lost Paradise relates.

CHAPTER XII.

The third Shift of them who esteem it a mere Judicial Law. Proved again to be a Law of moral Equity.

ANOTHER while it shall suffice them that it was not a moral but a judicial law, and so was abrogated: nay, rather, not abrogated because judicial, which law the ministry of Christ came not to deal with. And who put it in man's power to exempt, where Christ speaks in general of not abrogating "the least jot or tittle," and in special not that of divorce, because it follows among those laws which he promised expressly not to abrogate, but to vindicate from abusive traditions? Which is most evidently to be seen in the 16th of Luke, where this caution of not abrogating is inserted immediately, and not otherwise than purposely, when no other point of the law is touched but that of divorce. And if we mark the 31st verse of Matt. v. he there cites not the law of Moses, but the licentious gloss which traduced the law. That therefore which he cited, that he abrogated, and not only abrogated, but disallowed and flatly condemned; which could not be the law of Moses, for that had been foully to the rebuke of his great servant. To abrogate a law made with God's allowance, had been to tell us only that such a law was now to cease; but o refute it with an ignominious note of civilizing adultery, casts the reproof which was meant only to the Pharisees even upon him that made the law. But yet if that be judicial which belongs to a civil court, this law is less judicial than nine of the ten commandments: for antiquaries affirm that divorces proceeded among the Jews without knowledge of the magistrate, only with hands and seals under the testimony of some rabbis to be then present. Perkins, in a "Treatise of Conscience," grants, that what in the judicial law is of common equity binds also the Christian: and how to judge of this, prescribes two ways: if wise nations have enacted the like decree; or if it maintain the good of family, church, or commonwealth. This therefore is a pure moral economical law, too hastily imputed of tolerating sin; being rather so clear in nature and reason that it was left to a man's own arbitrement, to be determined between God and his own conscience; not only among the Jews, but in every wise nation: the restraint whereof, who is not too thick-sighted, may see how hurtful and distractive it is to the house, the church, and commonwealth. And that power which Christ never took from the master of a family, but rectified only to a right and wary use at home; that power the undiscerning canonist hath improperly usurped in his court-leet, and bescribbled with a thousand trifling impertinences, which yet have filled the life of man with serious trouble and calamity. Yet grant it were of old a judicial law, it need not be the less moral for that, being conversant as it is about virtue or vice. And our Saviour disputes not here the judicature, for that was not his office, but the morality of divorce, whether it be adultery or no. If therefore he touch the law of Moses at all, he touches the moral part thereof, which is absurd to imagine, that the covenant of grace should reform the exact and perfect law of works, eternal and immutable; or if he touch not the law at all, then is not the allowance thereof disallowed to us.

CHAPTER XIII.

The ridiculous Opinion that Divorce was permitted from the Custom in Egypt. That Moses gave not this Law unwillingly. Perkins confesses this Law was not abrogated.

OTHERS are so ridiculous as to allege, that this licence of divorcing was given them because they were so accustomed in Egypt. As if an ill custom were to be kept to all posterity; for the dispensation is both universal and of time unlimited, and so indeed no dispensation at all; for the over-dated dispensation of a thing unlawful serves for nothing but to increase hardness of heart, and makes men but wax more incorrigible; which were a great reproach to be said of any law or allowance that God should give us. In these opinions it would be more religion to advise well, lest we make ourselves juster than God by censuring rashly that for sin which his unspotted law without rebuke allows and his people without being conscious of displeasing him have used. And if we can think so of Moses, as that the Jewish obstinacy could compel him to write such impure permissions against the word of God and his own judgment; doubtless it was his part to have protested publicly what straits he was driven to, and to have declared his conscience, when he gave any law against his mind. For the law is the touchstone of sin and of conscience, and must not be intermixed with corrupt indulgences; for then it loses the greatest praise it has of being certain and infallible, not leading into error as the Jews were led by this connivance of Moses, if it were a connivance. But still they fly back to the primitive institution, and would have us re-enter Paradise against the sword that guards it. Whom I again thus reply to, that the place in Genesis contains the description of a fit and perfect marriage, with an interdict of ever divorcing such a union: but where nature is discovered to have never joined indeed, but vehemently seeks to part, it cannot be there conceived that God forbids it; nay, he commands it both in the law and in the prophet Malachi, which is to be our rule. And Perkins upon this chapter of Matthew deals plainly, that our Saviour here confutes not Moses's law, but the false glosses that depraved the law; which being true, Perkins must needs grant that something then is left to that law which Christ found no fault with; and what can that be but the conscionable use of such liberty, as the plain words import? So that by his own inference, Christ did not absolutely intend to restrain all divorces to the only cause of adultery. This therefore is the true scope of our Saviour's will, that he who looks upon the law concerning divorce, should also look back upon the institution, that he may endeavour what is perfectest: and he that looks upon the institution shall not refuse as sinful and unlawful those allowances which God affords him in his following law, lest he make himself purer than his Maker, and presuming above strength, slip into temptations irrecoverably. For this is wonderful, that in all those decrees concerning marriage God should never once mention the prime institution, to dissuade them from divorcing, and that he should forbid smaller sins as opposite to the hardness of their hearts and let this adulterous matter of divorce pass ever unreproved.

This is also to be marvelled, that seeing Christ did not condemn whatever it was that Moses suffered, and that thereupon the Christian magistrate permits usury and open stews, and here with us adultery to be so slightly punished which was punished by death to these hard-hearted Jews; why we should strain thus at the matter of divorce, which may stand so much with Charity to permit, and make no scruple to allow usury esteemed to be so much against Charity? But this it is to embroil ourselves against the righteous and all-wise judgments and statutes of God; which are not variable and contrarious, as we would make them, one while permitting, and another while forbidding, but are most constant and most harmonious each to other. For how can the uncorrupt and majestic Law of God, bearing in her hand the wages of life and death, harbour such a repugnance within herself as to require an unexempted and impartial obedience to all her decrees, either from us or from our Mediator, and yet debase herself to falter so many ages with circumcised adulteries by unclean and slubbering permissions?

CHAPTER XIV.

That Beza's Opinion of regulating Sin by Apostolic Law cannot be found.

YET Beza's opinion is, that a politic law (but what politic law I know not, unless one of Machiavel's) may regulate sin; may bear indeed, I grant, with imperfection for a time, as those canons of the Apostles did in ceremonial things; but as for sin, the essence of it cannot consist with rule; and if the law fall to regulate sin, and not to take it utterly away, it necessarily confirms and establishes sin. To make a regularity of sin by law, either the law must straighten sin into no sin, or sin must crook the law into no law. The judicial law can serve to no other end than to be the protector and champion of religion and honest civility, as is set down plainly, Rom. xiii., and is but the arm of moral law, which can no more be separate from justice, than justice from virtue. Their office also, in a different manner, steers the same course; the one teaches what is good by precept, the other unteaches what is bad by punishment. But if we give way to politic dispensations of lewd uncleanness, the first good consequence of such a relax will be the justifying of papal stews, joined with a toleration of epidemic whoredom. Justice must revolt from the end of her authority, and become the patron of that whereof she was created the punisher. The example of usury, which is commonly alleged, makes against the allegation which it brings, as I touched before. Besides that usury, so much as is permitted by the magistrate and demanded with common equity, is neither against the Word of God, nor the rule of Charity; as hath been often discussed by men of eminent learning and judgment. There must be therefore some other example found out to shew us wherein civil policy may with warrant from God settle wickedness by law, and make that lawful which is lawless. Although I doubt not but, upon deeper consideration, that which is true in physic will be found as true in policy, that as of bad pulses those that beat most in order, are much worse than those that keep the most inordinate circuit; so of popular vices, those that may be committed legally will be more pernicious than those that are left to their own course at peril, not under a stinted privilege to sin orderly and regularly, which is an implicit contradiction, but under due and fearless execution of punishment.

The political law, since it cannot regulate vice, is to restrain it by using all means to root it out. But if it suffer the weed to grow up to any pleasurable or contented height, upon what pretext soever, it fastens the root, it prunes and dresses vice as if it were a good plant. Let no man doubt therefore to affirm, that it is not so hurtful or dishonourable to a commonwealth, nor so much to the hardening of hearts, when those worse faults pretended to be feared are committed by who so dares under strict and executed penalty, as when those less faults tolerated for fear of greater, harden their faces, not their hearts only, under the protection of public authority. For what less indignity were this than as if justice herself, the queen of virtues, descending from her sceptered royalty, instead of conquering, should compound and treat with sin, her eternal adversary and rebel, upon ignoble terms? or as if the judicial law were like that untrusty steward in the Gospel, and instead of calling in the debts of his moral master, should give out subtile and sly acquittances to keep himself from begging? Or let us person him like some wretched itinerary judge, who, to gratify his delinquents before him, would let them basely break his head, lest they should pull him from the bench and throw him over the bar. Unless we had rather think both moral and judicial, full of malice and deadly purpose, conspired to let the debtor Israelite, the seed of Abraham, run on upon a bankrupt score, flatter with insufficient and ensnaring discharges, that so he might be haled to a more cruel forfeit for all the indulgent arrears which those judicial acquittances had engaged him in. No, no, this cannot be, that the Law whose integrity and faithfulness is next to God, should be either the shameless broker of our impunities, or the intended instrument of our destruction. The method of holy correction, such as became the commonwealth of Israel, is not to bribe sin with sin, to capitulate and hire out one crime with another; but with more noble and graceful severity than Popilius the Roman legate used with Antiochus to limit and level out the direct way from vice to virtue with straightest and exactest lines on either side, not winding or indenting so much as to the right hand of fair pretences. Violence indeed and insurrection may force the Law to suffer what it cannot mend; but to write a decree in allowance of sin, as soon can the hand of justice rot off. Let this be ever concluded as a truth that will outlive the faith of those that seek to bear it down.

CHAPTER XV.

That Divorce was not given for Wives only, as Beza and Paræus write. More of the Institution.

LASTLY, if divorce were granted, as Beza and others say, not for men, but to release afflicted wives; certainly, it is not only a dispensation, but a most merciful law. And why it should not yet be in force, being wholly as needful, I know not what can be in cause but senseless cruelty. But yet to say divorce was granted for relief of wives rather than of husbands, is but weakly conjectured, and is manifestly the extreme shift of a huddled exposition. Whenas it could not be found how hardness of heart should be lessened by liberty of divorce, a fancy was devised to hide the flaw, by commenting that divorce was permitted only for the help of wives. Palpably uxorious! who can be ignorant, that woman was created for man, and not man for woman, and that a husband may be injured as insufferably in marriage as a wife? What an injury is it after wedlock not to be beloved! what to be slighted! what to be contended with in point of house-rule who shall be the head; not for any parity of wisdom, for that were something reasonable, but out of a female pride! "I suffer not," saith St. Paul, "the woman to usurp authority over the man." If the apostle could not suffer it, into what mould is he mortified that can? Solomon saith, "that a bad wife is to her husband as rottenness to his bones, a continual dropping. Better dwell in the corner of a house-top, or in the wilderness," than with such a one. "Whoso hideth her, hideth the wind, and one of the four mischiefs which the earth cannot bear." If the Spirit of God wrote such aggravations as these, and—as may be guessed by these similitudes—counsels the man rather to divorce than to live with such a colleague; and yet on the other side expresses nothing of the wife's suffering with a bad husband; is it not most likely that God in his law had more pity towards man thus wedlocked than towards the woman that was created for another? The same Spirit relates to us the course which the Medes and Persians took by occasion of Vashti, whose mere denial to come at her husband's sending lost her the being queen any longer, and set up a wholesome law, "that every man should bear rule in his own house." And the divine relater shews us not the least sign of disliking what was done; how should he, if Moses long before was nothing less mindful of the honour and pre-eminence due to man? So that to say divorce was granted for woman rather than man, was but fondly invented. Esteeming therefore to have asserted thus an injured law of Moses from the unwarranted and guilty name of a dispensation to be again a most equal and requisite law, we have the word of Christ himself, that he came not to alter the least tittle of it; and signifies no small displeasure against him that shall teach to do so. On which relying, I shall not much waver to affirm, that those words which are made to intimate as if they forbade all divorce but for adultery—though Moses have constituted otherwise—those words taken circumscriptly, without regard to any precedent law of Moses or attestation of Christ himself, or without care to preserve those his fundamental and superior laws of nature and charity to which all other ordinances give up their seal, are as much against plain equity and the mercy of religion as those words of "Take, eat; this is my body," elementally understood, are against nature and sense.

And surely the restoring of this degraded law hath well recompensed the diligence was used, by enlightening us further to find out wherefore Christ took off the Pharisees from alleging the Law, and referred them to the first institution; not condemning, altering, or abolishing this precept of divorce, which is plainly moral, for that were against his truth, his promise, and his prophetic office; but knowing how fallaciously they had cited and concealed the particular and natural reason of the law, that they might justify any froward reason of their own he lets go that sophistry unconvinced; for that had been to teach them else, which his purpose was not. And since they had taken a liberty which the law gave not, he amuses and repels their tempting pride with a perfection of Paradise which the law required not; not thereby to oblige our performance to that whereto the law never enjoined the fallen estate of man. For if the first institution must make wedlock, whatever happen, inseparable to us, it must make it also as perfect, as meetly helpful, and as comfortable as God promised it should be, at least in some degree; otherwise it is not equal or proportionable to the strength of man that he should be reduced into such indissoluble bonds to his assured misery, if all the other conditions of that covenant be manifestly altered.

CHAPTER XVI.

How to be understood, that they must be one Flesh; and how that those whom God hath joined, Man should not sunder.

NEXT he saith, "They must be one flesh;" which when all conjecturing is done, will be found to import no more but to make legitimate and good the carnal act, which else might seem to have something of pollution in it: and infers thus much over, that the fit union of their souls be such as may even incorporate them to love and amity. But that can never be where no correspondence is of the mind; nay, instead of being one flesh, they will be rather two carcasses chained unnaturally together; or, as it may happen, a living soul bound to a dead corpse; a punishment too like that inflicted by the tyrant Mezentius, so little worthy to be received as that remedy of loneliness which God meant us. Since we know it is not the joining of another body will remove loneliness, but the uniting of another compliable mind; and that it is no blessing but a torment, nay, a base and brutish condition, to be one flesh, unless where nature can in some measure fix a unity of disposition. The meaning therefore of these words, " For this cause shall a man leave his father and his mother, and shall cleave to his wife," was first to shew us the dear affection which naturally grows in every not unnatural marriage, even to the leaving of parents or other familiarity whatsoever. Next, it justifies a man in so doing, that nothing is done undutifully to father or mother. But he that should be here sternly commanded to cleave to his error, a disposition which to his he finds will never cement, a quotidian of sorrow and discontent in his house; let us be excused to pause a little, and bethink us every way round ere we lay such a flat solecism upon the gracious, and certainly not inexorable, not ruthless and flinty, ordinance of marriage. For if the meaning of these words must be thus blocked up within their own letters from all equity and fair deduction, they will serve then well indeed their turn who affirm divorce to have been granted only for wives; whenas we see no word of this text binds women, but men only, what it binds. No marvel then if Salomith, sister to Herod, sent a writ of ease to Costobarus her husband, which, as Josephus there attests, was lawful only to men. No marvel though Placidia, the sister of Honorius, threatened the like to earl Constantius for a trivial cause, as Photius relates from Olympiodorus. No marvel anything, if letters must be turned into palisadoes, to stake out all requisite sense from entering to their due enlargement.

Lastly, Christ himself tells who should not be put asunder, namely, those whom God hath joined. A plain solution of this great controversy, if men would but use their eyes. For when is it that God may be said to join? When the parties and their friends consent? No, surely; for that may concur to lewdest ends. Or is it when Church rites are finished? Neither; for the efficacy of those depends upon the presupposed fitness of either party. Perhaps after carnal knowledge. Least of all; for that may join persons whom neither law nor nature dares join. It is left, that only then when the minds are fitly disposed and enabled to maintain a cheerful conversation, to the solace and love of each other, according as God intended and promised in the very first foundation of matrimony, "I will make him a help-meet for him;" for surely what God intended and promised, that only can be thought to be his joining, and not the contrary. So likewise the apostle witnesseth, 1 Cor. vii. 15, that in marriage "God hath called us to peace." And doubtless in what respect He hath called us to marriage, in that also He hath joined us. The rest, whom either disproportion, or deadness of spirit, or something distasteful and averse in the immutable bent of nature renders conjugal, error may have joined, but God never joined against the meaning of his own ordinance. And if He joined them not, then is there no power above their own consent to hinder them from unjoining, when they cannot reap the soberest ends of being together in any tolerable sort. Neither can it be said properly that such twain were ever divorced, but only parted from each other, as two persons unconjunctive are unmarriable together. But if, whom God hath made a fit help, frowardness or private injuries hath made unfit, that being the secret of marriage, God can better judge than man, neither is man indeed fit or able to decide this matter. However it be, undoubtedly a peaceful divorce is a less evil, and less in scandal than hateful, hard-hearted, and destructive continuance of marriage in the judgment of Moses and of Christ, that justifies him in choosing the less evil: which if it were an honest and civil prudence in the Law, what is there in the Gospel forbidding such a kind of legal wisdom, though we should admit the common expositors?

CHAPTER XVII.

The sentence of Christ concerning Divorce how to be expounded. What Grotius hath observed. Other additions.

HAVING thus unfolded those ambiguous reasons, wherewith Christ, as his wont was, gave to the Pharisees that came to sound him such an answer as they deserved, it will not be uneasy to explain the sentence itself that now follows: "Whosoever shall put away his wife, except it be for fornication, and shall marry another, committeth adultery." First therefore I will set down what is observed by Grotius upon this point, a man of general learning. Next, I produce what mine own thoughts gave me before I had seen his annotations. Origen, saith he, notes that Christ named adultery rather as one example of other like cases, than as one only exception; and that is frequent not only in human but in divine laws, to express one kind of fact, whereby other causes of like nature may have the like plea, as Exod. xxi. 18, 19, 20, 26; Deut. xix. 5. And from the maxims of civil law he shews, that even in sharpest penal laws the same reason hath the same right; and in gentler laws, that from like causes to like the law interprets rightly. But it may be objected, saith he, that nothing destroys the end of wedlock so much as adultery. To which he answers, that marriage was not ordained only for copulation, but for mutual help and comfort of life. And if we mark diligently the nature of our Saviour's commands, we shall find that both their beginning and their end consists in Charity: whose will is that we should so be good to others, as that we be not cruel to ourselves. And hence it appears why Mark, and Luke, and St. Paul to the Corinthians, mentioning this precept of Christ, add no exception, because exceptions that arise from natural equity are included silently under general terms: it would be considered therefore, whether the same equity may not have place in other cases less frequent. Thus far he. From hence is what I add: First, that this saying of Christ, as it is usually expounded, can be no law at all, that a man for no cause should separate but for adultery, except it be a supernatural law, not binding us as we now are. Had it been the law of nature, either the Jews, or some other wise and civil nation would have pressed it. Or let it be so, yet that law, Deut. xxiv. 1, whereby a man hath leave to part whenas, for just and natural cause discovered, he cannot love, is a law ancienter and deeper engraven in blameless nature than the other. Therefore the inspired lawgiver Moses took care, that this should be specified and allowed; the other he let vanish in silence, not once repeated in the volume of his law, even as the reason of it vanished with Paradise. Secondly, this can be no new command, for the Gospel enjoins no new morality, save only the infinite enlargement of Charity, which in this respect is called the new commandment by St. John, as being the accomplishment of every command. Thirdly, it is no command of perfection further than it partakes of Charity, which is "the bond of perfection." Those commands therefore, which compel us to self-cruelty above our strength, so hardly will help forward to perfection that they hinder and set backward in all the common rudiments of Christianity, as was proved. It being thus clear that the words of Christ can be no kind of command as they are vulgarly taken, we shall now see in what sense they may be a command, and that an excellent one, the same with that of Moses, and no other. Moses had granted, that only for a natural annoyance, defect, or dislike, whether in body or mind, for so the Hebrew word plainly notes, which a man could not force himself to live with, he might give a bill of divorce, thereby forbidding any other cause wherein amendment or reconciliation might have place. This law the Pharisees depraving extended to any slight contentious cause whatsoever. Christ therefore seeing where they halted, urges the negative part of the law, which is necessarily understood—for the determinate permission of Moses binds them from further licence—and checking their supercilious drift, declares that no accidental, temporary, or reconcilable offence, except fornication, can justify a divorce. He touches not here those natural and perpetual hinderances of society, whether in body or mind, which are not to be removed; for such as they are aptest to cause an unchangeable offence, so are they not capable of reconcilement because not of amendment: they do not break indeed, but they annihilate the bands of marriage more than adultery. For that fault committed argues not always a hatred either natural or incidental against whom it is committed; neither does it infer a disability of all future helpfulness, or loyalty, or loving agreement, being once past and pardoned, where it can be pardoned. But that which naturally distastes, and "finds no favour in the eyes" of matrimony, can never be concealed, never appeased, never intermitted, but proves a perpetual nullity of love and contentment, a solitude and dead vacation of all acceptable conversing. Moses therefore permits divorce, but in cases only that have no hands to join, and more need separating than adultery. Christ forbids it, but in matters only that may accord, and those less than fornication. Thus is Moses's law here plainly confirmed, and those causes which he permitted not a jot gainsaid. And that this is the true meaning of this place, I prove by no less an author than St. Paul himself, 1 Cor. vii. 10, 11; upon which text interpreters agree, that the Apostle only repeats the precept of Christ : where while he speaks of the "wife's reconcilement to her husband," he puts it out of controversy, that our Saviour meant chiefly matters of strife and reconcilement; of which sort he would not that any difference should be the occasion of divorce, except fornication. And that we may learn better how to value a grave and prudent law of Moses, and how unadvisedly we smatter with our lips when we talk of Christ's abolishing any judicial law of his great Father, except in some circumstances which are judaical rather than judicial and need no abolishing but cease of themselves; I say again, that this recited law of Moses contains a cause of divorce greater beyond compare than that for adultery: and whoso cannot so conceive it, errs and wrongs exceedingly a law of deep wisdom for want of well fathoming. For let him mark, no man urges the just divorcing of adultery as it is a sin, but as it is an injury to marriage; and though it be but once committed, and that without malice, whether through importunity or opportunity, the Gospel does not therefore dissuade him who would therefore divorce. But that natural hatred whenever it arises, is a greater evil in marriage than the accident of adultery, a greater defrauding, a greater injustice, and yet not blameable, he who understands not after all this representing, I doubt his will, like a hard spleen, draws faster than his understanding can well sanguify: nor did that man ever know or feel what it is to love truly, nor ever yet comprehend in his thoughts what the true intent of marriage is. And this also will be somewhat above his reach, but yet no less a truth for lack of his perspective, that as no man apprehends what vice is so well as he who is truly virtuous, no man knows hell like him who converses most in heaven, so there is none that can estimate the evil and the affliction of a natural hatred in matrimony, unless he have a soul gentle enough and spacious enough to contemplate what is true love.

And the reason why men so disesteem this wise judging law of God, and count hate, or "the not finding of favour," as it is there termed, a humorous, a dishonest, and slight cause of divorce, is because themselves apprehend so little of what true concord means. For if they did, they would be juster in their balancing between natural hatred and casual adultery; this being but a transient injury, and soon amended, I mean as to the party against whom the trespass is: but that other being an unspeakable and unremitting sorrow and offence, whereof no amends can be made, no cure, no ceasing but by divorce, which like a divine touch in one moment heals all, and, like the word of God, in one instant hushes outrageous tempests into a sudden stillness and peaceful calm. Yet all this so great a good of God's own enlarging to us is, by the hard reins of them that sit us, wholly diverted and embezzled from us. Maligners of mankind, but who hath taught you to mangle thus and make more gashes in the miseries of a blameless creature with the leaden daggers of your literal decrees, to whose ease you cannot add the tithe of one small atom but by letting alone your unhelpful surgery? As for such as think wandering concupiscence to be here newly and more precisely forbidden than it was before; if the Apostle can convince them, we know that we are to "know lust by the Law," and not by any new discovery of the Gospel. The Law of Moses knew what it permitted, and the Gospel knew what it forbid. He that under a peevish conceit of debarring concupiscence, shall go about to make a novice of Moses (not to say a worse thing, for reverence sake), and such a one of God himself as is a horror to think, to bind our Saviour in the default of a downright promise-breaking, and to bind the disunions of complaining nature in chains together, and curb them with a canon bit; it is he that commits all the whoredom and adultery which himself ajudges, besides the former guilt so manifold that lies upon him. And if none of these considerations, with all their weight and gravity, can avail to the dispossessing him of his precious literalism, let some one or other entreat him but to read on in the same 19th of Matt. till he comes to that place that says, "Some make themselves eunuchs for the kingdom of heaven's sake." And if then he please to make use of Origen's knife, he may do well to be his own carver.

CHAPTER XVIII.

Whether the Words of our Saviour be rightly expounded only of actual Fornication to be the Cause of Divorce. The opinion of Grotius, with other Reasons.

BUT because we know that Christ never gave a judicial law, and that the word fornication is variously significant in scripture, it will be much right done to our Saviour's words, to consider diligently whether it be meant here, that nothing but actual fornication, proved by witness, can warrant a divorce; for so our canon law judges. Nevertheless, as I find that Grotius on this place hath observed, the Christian emperors Theodosius the Second and Justinian, men of high wisdom and reputed piety, decreed it to be a divorcive fornication, if the wife attempted either against the knowledge, or obstinately against the will of her husband, such things as gave open suspicion of adulterising, as the wilful haunting of feasts, and invitations with men not of her near kindred, the lying forth of her house without probable cause, the frequenting of theatres against her husband's mind, her endeavour to prevent or destroy conception. Hence that of Jerome, "Where fornication is suspected, the wife may lawfully be divorced." Not that every motion of a jealous mind should be regarded; but that it should not be exacted to prove all things by the visibility of law witnessing, or else to hoodwink the mind: for the law is not able to judge of these things but by the rule of equity, and by permitting a wise man to walk the middle way of prudent circumspection, neither wretchedly jealous, nor stupidly and tamely patient. To this purpose hath Grotius in his notes. He shews also, that fornication is taken in Scripture for such a continual headstrong behaviour, as tends to plain contempt of the husband, and proves it out of Judges xix. 2, where the Levite's wife is said to have played the whore against him; which Josephus and the Septuagint, with the Chaldean, interpret only of stubbornness and rebellion against her husband. And to this I add, that Kimchi, and the two other rabbis who gloss the text, are in the same opinion. Ben Gersom reasons, that had it been whoredom, a Jew and a Levite would have disdained to fetch her again. And this I shall contribute, that had it been whoredom, she would have chosen any other place to run to than to her father's house, it being so infamous for a Hebrew woman to play the harlot, and so opprobrious to the parents. Fornication then in this place of the Judges is understood for stubborn disobedience against the husband, and not for adultery. A sin of that sudden activity, as to be already committed when no more is done but only looked unchastely: which yet I should be loath to judge worthy a divorce, though in our Saviour's language it be called adultery. Nevertheless when palpable and frequent signs are given, the law of God, Numb. v., so far gave way to the jealousy of a man, as that the woman set before the sanctuary with her head uncovered, was adjured by the priest to swear whether she were false or no, and constrained to drink that "bitter water," with an undoubted "curse of rottenness and tympany" to follow, unless she were innocent. And the jealous man had not been guiltless before God, as seems by the last verse, if having such a suspicion in his head he should neglect his trial; which if to this day it be not used, or be thought as uncertain of effect as our antiquated law of Ordalium, yet all equity will judge, that many adulterous demeanours, which are of lewd suspicion and example, may be held sufficient to incur a divorce, though the act itself hath not been proved. And seeing the generosity of our nation is so, as to account no reproach more abominable than to be nicknamed the husband of an adulteress; that our law should not be as ample as the law of God, to vindicate a man from that ignoble sufferance, is our barbarous unskilfulness, not considering that the law should be exasperated according to our estimation of the injury. And if it must be suffered till the act be visibly proved, Solomon himself, whose judgment will be granted to surpass the acuteness of any canonist, confesses, Prov. xxx. 19, 20, that for the act of adultery it is as difficult to be found as the "track of an eagle in the air, or the way of a ship in the sea;" so that a man may be put to unmanly indignities ere it be found out. This therefore may be enough to inform us that divorcive adultery is not limited by our Saviour to the utmost act, and that to be attested always by eyewitness, but may be extended also to divers obvious actions, which either plainly lead to adultery, or give such presumption whereby sensible men may suspect the deed to be already done. And this the rather may be thought in that our Saviour chose to use the word fornication, which word is found to signify other matrimonial transgressions of main breach to that covenant besides actual adultery. For that sin needed not the riddance of divorce, but of death by the law, which was active even till then, by the example of the woman taken in adultery; or if the law had been dormant, our Saviour was more likely to have told them of their neglect, than to have let a capital crime silently scape into a divorce. Or if it be said, his business was not to tell them what was criminal in the civil courts, but what was sinful at the bar of conscience, how dare they then, having no other ground than these our Saviour's words, draw that into the trial of law, which both by Moses and our Saviour was left to the jurisdiction of conscience? But we take from our Saviour, say they, only that it was adultery, and our law of itself applies the punishment. But by their leave that so argue, the great Lawgiver of all the world, who knew best what was adultery, both to the Jew and to the Gentile, appointed no such applying, and never likes when mortal men will be vainly presuming to outstrip his justice.

CHAPTER XIX.

Christ's manner of teaching. St. Paul adds to this matter of Divorce without command, to shew the matter to be of Equity, not of Rigour. That the Bondage of a Christian may be as much, and his Peace as little, in some other Marriages besides idolatrous. If those Arguments, therefore, be good in that one Case, why not in those other? Therefore the Apostle himself adds, ἐν τοῖς τοιούτοις.

THUS at length we see, both by this and other places, that there is scarce any one saying in the Gospel but must be read with limitations and distinctions to be rightly understood; for Christ gives no full comments or continued discourses, but, as Demetrius the rhetorician phrases it, speaks oft in monosyllables, like a master scattering the heavenly grain of his doctrine like pearls here and there, which requires a skilful and laborious gatherer, who must compare the words he finds with other precepts, with the end of every ordinance, and with the general analogy of evangelic doctrine. Otherwise many particular sayings would be but strange repugnant riddles, and the Church would offend in granting divorce for frigidity, which is not here excepted with adultery, but by them added. And this was it undoubtedly which gave reason to St. Paul, of his own authority, as he professes, and without command from the Lord, to enlarge the seeming construction of those places in the Gospel, by adding a case wherein a person deserted, which is something less than divorced, may lawfully marry again. And having declared his opinion in one case, he leaves a further liberty for Christian prudence to determine in cases of like importance, using words so plain as not to be shifted off, "that a brother or a sister is not under bondage in such cases;" adding also, that "God hath called us to peace" in marriage.

Now if it be plain that a Christian may be brought into unworthy bondage, and his religious peace not only interrupted now and then, but perpetually and finally hindered in wedlock, by misyoking with a diversity of nature as well as of religion, the reasons of St. Paul cannot be made special to that one case of infidelity, but are of equal moment to a divorce, wherever Christian liberty and peace are without fault equally obstructed: that the ordinance which God gave to our comfort may not be pinned upon us to our undeserved thraldom, to be cooped up, as it were, in mockery of wedlock, to a perpetual betrothed loneliness and discontent, if nothing worse ensue. There being nought else of marriage left between such but a displeasing and forced remedy against the sting of a brute desire; which fleshly accustoming without the soul's union and commixture of intellectual delight, as it is rather a soiling than a fulfilling of marriage rites, so is it enough to abase the mettle of a generous spirit, and sinks him to a low and vulgar pitch of endeavour in all his actions; or, which is worse, leaves him in a despairing plight of abject and hardened thoughts. Which condition rather than a good man should fall into, a man useful in the service of God and mankind, Christ himself hath taught us to dispense with the most sacred ordinance of his worship, even for a bodily healing to dispense with that holy and speculative rest of Sabbath, much more then with the erroneous observance of an ill-knotted marriage, for the sustaining of an overcharged faith and perseverance.

CHAPTER XX.

The Meaning of St. Paul, that "Charity believeth all Things." What is to be said to the Licence which is vainly feared will grow hereby. What to those who never have done prescribing Patience in this Case. The Papists most severe against Divorce, yet most easy to all Licence. Of all the miseries in Marriage God is to be cleared, and the faults to be laid on Man's unjust Laws.

AND though bad causes would take licence by this pretext, if that cannot be remedied, upon their conscience be it who shall so do. This was that hardness of heart, and abuse of a good law, which Moses was content to suffer, rather than good men should not have it at all to use needfully. And he who, to run after one lost sheep, left ninety-nine of his own flock at random in the wilderness, would little perplex his thoughts for the obduring of nine hundred and ninety such as will daily take worse liberties, whether they have permission or not. To conclude, as without Charity God hath given no commandment to men, so without it neither can men rightly believe any commandment given. For every act of true faith, as well that whereby we believe the law as that whereby we endeavour the law, is wrought in us by charity, according to that in the divine hymn of St. Paul, 1 Cor. xiii., "Charity believeth all things." Not as if she were so credulous, which is the exposition hitherto current, for that were a trivial praise; but to teach us that Charity is the high governess of our belief, and that we cannot safely assent to any precept written in the Bible, but as Charity commends it to us. Which agrees with that of the same Apostle to the Eph. iv. 14, 15; where he tells us, that the way to get a sure undoubted knowledge of things, is to hold that for Truth which accords most with Charity. Whose unerring guidance and conduct having followed as a loadstar with all diligence and fidelity in this question, I trust, through the help of that illuminating Spirit which hath favoured me, to have done no every day's work in asserting, after many the words of Christ, with other scriptures of great concernment, from burdensome and remorseless obscurity, tangled with manifold repugnances, to their native lustre and consent between each other; hereby also dissolving tedious and Gordian difficulties which have hitherto molested the church of God, and are now decided, not with the sword of Alexander, but with the immaculate hands of Charity, to the unspeakable good of Christendom. And let the extreme literalist sit down now, and revolve whether this in all necessity be not the due result of our Saviour's words; or if he persist to be otherwise opinioned, let him well advise, lest thinking to gripe fast the Gospel he be found instead with the Canon Law in his fist; whose boisterous edicts tyrannizing the blessed ordinance of marriage into the quality of a most unnatural and unchristianly yoke, hath given the flesh this advantage to hate it and turn aside, ofttimes unwillingly, to all dissolute uncleanness, even till punishment itself is weary of and overcome by the incredible frequency of trading lust and uncontrolled adulteries. Yet men whose creed is Custom, I doubt not will be still endeavouring to hide the sloth of their own timorous capacities with this pretext, that for all this it is better to endure with patience and silence this affliction which God hath sent. And I agree it is true, if this be exhorted and not enjoined; but withal it will be wisely done to be as sure as may be that what man's iniquity hath laid on be not imputed to God's sending, lest under the colour of an affected patience we detain ourselves at the gulf's mouth of many hideous temptations, not to be withstood without proper gifts, which, as Perkins well notes, God gives not ordinarily, no, not to most earnest prayers. Therefore we pray, "Lead us not into temptation;" a vain prayer, if, having led ourselves thither, we love to stay in that perilous condition. God sends remedies as well as evils, under which he who lies and groans, that may lawfully acquit himself, is accessory to his own ruin. Nor will it excuse him though he suffer through a sluggish fearfulness to search thoroughly what is lawful, for fear of disquieting the secure falsity of an old opinion. Who doubts not but that it may be piously said, to him who would dismiss his frigidity, Bear your trial; take it as if God would have you live this life of continence? If he exhort this, I hear him as an angel, though he speak without warrant. But if he would compel me, I know him for Satan. To him who divorces an adulteress, piety might say, Pardon her; you may shew much mercy, you may win a soul. Yet the law both of God and man leaves it freely to him; for God loves not to plough out the heart of our endeavours with overhard and sad tasks. God delights not to make a drudge of virtue, whose actions must be all elective and unconstrained. Forced virtue is as a bolt overshot, it goes neither forward nor backward, and does no good as it stands. Seeing, therefore, that neither Scripture nor Reason hath laid this unjust austerity upon divorce, we may resolve that nothing else hath wrought it but that letter-bound servility of the canon doctors, supposing marriage to be a sacrament, and out of the art they have to lay unnecessary burdens upon all men, to make a fair shew in the fleshly observance of matrimony, though peace and love with all other conjugal respects fare never so ill. And, indeed, the papists, who are the strictest forbidders of divorce, are the easiest libertines to admit of grossest uncleanness; as if they had a design by making wedlock a supportless yoke, to violate it most, under colour of preserving it most inviolable; and withal delighting, as their mystery is, to make men the day labourers of their own afflictions, as if there were such a scarcity of miseries from abroad, that we should be made to melt our choicest home blessings and coin them into crosses, for want whereby to hold commerce with patience. If any, therefore, who shall hap to read this discourse, hath been through misadventure ill engaged in this contracted evil here complained of, and finds the fits and workings of a high impatience frequently upon him; of all those wild words which men in misery think to ease themselves by uttering, let him not open his lips against the providence of Heaven, or tax the ways of God and his divine truth. For they are equal, easy, and not burdensome; nor do they ever cross the just and reasonable desires of men, nor involve this our portion of mortal life into a necessity of sadness and malcontent, by laws commanding over the unreducible antipathies of nature, sooner or later found; but allow us to remedy and shake off those evils into which human error hath led us through the midst of our best intentions, and to support our incident extremities by that authentic precept of sovereign Charity, whose grand commission is to do and to dispose over all the ordinances of God to man, that love and truth may advance each other to everlasting. While we, literally superstitious, through customary faintness of heart not venturing to pierce with our free thoughts into the full latitude of nature and religion, abandon ourselves to serve under the tyranny of usurped opinions, suffering those ordinances which were allotted to our solace and reviving, to trample over us, and hale us into a multitude of sorrows, which God never meant us. And where He sets us in a fair allowance of way, with honest liberty and prudence to our guard, we never leave subtilizing and casuisting till we have straitened and pared that liberal path into a razor's edge to walk on, between a precipice of unnecessary mischief on either side; and starting at every false alarm, we do not know which way to set a foot forward with manly confidence and Christian resolution, through the confused ringing in our ears of panic scruples and amazements.

CHAPTER XXI.

That the Matter of Divorce is not to be tried by Law, but by Conscience, as many other Sins are. The Magistrate can only see that the Condition of the Divorce be just and equal. The Opinion of Fagius, and the Reasons of the Assertion.

ANOTHER act of papal encroachment it was to pluck the power and arbitrement of divorce from the master of the family, into whose hands God and the law of all nations had put it, and Christ so left it, preaching only to the Conscience, and not authorizing a judicial court to toss about and divulge the unaccountable and secret reason of disaffection between man and wife,

as a thing most improperly answerable to any such kind of trial.
But the popes of Rome, perceiving the great revenue and high
authority it would give them even over princes, to have the
judging and deciding of such a main consequence in the life of
man as was divorce, wrought so upon the superstition of those
ages, as to divest them of that right, which God from the beginning had entrusted to the husband. By which means they subjected
that ancient and naturally domestic prerogative to an external
and unbefitting judicature. For although differences in divorce
about dowries, jointures, and the like, besides the punishing of
adultery, ought not to pass without referring, if need be, to the
magistrate; yet that the absolute and final hindering of divorce
cannot belong to any civil or earthly power, against the will and
consent of both parties, or of the husband alone, some reasons
will be here urged as shall not need to decline the touch. But
first I shall recite what hath been already yielded by others in
favour of this opinion. Grotius and many more agree, that notwithstanding what Christ spake therein to the conscience, the
magistrate is not thereby enjoined aught against the preservation
of civil peace, of equity, and of convenience. And among these
Fagius is most remarkable, and gives the same liberty of pro-
nouncing divorce to the Christian magistrate as the Mosaic had.
"For whatever," saith he, "Christ spake to the regenerate, the
judge hath to deal with the vulgar: if therefore any through
hardness of heart will not be a tolerable wife to her husband, it
will be lawful as well now as of old to pass the bill of divorce,
not by private but by public authority. Nor doth man separate
them then, but God by his law of divorce given by Moses.
What can hinder the magistrate from so doing, to whose government all outward things are subject, to separate and remove
from perpetual vexation and no small danger those bodies
whose minds are already separate; it being his office to procure
peaceable and convenient living in the commonwealth; and
being as certain also, that they so necessarily separated cannot
all receive a single life?" And this I observe, that our divines
do generally condemn separation of bed and board without

the liberty of second choice: if that therefore in some cases be most purely necessary—as who so blockish to deny?—then is this also as needful. Thus far by others is already well stepped, to inform us that divorce is not a matter of law, but of charity. If there remain a furlong yet to end the question, these following reasons may serve to gain it with any apprehension not too unlearned or too wayward. First because ofttimes the causes of seeking divorce reside so deeply in the radical and innocent affections of nature, as is not within the diocese of law to tamper with. Other relations may aptly enough be held together by a civil and virtuous love: but the duties of man and wife are such as are chiefly conversant in that love which is most ancient and merely natural, whose two prime statutes are to join itself to that which is good, and acceptable, and friendly; and to turn aside and depart from what is disagreeable, displeasing, and unlike. Of the two this latter is the strongest, and most equal to be regarded; for although a man may often be unjust in seeking that which he loves, yet he can never be unjust or blameable in retiring from his endless trouble and distaste, whenas his tarrying can redound to no true content on either side. Hate is of all things the mightiest divider; nay, is division itself. To couple hatred therefore, though wedlock try all her golden links and borrow to her aid all the iron manacles and fetters of law, it does but seek to twist a rope of sand, which was a task they say that posed the devil: and that sluggish fiend in hell, Ocnus, whom the poems tell of, brought his idle cordage to as good effect, which never served to bind with, but to feed the ass that stood at his elbow. And that the restrictive law against divorce attains as little to bind anything truly in a disjointed marriage, or to keep it bound, but serves only to feed the ignorance and definite impertinence of a doltish canon, were no absurd allusion. To hinder therefore those deep and serious regresses of nature in a reasonable soul, parting from that mistaken help which he justly seeks in a person created for him, recollecting himself from an unmeet help which was never meant, and to detain him by compulsion in such an unpredestined misery as this, is in diameter against both nature and institution. But to interpose a jurisdictive power over the inward and irremediable disposition of man, to command love and sympathy, to forbid dislike against the guiltless instinct of nature, is not within the province of any law to reach; and were indeed an uncommodious rudeness, not a just power. For that law may bandy with nature, and traverse her sage motions, was an error in Callicles the rhetorician, whom Socrates from high principles confutes in Plato's Gorgias. If therefore divorce may be so natural, and that law and nature are not to go contrary; then to forbid divorce compulsively is not only against nature but against law.

Next, it must be remembered, that all law is for some good that may be frequently attained without the admixture of a worse inconvenience; and therefore many gross faults, as ingratitude and the like, which are too far within the soul to be cured by constraint of law, are left only to be wrought on by conscience and persuasion. Which made Aristotle, in the 10th of his Ethics to Nicomachus, aim at a kind of division of law into private or persuasive, and public or compulsive. Hence it is, that the law forbidding divorce never attains to any good end of such prohibition but rather multiplies evil. For if nature's resistless sway in love or hate be once compelled, it grows careless of itself, vicious, useless to friends, unserviceable and spiritless to the commonwealth. Which Moses rightly foresaw, and all wise lawgivers that ever knew man, what kind of creature he was. The parliament also and clergy of England were not ignorant of this, when they consented that Harry VIII. might put away his queen Anne of Cleve, whom he could not like after he had been wedded half a year; unless it were that, contrary to the proverb, they made a necessity of that which might have been a virtue in them to do; for even the freedom and eminence of man's creation gives him to be a law in this matter to himself, being the head of the other sex which was made for him: whom therefore though he ought not to injure, yet neither should he be forced to retain in society to his own overthrow, nor to hear any judge therein above himself: it being also an unseemly affront to the sequestered and veiled modesty of that sex, to have her unpleasingness and other concealments bandied up and down, and aggravated in open court by those hired masters of tongue-fence. Such uncomely exigencies it befell no less a majesty than Henry VIII. to be reduced to, who, finding just reason in his conscience to forego his brother's wife, after many indignities of being deluded and made a boy of by those his two cardinal judges, was constrained at last, for want of other proof that she had been carnally known by Prince Arthur, even to uncover the nakedness of that virtuous lady and to recite openly the obscene evidence of his brother's chamberlain. Yet it pleased God to make him see all the tyranny of Rome, by discovering this which they exercised over divorce, and to make him the beginner of a reformation to this whole kingdom, by first asserting into his familiary power the right of just divorce. It is true, an adulteress cannot be shamed enough by any public proceeding; but the woman whose honour is not appeached is less injured by a silent dismission, being otherwise not illiberally dealt with, than to endure a clamouring debate of utterless things, in a business of that civil secrecy and difficult discerning as not to be overmuch questioned by nearest friends. Which drew that answer from the greatest and worthiest Roman of his time, Paulus Æmilius, being demanded why he would put away his wife for no visible reason? "This shoe," said he, and held it out on his foot, "is a neat shoe, a new shoe, and yet none of you know where it wrings me:" much less by the unfamiliar cognizance of a feed gamester can such a private difference be examined, neither ought it.

Again, if law aim at the firm establishment and preservation of matrimonial faith, we know that cannot thrive under violent means, but is the more violated. It is not when two unfortunately met are by the canon forced to draw in that yoke an unmerciful day's work of sorrow till death unharness them, that then the law keeps marriage most unviolated and unbroken; but when the law takes order that marriage be accountant and responsible to perform that society, whether it be religious, civil, or corporal, which may be conscionably required and claimed therein, or else to be dissolved if it cannot be undergone. This is to make marriage most indissoluble, by making it a just and equal dealer, a performer of those due helps, which instituted the covenant; being otherwise a most unjust contract, and no more to be maintained under tuition of law, than the vilest fraud, or cheat, or theft, that may be committed. But because this is such a secret kind of fraud or theft as cannot be discerned by law but only by the plaintiff himself; therefore to divorce was never counted a political or civil offence, neither to Jew nor Gentile, nor by any judicial intendment of Christ, further than could be discerned to transgress the allowance of Moses, which was of necessity so large that it doth all one as if it sent back the matter undeterminable at law, and intractable by rough dealing, to have instructions and admonitions bestowed about it by them whose spiritual office is to adjure and to denounce, and so left to the conscience. The law can only appoint the just and equal conditions of divorce; and is to look how it is an injury to the divorced, which in truth it can be none, as a mere separation; for if she consent, wherein has the law to right her? or consent not, then is it either just and so deserved, or if unjust such in all likelihood was the divorcer, and to part from an unjust man is a happiness, and no injury to be lamented. But suppose it to be an injury, the law is not able to amend it, unless she think it other than a miserable redress to return back from whence she was expelled or but entreated to be gone, or else to live apart, still married without marriage, a married widow. Last, if it be to chasten the divorcer, what law punishes a deed which is not moral but natural, a deed which cannot certainly be found to be an injury; or how can it be punished by prohibiting the divorce, but that the innocent must equally partake both in the shame and in the smart? So that which way soever we look, the law can to no rational purpose forbid divorce, it can only take care that the conditions of divorce be not injurious. Thus then we see the trial of law, how impertinent it is to the question of divorce, how helpless next, and then how hurtful.

CHAPTER XXII.

The last Reason why Divorce is not to be restrained by Law, it being against the Law of Nature and of Nations. The larger Proof whereof referred to Mr. Selden's Book, "De Jure Naturali et Gentium." An Objection of Paræus answered. How it ought to be ordered by the Church. That this will not breed any worse Inconvenience, nor so bad as is now suffered.

THEREFORE the last reason why it should not be, is the example we have, not only from the noblest and wisest commonwealths guided by the clearest light of human knowledge, but also from the divine testimonies of God himself lawgiving in person to a sanctified people. That all this is true whoso desires to know at large with least pains, and expects not here overlong rehearsals of that which is by others already so judiciously gathered, let him hasten to be acquainted with that noble volume written by our learned Selden, "Of the Law of Nature and of Nations," a work more useful and more worthy to be perused by whosoever studies to be a great man in wisdom, equity, and justice, than all those "decretals and sumless sums," which the pontifical clerks have doted on, ever since that unfortunate mother famously sinned thrice, and died impenitent of her bringing into the world those two misbegotten infants, and for ever infants, Lombard and Gratian, him the compiler of canon iniquity, the other the Tubal Cain of scholastic sophistry, whose overspreading barbarism hath not only infused their own bastardy upon the fruitfullest part of human learning, not only dissipated and dejected the clear light of nature in us, and of nations, but hath tainted also the fountains of divine doctrine, and rendered the pure and solid law of God unbeneficial to us by their calumnious dunceries. Yet this law which their unskilfulness hath made liable to all ignominy, the purity and wisdom of this law shall be the buckler of our dispute. Liberty of divorce we

T

claim not, we think not, but from this law; the dignity, the faith, the authority thereof is now grown among Christians, O astonishment, a labour of no mean difficulty and envy to defend. That it should not be counted a faltering dispense a flattering permission of sin, the bill of adultery a snare, is the expense of all this Apology. And all that we solicit is, that it may be suffered to stand in the place where God set it, amidst the firmament of His Holy Laws, to shine, as it was wont, upon the weaknesses and errors of men, perishing else in the sincerity of their honest purposes. For certain there is no memory of whoredoms and adulteries left among us now, when this warranted freedom of God's own giving is made dangerous, and discarded for a scroll of licence. It must be your suffrages and votes, O Englishmen, that this exploded decree of God and Moses may scape and come off fair, without the censure of a shameful abrogating: which, if yonder sun ride sure and means not to break word with us to-morrow, was never yet abrogated by our Saviour. Give sentence if you please that the frivolous canon may reverse the infallible judgment of Moses and his great director. Or if it be the Reformed writers, whose doctrine persuades this rather, their reasons I dare affirm are all silenced, unless it be only this. Paræus, on the Corinthians, would prove, that hardness of heart in divorce is no more now to be permitted, but to be amerced with fine and imprisonment. I am not willing to discover the forgettings of reverend men, yet here I must: what article or clause of the whole new covenant can Paræus bring, to exasperate the judicial law upon any infirmity under the Gospel? I say infirmity, for if it were the high hand of sin, the Law as little would have endured it as the Gospel. It would not stretch to the dividing of an inheritance; it refused to condemn adultery, not that these things should not be done at law, but to shew that the Gospel hath not the least influence upon judicial courts, much less to make them sharper and more heavy, least of all to arraign before a temporal judge that which the law without summons acquitted. "But," saith he, "the Law was the time of youth, under violent affections; the Gospel in us is mature age, and ought to subdue affections."

True, and so ought the Law too, if they be found inordinate, and not merely natural and blameless. Next I distinguish, that the time of the Law is compared to youth and pupilage in respect of the ceremonial part, which led the Jews as children through corporal and garish rudiments, until the fulness of time should reveal to them the higher lessons of faith and redemption. This is not meant of the moral part; therein it soberly concerned them not to be babies, but to be men in good earnest. The sad and awful majesty of that Law was not to be jested with. To bring a bearded nonage with lascivious dispensations before that throne had been a lewd affront, as it is now a gross mistake. But what discipline is this, Paræus, to nourish violent affections in youth by cockering and wanton indulgencies, and to chastise them in mature age with a boyish rod of correction? How much more coherent is it to Scripture, that the Law, as a strict schoolmaster, should have punished every trespass without indulgence so baneful to youth, and that the Gospel should now correct that by admonition and reproof only, in free and mature age, which was punished with stripes in the childhood and bondage of the Law? What, therefore, it allowed them so fairly, much less is to be whipped now, especially in penal courts: and if it ought now to trouble the conscience, why did that angry accuser and condemner Law reprieve it? So then, neither from Moses nor from Christ hath the magistrate any authority to proceed against it.

But what, shall then the disposal of that power return again to the master of a family? Wherefore not, since God there put it, and the presumptuous canon thence bereft it? This only must be provided, that the ancient manner be observed in the presence of the minister and other grave selected elders, who after they shall have admonished and pressed upon him the words of our Saviour, and he shall have protested, in the faith of the eternal Gospel, and the hope he has of happy resurrection, that otherwise than thus he cannot do, and thinks himself and this his case not contained in that prohibition of divorce which Christ pronounced, the matter not being of malice, but of nature, and so not capable of reconciling; to constrain him further were to unchristian him, to unman him, to throw the mountain of Sinai upon him, with the weight of the whole law to boot, flat against the liberty and essence of the gospel; and yet nothing available either to the sanctity of marriage, the good of husband, wife, or children, nothing profitable either to Church or Commonwealth, but hurtful and pernicious in all these respects. But this will bring in confusion: yet these cautious mistrusters might consider, that what they thus object lights not upon this book, but upon that which I engage against them, the Book of God and Moses, with all the wisdom and providence which had forecast the worst of confusion that could succeed, and yet thought fit of such a permission. But let them be of good cheer, it wrought so little disorder among the Jews, that from Moses till after the captivity, not one of the prophets thought it worth the rebuking; for that of Malachi well looked into will appear to be not against divorcing, but rather against keeping strange concubines, to the vexation of their Hebrew wives. If, therefore, we Christians may be thought as good and tractable as the Jews were—and certainly the prohibitors of divorce presume us to be better—then less confusion is to be feared for this among us than was among them. If we be worse, or but as bad, which lamentable examples confirm we are, then have we more, or at least as much, need of this permitted law as they to whom God therefore gave it, as they say, under a harsher covenant. Let not, therefore, the frailty of man go on thus inventing needless troubles to itself, to groan under the false imagination of a strictness never imposed from above; enjoining that for duty which is an impossible and vain supererogating. "Be not righteous overmuch," is the counsel of Ecclesiastes; "why shouldst thou destroy thyself?" Let us not be thus overcurious to strain at atoms, and yet to stop every vent and cranny of permissive liberty, lest nature, wanting those needful pores and breathing-places which God hath not debarred our weakness, either suddenly break out into some wide rupture of open vice and frantic heresy, or else inwardly fester with repining and blasphemous thoughts under an unreasonable and fruitless rigour of unwarranted law. Against which evils nothing can more beseem the Religion of the Church, or the Wisdom of the State, than to consider timely and provide. And in so doing let them not doubt but they shall vindicate the misreputed honour of God and his great lawgiver, by suffering him to give his own laws according to the condition of man's nature best known to him, without the unsufferable imputation of dispensing legally with many ages of ratified adultery. They shall recover the misattended words of Christ to the sincerity of their true sense from manifold contradictions, and shall open them with the key of Charity. Many helpless Christians they shall raise from the depth of sadness and distress, utterly unfitted as they are to serve God or man. Many they shall reclaim from obscure and giddy sects, many regain from dissolute and brutish licence, many from desperate hardness, if ever that were justly pleaded. They shall set free many daughters of Israel not wanting much of her sad plight whom "Satan had bound eighteen years." Man they shall restore to his just dignity and prerogative in nature, preferring the soul's free peace before the promiscuous draining of a carnal rage. Marriage, from a perilous hazard and snare, they shall reduce to be a more certain haven and retirement of happy society; when they shall judge according to God and Moses—and how not then according to Christ—when they shall judge it more wisdom and goodness to break that covenant seemingly and keep it really, than by compulsion of law to keep it seemingly and by compulsion of blameless nature to break it really, at least if it were ever truly joined. The vigour of discipline they may then turn with better success upon the prostitute looseness of the times, when men, finding in themselves the infirmities of former ages, shall not be constrained above the gift of God in them to unprofitable and impossible observances, never required from the civilest, the wisest, the holiest nations, whose other excellencies in moral virtue they never yet could equal. Last of all, to those whose mind is still to maintain textual restrictions, whereof the bare sound cannot consist sometimes with humanity, much less with Charity; I would ever answer, by putting them in remembrance of a command above all commands, which they seem to have forgot, and who spake it: in comparison whereof, this which they so exalt is but a petty and subordinate precept. "Let them go," therefore, with whom I am loth to couple them, yet they will needs run into the same blindness with the Pharisees; "let them go therefore," and consider well what this lesson means, "I will have mercy and not sacrifice;" for on that saying all the law and prophets depend; much more the Gospel, whose end and excellence is mercy and peace. Or if they cannot learn that, how will they hear this, which yet I shall not doubt to leave with them as a conclusion, that God the Son hath put all other things under his own feet, but his commandments he hath left all under the feet of Charity.

MAN AND CHILD.

"How charming is divine Philosophy!
Not harsh and crabbed as dull fools suppose,
But musical as is Apollo's lute,
And a perpetual feast of nectared sweets
Where no crude surfeit reigns."
—*Comus.*

OF EDUCATION.

MASTER HARTLIB,—I am long since persuaded that to say and do aught worth memory and imitation, no purpose or respect should sooner move us than simply the love of God and of mankind. Nevertheless, to write now the reforming of Education, though it be one of the greatest and noblest designs that can be thought on, and for the want whereof this nation perishes, I had not yet at this time been induced but by your earnest entreaties and serious conjurements; as having my mind diverted for the present in the pursuance of some other assertions, the knowledge and the use of which cannot but be a great furtherance both to the enlargement of truth and honest living with much more peace. Nor should the laws of any private friendship have prevailed with me to divide thus or transpose my former thoughts; but that I see those aims, those actions which have won you with me the esteem of a person sent hither by some good providence from a far country to be the occasion and incitement of great good to this island, and as I hear you have obtained the same repute with men of most approved wisdom and some of the highest authority among us, not to mention the learned correspondence which you hold in foreign parts, and the extraordinary pains and diligence which you have used in this matter both here and beyond the seas, either by the definite will of God so ruling, or the peculiar sway of nature, which also is God's working. Neither can I think, that so reputed and so valued as you are, you would, to the forfeit of your own discerning ability, impose upon me an unfit and overponderous argument; but that the satisfaction which you profess to have received from those incidental discourses which we have wandered into hath pressed and almost constrained you into a persuasion, that what you require from me in this point I neither ought nor can in conscience defer beyond this time both of so much need at once and so much opportunity to try what God hath determined. I will not resist, therefore, whatever it is either of divine or human obligement that you lay upon me; but will forthwith set down in writing, as you request me, that voluntary idea, which hath long in silence presented itself to me, of a better education, in extent and comprehension far more large, and yet of time far shorter and of attainment far more certain, than hath been yet in practice. Brief I shall endeavour to be; for that which I have to say assuredly this nation hath extreme need should be done sooner than spoken. To tell you, therefore, that I have benefited herein among old renowned authors I shall spare; and to search what many modern Januas and Didactics more than ever I shall read have projected, my inclination leads me not. But if you can accept of these few observations which have flowered off, and are, as it were, the burnishing of many contemplative years altogether spent in the search of religious and civil knowledge, and such as pleased you so well in the relating, I here give you them to dispose of."

The end, then, of learning is, to repair the ruins of our first parents by regaining to know God aright, and out of that knowledge to love him, to imitate him, to be like him, as we may the nearest by possessing our souls of true virtue, which, being united to the heavenly grace of faith, makes up the highest perfection. But because our understanding cannot in this body found itself but on sensible things, nor arrive so clearly to the knowledge of God and things invisible as by orderly conning over the visible and inferior creature, the same method is necessarily to be followed in all discreet teaching. And seeing every nation affords not experience and tradition enough for all kind of learning, therefore we are chiefly taught the languages of those people who have at any time been most industrious after Wisdom; so that Language is but the instrument conveying to us things useful to be known. And though a linguist should pride himself to have all the tongues that Babel cleft the world into, yet if he have not studied the solid things in them as well as the words and lexicons, he were nothing so much to be esteemed a learned man as any yeoman or tradesman competently wise in his mother-dialect only. Hence appear the many mistakes which have made learning generally so unpleasing and so unsuccessful. First, we do amiss to spend seven or eight years merely in scraping together so much miserable Latin and Greek as might be learned otherwise easily and delightfully in one year. And that which casts our proficiency therein so much behind, is our time lost in too oft idle vacancies given both to schools and universities; partly in a preposterous exaction, forcing the empty wits of children to compose themes, verses, and orations, which are the acts of ripest judgment, and the final work of a head filled by long reading and observing with elegant maxims and copious invention. These are not matters to be wrung from poor striplings, like blood out of the nose, or the plucking of untimely fruit; besides the ill habit which they get of wretched barbarising against the Latin and Greek idiom with their untutored Anglicisms, odious to be read, yet not to be avoided without a well-continued and judicious conversing among pure authors, digested, which they scarce taste. Whereas, if after some preparatory grounds of speech by their certain forms got into memory, they were led to the praxis hereof in some chosen short book lessened thoroughly to them, they might then forthwith proceed to learn the substance of good things and arts in due order, which would bring the whole language quickly into their power. This I take to be the most rational and most profitable way of learning Languages, and whereby we may best hope to give account to God of our youth spent herein. And for the usual method of teaching Arts, I deem it to be an old error of Universities, not yet well recovered from the scholastic grossness of barbarous ages, that instead of beginning with arts most easy (and those be such as are most obvious to the sense), they present their young unmatriculated novices at first coming with the most intellective abstractions of logic and metaphysics; so that they having but newly left those grammatic flats and shallows where they stuck unreasonably to learn a few words with lamentable construction, and now on the sudden transported under another climate to be tossed and turmoiled with their unballasted wits in fathomless and unquiet deeps of controversy, do, for the most part, grow into hatred and contempt of learning, mocked and deluded all this while with ragged notions and babblements, while they expected worthy and delightful knowledge; till poverty or youthful years call them importunately their several ways, and hasten them, with the sway of friends, either to an ambitious and mercenary, or ignorantly zealous Divinity: some allured to the trade of Law, grounding their purposes not on the prudent and heavenly contemplation of justice and equity, which was never taught them, but on the promising and pleasing thoughts of litigious terms, fat contentions, and flowing fees: others betake them to State Affairs with souls so unprincipled in virtue and true generous breeding, that flattery, and court-shifts, and tyrannous aphorisms appear to them the highest points of wisdom, instilling their barren hearts with a conscientious slavery, if, as I rather think, it be not feigned: others, lastly, of a more delicious and airy spirit, retire themselves, knowing no better, to the enjoyments of ease and luxury, living out their days in feast and jollity, which, indeed, is the wisest and safest course of all these, unless they were with more integrity undertaken. And these are the errors, and these are the fruits of mis-spending our prime youth at the schools and universities, as we do, either in learning mere words, or such things chiefly as were better unlearnt.

I shall detain you no longer in the demonstration of what we should not do, but straight conduct you to a hillside, where I will point you out the right path of a virtuous and noble education; laborious indeed at the first ascent, but else so smooth, so green, so full of goodly prospect and melodious sounds on every side, that the harp of Orpheus was not more charming. I doubt not but ye shall have more ado to drive our dullest and laziest youth, our stocks and stubs, from the infinite desire of such a happy nurture, than we have now to haul and drag our choicest and hopefullest wits to that asinine feast of sow-thistles and brambles which is commonly set before them as all the food and entertainment of their tenderest and most docible age. I call, therefore, a complete and generous Education, that which fits a man to perform justly, skilfully, and magnanimously all the offices, both private and public, of peace and war. And how all this may be done between twelve and one-and-twenty, less time than is now bestowed in pure trifling at grammar and sophistry, is to be thus ordered :—

First, to find out a spacious house and ground about it fit for an Academy, and big enough to lodge one hundred and fifty persons, whereof twenty or thereabout may be attendants, all under the government of one who shall be thought of desert sufficient and ability either to do all or wisely to direct and oversee it done. This place should be at once both School and University, not needing a remove to any other house of scholarship, except it be some peculiar college of law or physic where they mean to be practitioners; but as for those general studies which take up all our time from Lilly to the commencing, as they term it, Master of Art, it should be absolute. After this pattern as many edifices may be converted to this use as shall be needful in every city throughout this land, which would tend much to the increase of learning and civility everywhere. This number, less or more, thus collected, to the convenience of a foot-company or interchangeably two troops of cavalry, should divide their day's work into three parts, as it lies orderly—their Studies, their Exercise, and their Diet.

For their Studies: first, they should begin with the chief and necessary rules of some good grammar, either that now used, or any better; and while this is doing, their speech is to be fashioned to a distinct and clear pronunciation, as near as may be to the Italian, especially in the vowels. For we Englishmen, being far northerly, do not open our mouths in the cold air wide enough to grace a southern tongue, but are observed by all other nations to speak exceeding close and inward; so that to smatter Latin with an English mouth is as ill a hearing as Law French. Next, to make them expert in the usefullest points of grammar, and withal to season them and win them early to the love of virtue and true labour, ere any flattering seducement or vain principle seize them wandering, some easy and delightful book of education should be read to them, whereof the Greeks have store, as Cebes, Plutarch, and other Socratic discourses; but in Latin we have none of classic authority extant, except the two or three first books of Quintilian and some select pieces elsewhere. But here the main skill and groundwork will be to temper them with such lectures and explanations upon every opportunity as may lead and draw them in willing obedience, inflamed with the study of learning and the admiration of virtue, stirred up with high hopes of living to be brave men and worthy patriots, dear to God and famous to all ages: that they may despise and scorn all their childish and ill-taught qualities, to delight in manly and liberal exercises; which he who hath the art and proper eloquence to catch them with, what with mild and effectual persuasions, and what with the intimation of some fear, if need be, but chiefly by his own example, might in a short space gain them to an incredible diligence and courage, infusing into their young breasts such an ingenuous and noble ardour as would not fail to make many of them renowned and matchless men. At the same time, some other hour of the day might be taught them the rules of arithmetic, and, soon after, the elements of geometry, even playing, as the old manner was. After evening repast till bed-time their thoughts would be best taken up in the easy grounds of Religion and the story of Scripture. The next step would be to the authors of agriculture, Cato, Varro, and Columella, for the matter is most easy; and if the language is difficult, so much the better; it is not a difficulty above their years. And here will be an occasion of inciting and enabling them hereafter to improve the tillage of their country, to recover the bad soil, and to remedy the waste that is made of good; for this was one of Hercules' praises. Ere half these authors be read (which will soon be, with plying hard and daily) they cannot choose but be masters of an ordinary prose: so that it will be then seasonable for them to learn in any modern author the use of the globes and all the maps, first with the old names and then with the new. Or they might then be capable to read any compendious method of natural philosophy; and, at the same time, might be entering into the Greek tongue, after the same manner as was before prescribed for the Latin; whereby the difficulties of grammar being soon overcome, all the historical physiology of Aristotle and Theophrastus are open before them, and, as I may say, under contribution. The like access will be to Vitruvius, to Seneca's "Natural Questions," to Mela, Celsus, Pliny, or Solinus. And having thus past the principles of arithmetic, geometry, astronomy, and geography, with a general compact of physics, they may descend in mathematics to the instrumental science of trigonometry, and from thence to fortification, architecture, enginery, or navigation. And in natural philosophy they may proceed leisurely from the history of meteors, minerals, plants, and living creatures, as far as anatomy. Then also in course might be read to them out of some not tedious writer the institution of physic; that they may know the tempers, the humours, the seasons, and how to manage a crudity, which he who can wisely and timely do is not only a great physician to himself and to his friends, but also may at some time or other save an army by this frugal and expenseless means only, and not let the healthy and stout bodies of young men rot away under him for want of this discipline, which is a great pity, and no less a shame to the commander. To set forward all these proceedings in nature and mathematics, what hinders but that they may procure, as oft as shall be needful, the helpful experiences of hunters, fowlers, fishermen, shepherds, gardeners, apothecaries; and in other sciences, architects, engineers, mariners, anatomists, who, doubtless, would be ready, some for reward and some to favour such a hopeful seminary. And this would give them such a real tincture of natural knowledge as they shall never forget, but daily augment with delight. Then also those poets which are now counted most hard will be both facile and pleasant, Orpheus, Hesiod, Theocritus, Aratus, Nicander, Oppian, Dionysius; and, in Latin, Lucretius, Manilius, and the rural part of Virgil.

By this time years and good general precepts will have furnished them more distinctly with that act of reason which in ethics is called proairesis, that they may with some judgment contemplate upon moral good and evil. Then will be required a special reinforcement of constant and sound endoctrinating to set them right and firm, instructing them more amply in the knowledge of virtue and the hatred of vice, while their young and pliant affections are led through all the moral works of Plato, Xenophon, Cicero, Plutarch, Laertius, and those Locrian remnants; but still to be reduced in their nightward studies, wherewith they close the day's work, under the determinate sentence of David or Solomon, or the Evangels and Apostolic Scriptures. Being perfect in the knowledge of personal duty, they may then begin the study of economics. And either now or before this they may have easily learned at any odd hour the Italian tongue. And soon after, but with wariness and good antidote, it would be wholesome enough to let them taste some choice comedies, Greek, Latin, or Italian; those tragedies also that treat of household matters, as Trachiniæ, Alcestis, and the like. The next remove must be to the study of politics; to know the beginning, end, and reasons of political societies, that they may not, in a dangerous fit of the commonwealth, be such poor shaken uncertain reeds, of such a tottering conscience as many of our great councillors have lately shown themselves, but steadfast pillars of the State. After this they are to dive into the grounds of law and legal justice, delivered first and with best warrant by Moses, and, as far as human prudence can be trusted, in those extolled remains of Grecian lawgivers, Lycurgus, Solon, Zaleucus, Charondas; and thence to all the Roman edicts and tables, with their Justinian; and so down to the Saxon and common laws of England and the statutes. Sundays also and every evening may now be understandingly spent in the highest matters of theology and church history, ancient and modern: and ere this time at a set hour the Hebrew tongue might have been gained, that the Scriptures may be now read in their own original; whereto it would be no impossibility to add the Chaldee and the Syrian dialect. When all these employments are well conquered, then will the choice histories, heroic poems, and Attic tragedies of stateliest and most regal argument, with all the famous political orations, offer themselves; which, if they were not only read, but some of them got by memory, and solemnly pronounced with right accent and grace, as might be taught, would endue them even with the spirit and vigour of Demosthenes or Cicero, Euripides or Sophocles. And now, lastly, will be the time to read with them those organic arts which enable men to discourse and write perspicuously, elegantly, and according to the fitted style of lofty, mean, or lowly. Logic, therefore, so much as is useful, is to be referred to this due place, with all her well-couched heads and topics, until it be time to open her contracted palm into a graceful and ornate rhetoric taught out of the rule of Plato, Aristotle, Phalereus, Cicero, Hermogenes, Longinus. To which poetry would be made subsequent, or, indeed, rather precedent, as being less subtile and fine, but more simple, sensuous, and passionate; I mean not here the prosody of a verse, which they could not but have hit on before among the rudiments of grammar, but that sublime art which in Aristotle's Poetics, in Horace, and the Italian commentaries of Castelvetro, Tasso, Mazzoni, and others, teaches what the laws are of a true epic poem, what of a dramatic, what of a lyric, what decorum is, which is the grand masterpiece to observe. This would make them soon perceive what despicable creatures our common rhymers and playwriters be; and show them what religious, what glorious and magnificent use might be made of poetry, both in divine and human things. From hence, and not till now, will be the right season of forming them to be able writers and composers in every excellent matter, when they shall be thus fraught with an universal insight into things: or whether they be to speak in parliament or council, honour and attention would be waiting on their lips. There would then appear in pulpits other visages, other gestures, and stuff otherwise wrought than we now sit under, ofttimes to as great a trial of our patience as any other that they preach to us. These are the studies wherein our noble and our gentle youth ought to bestow their time in a disciplinary way from twelve to one-and-twenty, unless they rely more upon their ancestors dead than upon themselves living. In which methodical course it is so supposed they must proceed by the steady pace of learning onward, as at convenient times for memory's sake to retire back into the middle ward, and sometimes into the rear of what they have been taught, until they have confirmed and solidly united the whole body of their perfected knowledge, like the last embattling of a Roman legion.

Now will be worth the seeing what exercises and recreations may best agree and become those studies.

THEIR EXERCISE.

The Course of Study hitherto briefly described is, what I can guess by reading, likest to those ancient and famous Schools of Pythagoras, Plato, Isocrates, Aristotle, and such others, out of which were bred such a number of renowned philosophers, orators, historians, poets, and princes all over Greece, Italy, and Asia, besides the flourishing studies of Cyrene and Alexandria. But herein it shall exceed them, and supply a defect as great as that which Plato noted in the commonwealth of Sparta. Whereas that city trained up their youth most for war, and these in their Academies and Lycæum all for the gown, this institution of breeding which I here delineate shall be equally good both for peace and war. Therefore, about an hour and a half ere they eat at noon should be allowed them for exercise, and due rest afterwards; but the time for this may be enlarged at pleasure, according as their rising in the morning shall be early. The exercise which I commend first is the exact use of their weapon, to guard, and to strike safely with edge or point. This will keep them healthy, nimble, strong, and well in breath; is also the likeliest means to make them grow large and tall, and to inspire them with a gallant and fearless courage, which being tempered with seasonable lectures and precepts to make them of true fortitude and patience, will turn into a native and heroic valour, and make them hate the cowardice of doing wrong. They must be also practised in all the locks and gripes of wrestling, wherein Englishmen are wont to excel, as need may often be in fight to tug, to grapple, and to close. And this, perhaps, will be enough wherein to prove and heat their single strength. The interim of unsweating themselves regularly, and convenient rest before meat, may both with profit and delight be taken up in recreating and composing their travailed spirits with the solemn and divine harmonies of music heard or learned, either whilst the skilful organist plies his grave and fancied descant in lofty fugues, or the whole symphony with artful and unimaginable touches adorn and grace the well-studied chords of some choice composer; sometimes the lute or soft organ-stop, waiting on elegant voices either to religious, martial, or civil ditties, which, if wise men and prophets be not extremely out, have a great power over dispositions and manners to smooth and make them gentle from rustic harshness and distempered passions. The like also would not be unexpedient after meat, to assist and cherish nature in her first concoction, and send their minds back to study in good tune and satisfaction.

Where having followed it under vigilant eyes until about two hours before supper, they are, by a sudden alarum or watchword, to be called out of their military motions, under sky or covert, according to the season, as was the Roman wont; first on foot, then, as their age permits, on horseback to all the art of cavalry; that having in sport, but with much exactness and daily muster, served out the rudiments of their soldiership in all the skill of embattling, marching, encamping, fortifying, besieging, and battering, with all the helps of ancient and modern stratagems, tactics, and warlike maxims, they may, as it were out of a long war, come forth renowned and perfect commanders in the service of their country. They would not then, if they were trusted with fair and hopeful armies, suffer them for want of just and wise discipline to shed away from about them like sick feathers, though they be never so oft supplied; they would not suffer their empty and unrecruitable colonels of twenty men in a company to quaff out or convey into secret hoards the wages of a delusive list and miserable remnant, yet in the meanwhile to be overmastered with a score or two of drunkards, the only soldiery left about them, or else to comply with all rapines and violences. No, certainly, if they knew aught of that knowledge which belongs to good men or good governors they would not suffer these things.

But to return to our own institute. Besides these constant exercises at home, there is another opportunity of gaining experience to be won from pleasure itself abroad. In those vernal seasons of the year, when the air is calm and pleasant, it were an injury and sullenness against nature not to go out and see her riches and partake in her rejoicing with heaven and earth. I should not, therefore, be a persuader to them of studying much then, after two or three years that they have well laid their grounds, but to ride out in companies with prudent and staid guides to all the quarters of the land, learning and observing all places of strength, all commodities of building and of soil for towns and tillage, harbours, and ports for trade. Sometimes taking sea as far as to our navy, to learn there also what they can in the practical knowledge of sailing and sea-fight. These ways would try all their peculiar gifts of nature, and if there were any secret excellence among them, would fetch it out and give it fair opportunities to advance itself by, which could not but mightily redound to the good of this nation, and bring into fashion again those old admired virtues and excellencies with far more advantage now in this purity of Christian knowledge. Nor shall we then need the monsieurs of Paris to take our hopeful youth into their slight and prodigal custodies, and send them over back again transformed into mimics, apes, and kekshose. But if they desire to see other countries at three or four and twenty years of age, not to learn principles but to enlarge experience and make wise observation, they will by that time be such as shall deserve the regard and honour of all men where they pass, and the society and friendship of those in all places who are best and most eminent. And perhaps then other nations will be glad to visit us for their breeding, or else to imitate us in their own country.

Now, lastly, for their Diet there cannot be much to say, save only that it would be best in the same house; for much time else would be lost abroad, and many ill habits got; and that it should be plain, healthful, and moderate I suppose is out of controversy.

Thus, Mr. Hartlib, you have a general view in writing, as your desire was, of that which at several times I had discoursed with you concerning the best and noblest way of education; not beginning, as some have done, from the cradle, which yet might be worth many considerations, if brevity had not been my scope. Many other circumstances also I could have mentioned, but this, to such as have the worth in them to make trial, for light and direction may be enough. Only I believe that this is not a bow for every man to shoot in that counts himself a teacher, but will require sinews almost equal to those which Homer gave Ulysses; yet I am withal persuaded that it may prove much more easy in the assay than it now seems at distance, and much more illustrious: howbeit not more difficult than I imagine, and that imagination presents me with nothing but very happy and very possible according to best wishes, if God have so decreed, and this age have spirit and capacity enough to apprehend.

MAN AND MAN.

"Liberty
. . . always with right Reason dwells
Twinned, and from her hath no dividual being
Reason in Man obscured, or not obeyed,
Immediately inordinate Desires
And upstart Passions catch the Government
From Reason, and to Servitude reduce
Man till then free. Therefore, since he permits
Within himself unworthy powers to reign
Over free Reason, God, in Judgment just,
Subjects him from without to violent Lords,
Who oft as undeservedly enthral
His outward Freedom : Tyranny must be ;
Though to the Tyrant thereby no excuse."
—*Paradise Lost.* Book xii.

AREOPAGITICA:

A SPEECH FOR THE LIBERTY OF UNLICENSED PRINTING.

To the Parliament of England.

THEY, who to states and governors of the Commonwealth direct their speech, high Court of Parliament, or wanting such access in a private condition, write that which they foresee may advance the public good, I suppose them, as at the beginning of no mean endeavour, not a little altered and moved inwardly in their minds; some with doubt of what will be the success, others with fear of what will be the censure, some with hope, others with confidence of what they have to speak. And me perhaps each of these dispositions, as the subject was whereon I entered, may have at other times variously affected; and likely might in these foremost expressions now also disclose which of them swayed most, but that the very attempt of this address thus made, and the thought of whom it hath recourse to, hath got the power within me to a passion far more welcome than incidental to a preface.

Which though I stay not to confess ere any ask I shall be blameless, if it be no other than the joy and gratulation which it brings to all who wish to promote their country's liberty, whereof this whole discourse proposed will be a certain testimony, if not a trophy. For this is not the liberty which we can hope, that no grievance ever should arise in the Commonwealth, that let no man in this world expect; but when complaints are freely heard, deeply considered, and speedily reformed, then is the utmost bound of civil liberty obtained that wise men look for. To which if I now manifest, by the very sound of this which I shall utter, that we are already in good part arrived, and yet from such a steep disadvantage of tyranny and superstition grounded into our principles as was beyond the manhood of a Roman recovery, it will be attributed first, as is most due, to the strong assistance of God, our deliverer; next, to your faithful guidance and undaunted wisdom, Lords and Commons of England. Neither is it in God's esteem, the diminution of His glory, when honourable things are spoken of good men, and worthy magistrates; which if I now first should begin to do, after so fair a progress of your laudable deeds and such a long obligement upon the whole realm to your indefatigable virtues, I might be justly reckoned among the tardiest and the unwillingest of them that praise ye.

Nevertheless there being three principal things, without which all praising is but courtship and flattery: first, when that only is praised which is solidly worth praise; next, when greatest likelihoods are brought that such things are truly and really in those persons to whom they are ascribed; the other, when he who praises, by showing that such his actual persuasion is of whom he writes, can demonstrate that he flatters not: the former two of these I have heretofore endeavoured, rescuing the employment from him who went about to impair your merits with a trivial and malignant encomium; the latter, as belonging chiefly to mine own acquittal, that whom I so extolled I did not flatter, hath been reserved opportunely to this occasion. For he who freely magnifies what hath been nobly done and fears not to declare as freely what might be done better, gives ye the best covenant of his fidelity, and that his loyalest affection and his hope waits on your proceedings. His highest praising is not flattery, and his plainest advice is a kind of praising. For though I should affirm and hold by argument, that it would fare better with truth, with learning, and the commonwealth, if one of your published orders, which I should name, were called in; yet at the same time it could not but much redound to the lustre of your mild and equal government, whenas private persons are hereby animated to think ye better pleased with public advice than other statists have been delighted heretofore with public flattery. And men will then see what difference there is between the magnanimity of a triennial parliament and that jealous haughtiness of prelates and cabin counsellors that usurped of late, whenas they shall observe ye in the midst of your victories and successes more gently brooking written exceptions against a voted order, than other courts, which had produced nothing worth memory but the weak ostentation of wealth, would have endured the least signified dislike at any sudden proclamation.

If I should thus far presume upon the meek demeanour of your civil and gentle greatness, Lords and Commons, as what your published order hath directly said that to gainsay, I might defend myself with ease if any should accuse me of being new or insolent, did they but know how much better I find ye esteem it to imitate the old and elegant humanity of Greece than the barbaric pride of a Hunnish and Norwegian stateliness. And out of those ages to whose polite wisdom and letters we owe that we are not yet Goths and Jutlanders, I could name him who from his private house wrote that discourse to the Parliament of Athens that persuades them to change the form of democracy which was then established. Such honour was done in those days to men who professed the study of wisdom and eloquence, not only in their own country but in other lands, that cities and signiories heard them gladly and with great respect, if they had aught in public to admonish the state. Thus did Dion Prusæus, a stranger and a private orator, counsel the Rhodians against a former edict; and I abound with other like examples, which to set here would be superfluous. But if from the industry of a life wholly dedicated to studious labours and those natural endowments haply not the worst for two and fifty degrees of northern latitude so much must be derogated as to count me not equal to any of those who had this privilege, I would obtain to be thought not so inferior, as yourselves are superior to the most of them who received their counsel; and how far you excel them, be assured, Lords and Commons, there can no greater testimony appear than when your prudent spirit acknowledges and obeys the voice of reason, from what quarter soever it be heard speaking; and renders ye as willing to repeal any act of your own setting forth as any set forth by your predecessors.

If ye be thus resolved, as it were injury to think ye were not, I know not what should withhold me from presenting ye with a fit instance wherein to show both that love of truth which ye eminently profess and that uprightness of your judgment which is not wont to be partial to yourselves, by judging over again that order which ye have ordained "to regulate printing: that no book, pamphlet, or paper shall be henceforth printed, unless the same be first approved and licensed by such, or at least one of such, as shall be thereto appointed." For that part which preserves justly every man's copy to himself, or provides for the poor, I touch not; only wish they be not made pretences to abuse and persecute honest and painful men who offend not in either of these particulars. But that other clause of licensing books, which we thought had died with his brother quadragesimal and matrimonial when the prelates expired, I shall now attend with such a homily as shall lay before ye, first, the inventors of it to be those whom ye will be loath to own; next, what is to be thought in general of reading, whatever sort the books be; and that this order avails nothing to the suppressing of scandalous, seditious, and libellous books, which were mainly intended to be suppressed. Last, that it will be primely to the discouragement of all learning, and the stop of truth, not only by disexercising and blunting our abilities in what we know already, but by hindering and cropping the discovery that might be yet further made both in religious and civil wisdom.

I deny not but that it is of greatest concernment in the Church and Commonwealth, to have a vigilant eye how books demean themselves, as well as men; and thereafter to confine, imprison, and do sharpest justice on them as malefactors. For books are not absolutely dead things, but do contain a potency of life in them to be as active as that soul was whose progeny they are; nay, they do preserve as in a vial the purest efficacy and extraction of that living intellect that bred them. I know they are as lively and as vigorously productive as those fabulous dragon's teeth: and being sown up and down, may chance to spring up armed men. And yet, on the other hand, unless wariness be used, as good almost kill a man as kill a good book. Who kills a man kills a reasonable creature, God's image; but he who destroys a good book, kills Reason itself, kills the image of God, as it were, in the eye. Many a man lives a burden to the earth; but a good book is the precious life blood of a master-spirit, embalmed and treasured up on purpose to a life beyond life. It is true, no age can restore a life, whereof, perhaps, there is no great loss; and revolutions of ages do not oft recover the loss of a rejected truth, for the want of which whole nations fare the worse. We should be wary, therefore, what persecution we raise against the living labours of public men, how we spill that seasoned life of man preserved and stored up in books; since we see a kind of homicide may be thus committed, sometimes a martyrdom, and if it extend to the whole impression, a kind of massacre, whereof the execution ends not in the slaying of an elemental life, but strikes at the ethereal and fifth essence, the breath of reason itself; slays an immortality rather than a life. But lest I should be condemned of introducing licence while I oppose licensing, I refuse not the pains to be so much historical as will serve to show what hath been done by ancient and famous commonwealths against this disorder till the very time that this project of licensing, crept out of the inquisition, was catched up by our prelates, and hath caught some of our presbyters.

In Athens, where books and wits were ever busier than in any other part of Greece; I find but only two sorts of writings which the magistrate cared to take notice of; those either blasphemous and atheistical, or libellous. Thus the books of Protagoras were by the judges of Areopagus commanded to be burnt, and himself banished the territory, for a discourse begun with his confessing not to know "whether there were gods, or whether not." And against defaming, it was agreed that none should be traduced by name, as was the manner of Vetus Comœdia, whereby we may guess how they censured libelling. And this course was quick enough, as Cicero writes, to quell both the desperate wits of other atheists and the open way of defaming, as the event showed. Of other sects and opinions, though tending to voluptuousness and the denying of divine Providence, they took no heed. Therefore we do not read that either Epicurus or that libertine school of Cyrene, or what the Cynic impudence uttered, was ever questioned by the laws. Neither is it recorded that the writings of those old comedians were suppressed, though the acting of them were forbid. And that Plato commended the reading of Aristophanes, the loosest of them all, to his royal scholar, Dionysius, is commonly known, and may be excused if holy Chrysostom, as is reported, nightly studied so much the same author, and had the art to cleanse a scurrilous vehemence into the style of a rousing sermon.

That other leading city of Greece, Lacedæmon, considering that Lycurgus their lawgiver was so addicted to elegant learning as to have been the first that brought out of Ionia the scattered works of Homer, and sent the poet Thales from Crete to prepare and mollify the Spartan surliness with his smooth songs and odes, the better to plant among them law and civility, it is to be wondered how Museless and unbookish they were, minding nought but the feats of war. There needed no licensing of books among them, for they disliked all but their own Laconic apophthegms, and took a slight occasion to chase Archilochus out of their city, perhaps for composing in a higher strain than their own soldiery ballads and roundels could reach to; or if it were for his broad verses, they were not therein so cautious but they were as dissolute in their promiscuous conversing; whence Euripides affirms, in Andromache, that their women were all unchaste.

This much may give us light after what sort of books were prohibited among the Greeks. 'The Romans, also for many ages trained up only to a military roughness, resembling most the Lacedæmonian guise, knew of learning little but what their twelve tables and the pontific college with their augurs and flamens taught them in religion and law; so unacquainted with other learning, that when Carneades and Critolaus, with the stoic Diogenes, coming ambassadors to Rome, took thereby occasion to give the city a taste of their philosophy, they were suspected for seducers by no less a man than Cato the Censor, who moved it in the Senate to dismiss them speedily, and to banish all such Attic babblers out of Italy. But Scipio and others of the noblest senators withstood him and his old Sabine austerity; honoured and admired the men; and the Censor himself at last, in his old age, fell to the study of that whereof before he was so scrupulous. And yet, at the same time, Nævius and Plautus, the first Latin comedians, had filled the city with all the borrowed scenes of Menander and Philemon. Then began to be considered there also what was to be done to libellous books and authors; for Nævius was quickly cast into prison for his unbridled pen, and released by the tribunes upon his recantation: we read also that libels were burnt, and the makers punished, by Augustus.

The like severity, no doubt, was used, if aught were impiously written against their esteemed gods. Except in these two points, how the world went in books, the magistrate kept no reckoning. And therefore Lucretius, without impeachment, versifies his Epicurism to Memmius, and had the honour to be set forth the second time by Cicero, so great a father of the commonwealth; although himself disputes against that opinion in his own writings. Nor was the satirical sharpness or naked plainness of Lucilius, or Catullus, or Flaccus, by any order prohibited. And for matters of State, the story of Titus Livius, though it extolled that part which Pompey held, was not therefore suppressed by Octavius Cæsar, of the other faction. But that Naso was by him banished in his old age, for the wanton poems of his youth, was but a mere covert of state over some secret cause; and besides, the books were neither banished nor called in. From hence, we shall meet with little else but tyranny in the Roman empire, that we may not marvel if not so often bad as good books were silenced. I shall therefore deem to have been large enough, in producing what among the ancients was punishable to write, save only which, all other arguments were free to treat on.

By this time the emperors were become Christians, whose discipline in this point I do not find to have been more severe than what was formerly in practice. The books of those whom they took to be grand heretics were examined, refuted, and condemned in the General Councils; and not till then were prohibited, or burnt, by authority of the emperor. As for the writings of heathen authors, unless they were plain invectives against Christianity, as those of Porphyrius and Proclus, they met with no interdict that can be cited, till about the year 400, in a Carthaginian Council, wherein bishops themselves were forbid to read the books of Gentiles, but heresies they might read; while others long before them, on the contrary, scrupled more the books of heretics, than of Gentiles. And that the primitive Councils and bishops were wont only to declare what books were not commendable, passing no further, but leaving it to each one's conscience to read or to lay by, till after the year 800, is observed already by Padre Paolo, the great unmasker of the Trentine council. After which time the popes of Rome, engrossing what they pleased of political rule into their own hands, extended their dominion over men's eyes, as they had before over their judgments, burning and prohibiting to be read what they fancied not; yet sparing in their censures, and the books not many which they so dealt with; till Martin the Fifth, by his bull, not only prohibited, but was the first that excommunicated the reading of heretical books; for about that time Wyclif and Huss growing terrible, were they who first drove the papal court to a stricter policy of prohibiting. Which course Leo the Tenth and his successors followed, until the Council of Trent and the Spanish Inquisition engendering together, brought forth or perfected those catalogues and expurging indexes that rake through the entrails of many an old good author, with a violation worse than any could be offered to his tomb.

Nor did they stay in matters heretical, but any subject that was not to their palate they either condemned in a prohibition, or had it straight into the new purgatory of an index. To fill up the measure of encroachment, their last invention was to ordain that no book, pamphlet, or paper should be printed—as if St. Peter had bequeathed them the keys of the press also as well as of Paradise) unless it were approved and licensed under the hands of two or three gluttonous friars. For example:—

"Let the chancellor Cini be pleased to see if in this present work be contained aught that may withstand the printing.
"Vincent Rabbata, Vicar of Florence."

"I have seen this present work, and find nothing athwart the Catholic faith and good manners: in witness whereof I have given, &c. "Nicolo Cini, Chancellor of Florence."

"Attending the precedent relation, it is allowed that this present work of Davanzati may be printed.
"Vincent Rabbata, &c."

"It may be printed, July 15.
"Friar Simon Mompei d'Amelia, Chancellor of the Holy Office in Florence."

Sure they have a conceit, if he of the bottomless pit had not long since broke prison, that this quadruple exorcism would bar him down. I fear their next design will be to get into their custody the licensing of that which they say Claudius intended,*

* "Quo veniam daret flatum crepitumque ventris in convivio emittendi."— *Suelon, in Claudio.*

but went not through with. Vouchsafe to see another of their forms, the Roman stamp:—

> "Imprimatur, If it seem good to the reverend master of the Holy Palace. "Belcastro, Vicegerent."
>
> "Imprimatur,
> "Friar Nicholo Rodolphi, Master of the Holy Palace."

Sometimes five imprimaturs are seen together, dialogue wise, in the piazza of one titlepage, complimenting and ducking each to other with their shaven reverences, whether the author, who stands by in perplexity at the foot of his epistle, shall to the press or to the sponge. These are the pretty responsories, these are the dear antiphonies, that so bewitched of late our prelates and their chaplains, with the goodly echo they made; and besotted us to the gay imitation of a lordly Imprimatur, one from Lambeth-house, another from the west end of Paul's; so apishly romanizing, that the word of command still was set down in Latin; as if the learned grammatical pen that wrote it would cast no ink without Latin; or perhaps, as they thought, because no vulgar tongue was worthy to express the pure conceit of an Imprimatur; but rather, as I hope, for that our English, the language of men ever famous and foremost in the achievements of liberty, will not easily find servile letters enow to spell such a dictatory presumption Englished.

And thus ye have the inventors and the original of Book Licensing ripped up and drawn as lineally as any pedigree. We have it not, that can be heard of, from any ancient state, or polity, or church, nor by any statute left us by our ancestors elder or later; nor from the modern custom of any reformed city or church abroad; but from the most Antichristian Council, and the most tyrannous Inquisition that ever inquired. Till then books were ever as freely admitted into the world as any other birth; the issue of the brain was no more stifled than the issue of the womb: no envious Juno sat cross-legged over the nativity of any man's intellectual offspring; but if it proved a monster, who denies but that it was justly burnt, or sunk into the sea? But that a book, in worse condition than a peccant soul, should be to stand before a jury ere it be born to the world, and undergo yet in darkness the judgment of Rhadamanth and his colleagues, ere it can pass the ferry backward into light, was never heard before, till that mysterious iniquity, provoked and troubled at the first entrance of Reformation, sought out new limbos and new hells wherein they might include our books also within the number of their damned. And this was the rare morsel so officiously snatched up, and so ill-favouredly imitated by our inquisiturient bishops, and the attendant minorities, their chaplains. That ye like not now these most certain authors of this licensing order, and that all sinister intention was far distant from your thoughts when ye were importuned the passing it, all men who know the integrity of your actions, and how ye honour truth, will clear ye readily.

But some will say, what though the inventors were bad, the thing for all that may be good. It may so; yet if that thing be no such deep invention, but obvious and easy for any man to light on, and yet best and wisest commonwealths through all ages and occasions have forborne to use it, and falsest seducers and oppressors of men were the first who took it up, and to no other purpose but to obstruct and hinder the first approach of reformation; I am of those who believe, it will be a harder alchymy than Lullius ever knew, to sublimate any good use out of such an invention. Yet this only is what I request to gain from this reason, that it may be held a dangerous and suspicious fruit, as certainly it deserves, for the tree that bore it, until I can dissect one by one the properties it has. But I have first to finish, as was propounded, what is to be thought in general of reading books, whatever sort they be, and whether be more the benefit or the harm that thence proceeds.

Not to insist upon the examples of Moses, Daniel, and Paul, who were skilful in all the learning of the Egyptians, Chaldeans, and Greeks, which could not probably be without reading their books of all sorts, in Paul especially, who thought it no defilement to insert into Holy Scripture the sentences of three Greek poets, and one of them a tragedian; the question was notwithstanding sometimes controverted among the primitive doctors, but with great odds on that side which affirmed it both lawful and profitable, as was then evidently perceived when Julian the Apostate and subtlest enemy to our faith made a decree forbidding Christians the study of heathen learning; for, said he, they wound us with our own weapons, and with our own arts and sciences they overcome us. And indeed the Christians were put so to their shifts by this crafty means, and so much in danger to decline into all ignorance, that the two Appollinarii were fain, as a man may say, to coin all the seven liberal sciences out of the Bible, reducing it into divers forms of orations, poems, dialogues, even to the calculating of a new Christian grammar.

But, saith the historian Socrates, the providence of God provided better than the industry of Appollinarius and his son, by taking away that illiterate law with the life of him who devised it. So great an injury they then held it to be deprived of Hellenic learning; and thought it a persecution more undermining, and secretly decaying the Church, than the open cruelty of Decius or Diocletian. And perhaps it was with the same politic drift that the devil whipped St. Jerome in a lenten dream, for reading Cicero; or else it was a phantasm bred by the fever which had then seized him. For had an angel been his discipliner, unless it were for dwelling too much on Ciceronianisms, and had chastised the reading, not the vanity, it had been plainly partial, first, to correct him for grave Cicero, and not for scurril Plautus, whom he confesses to have been reading not long before; next to correct him only, and let so many more ancient Fathers wax old in those pleasant and florid studies, without the lash of such a tutoring apparition; insomuch that Basil teaches how some good use may be made of Margites, a sportful poem, not now extant, writ by Homer; and why not then of Morgante, an Italian romance much to the same purpose?

But if it be agreed we shall be tried by visions, there is a vision recorded by Eusebius, far ancienter than this tale of Jerome to the nun Eustochium, and besides, has nothing of a fever in it. Dionysius Alexandrinus was, about the year 240, a person of great name in the Church, for piety and learning, who had wont to avail himself much against heretics by being conversant in their books; until a certain presbyter laid it scrupulously to his conscience, how he durst venture himself among those defiling volumes. The worthy man, loth to give offence, fell into a new debate with himself, what was to be thought; when suddenly a vision sent from God (it is his own epistle that so avers it) confirmed him in these words: "Read any books whatever come to thy hands, for thou art sufficient both to judge aright, and to examine each matter." To this revelation he assented the sooner, as he confesses, because it was answerable to that of the Apostle to the Thessalonians: "Prove all things, hold fast that which is good."

And he might have added another remarkable saying of the same author: "To the pure, all things are pure;" not only meats and drinks, but all kind of knowledge whether of good or evil: the knowledge cannot defile, nor consequently the books, if the will and conscience be not defiled. For books are as meats and viands are; some of good, some of evil substance; and yet God in that unapocryphal vision said without exception, "Rise, Peter, kill and eat:" leaving the choice to each man's discretion. Wholesome meats to a vitiated stomach differ little or nothing from unwholesome; and best books to a naughty mind are not unapplicable to occasions of evil. Bad meats will scarce breed good nourishment in the healthiest concoction; but herein the difference is of bad books, that they to a discreet and judicious reader serve in many respects to discover, to confute, to forewarn, and to illustrate. Whereof what better witness can ye expect I should produce, than one of your own now sitting in Parliament, the chief of learned men reputed in this land, Mr. Selden; whose volume of Natural and National Laws proves, not only by great authorities brought together, but by exquisite reasons and theorems almost mathematically demonstrative, that all opinions, yea, errors, known, read, and collated, are of main service and assistance toward the speedy attainment of what is truest.

I conceive, therefore, that when God did enlarge the universal diet of man's body (saving ever the rules of temperance), he then also, as before, left arbitrary the dieting and repasting of our minds; as wherein every mature man might have to exercise his own leading capacity. How great a virtue is temperance, how much of moment through the whole life of man! Yet God commits the managing so great a trust, without particular law or prescription, wholly to the demeanour of every grown man. And therefore when he himself tabled the Jews from heaven, that omer, which was every man's daily portion of manna, is computed to have been more than might have well sufficed the heartiest feeder thrice as many meals. For those actions which enter into a man rather than issue out of him, and therefore defile not, God uses not to captivate under a perpetual childhood of prescription, but trusts him with the gift of reason to be his own chooser; there were but little work left for preaching, if law and compulsion should grow so fast upon those things which heretofore were governed only by exhortation. Solomon informs us, that much reading is a weariness to the flesh; but neither he, nor other inspired author, tells us that such or such reading is unlawful; yet certainly had God thought good to limit us herein, it had been much more expedient to have told us what was unlawful than what was wearisome.

As for the burning of those Ephesian books by St. Paul's converts, it is replied, the books were magic, the Syriac so renders them. It was a private act, a voluntary act, and leaves us to a voluntary imitation: the men in remorse burnt those books which were their own; the magistrate by this example is not appointed; these men practised the books, another might perhaps have read them in some sort usefully. Good and evil we know in the field of this world grow up together almost inseparably; and the knowledge of good is so involved and interwoven with the knowledge of evil, and in so many cunning resemblances hardly to be discerned, that those confused seeds which were imposed upon Psyche as an incessant labour to cull out, and sort asunder, were not more intermixed. It was from out the rind of one apple tasted, that the knowledge of good and evil, as two twins cleaving together, leaped forth into the world. And perhaps this is that doom which Adam fell into, of knowing good and evil; that is to say, of knowing good by evil.

As therefore the state of man now is; what wisdom can there be to choose, what continence to forbear, without the knowledge of evil? He that can apprehend and consider vice with all her baits and seeming pleasures, and yet abstain, and yet distinguish, and yet prefer that which is truly better, he is the true warfaring Christian. I cannot praise a fugitive and cloistered virtue unexercised and unbreathed, that never sallies out and seeks her adversary, but slinks out of the race where that immortal garland is to be run for, not without dust and heat. Assuredly we bring not innocence into the world, we bring impurity much rather; that which purifies us is trial, and trial is by what is contrary. That virtue therefore which is but a youngling in the contemplation of evil, and knows not the utmost that vice promises to her followers, and rejects it, is but a blank virtue, not a pure; her whiteness is but an excremental whiteness; which was the reason why our sage and serious poet Spenser (whom I dare be known to think a better teacher than Scotus or Aquinas), describing true temperance under the person of Guyon, brings him in with his palmer through the cave of Mammon, and the bower of earthly bliss, that he might see and know, and yet abstain.

Since therefore the knowledge and survey of vice is in this world so necessary to the constituting of human virtue, and the scanning of error to the confirmation of truth, how can we more safely, and with less danger, scout into the regions of sin and falsity, than by reading all manner of tractates and hearing all manner of reason? And this is the benefit which may be had of books promiscuously read. But of the harm that may result hence, three kinds are usually reckoned. First, is feared the infection, that may spread: but then, all human learning and controversy in religious points must remove out of the world, yea, the Bible itself; for that ofttimes relates blasphemy not nicely, it describes the carnal sense of wicked men not unelegantly, it brings in holiest men passionately murmuring against Providence through all the arguments of Epicurus: in other great disputes it answers dubiously and darkly to the common reader; and ask a Talmudist what ails the modesty of his marginal Keri, that Moses and all the prophets cannot persuade him to pronounce the textual Chetiv. For these causes we all know the Bible itself put by the papist into the first rank of prohibited books. The ancientest Fathers must be next removed, as Clement of Alexandria, and that Eusebian book of Evangelic Preparation, transmitting our ears through a hoard of heathenish obscenities to receive the Gospel. Who finds not that Irenæus, Epiphanius, Jerome, and others discover more heresies than they well confute, and that oft for heresy which is the truer opinion?

Nor boots it to say for these, and all the heathen writers of greatest infection, if it must be thought so, with whom is bound up the life of human learning, that they wrote in an unknown tongue, so long as we are sure those languages are known as well to the worst of men, who are both most able and most diligent to instil the poison they suck, first into the courts of princes, acquainting them with the choicest delights and criticisms of sin.

As perhaps did that Petronius, whom Nero called his Arbiter, the master of his revels; and that notorious ribald of Arezzo, dreaded and yet dear to the Italian courtiers. I name not him, for posterity's sake, whom Henry the Eighth named in merriment his vicar of hell. By which compendious way all the contagion that foreign books can infuse will find a passage to the people far easier and shorter than an Indian voyage, though it could be sailed either by the north of Cataio eastward, or of Canada westward, while our Spanish Licensing gags the English press never so severely.

But, on the other side, that infection which is from books of controversy in religion, is more doubtful and dangerous to the learned than to the ignorant; and yet those books must be permitted untouched by the licenser. It will be hard to instance where any ignorant man hath been ever seduced by any papistical book in English, unless it were commended and expounded to him by some of that clergy; and indeed all such tractates, whether false or true, are as the prophecy of Isaiah was to the eunuch, not to be "understood without a guide." But of our priests and doctors how many have been corrupted by studying the comments of Jesuits and Sorbonnists, and how fast they could transfuse that corruption into the people, our experience is both late and sad. It is not forgot, since the acute and distinct Arminius was perverted merely by the perusing of a nameless discourse written at Delft, which at first he took in hand to confute.

Seeing therefore that those books, and those in great abundance, which are likeliest to taint both life and doctrine, cannot be suppressed without the fall of learning, and of all ability in disputation and that these books of either sort are most and soonest catching to the learned—from whom to the common people whatever is heretical or dissolute may quickly be conveyed;—and that evil manners are as perfectly learnt without books a thousand other ways which cannot be stopped; and evil doctrine not with books can propagate; except a teacher guide, which he might also do without writing, and so beyond prohibiting; I am not unable to unfold, how this cautelous enterprise of licensing can be exempted from the number of vain and impossible attempts. And he who were pleasantly disposed, could not well avoid to liken it to the exploit of that gallant man, who thought to pound up the crows by shutting his park gate.

Besides another inconvenience,—if learned men be the first receivers out of books, and dispreaders both of vice and error, how shall the licensers themselves be confided in, unless we can confer upon them, or they assume to themselves, above all others in the land, the grace of infallibility and uncorruptedness? And again, if it be true, that a wise man, like a good refiner, can gather gold out of the drossiest volume, and that a fool will be a fool with the best book, yea, or without book; there is no reason that we should deprive a wise man of any advantage to his wisdom, while we seek to restrain from a fool that which being restrained will be no hindrance to his folly. For if there should be so much exactness always used to keep that from him which is unfit for his reading, we should in the judgment of Aristotle not only, but of Solomon, and of our Saviour, not vouchsafe him good precepts, and by consequence not willingly admit him to good books; as being certain that a wise man will make better use of an idle pamphlet than a fool will do of sacred Scripture.

It is next alleged, we must not expose ourselves to temptations without necessity; and next to that, not employ our time in vain things. To both these objections one answer will serve, out of the grounds already laid, that to all men such books are not temptations, nor vanities, but useful drugs and materials wherewith to temper and compose effective and strong medicines, which man's life cannot want. The rest, as children and childish men who have not the art to qualify and prepare these working minerals, well may be exhorted to forbear; but hindered forcibly they cannot be, by all the licensing that sainted Inquisition could ever yet contrive; which is what I promised to deliver next: that this Order of Licensing conduces nothing to the end for which it was framed; and hath almost prevented me by being clear already while thus much hath been explaining. See the ingenuity of truth, who, when she gets a free and willing hand, opens herself faster than the pace of method and discourse can overtake her. It was the task which I began with, to show that no nation or well instituted state, if they valued books at all, did ever use this way of licensing; and it might be answered, that this is a piece of prudence lately discovered.

To which I return, that as it was a thing slight and obvious to think on, so if it had been difficult to find out, there wanted not among them long since who suggested such a course ; which they not following, leave us a pattern of their judgment that it was not the not knowing, but the not approving, which was the cause of their not using it. Plato, a man of high authority indeed, but least of all for his Commonwealth, in the book of his Laws, which no city ever yet received, fed his fancy with making many edicts to his airy burgomasters, which they who otherwise admire him, wish had been rather buried and excused in the genial cups of an academic night sitting. By which Laws he seems to tolerate no kind of learning, but by unalterable decree, consisting most of practical traditions, to the attainment whereof a library of smaller bulk than his own Dialogues would be abundant. And there also enacts, that no poet should so much as read to any private man what he had written, until the judges and law keepers had seen it, and allowed it. But that Plato meant this law peculiarly to that Commonwealth which he had imagined, and to no other, is evident. Why was he not else a lawgiver to himself but a transgressor, and to be expelled by his own magistrates, both for the wanton epigrams and dialogues which he made, and his perpetual reading of Sophron Mimus and Aristophanes, books of grossest infamy; and also for commending the latter of them, though he were the malicious libeller of his chief friends, to be read by the tyrant Dionysius, who had little need of such trash to spend his time on? But that he knew this licensing of poems had reference and dependence to many other provisoes there set down in his fancied Republic, which in this world could have no place ; and so neither he himself, nor any magistrate or city, ever imitated that course, which, taken apart from those other collateral injunctions, must needs be vain and fruitless.

For if they fell upon one kind of strictness, unless their care were equal to regulate all other things of like aptness to corrupt the mind, that single endeavour they knew would be but a fond labour; to shut and fortify one gate against corruption, and be necessitated to leave others round about wide open. If we think to regulate printing thereby to rectify manners, we must regulate all recreations and pastimes, all that is delightful to man. No music must be heard, no song be set or sung, but what is grave and Doric. There must be licensing dancers, that no gesture, motion, or deportment be taught our youth, but what by their allowance shall be thought honest; for such Plato was provided of. It will ask more than the work of twenty licensers to examine all the lutes, the violins, and the guitars in every house; they must not be suffered to prattle as they do, but must be licensed what they may say. And who shall silence all the airs and madrigals that whisper softness in chambers? The windows also and the balconies must be thought on; these are shrewd books, with dangerous frontispieces, set to sale: who shall prohibit them, shall twenty licensers? The villages also must have their visitors to inquire what lectures the bagpipe and the rebeck reads, even to the ballatry and the gamut of every municipal fiddler; for these are the countryman's Arcadias, and his Montemayors.

Next, what more national corruption, for which England hears ill abroad, than household gluttony? Who shall be the rectors of our daily rioting? And what shall be done to inhibit the multitudes that frequent those houses where drunkenness is sold and harboured? Our garments also should be referred to the licensing of some more sober workmasters, to see them cut into a less wanton garb. Who shall regulate all the mixed conversation of our youth, male and female together, as is the fashion of this country? Who shall still appoint what shall be discoursed, what presumed, and no further? Lastly, who shall forbid and separate all idle resort, all evil company? These things will be, and must be; but how they shall be least hurtful, how least enticing, herein consists the grave and governing wisdom of a state.

To sequester out of the world into Atlantic and Utopian politics, which never can be drawn into use, will not mend our condition; but to ordain wisely as in this world of evil, in the midst whereof God hath placed us unavoidably. Nor is it Plato's licensing of books will do this, which necessarily pulls along with it so many other kinds of licensing, as will make us all both ridiculous and weary, and yet frustrate; but those unwritten, or at least unconstraining laws of virtuous education, religious and civil nurture, which Plato there mentions, as the bonds and ligaments of the commonwealth, the pillars and the sustainers of every written statute: these they be, which will bear chief sway in such matters as these, when all licensing will be easily eluded. Impunity and remissness for certain are the bane of a commonwealth; but here the great art lies, to discern in what the law is to bid restraint and punishment, and in what things persuasion only is to work. If every action which is good or evil in man at ripe years were to be under pittance, prescription, and compulsion, what were virtue but a name, what praise could be then due to well doing, what gramercy to be sober, just, or continent?.

Many there be that complain of divine Providence for suffering Adam to transgress. Foolish tongues! when God gave him reason, he gave him freedom to choose, for reason is but choosing; he had been else a mere artificial Adam, such an Adam as he is in the motions. We ourselves esteem not of that obedience, or love, or gift, which is of force; God therefore left him free, set before him a provoking object ever almost in his eyes; herein consisted his merit, herein the right of his reward, the praise of his abstinence. Wherefore did he create passions within us, pleasures round about us, but that these rightly tempered are the very ingredients of virtue? They are not skilful considerers of human things, who imagine to remove sin by removing the matter of sin; for besides that it is a huge heap increasing under the very act of diminishing, though some part of it may for a time be withdrawn from some persons it cannot from all, in such a universal thing as books are; and when this is done, yet the sin remains entire. Though ye take from a covetous man all his treasure, he has yet one jewel left, ye cannot bereave him of his covetousness. Banish all objects of lust, shut up all youth into the severest discipline that can be exercised in any hermitage, ye cannot make them chaste that came not thither so: such great care and wisdom is required to the right managing of this point.

Suppose we could expel sin by this means; look how much we thus expel of sin, so much we expel of virtue: for the matter of them both is the same: remove that, and ye remove them both alike. This justifies the high providence of God, who, though he commands us temperance, justice, continence, yet pours out before us even to a profuseness all desirable things, and gives us minds that can wander beyond all limit and satiety. Why should we then affect a rigour contrary to the manner of God and of nature, by abridging or scanting those means, which books freely permitted are, both to the trial of virtue and the exercise of truth?

It would be better done, to learn that the law must needs be frivolous which goes to restrain things uncertainly and yet equally working to good and to evil. And were I the chooser, a dram of well-doing should be preferred before many times as much the forcible hindrance of evil doing. For God sure esteems the growth and completing of one virtuous person, more than the restraint of ten vicious. And albeit, whatever thing we hear or see, sitting, walking, travelling, or conversing, may be fitly called our book, and is of the same effect that writings are; yet grant the thing to be prohibited were only books, it appears that this order hitherto is far insufficient to the end which it intends. Do we not see, not once or oftener, but weekly, that continued court-libel against the parliament and city, printed, as the wet sheets can witness, and dispersed among us for all that licensing can do? Yet this is the prime service a man would think wherein this order should give proof of itself. If it were executed, you will say. But certain, if execution be remiss or blindfold now, and in this particular, what will it be hereafter, and in other books?

If then the Order shall not be vain and frustrate, behold a new labour, Lords and Commons, ye must repeal and proscribe all scandalous and unlicensed books already printed and divulged; after ye have drawn them up into a list, that all may know which are condemned, and which not; and ordain that no foreign books be delivered out of custody till they have been read over. This office will require the whole time of not a few overseers, and those no vulgar men. There be also books which are partly useful and excellent, partly culpable and pernicious; this work will ask as many more officials, to make expurgations and expunctions, that the commonwealth of learning be not damnified. In fine, when the multitude of books increase upon their hands, ye must be fain to catalogue all those printers who are found frequently offending, and forbid the importation of their whole suspected typography. In a word, that this your order may be exact, and not deficient, ye must reform it perfectly, according to the model of Trent and Seville, which I know ye abhor to do.

Yet though ye should condescend to this, which God forbid, the Order still would be but fruitless and defective to that end whereto ye meant it. If to prevent sects and schisms, who is so unread or uncatechised in story that hath not heard of many sects refusing books as a hindrance, and preserving their doctrine unmixed for many ages only by unwritten traditions? The

Christian faith (for that was once a schism) is not unknown to have spread all over Asia, ere any Gospel or Epistle was seen in writing. If the amendment of manners be aimed at, look into Italy and Spain, whether those places be one scruple the better, the honester, the wiser, the chaster, since all the inquisitional rigour that hath been executed upon books.

Another reason, whereby to make it plain that this Order will miss the end it seeks, consider by the quality which ought to be in every licenser. It cannot be denied, but that he who is made judge to sit upon the birth or death of books, whether they may be wafted into this world or not, had need to be a man above the common measure, both studious, learned, and judicious; there may be else no mean mistakes in the censure of what is passable or not; which is also no mean injury. If he be of such worth as behoves him, there cannot be a more tedious and unpleasing journey-work, a greater loss of time levied upon his head, than to be made the perpetual reader of unchosen books and pamphlets, ofttimes huge volumes. There is no book that is acceptable, unless at certain seasons; but to be enjoined the reading of that at all times, and in a hand scarce legible, whereof three pages would not down at any time in the fairest print, is an imposition I cannot believe how he that values time and his own studies, or is but of a sensible nostril, should be able to endure. In this one thing I crave leave of the present licensers to be pardoned for so thinking: who doubtless took this office up, looking on it through their obedience to the parliament, whose command perhaps made all things seem easy and unlaborious to them; but that this short trial hath wearied them out already, their own expressions and excuses to them who make so many journeys to solicit their licence, are testimony enough. Seeing therefore those who now possess the employment, by all evident signs wish themselves well rid of it, and that no man of worth, none that is not a plain unthrift of his own hours, is ever likely to succeed them, except he mean to put himself to the salary of a press correcter, we may easily foresee what kind of licensers we are to expect hereafter, either ignorant, imperious, and remiss, or basely pecuniary. This is what I had to show, wherein this Order cannot conduce to that end whereof it bears the intention. —

I lastly proceed from the no good it can do, to the manifest hurt it causes, in being first the greatest discouragement and affront that can be offered to learning and to learned men. It was the complaint and lamentation of prelates, upon every least of a motion to remove pluralities and distribute more equally Church revenues, that then all learning would be for ever dashed and discouraged. But as for that opinion, I never found cause to think that the tenth part of learning stood or fell with the clergy: nor could I ever but hold it for a sordid and unworthy speech of any Churchman, who had a competency left him. If therefore ye be loth to dishearten utterly and discontent, not the mercenary crew of false pretenders to learning, but the free and ingenious sort of such as evidently were born to study and love learning for itself, not for lucre, or any other end, but the service of God and of truth, and perhaps that lasting fame and perpetuity of praise which God and good men have consented shall be the reward of those whose published labours advance the good of mankind: then know, that so far to distrust the judgment and the honesty of one who hath but a common repute in learning, and never yet offended, as not to count him fit to print his mind without a tutor and examiner, lest he should drop a schism, or something of corruption, is the greatest displeasure and indignity to a free and knowing spirit that can be put upon him.

What advantage is it to be a man, over it is to be a boy at school, if we have only escaped the ferula, to come under the fescue of an Imprimatur? if serious and elaborate writings, as if they were no more than the theme of a grammar-lad under his pedagogue, must not be uttered without the cursory eyes of a temporizing and extemporizing licenser? He who is not trusted with his own actions, his drift not being known to be evil, and standing to the hazard of law and penalty, has no great argument to think himself reputed in the commonwealth wherein he was born for other than a fool or a foreigner. When a man writes to the world, he summons up all his reason and deliberation to assist him; he searches, meditates, is industrious, and likely consults and confers with his judicious friends; after all which done, he takes himself to be informed in what he writes, as well as any that wrote before him; if in this, the most consummate act of his fidelity and ripeness, no years, no industry, no former proof of his abilities, can bring him to that state of maturity, as not to be still mistrusted and suspected, unless he carry all his considerate diligence, all his midnight watchings, and expense of Palladian oil, to the hasty view of an unleisured licenser, perhaps much his younger, perhaps far his inferior in judgment, perhaps one who never knew the labour of bookwriting; and if he be not repulsed, or slighted, must appear in print like a puny with his guardian, and his censor's hand on the back of his title to be his bail and surety, that he is no idiot or seducer; it cannot be but a dishonour and derogation to the author, to the book, to the privilege and dignity of learning.

And what if the author shall be one so copious of fancy, as to have many things, well worth the adding, come into his mind after licensing, while the book is yet under the press, which not seldom[4] happens to the best and diligentest writers: and that perhaps a dozen times in one book. The printer dares not go beyond his licensed copy; so often then must the author trudge to his leave-giver, that those his new insertions may be viewed; and many a jaunt will be made ere that licenser, for it must be the same man, can either be found, or found at leisure; meanwhile either the press must stand still, which is no small damage, or the author lose his accuratest thoughts, and send the book forth worse than he had made it, which to a diligent writer is the greatest melancholy and vexation that can befall.

And how can a man teach with authority, which is the life of teaching; how can he be a doctor in his book, as he ought to be, or else had better be silent; whenas all he teaches, all he delivers, is but under the tuition, under the correction of his patriarchal licenser, to blot or alter what precisely accords not with the hide-bound humour which he calls his judgment? When every acute reader, upon the first sight of a pedantic licence, will be ready with these like words to ding the book a quoit's distance from him:—'I hate a pupil teacher; I endure not an instructor that comes to me under the wardship of an overseeing fist. I know nothing of the licenser, but that I have his own hand here for his arrogance; who shall warrant me his judgment?' 'The State, sir,' replies the stationer: but has a quick return:—'The State shall be my governors, but not my critics; they may be mistaken in the choice of a licenser, as easily as this licenser may be mistaken in an author. This is some common stuff:' and he might add from Sir Francis Bacon, that 'such authorized books are but the language of the times.' For though a licenser should happen to be judicious more than ordinary, which will be a great jeopardy of the next succession, yet his very office and his commission enjoins him to let pass nothing but what is vulgarly received already.

Nay, which is more lamentable, if the work of any deceased author, though never so famous in his lifetime, and even to this day, comes to their hands for licence to be printed or reprinted, if there be found in his book one sentence of a venturous edge, uttered in the height of zeal—and who knows whether it might not be the dictate of a divine spirit?—yet, not suiting with every low decrepit humour of their own, though it were Knox himself, the reformer of a kingdom, that spake it, they will not pardon him their dash; the sense of that great man shall to all posterity be lost, for the fearfulness, or the presumptuous rashness of a perfunctory licenser. And to what an author this violence hath been lately done, and in what book, of greatest consequence to be faithfully published, I could now instance, but shall forbear till a more convenient season. Yet if these things be not resented seriously and timely by them who have the remedy in their power, but that such ironmoulds as these shall have authority to gnaw out the choicest periods of exquisitest books, and to commit such a treacherous fraud against the orphan remainders of worthiest men after death, the more sorrow will belong to that hapless race of men, whose misfortune it is to have understanding. Henceforth let no man care to learn, or care to be more than worldly wise; for certainly in higher matters to be ignorant and slothful, to be a common steadfast dunce, will be the only pleasant life, and only in request.

And as it is a particular disesteem of every knowing person alive, and most injurious to the written labours and monuments of the dead, so to me it seems an undervaluing and vilifying of the whole nation. I cannot set so light by all the invention, the art, the wit, the grave and solid judgment which is in England, as that it can be comprehended in any twenty capacities, how good soever; much less that it should not pass except their superintendence be over it, except it be sifted and strained with their strainers, that it should be uncurrent without their manual stamp. Truth and understanding are not such wares as to be monopolized and traded in by tickets, and statutes, and standards. We must not think to make a staple commodity of all the knowledge in the land, to mark and license it like our broadcloth and our woolpacks. What is it but a servitude like that imposed by the Philistines, not to be allowed the sharpening of our own axes and coulters, but we must repair from all quarters to twenty licensing forges?

Had any one written and divulged erroneous things and scandalous to honest life, misusing and forfeiting the esteem had of his reason among men, if after conviction this only censure were adjudged him, that he should never henceforth write but what were first examined by an appointed officer, whose hand should be annexed to pass his credit for him that now he might be safely read; it could not be apprehended less than a disgraceful punishment. Whence to include the whole nation, and those that never yet thus offended, under such a diffident and suspectful prohibition, may plainly be understood what a disparagement it is. So much the more whenas debtors and delinquents may walk abroad without a keeper, but unoffensive books must not stir forth without a visible jailor in their title. Nor is it to the common people less than a reproach; for if we be so jealous over them, as that we dare not trust them with an English pamphlet, what do we but censure them for a giddy, vicious, and ungrounded people; in such a sick and weak state of faith and discretion, as to be able to take nothing down but through the pipe of a licenser? That this is care or love of them, we cannot pretend, whenas in those popish places, where the laity are most hated and despised, the same strictness is used over them. Wisdom we cannot call it, because it stops but one breach of licence, nor that neither: whenas those corruptions which it seeks to prevent break in faster at other doors, which cannot be shut.

And, in conclusion, it reflects to the disrepute of our ministers also, of whose labours we should hope better, and of their proficiency which their flock reaps by them, than that after all this light of the Gospel which is, and is to be, and all this continual preaching, they should be still frequented with such an unprincipled, unedified, and laic rabble, as that the whiff of every new pamphlet should stagger them out of their catechism and

Christian walking. This may have much reason to discourage the ministers, when such a low conceit is had of all their exhortations and the benefiting of their hearers as that they are not thought fit to be turned loose to three sheets of paper without a licenser; that all the sermons, all the lectures preached, printed, vended in such numbers and such volumes as have now well-nigh made all other books unsaleable, should not be armour enough against one single Enchiridion, without the castle of St. Angelo of an Imprimatur.

And lest some should persuade ye, Lords and Commons, that these arguments of learned men's discouragement at this your order are mere flourishes, and not real, I could recount what I have seen and heard in other countries, where this kind of inquisition tyrannizes; when I have sat among their learned men (for that honour I had), and been counted happy to be born in such a place of philosophic freedom as they supposed England was, while themselves did nothing but bemoan the servile condition into which learning amongst them was brought; that this was it which had damped the glory of Italian wits; that nothing had been there written now these many years but flattery and fustian. There it was that I found and visited the famous Galileo, grown old, a prisoner to the inquisition, for thinking in astronomy otherwise than the Franciscan and Dominican licensers thought. And though I knew that England then was groaning loudest under the prelatical yoke, nevertheless I took it as a pledge of future happiness, that other nations were so persuaded of her liberty.

Yet was it beyond my hope, that those worthies were then breathing in her air who should be her leaders to such a deliverance as shall never be forgotten by any revolution of time that this world hath to finish. When that was once begun, it was as little in my fear, that what words of complaint I heard among learned men of other parts uttered against the Inquisition, the same I should hear, by as learned men at home, uttered in time of Parliament against an Order of Licensing; and that so generally, that when I had disclosed myself a companion of their discontent, I might say, if without envy, that he whom an honest quæstorship had endeared to the Sicilians was not more by them importuned against Verres, than the favourable opinion which I had among many who honour ye, and are known and respected by ye, loaded me with entreaties and persuasions that I would not despair to lay together that which just reason should bring into my mind towards the removal of an undeserved thraldom upon learning.

That this is not therefore the disburdening of a particular fancy, but the common grievance of all those who had prepared their minds and studies above the vulgar pitch to advance truth in others and from others to entertain it, thus much may satisfy. And in their name I shall for neither friend nor foe conceal what the general murmur is; that if it come to Inquisitioning again, and Licensing, and that we are so timorous of ourselves and suspicious of all men as to fear each book and the shaking of each leaf before we know what the contents are; if some who but of late were little better than silenced from preaching, shall come now to silence us from reading except what they please, it cannot be guessed what is intended by some but a second tyranny over learning: and will soon put it out of controversy that bishops and presbyters are the same to us, both name and thing.

That those evils of prelaty which before from five or six and twenty sees were distributively charged upon the whole people will now light wholly upon learning, is not obscure to us, whenas now the pastor of a small unlearned parish, on the sudden shall be exalted archbishop over a large diocess of books, and yet not remove, but keep his other cure too, a mystical pluralist. He who but of late cried down the sole ordination of every novice Bachelor of Art, and denied sole jurisdiction over the simplest parishioner, shall now, at home in his private chair, assume both these over worthiest and excellentest books, and ablest authors that write them. This is not the covenants and protestations that we have made! This is not to put down prelacy; this is but to chop an episcopacy; this is but to translate the palace metropolitan from one kind of dominion into another; this is but an old canonical sleight of commuting our penance. To startle thus betimes at a mere unlicensed pamphlet, will, after a while, be afraid of every conventicle, and a while after will make a conventicle of every Christian meeting.

But I am certain that a State governed by the rules of justice and fortitude, or a Church built and founded upon the rock of faith and true knowledge, cannot be so pusillanimous. While things are yet not constituted in religion, that freedom of writing should be restrained by a discipline imitated from the prelates and learned by them from the Inquisition to shut us up all again into the breast of a Licenser, must needs give cause of doubt and discouragement to all learned and religious men; who cannot but discern the fineness of this politic drift, and who are the contrivers: that while bishops were to be baited down, then all presses might be open; it was the people's birthright and privilege in time of Parliament, it was the breaking forth of light.

But now the bishops abrogated and voided out of the Church, as if our Reformation sought no more but to make room for others into their seats under another name; the episcopal arts begin to bud again; the cruise of truth must run no more oil; liberty of printing must be enthralled again, under a prelatical commission of twenty; the privilege of the people nullified; and, which is worse, the freedom of learning must groan again, and to her old fetters: all this the Parliament yet sitting. Although their own late arguments and defences against the prelates might remember them, that this obstructing violence meets for the most part with an event utterly opposite to the end which it drives at. Instead of suppressing sects and schisms, it raises them and invests them with a reputation: "The punishing of wits enhances their authority," saith the Viscount St. Albans; "and a forbidden writing is thought to be a certain spark of truth, that flies up in the faces of them who seek to tread it out." This order, therefore, may prove a nursing mother to sects, but I shall easily show how it will be a stepdame to truth: and first, by disenabling us to the maintenance of what is known already.

Well knows he who uses to consider, that our faith and knowledge thrives by exercise, as well as our limbs and complexion. Truth is compared in Scripture to a streaming fountain; if her waters flow not in a perpetual progression, they sicken into a muddy pool of conformity and tradition. A man may be a heretic in the truth; and if he believe things only because his pastor says so, or the Assembly so determines, without knowing other reason, though his belief be true, yet the very truth he holds becomes his heresy. There is not any burden that some would gladlier post off to another, than the charge and care of their religion. There be—who knows not that there be?—of Protestants and professors, who live and die in as errant and implicit faith, as any lay papist of Loretto.

A wealthy man, addicted to his pleasure and to his profits, finds Religion to be a traffic so entangled, and of so many piddling accounts, that of all mysteries he cannot skill to keep a stock going upon that trade. What should he do? Fain he would have the name to be religious, fain he would bear up with his neighbours in that. What does he, therefore, but resolves to give over toiling, and to find himself out some factor, to whose care and credit he may commit the whole managing of his religious affairs; some divine of note and estimation that must be. To him he adheres, resigns the whole warehouse of his religion, with all the locks and keys, into his custody; and indeed makes the very person of that man his religion; esteems his associating with him a sufficient evidence and commendatory of his own piety. So that a man may say his religion is now no more within himself, but is become a dividual movable, and goes and comes near him, according as that good man frequents the house. He entertains him, gives him gifts, feasts him, lodges him; his religion comes home at night, prays, is liberally supped, and sumptuously laid to sleep; rises, is saluted, and after the malmsey, or some well-spiced bruage, and better breakfasted than He whose morning appetite would have gladly fed on green figs between Bethany and Jerusalem, his religion walks abroad at eight, and leaves his kind entertainer in the shop trading all day without his religion.

Another sort there be, who when they hear that all things shall be ordered, all things regulated and settled; nothing written but what passes through the custom-house of certain publicans that have the tonnaging and poundaging of all free-spoken truth; will straight give themselves up into your hands, make them and cut them out what religion ye please. There be delights, there be recreations and jolly pastimes, that will fetch the day about from sun to sun, and rock the tedious year as in a delightful dream. What need they torture their heads with that which others have taken so strictly and so unalterably into their own purveying? These are the fruits which a dull ease and cessation of our knowledge will bring forth among the people. How goodly, and how to be wished were such an obedient unanimity as this! What a fine conformity would it starch us all into! Doubtless a staunch and solid piece of framework, as any January could freeze together.

Nor much better will be the consequence even among the

clergy themselves. It is no new thing never heard of before, for a parochial minister, who has his reward, and is at his Hercules pillars in a warm benefice, to be easily inclinable, if he have nothing else that may rouse up his studies, to finish his circuit in an English Concordance and a topic folio, the gatherings and savings of a sober graduateship, a Harmony and a Catena, treading the constant round of certain common doctrinal heads, attended with their uses, motives, marks, and means; out of which, as out of an alphabet or sol-fa, by forming and transforming, joining and disjoining variously, a little bookcraft, and two hours' meditation, might furnish him unspeakably to the performance of more than a weekly charge of sermoning: not to reckon up the infinite helps of interliniaries, breviaries, synopses, and other loitering gear. But as for the multitude of sermons ready printed and piled up, on every text that is not difficult, our London trading St. Thomas in his vestry, and add to boot St. Martin and St. Hugh, have not within their hallowed limits more vendible ware of all sorts ready made: so that penury he never need fear of pulpit provision, having where so plenteously to refresh his magazine. But if his rear and flanks be not impaled, if his back door be not secured by the rigid licenser, but that a bold book may now and then issue forth and give the assault to some of his old collections in their trenches, it will concern him then to keep waking, to stand in watch, to set good guards and sentinels about his received opinions, to walk the round and counter-round with his fellow-inspectors, fearing lest any of his flock be seduced who also then would be better instructed, better exercised, and disciplined. And God send that the fear of this diligence, which must then be used, do not make us affect the laziness of a licensing church?

For if we be sure we are in the right, and do not hold the truth guiltily, which becomes not, if we ourselves condemn not our own weak and frivolous teaching, and the people for an untaught and irreligious gadding route; what can be more fair, than when a man judicious, learned, and of a conscience, for aught we know, as good as theirs that taught us what we know, shall—not privily from house to house, which is more dangerous, but openly—by writing, publish to the world what his opinion is, what his reasons, and wherefore that which is now thought cannot be sound? Christ urged it as wherewith to justify himself, that he preached in public; yet writing is more public than preaching; and more easy to refutation if need be, there being so many whose business and profession merely it is to be the champions of truth; which if they neglect, what can be imputed but their sloth or inability?

Thus much we are hindered and disinured by this course of licensing towards the true knowledge of what we seem to know. For how much it hurts and hinders the licensers themselves in the calling of their ministry, more than any secular employment, if they will discharge that office as they ought, so that of necessity they must neglect either the one duty or the other, I insist not, because it is a particular, but leave it to their own conscience how they will decide it there.

There is yet behind of what I purposed to lay open, the incredible loss and detriment that this plot of licensing puts us to, more than if some enemy at sea should stop up all our havens, and ports, and creeks; it hinders and retards the importation of our richest merchandise,—truth. Nay, it was first established and put in practice by anti-Christian malice and mystery, or set purpose to extinguish, if it were possible, the light of reformation, and to settle falsehood; little differing from that policy wherewith the Turk upholds his Alcoran, by the prohibiting of printing. It is not denied, but gladly confessed, we are to send our thanks and vows to heaven louder than most of nations, for that great measure of truth which we enjoy, especially in those main points between us and the pope, with his appurtenances the prelates. But he who thinks we are to pitch our tent here, and have attained the utmost prospect of reformation that the mortal glass wherein we contemplate can show us till we come to beatific vision, that man by this very opinion declares that he is yet far short of truth.

Truth indeed came once into the world with her Divine Master, and was a perfect shape most glorious to look on: but when he ascended, and his apostles after him were laid asleep, then straight arose a wicked race of deceivers, who, as that story goes of the Egyptian Typhon with his conspirators, how they dealt with the good Osiris, took the virgin Truth, hewed her lovely form into a thousand pieces, and scattered them to the four winds. From that time ever since, the sad friends of Truth, such as durst appear, imitating the careful search that Isis made for the mangled body of Osiris, went up and down gathering up limb by limb still as they could find them. We have not yet found them all, Lords and Commons, nor ever shall do, till her Master's second coming; he shall bring together every joint and member, and shall mould them into an immortal feature of loveliness and perfection. Suffer not these licensing prohibitions to stand at every place of opportunity forbidding and disturbing them that continue seeking, that continue to do our obsequies to the torn body of our martyred saint.

We boast our light; but if we look not wisely on the sun itself, it smites us into darkness. Who can discern those planets that are oft combust, and those stars of brightest magnitude that rise and set with the sun, until the opposite motion of their orbs bring them to such a place in the firmament where they may be seen evening or morning? The light which we have gained was given us, not to be ever staring on, but by it to discover onward things more remote from our knowledge. It is not the unfrocking of a priest, the unmitring of a bishop, and the removing him from off the Presbyterian shoulders, that will make us a happy nation. No; if other things as great in the Church, and in the rule of life both economical and political, be not looked into and reformed, we have looked so long upon the blaze that Zuinglius and Calvin have beaconed up to us that we are stark blind.

There be who perpetually complain of schisms and sects, and make it such a calamity that any man dissents from their maxims. It is their own pride and ignorance which causes the disturbing, who neither will hear with meekness nor can convince, yet all must be suppressed which is not found in their Syntagma. They are the troublers, they are the dividers of unity, who neglect and permit not others to unite those dissevered pieces, which are yet wanting to the body of Truth. To be still searching what we know not by what we know, still closing up truth to truth as we find it (for all her body is homogeneal, and proportional), this is the golden rule in theology as well as in arithmetic, and makes up the best harmony in a Church; not the forced and outward union of cold, and neutral, and inwardly divided minds.

Lords and Commons of England! consider what nation it is whereof ye are, and whereof ye are the governors: a nation not slow and dull, but of a quick, ingenious, and piercing spirit; acute to invent, subtile and sinewy to discourse, not beneath the reach of any point the highest that human capacity can soar to. Therefore the studies of learning in her deepest sciences have been so ancient and so eminent among us, that writers of good antiquity and able judgment have been persuaded that even the school of Pythagoras and the Persian wisdom took beginning from the old philosophy of this island. And that wise and civil Roman, Julius Agricola, who governed once here for Cæsar, preferred the natural wits of Britain before the laboured studies of the French.

Nor is it for nothing that the grave and frugal Transylvanian sends out yearly from as far as the mountainous borders of Russia and beyond the Hercynian wilderness, not their youth, but their staid men, to learn our language and our theological arts. Yet that which is above all this, the favour and the love of Heaven, we have great argument to think in a peculiar manner propitious and propending towards us. Why else was this nation chosen before any other, that out of her as out of Sion should be proclaimed and sounded forth the first tidings and trumpet of reformation to all Europe? And had it not been the obstinate perverseness of our prelates against the divine and admirable spirit of Wyclif, to suppress him as a schismatic and innovator, perhaps neither the Bohemian Huss and Jerome, no, nor the name of Luther or of Calvin, had been ever known: the glory of reforming all our neighbours had been completely ours. But now, as our obdurate clergy have with violence demeaned the matter, we are become hitherto the latest and the backwardest scholars, of whom God offered to have made us the teachers.

Now once again by all concurrence of signs, and by the general instinct of holy and devout men, as they daily and solemnly express their thoughts, God is decreeing to begin some new and great period in His Church, even to the reforming of Reformation itself; what does he then but reveal himself to his servants, and as his manner is, first to his Englishmen? I say, as his manner is, first to us; though we mark not the method of his counsels and are unworthy. Behold now this vast city, a city of refuge, the mansion-house of liberty, encompassed and surrounded with his protection; the shop of war hath not there more anvils and hammers working to fashion out the plates and instruments of armed justice in defence of beleagured truth, than there be pens and heads there, sitting by their studious lamps, musing, searching, revolving new notions and ideas wherewith to present, as with their homage and their fealty, the approaching Reformation: others as fast reading, trying all things, assenting to the force of reason and convincement.

What could a man require more from a nation so pliant and so prone to seek after knowledge? What wants there to such a towardly and pregnant soil, but wise and faithful labourers, to make a knowing people, a nation of prophets, of sages, and of worthies? We reckon more than five months yet to harvest; there need not be five weeks, had we but eyes to lift up, the fields are white already. Where there is much desire to learn, there of necessity will be much arguing, much writing, many opinions; for opinion in good men is but knowledge in the making. Under these fantastic terrors of sect and schism, we wrong the earnest and zealous thirst after knowledge and understanding which God hath stirred up in this city. What some lament of, we rather should rejoice at, should rather praise this pious forwardness among men to reassume the ill-deputed care of their religion into their own hands again. A little generous prudence, a little forbearance of one another, and some grain of charity might win all these diligencies to join and unite into one general and brotherly search after truth; could we but forego this prelatical tradition of crowding free consciences and Christian liberties into canons and precepts of men. I doubt not, if some great and worthy stranger should come among us, wise to discern the mould and temper of a people and how to govern it, observing the high hopes and aims, the diligent alacrity of our extended thoughts and reasonings in the pursuance of truth and freedom, but that he would cry out as Pyrrhus did, admiring the Roman docility and courage, "If such were my Epirots, I would not despair the greatest design that could be attempted to make a Church or Kingdom happy."

Yet these are the men cried out against for schismatics and sectaries, as if, while the temple of the Lord was building, some cutting, some squaring the marble, others hewing the cedars, there should be a sort of irrational men, who could not consider there must be many schisms and many dissections made in the quarry and in the timber ere the house of God can be built. And when every stone is laid artfully together, it cannot be united into a continuity, it can but be contiguous in this world. Neither can every piece of the building be of one form; nay, rather the perfection consists in this, that out of many moderate varieties and brotherly dissimilitudes that are not vastly disproportional, arises the goodly and the graceful symmetry that commends the whole pile and structure.

Let us therefore be more considerate builders, more wise in spiritual architecture, when great reformation is expected. For now the time seems come, wherein Moses, the great prophet, may sit in heaven rejoicing to see that memorable and glorious wish of his fulfilled, when not only our seventy elders, but all the Lord's people, are become prophets. No marvel then though some men, and some good men too perhaps, but young in goodness, as Joshua then was, envy them. They fret, and out of their own weakness are in agony, lest these divisions and subdivisions will undo us. The adversary again applauds, and waits the hour: when they have branched themselves out, saith he, small enough into parties and partitions, then will be our time. Fool! he sees not the firm root, out of which we all grow, though into branches; nor will beware, until he see our small divided maniples cutting through at every angle of his ill-united and unwieldy brigade. And that we are to hope better of all these supposed sects and schisms, and that we shall not need that solicitude, honest perhaps though over-timorous, of them that vex in this behalf, but shall laugh in the end at those malicious applauders of our differences, I have these reasons to persuade me.

. First, when a city shall be as it were besieged and blocked about, her navigable river infested, inroads and incursions round, defiance and battle oft rumoured to be marching up, even to her walls and suburb trenches; that then the people, or the greater part, more than at other times, wholly taken up with the study of highest and most important matters to be reformed, should be disputing, reasoning, reading, inventing, discoursing, even to a rarity and admiration, things not before discoursed or written of, argues first a singular good will, contentedness, and confidence in your prudent foresight, and safe government, Lords and Commons; and from thence derives itself to a gallant bravery and well-grounded contempt of their enemies, as if there were no small number of as great spirits among us as his was who, when Rome was nigh besieged by Hannibal, being in the city, bought that piece of ground at no cheap rate whereon Hannibal himself encamped his own regiment.

Next, it is a lively and cheerful presage of our happy success and victory. For as in a body when the blood is fresh, the spirits pure and vigorous, not only to vital but to rational faculties, and those in the acutest and the pertest operations of wit and subtlety, it argues in what good plight and constitution the body is; so when the cheerfulness of the people is so sprightly up, as that it has not only wherewith to guard well its own freedom and safety, but to spare, and to bestow upon the solidest and sublimest points of controversy and new invention, it betokens us not degenerated, nor drooping to a fatal decay, by casting off the old and wrinkled skin of corruption to outlive these pangs and wax young again, entering the glorious ways of truth and prosperous virtue, destined to become great and honourable in these latter ages. Methinks I see in my mind a noble and puissant nation rousing herself like a strong man after sleep, and shaking her invincible locks. Methinks I see her as an eagle mewing her mighty youth, and kindling her undazzled eyes at the full midday beam; purging and unscaling her long-abused sight at the fountain itself of heavenly radiance; while the whole noise of timorous and flocking birds, with those also that love the twilight, flutter about, amazed at what she means, and in their envious gabble would prognosticate a year of sects and schisms.

What should ye do then, should ye suppress all this flowery crop of knowledge and new light sprung up and yet springing daily in this city? Should ye set an oligarchy of twenty engrossers over it, to bring a famine upon our minds again, when we shall know nothing but what is measured to us by their bushel? Believe it, Lords and Commons! they who counsel ye to such a suppressing, do as good as bid ye suppress yourselves; and I will soon show how. If it be desired to know the immediate cause of all this free writing and free speaking, there cannot be assigned a truer than your own mild, and free, and humane government; it is the liberty, Lords and Commons, which your own valorous and happy counsels have purchased us; liberty which is the nurse of all great wits: this is that which hath rarified and enlightened our spirits like the influence of heaven: this is that which hath enfranchised, enlarged, and lifted up our apprehensions degrees above themselves. Ye cannot make us now less capable, less knowing, less eagerly pursuing of the truth, unless ye first make yourselves, that made us so, less the lovers, less the founders of our true liberty. We can grow ignorant again, brutish, formal, and slavish, as ye found us; but you then must first become that which ye cannot be, oppressive, arbitrary, and tyrannous, as they were from whom ye have freed us. That our hearts are now more capacious, our thoughts more erected to the search and expectation of greatest and exactest things, is the issue of your own virtue propagated in us; ye cannot suppress that, unless ye reinforce an abrogated and merciless law, that fathers may dispatch at will their own children. And who shall then stick closest to ye and excite others? Not he who takes up arms for coat and conduct, and his four nobles of Danegelt. Although I dispraise not the defence of just immunities, yet love my peace better, if that were all. <u>Give me the liberty to know</u>, to utter, and to argue freely according to conscience, above all liberties.

What would be best advised then, if it be found so hurtful and so unequal to suppress opinions for the newness or the unsuitableness to a customary acceptance, will not be my task to say. I shall only repeat what I have learned from one of your own honourable number, a right noble and pious lord, who had he not sacrificed his life and fortunes to the Church and commonwealth, we had not now missed and bewailed a worthy and undoubted patron of this argument. Ye know him, I am sure; yet I for honour's sake, and may it be eternal to him, shall name him, the Lord Brook. He writing of episcopacy, and by the way treating of sects and schisms, left ye his vote, or rather now the last words of his dying charge, which I know will ever be of dear and honoured regard with ye, so full of meekness and breathing charity, that next to His last testament who bequeathed love and peace to His disciples, I cannot call to mind where I have read or heard words more mild and peaceful. He there exhorts us to hear with patience and humility those, however they be miscalled, that desire to live purely in such a use of God's ordinances as the best guidance of their conscience gives them, and to tolerate them, though in some disconformity to ourselves. The book itself will tell us more at large, being published to the world, and dedicated to the Parliament by him, who both for his life and for his death deserves that what advice he left be not laid by without perusal.

And now the time in special is, by privilege to write and speak what may help to the further discussing of matters in agitation. The temple of Janus, with his two controversial faces, might now not unsignificantly be set open. And though all the winds of doctrine were let loose to play upon the earth, so Truth be in the field, we do injuriously by licensing and prohibiting to misdoubt her strength. Let her and Falsehood grapple; who ever knew Truth put to the worse, in a free and open encounter? Her confuting is the best and surest suppressing. He who hears what praying there is for light and clear knowledge to be sent down among us, would think of other matters to be constituted beyond the discipline of Geneva, framed and fabricated already to our hands.

Yet when the new light which we beg for shines in upon us, there be who envy and oppose if it come not first in at their casements. What a collusion is this, whenas we are exhorted by the wise man to use diligence, "to seek for wisdom as for hidden treasures," early and late, that another order shall enjoin us, to know nothing but by statute? When a man hath been labouring the hardest labour in the deep mines of knowledge, hath furnished out his findings in all their equipage, drawn forth his reasons as it were a battle ranged, scattered and defeated all objections in his way, calls out his adversary into the plain, offers him the advantage of wind and sun, if he please, only that he may try the matter by dint of argument; for his opponents then to skulk, to lay ambushments, to keep a narrow bridge of licensing where the challenger should pass, though it be valour enough in soldiership, is but weakness and cowardice in the wars of Truth. For who knows not that Truth is strong, next to the Almighty; she needs no policies, nor stratagems, nor licensings to make her victorious, those are the shifts and the defences that Error uses against her power. Give her but room, and do not bind her when she sleeps, for then she speaks not true as the old Proteus did who spake oracles only when he was caught and bound, but then rather she turns herself into all shapes except her own, and perhaps tunes her voice according to the time as Micaiah did before Ahab, until she be adjured into her own likeness.

Yet is it not impossible that she may have more shapes than one. What else is all that rank of things indifferent, wherein Truth may be on this side, or on the other, without being unlike herself? What but a vain shadow else is the abolition of "those ordinances, that hand-writing nailed to the cross?" What great purchase is this Christian liberty which Paul so often boasts of? His doctrine is, that he who eats or eats not, regards a day or regards it not, may do either to the Lord. How many other things might be tolerated in peace, and left to conscience, had we but Charity, and were it not the chief stronghold of our hypocrisy to be ever judging one another? I fear yet this iron yoke of outward conformity hath left a slavish print upon our necks; the ghost of a linen decency yet haunts us. We stumble, and are impatient at the least dividing of one visible congregation from another, though it be not in fundamentals. And through our forwardness to suppress, and our backwardness to recover any enthralled piece of Truth out of the grip of custom, we care not to keep Truth separated from Truth, which is the fiercest rent and disunion of all. We do not see that while we still affect by all means a rigid external formality we may as soon fall again into a gross conforming stupidity, a stark and dead congealment of "wood and hay and stubble" forced and frozen together, which is more to the sudden degenerating of a Church than many sub-dichotomies of petty schisms.

Not that I can think well of every light separation; or that all in a church is to be expected "gold and silver, and precious stones;" it is not possible for man to sever the wheat from the tares, the good fish from the other fry; that must be the angels' ministry at the end of mortal things. Yet if all cannot be of one mind, as who looks they should be? this doubtless is more wholesome, more prudent, and more Christian, that many be tolerated rather than all compelled. I mean not tolerated popery and open superstition, which as it extirpates all religions and civil supremacies so itself should be extirpate, provided first that all charitable and compassionate means be used to win and regain the weak and the misled. That also which is impious or evil absolutely either against faith or manners, no law can possibly permit that intends not to unlaw itself. But those neighbouring differences, or rather indifferences, are what I speak of, whether in some point of doctrine or of discipline, which though they may be many yet need not interrupt the unity of spirit, if we could but find among us the bond of peace.

In the meanwhile, if any one would write, and bring his helpful hand to the slow-moving reformation which we labour under, if truth have spoken to him before others, or but seemed at least to speak, who hath so bejesuited us, that we should trouble that man with asking licence to do so worthy a deed; and not consider this, that if it come to prohibiting, there is not aught more likely to be prohibited than Truth itself; whose first appearance to our eyes, bleared and dimmed with prejudice and custom, is more unsightly and unplausible than many errors; even as the person is of many a great man slight and contemptible to see to. And what do they tell us vainly of new opinions, when this very opinion of theirs that none must be heard but whom they like, is the worst and newest opinion of all others; and is the chief cause why sects and schisms do so much abound and true knowledge is kept at distance from us; besides yet a greater danger which is in it. For when God shakes a kingdom with strong and healthful commotions to a general reforming, it is not untrue that many sectaries and false teachers are then busiest in seducing.

But yet more true it is, that God then raises to his own work men of rare abilities and more than common industry, not only to look back and revive what hath been taught heretofore, but to gain further, and to go on some new enlightened steps in the discovery of truth. For such is the order of God's enlightening his Church, to dispense and deal out by degrees his beam, so as our earthly eyes may best sustain it. Neither is God appointed and confined, where and out of what place these his chosen shall be first heard to speak; for He sees not as man sees, chooses not as man chooses, lest we should devote ourselves again to set places and assemblies and outward callings of men; planting our faith one while in the old Convocation house; and another while in the chapel at Westminster; when all the faith and religion that shall be there canonized is not sufficient, without plain convincement and the charity of patient instruction, to supple the least bruise of conscience, to edify the meanest Christian who desires to walk in the spirit and not in the letter of human trust, for all the number of voices that can be there made; no, though Harry the Seventh himself there, with all his liege tombs about him, should lend them voices from the dead to swell their number.

And if the men be erroneous who appear to be the leading schismatics, what withholds us but our sloth, our self-will, and distrust in the right cause, that we do not give them gentle meetings and gentle dismissions, that we debate not and examine the matter thoroughly with liberal and frequent audience; if not for their sakes yet for our own? seeing no man who hath tasted learning, but will confess the many ways of profiting by those who, not contented with stale receipts, are able to manage and set forth new positions to the world. And were they but as the dust and cinders of our feet, so long as in that notion they may yet serve to polish and brighten the armoury of truth even for that respect they were not utterly to be cast away. But if they be of those whom God hath fitted for the special use of these times with eminent and ample gifts, and those perhaps neither among the priests, nor among the Pharisees, and we, in the haste of a precipitant zeal, shall make no distinction, but resolve to stop their mouths because we fear they come with new and dangerous opinions, as we commonly forejudge them ere we understand them; no less than woe to us! While thinking thus to defend the Gospel, we are found the persecutors.

There have been not a few since the beginning of this parliament, both of the presbytery and others, who by their unlicensed books to the contempt of an Imprimatur first broke that triple ice clung about our hearts, and taught the people to see day. I hope that none of those were the persuaders to renew upon us this bondage, which they themselves have wrought so much good by contemning. But if neither the check that Moses gave to young Joshua, nor the countermand which our Saviour gave to young John, who was so ready to prohibit those whom he thought unlicensed, be not enough to admonish our elders how unacceptable to God their testy mood of prohibiting is; if neither their own remembrance what evil hath abounded in the Church by this lett of licensing, and what good they themselves have begun by transgressing it, be not enough, but that they will persuade and execute the most Dominican part of the Inquisition over us, and are already with one foot in the stirrup so active at suppressing, it would be no unequal distribution in the first place to suppress the suppressors themselves; whom the change of their condition hath puffed up, more than their late experience of harder times hath made wise.

And as for regulating the press, let no man think to have the honour of advising ye better than yourselves have done in that

Order published next before this, "That no book be printed, unless the printer's and the author's name, or at least the printer's be registered." Those which otherwise come forth, if they be found mischievous and libellous, the fire and the executioner will be the timeliest and the most effectual remedy that man's prevention can use. For this authentic Spanish policy of licensing books, if I have said aught, will prove the most unlicensed book itself within a short while; and was the immediate image of a Star Chamber Decree to that purpose made in those times when that court did the rest of those her pious works, for which she is now fallen from the stars with Lucifer. Whereby ye may guess what kind of state prudence, what love of the people, what care of religion or good manners there was at the contriving, although with singular hypocrisy it pretended to bind books to their good behaviour. And how it got the upper hand of your precedent order so well constituted before, if we may believe those men whose profession gives them cause to inquire most, it may be doubted there was in it the fraud of some old patentees and monopolizers, in the trade of bookselling; who, under pretence of the poor in their company not to be defrauded, and the just retaining of each man his several copy—which God forbid should be gainsaid—brought divers glossing colours to the House, which were indeed but colours, and serving to no end except it be to exercise a superiority over their neighbours; men who do not therefore labour in an honest profession to which learning is indebted that they should be made other men's vassals. Another end is thought was aimed at by some of them in procuring by petition this Order, that having power in their hands, malignant books might the easier escape abroad, as the event shows. But of these sophisms and elenchs of merchandise I skill not. This I know, that errors in a good government and in a bad are equally almost incident; for what magistrate may not be misinformed, and much the sooner if Liberty of Printing be reduced into the power of a few? But to redress willingly and speedily what hath been erred, and in highest authority to esteem a plain advertisement more than others have done a sumptuous bride, is a virtue, honoured Lords and Commons, answerable to your highest actions, and whereof none can participate but greatest and wisest men.

THE TENURE OF KINGS AND MAGISTRATES:

PROVING

That it is Lawful, and hath been held so through all ages, for any, who have the power, to call to account a Tyrant, or wicked King, and after due Conviction, to Depose, and put him to Death, if the ordinary Magistrate have neglected or denied to do it. And that they who of late so much blame Deposing, are the Men that did it themselves.

IF men within themselves would be governed by Reason and not generally give up their understanding to a double tyranny, of Custom from without, and blind Affections within, they would discern better what it is to favour and uphold the tyrant of a nation. But, being slaves within doors, no wonder that they strive so much to have the public state conformably governed to the inward vicious rule by which they govern themselves. For, indeed, none can love freedom heartily but good men; the rest love not freedom but licence, which never hath more scope, or more indulgence than under tyrants. Hence is it that tyrants are not oft offended, nor stand much in doubt of bad men, as being all naturally servile; but in whom virtue and true worth most is eminent, them they fear in earnest, as by right their masters; against them lies all their hatred and suspicion. Consequently, neither do bad men hate tyrants, but have been always readiest, with the falsified names of loyalty and obedience, to colour over their base compliances.

And although sometimes for shame, and when it comes to their own grievances, of purse especially, they would seem good patriots and side with the better cause, yet when others, for the deliverance of their country, endued with fortitude and heroic virtue to fear nothing but the curse written against those "that do the work of the Lord negligently," would go on to remove, not only the calamities and thraldoms of a people, but the roots and causes whence they spring; straight these men and sure helpers at need, as if they hated only the miseries but not the mischiefs, after they have juggled and paltered with the world, bandied and borne arms against their king, divested him, disanointed him, nay, cursed him all over in their pulpits and their pamphlets, to the engaging of sincere and real men beyond what is possible or honest to retreat from, not only turn revolters from those principles which only could at first move them, but lay the strain of disloyalty, and worse, on those proceedings which are the necessary consequences of their own former actions; nor disliked by themselves, were they managed to the entire advantages of their own faction: not considering the while that he toward whom they boasted their new fidelity, counted them accessory, and by those statutes and laws which they so impotently brandish against others would have doomed them to a traitor's death for what they have done already.

It is true that most men are apt enough to civil wars and commotions as a novelty, and for a flash hot and active, but through sloth or inconstancy and weakness of spirit, either fainting ere their own pretences, though never so just, be half attained, or through an inbred falsehood and wickedness, betray ofttimes to destruction with themselves men of noblest temper joined with them for causes whereof they in their rash undertakings were not capable. If God and a good cause give them victory, the prosecution whereof for the most part inevitably draws after it the alteration of laws, change of government, downfall of princes with their families; then comes the task to those worthies which are the soul of that enterprise, to be sweat and laboured out amidst the throng and noses of vulgar and irrational men. Some contesting for privileges, customs, forms, and that old entanglement of iniquity, their gibberish laws, though the badge of their ancient slavery. Others, who have been fiercest against their prince under the notion of a tyrant, and no mean incendiaries of the war against him, when God, out of his providence and high disposal hath delivered him into the hand of their brethren, on a sudden and in a new garb of allegiance which their doings have long since cancelled, they plead for him, pity him, extol him, protest against those that talk of bringing him to the trial of justice, which is the sword of God, superior to all mortal things, in whose hand soever by apparent signs his testified will is to put it.

But certainly, if we consider who and what they are, on a sudden grown so pitiful, we may conclude their pity can be no true and Christian commiseration, but either levity and shallowness of mind, or else a carnal admiring of that worldly pomp and greatness from whence they see him fallen; or rather, lastly, a dissembled and seditious pity, feigned of industry to beget new discord. As for mercy, if it be to a tyrant, under which name they themselves have cited him so oft in the hearing of God, of angels, and the holy Church assembled, and there charged him with the spilling of more innocent blood by far than ever Nero did, undoubtedly the mercy which they pretend is the mercy of wicked men,—and "their mercies," we read, "are cruelties,"—hazarding the welfare of a whole nation, to have saved one whom they so oft have termed Agag, and vilifying the blood of many Jonathans who have saved Israel; insisting with much niceness on the unnecessariest clause of their covenant wrested, wherein the fear of change and the absurd contradiction of a flattering hostility had hampered them, but not scrupling to give away for compliments to an implacable revenge, the heads of many thousand Christians more.

Another sort there is, who coming in the course of these affairs to have their share in great actions above the form of law or custom, at least to give their voice and approbation, begin to swerve and almost shiver at the majesty and grandeur of some noble deed, as if they were newly entered into a great sin; disputing precedents, forms, and circumstances, when the commonwealth nigh perishes for want of deeds in substance, done with just and faithful expedition. To these I wish better instruction, and virtue equal to their calling; the former of which, that is to say, instruction, I shall endeavour, as my duty is, to bestow on them; and exhort them not to startle from the just and pious resolution of adhering, with all their strength and assistance, to the present Parliament and Army, in the glorious way wherein justice and victory hath set them—the only warrants through all ages, next under immediate revelation, to exercise supreme power—in those proceedings, which hitherto appear equal to what hath been done in any age or nation heretofore justly or magnanimously.

Nor let them be discouraged or deterred by any new apostate scarecrows, who, under show of giving counsel, send out their barking monitories and mementoes, empty of aught else but the spleen of a frustrated faction. For how can that pretended counsel be either sound or faithful, when they that give it see not, for madness and vexation of their ends lost, that those Statutes and Scriptures which both falsely and scandalously they wrest against their friends and associates, would, by sentence of the common adversary, fall first and heaviest upon their own heads? Neither by mild and tender dispositions be foolishly softened from their duty and perseverance with the unmasculine rhetoric of any puling priest or chaplain, sent as a friendly letter of advice, for fashion's sake in private, and forthwith published by the sender himself that we may know how much of friend there was in it, to cast an odious envy upon them to whom it was pretended to be sent in charity. Nor let any man be deluded by either the ignorance or the notorious hypocrisy and self-repugnance of our dancing divines, who have the conscience and the boldness to come with Scripture in their mouths, glossed and fitted for their turns with a double contradictory sense, transforming the sacred verity of God to an idol with two faces, looking at once two several ways; and with the same quotations to charge others, which in the same case they made serve to justify themselves. For while the hope to be made classic and provincial lords led them on, while pluralities greased them thick and deep, to the shame and scandal of religion more than all the sects and heresies they exclaim against; then to fight against the king's person, and no less a party of his Lords and Commons, or to put force upon both the Houses, was good, was lawful, was no resisting of superior powers; they only were powers not to be resisted who countenanced the good and punished the evil.

But now that their censorious domineering is not suffered to be universal, truth and conscience to be freed, tithes and pluralities to be no more,—though competent allowance provided,—and the warm experience of large gifts, and they so good at taking them; yet now to exclude and seize upon impeached members, to bring delinquents without exemption to a fair tribunal by the common national law against murder, is now to be no less than Korah, Dathan, and Abiram. He who but erewhile in the pulpits was a cursed tyrant, an enemy to God and saints, laden with all the innocent blood spilt in three kingdoms, and so to be fought against; is now, though nothing penitent or altered from his first principles, a lawful magistrate, a sovereign lord, the Lord's anointed, not to be touched, though by themselves imprisoned. As if this only were obedience, to preserve the mere useless bulk of his person, and that only in prison not in the field, not to disobey his commands, deny him his dignity and office, everywhere to resist his power, but where they think it only surviving in their own faction.

But who in particular is a tyrant, cannot be determined in a general discourse, otherwise than by supposition; his particular charge, and the sufficient proof of it, must determine that. Which I leave to magistrates, at least to the uprighter sort of them, and of the people, though in number less by many, in whom faction least hath prevailed above the law of nature and right reason, to judge as they find cause. But this I dare own as part of my faith, that if such a one there be, by whose commission whole massacres have been committed on his faithful subjects, his provinces offered to pawn or alienation as the hire of those whom he had solicited to come in and destroy whole cities and countries; be he king, or tyrant, or emperor, the sword of justice is above him; in whose hand soever is found sufficient power to avenge the effusion and so great a deluge of innocent blood. For if all human power to execute, not accidentally but intendedly, the wrath of God upon evil-doers without exception, be of God; then that power, whether ordinary, or if that fail, extraordinary, so executing that intent of God, is lawful, and not to be resisted. But to unfold more at large this whole question, though with all expedient brevity, I shall here set down, from first beginning, the original of kings; how and wherefore exalted to that dignity above their brethren; and from thence shall prove, that turning to tyranny they may be as lawfully deposed and punished, as they were at first elected. This I shall do by authorities and reasons, not learnt in corners among schisms and heresies as our doubting divines are ready to calumniate, but fetched out of the midst of choicest and most authentic learning, and no prohibited authors; nor many heathen, but Mosaical, Christian, orthodoxal, and, which must needs be more convincing to our adversaries, presbyterial.

No man, who knows aught, can be so stupid to deny, that all men naturally were born free, being the image and resemblance of God himself, and were, by privilege above all the creatures, born to command, and not to obey. And that they lived so, till from the root of Adam's transgression falling among themselves to do wrong and violence, and foreseeing that such courses must needs tend to the destruction of them all, they agreed by common league to bind each other from mutual injury, and jointly to defend themselves against any that gave disturbance or opposition to such agreement. Hence came cities, towns, and commonwealths. And because no faith in all was found sufficiently binding, they saw it needful to ordain some authority that might restrain by force and punishment what was violated against peace and common right.

This authority and power of self-defence and preservation being originally and naturally in every one of them, and unitedly in them all; for ease, for order, and lest each man should be his own partial judge, they communicated and derived either to one whom for the eminence of his wisdom and integrity they chose above the rest, or to more than one, whom they thought of equal deserving: the first was called a king; the other, magistrates: not to be their lords and masters—though afterwards those names in some places were given voluntarily to such as had been authors of inestimable good to the people—but to be their deputies and commissioners, to execute, by virtue of their intrusted power, that justice, which else every man by the bond of nature and of covenant must have executed for himself, and for one another. And to him that shall consider well, why among free persons one man by civil right should bear authority and jurisdiction over another, no other end or reason can be imaginable.

These for a while governed well, and with much equity decided all things at their own arbitrement; till the temptation of such a power left absolute in their hands, perverted them at length to injustice and partiality. Then did they who now by trial had found the danger and inconveniencies of committing arbitrary power to any, invent laws, either framed or consented to by all, that should confine and limit the authority of whom they chose to govern them: that so Man, of whose failing they had proof, might no more rule over them, but Law and Reason, abstracted as much as might be from personal errors and frailties. "While, as the magistrate was set above the people, so the law was set above the magistrate." When this would not serve, but that the law was either not executed, or misapplied, they were constrained from that time, the only remedy left them, to put conditions and take oaths from all kings and magistrates at their first instalment, to do impartial justice by law: who, upon those terms and no other, received allegiance from the people, that is to say, bond or covenant to obey them in execution of those laws, which they, the people, had themselves made or assented to. And this ofttimes with express warning, that if the king or magistrate proved unfaithful to his trust, the people would be disengaged. They added also counsellors and parliaments, not to be only at his beck, but, with him or without him, at set times, or at all times, when any danger threatened, to have care of the public safety. Therefore saith Claudius Sesell, a French statesman, "The Parliament was set as a bridle to the king;" which I instance rather, not because our English lawyers have not said the same long before, but because that French monarchy is granted by all to be a far more absolute one than ours. That this and the rest of what hath hitherto been spoken is most true, might be copiously made appear through all stories, heathen and Christian; even of those nations where kings and emperors have sought means to abolish all ancient memory of the people's right by their encroachments and usurpations. But I spare long insertions, appealing to the German, French, Italian, Arragonian, English, and not least the Scottish histories; not forgetting this only by the way, that William the Norman, though a conqueror, and not unsworn at his coronation, was compelled a second time to take oath at St. Alban's ere the people would be brought to yield obedience.

It being thus manifest, that the Power of Kings and Magistrates is nothing else but what is only derivative, transferred, and committed to them in trust from the People to the common good of them all, in whom the power yet remains fundamentally and cannot be taken from them without a violation of their natural birthright; and seeing that from hence Aristotle and the best of political writers have defined a king, "him who governs to the good and profit of his people, and not for his own ends;" it follows from necessary causes, that the titles of sovereign lord, natural lord and the like are either arrogancies or flatteries, not admitted by emperors and kings of best note, and disliked by the Church both of Jews (Isa. xxvi. 13) and ancient Christians, as appears by Tertullian and others. Although generally the people of Asia, and with them the Jews also, especially since the time they chose a king against the advice and counsel of God, are noted by wise authors much inclinable to slavery.

Secondly, that to say, as is usual, the King hath as good right to his crown and dignity as any man to his inheritance, is to make the subject no better than the king's slave, his chattel, or his possession that may be bought and sold: and doubtless, if hereditary title were sufficiently inquired, the best foundation of it would be found but either in courtesy or convenience. But suppose it to be of right hereditary, what can be more just and legal, if a subject for certain crimes be to forfeit by law from himself and posterity all his inheritance to the king, than that a king, for crimes proportional, should forfeit all his title and inheritance to the people? Unless the people must be thought created all for him, he not for them, and they all in one body inferior to him single; which were a kind of treason against the dignity of mankind to affirm.

Thirdly, it follows, that to say Kings are accountable to none but God, is the overcoming of all law and government. For if they may refuse to give account, then all covenants made with them at coronation, all oaths are in vain, and mere mockeries; all laws which they swear to keep, made to no purpose: for if the king fear not God—as how many of them do not—we hold then our lives and estates by the tenure of his mere grace and mercy, as from a god, not a mortal magistrate; a position that none but court parasites or men besotted would maintain. Aristotle, therefore, whom we commonly allow for one of the best interpreters of nature and morality, writes in the fourth of his Politics, chap. x., that "monarchy unaccountable is the worst sort of tyranny, and least of all to be endured by free-born men."

And surely no Christian prince, not drunk with high mind and prouder than those pagan Cæsars that deified themselves, would arrogate so unreasonably above human condition, or derogate so basely from a whole nation of men, his brethren, as if for him only subsisting and to serve his glory, valuing them in comparison of his own brute will and pleasure no more than so many beasts, or vermin under his feet not to be reasoned with but to be trod on; among whom there might be found so many thousand men for wisdom, virtue, nobleness of mind, and all other respects but the fortune of his dignity, far above him. Yet some would persuade us that this absurd opinion was King David's, because in the 51st Psalm he cries out to God, "Against thee only have I sinned;" as if David had imagined, that to murder Uriah and adulterate his wife had been no sin against his neighbour, whenas that law of Moses was to the king expressly (Deut. xvii.) not to think so highly of himself above his brethren. David, therefore, by those words, could mean no other, than either that the depth of his guiltiness was known to God only, or to so few as had not the will or power to question him, or that the sin against God was greater beyond compare than against Uriah. Whatever his meaning were, any wise man will see, that the pathetical words of a psalm can be no certain decision to a point that hath abundantly more certain rules to go by.

How much more rationally spake the heathen king Demophoön, in a tragedy of Euripides, than these interpreters would put upon King David! "I rule not my people by tyranny, as if they were barbarians; but am myself liable, if I do unjustly, to suffer justly." Not unlike was the speech of Trajan, the worthy emperor, to one whom he made general of his prætorian forces: "Take this drawn sword," saith he, "to use for me if I reign well; if not, to use against me." Thus Dion relates. And not Trajan only, but Theodosius, the younger, a Christian emperor, and one of the best, caused it to be enacted as a rule undeniable and fit to be acknowledged by all kings and emperors, that a prince is bound to the laws; that on the authority of law the authority of a prince depends, and to the laws ought to submit. Which edict of his remains yet unrepealed in the code of Justinian (l. i. tit. 24), as a sacred constitution to all the succeeding emperors. How can any king in Europe maintain and write himself accountable to none but God, when emperors in their own imperial statutes have written and decreed themselves accountable to law? And indeed where such account is not feared, he that bids a man reign over him above law, may bid as well a savage beast.

.It follows, lastly, that since the King or Magistrate holds his authority of the People, both originally and naturally for their good, in the first place, and not his own, then may the people, as oft as they shall judge it for the best, either choose him or reject him, retain him or depose him, though no tyannt, merely by the liberty and right of freeborn men to <u>be governed as seems to them best.</u> This, though it cannot but stand with plain reason, shall be made good also by Scripture (Deut. xvii. 14): "When thou art come into the land which the Lord thy God giveth thee, and shalt say, I will set a king over me, like as all the nations about me." These words confirm us that the right of choosing, yea of changing their own government, is by the grant of God himself in the people. And therefore when they desired a king, though then under another form of government, and though their changing displeased him, yet he that was himself their king, and rejected by them, would not be a hindrance to what they intended, further than by persuasion, but that they might do therein as they saw good (1 Sam. viii.), only he reserved to himself the nomination of who should reign over them. Neither did that exempt the king, as if he were to God only accountable, though by his especial command anointed. Therefore "David first made a covenant with the elders of Israel, and so was by them anointed king" (2 Sam. v. 3; 1 Chron. xi.). And Jehoiada the priest, making Jehoash king, made a covenant between him and the people (2 Kings xi. 17). Therefore when Rehoboam, at his coming to the crown, rejected those conditions which the Israelites brought him, hear what they answer him: "What portion have we in David, or inheritance in the son of Jesse? See to thine own house, David." And for the like conditions not performed, all Israel before that time deposed Samuel; not for his own default, but for the misgovernment of his sons.

But some will say to both these examples, it was evilly done. I answer, that not the latter, because it was expressly allowed them in the Law, to set up a king if they pleased; and God himself joined with them in the work; though in some sort it was at that time displeasing to him, in respect of old Samuel, who had governed them uprightly; as Livy praises the Romans, who took occasion from Tarquinius, a wicked prince, to gain their liberty, which to have extorted, saith he, from Numa, or any of the good kings before, had not been seasonable. Nor was it in the former example done unlawfully; for when Rehoboam had prepared a huge army to reduce the Israelites, he was forbidden by the prophet (1 Kings xii. 24): "Thus saith the Lord, ye shall not go up, nor fight against your brethren, for this thing is from me." He calls them their brethren, not rebels, and forbids to be proceeded against them, owning the thing himself, not by single providence but by approbation, and that not only of the act, as in the former example, but of the fit season also: he had not otherwise forbid to molest them. And those grave and wise counsellors, whom Rehoboam first advised with, spake no such thing as our old grey-headed flatterers now are wont—'Stand upon your birthright, scorn to capitulate; you hold of God, not of them;'—for they knew no such matter, unless conditionally, but gave him politic counsel, as in a civil transaction.

Therefore Kingdom and Magistracy, whether supreme or subordinate, is called "a human ordinance" (1 Pet. ii. 13, &c.), which we are there taught is the will of God we should submit to, so far as for the punishment of evil-doers and the encouragement of them that do well. "Submit," saith he, "as free men." But to any civil power unaccountable, unquestionable, and not to be resisted, no, not in wickedness, and violent actions, how can we submit as free men? "There is no power but of God," saith Paul (Rom. xiii.); as much as to say, God put it into man's heart to find out that way at first for common peace and preservation, approving the exercise thereof; else it contradicts Peter, who calls the same authority an ordinance of man. It must be also understood of lawful and just power, else we read of great power in the affairs and kingdoms of the world permitted to the devil: for saith he to Christ (Luke iv. 6), "All this power will I give thee, and the glory of them, for it is delivered to me, and to whomsoever I will, I give it." Neither did he lie, or Christ gainsay what he affirmed; for in the thirteenth of the Revelation, we read how the Dragon gave to the Beast his power, his seat, and great authority: which beast so authorized most expound to be the tyrannical powers and kingdoms of the earth. Therefore Saint Paul in the forecited chapter tells us, that such magistrates he means as are not a terror to the good but to the evil; such as bear not the sword in vain, but to punish offenders, and to encourage the good.

If such only be mentioned here as powers to be obeyed, and our submission to them only required, then doubtless those powers that do the contrary are no powers ordained of God; and by consequence no obligation laid upon us to obey or not to resist them. And it may be well observed, that both these Apostles, whenever they give this precept, express it in terms not concrete, but abstract, as logicians are wont to speak; that is, they mention the ordinance, the power, the authority, before the persons that execute it; and what that power is, lest we should be deceived, they describe exactly. So that if the power be not such, or the person execute not such power, neither the one nor the other is of God, but of the devil, and by consequence to be resisted. From this exposition Chrysostom also, on the same place, dissents not; explaining that these words were not written in behalf of a tyrant. And this is verified by David, himself a king, and likeliest to be author of the Psalm (xciv. 20) which saith, "Shall the throne of iniquity have fellowship with thee?" And it were worth the knowing, since kings in these days, and that by Scripture, boast the justness of their title by holding it immediately of God yet cannot show the time when God ever set on the throne them or their forefathers, but only when the people chose them; why by the same reason, since God ascribes as oft to himself the casting down of princes from the throne, it should not be thought as lawful, and as much from God, when none are seen to do it but the people, and that for just causes. For if it needs must be a sin in them to depose, it may as likely be a sin to have elected. And contrary, if the people's act in election be pleaded by a king as the act of God and the most just title to enthrone him, why may not the people's act of rejection be as well pleaded by the people as the act of God and the most just reason to depose him? So that we see the title and just right of reigning or deposing, in reference to God, is found in Scripture to be all one; visible only in the people, and depending merely upon justice and demerit. Thus far hath been considered chiefly the Power of Kings and

Magistrates; how it was and is originally the people's, and by them conferred in trust only to be employed to the common peace and benefit; with liberty therefore and right remaining in them, to reassume it to themselves, if by kings or magistrates it be abused; or to dispose of it by any alteration, as they shall judge most conducing to the public good.

We may from hence with more ease and force of argument determine what a tyrant is, and what the people may do against him. A tyrant, whether by wrong or by right coming to the crown, is he who, regarding neither law nor the common good, reigns only for himself and his faction: thus St. Basil, among others, defines him. And because his power is great, his will boundless and exorbitant, the fulfilling whereof is for the most part accompanied with innumerable wrongs and oppressions of the people, murders, massacres, rapes, adulteries, desolation, and subversion of cities and whole provinces; look how great a good and happiness a just king is so great a mischief is a tyrant; as he the public father of his country, so this the common enemy against whom what the people lawfully may do, as against a common pest and destroyer of mankind, I suppose no man of clear judgment need go further to be guided than by the very principles of nature in him.

But because it is the vulgar folly of men to desert their own reason, and shutting their eyes to think they see best with other men's, I shall show, by such examples as ought to have most weight with us, what hath been done in this case heretofore. The Greeks and Romans, as their prime authors witness, held it not only lawful, but a glorious and heroic deed, rewarded publicly with statues and garlands, to kill an infamous tyrant at any time without trial; and but reason, that he who trod down all law should not be vouchsafed the benefit of law. Insomuch that Seneca, the tragedian, brings in Hercules, the grand suppressor of tyrants, thus speaking :—

         "Victima haud ulla amplior
Potest, magisque opima mactari Jovi
Quam rex iniquus."

         "There can be slain
No sacrifice to God more acceptable
Than an unjust and wicked king."

But of these I name no more, lest it be objected they were heathen; and come to produce another sort of men, that had the knowledge of true religion. Among the Jews this custom of tyrant-killing was not unusual. First, Ehud, a man whom God had raised to deliver Israel from Eglon, King of Moab, who had conquered and ruled over them eighteen years, being sent to him as an ambassador with a present, slew him in his own house. But he was a foreign prince, an enemy, and Ehud besides had special warrant from God. To the first I answer, it imports not whether foreign or native: for no prince so native but professes to hold by Law; which when he himself overturns, breaking all the covenants and oaths that gave title to his dignity and were the bond and alliance between him and his people, what differs he from an outlandish king or from an enemy?

For look how much right the King of Spain hath to govern us at all, so much right hath the King of England to govern us tyrannically. If he, though not bound to us by any league, coming from Spain in person to subdue us or to destroy us, might lawfully by the people of England either be slain in fight or put to death in captivity, what hath a native king to plead,— bound by so many covenants, benefits, and honours, to the welfare of his people,—why he through the contempt of all laws and parliaments, the only tie of our obedience to him, for his own will's sake, and a boasted prerogative unaccountable, after seven years' warring and destroying of his best subjects, overcome, and yielded prisoner, should think to scape unquestionable as a thing divine, in respect of whom so many thousand Christians destroyed should lie unaccounted for, polluting with their slaughtered carcasses all the land over and crying for vengeance against the living that should have righted them? Who knows not that there is a mutual bond of amity and brotherhood between Man and Man over all the world, neither is it the English sea that can sever us from that duty and relation: a straiter bond yet there is between fellow-subjects, neighbours, and friends. But when any of these do one to another so as hostility could do no worse, what doth the law decree less against them, than open enemies and invaders? or if the law be not present or too weak, what doth it warrant us to less than single defence or civil war? and from that time forward the law of civil defensive war differs nothing from the law of foreign hostility. Nor is it distance of place that makes enmity, but enmity that makes distance. He, therefore, that keeps peace with me, near or remote, of whatsoever nation, is to me, as far as all civil and human offices, an Englishman and a neighbour: but if an Englishman, forgetting all laws, human, civil, and religious, offend against life and liberty, to him offended, and to the Law in his behalf, though born in the same womb, he is no better than a Turk, a Saracen, a heathen.

This is Gospel, and this was ever law among equals; how much rather then in force against any king whatever who in respect of the people is confessed inferior and not equal: to distinguish, therefore, of a tyrant by outlandish, or domestic, is a weak evasion. To the second, that he was an enemy, I answer, what tyrant is not? yet Eglon by the Jews had been acknowledged as their sovereign, they had served him eighteen years, as long almost as we our William the Conqueror, in all which he could not be so unwise a statesman but to have taken of them oaths of fealty and allegiance; by which they made themselves his proper subjects, as their homage and present sent by Ehud testified. To the third, that he had special warrant to kill Eglon in that manner, it cannot be granted, because not expressed; it is plain that he was raised by God to be a deliverer, and went on just principles, such as were then and ever held allowable to deal so by a tyrant that could no otherwise be dealt with.

Neither did Samuel, though a prophet, with his own hand abstain from Agag; a foreign enemy no doubt; but mark the reason: "As thy sword has made women childless;" a cause that by the sentence of law itself nullifies all relations. And as the Law is between brother and brother, father and son, master and servant, wherefore not between king, or rather tyrant, and people? And whereas Jehu had special command to slay Jehoram, a successive and hereditary tyrant, it seems not the less imitable for that; for where a thing grounded so much on natural reason hath the addition of a command from God, what does it but establish the lawfulness of such an act? Nor is it likely that God, who had so many ways of punishing the house of Ahab, would have sent a subject against his prince, if the fact in itself, as done to a tyrant, had been of bad example. And if David refused to lift his hand against the Lord's anointed, the matter between them was not tyranny, but private enmity; and David, as a private person, had been his own revenger, not so much the people's. But when any tyrant at this day can show himself to be the Lord's anointed, the only mentioned reason why David withheld his hand, he may then, but not till then, presume on the same privilege.

We may pass, therefore, hence to Christian times. And first, our Saviour himself, how much he favoured tyrants and how much intended they should be found or honoured among Christians, declared his mind not obscurely; accounting their absolute authority no better than Gentilism, yea, though they flourished it over with the splendid name of benefactors; charging those that would be his disciples to usurp no such dominion; but that they who were to be of most authority among them, should esteem themselves ministers and servants to the public, Matt. xx. 25: "The princes of the Gentiles exercise lordship over them;" and Mark x. 42: "They that seem to rule," saith he, either slighting or accounting them no lawful rulers; "but ye shall not be so, but the greatest among you shall be your servant." And although he himself were the meekest, and came on earth to be so, yet to a tyrant we hear him not vouchsafe an humble word: but, "Tell that fox," Luke xiii. So far we ought to be from thinking that Christ and his Gospel should be made a sanctuary for tyrants from justice, to whom his law before never gave such protection. And wherefore did his mother, the Virgin Mary, give such praise to God in her prophetic song, that he had now, by the coming of Christ, cut down dynastas, or proud monarchs, from the throne, if the Church, when God manifests his power in them to do so, should rather choose all misery and vassalage to serve them, and let them still sit on their potent seats to be adored for doing mischief?

Surely it is not for nothing that tyrants, by a kind of natural instinct, both hate and fear none more than the true Church and saints of God, as the most dangerous enemies and subverters of monarchy, though indeed of tyranny. Hath not this been the perpetual cry of courtiers and court-prelates? Whereof no likelier cause can be alleged, but that they well discerned the mind and principles of most devout and zealous men, and indeed the very discipline of Church, tending to the dissolution of all tyranny.

No marvel then if since the faith of Christ received, in purer or impurer times, to depose a king and put him to death for tyranny hath been accounted so just and requisite, that neighbour kings have both upheld and taken part with subjects in the action. And Ludovicus Pius, himself an emperor, and son of Charles the Great, being made judge (du Haillan is my author) between Milegast, king of the Vultzes, and his subjects, who had deposed him, gave his verdict for the subjects, and for him whom they had chosen in his room. Note here, that the right of electing whom they please is, by the impartial testimony of an emperor, in the people: for, said he, "A just prince ought to be preferred before an unjust, and the end of government before the prerogative."

And Constantinus Leo, another emperor, in the Byzantine laws, saith, "That the end of a king is for the general good, which he not performing, is but the counterfeit of a king." And to prove that some of our own monarchs have acknowledged that their high office exempted them not from punishment, they had the sword of St. Edward borne before them by an officer, who was called earl of the palace, even at the times of their highest pomp and solemnities; to mind them, saith Matthew Paris, the best of our historians, "that if they erred, the sword had power to restrain them." And what restraint the sword comes to at length, having both edge and point, if any sceptic will doubt, let him feel. It is also affirmed from diligent search made in our ancient books of law, that the peers and barons of England had a legal right to judge the king: which was the cause most likely—for it could be no slight cause—that they were called his peers, or equals. This, however, may stand immovable, so long as man hath to deal with no better than man; that if our law judge all men to the lowest by their peers, it should, in all equity, ascend also, and judge the highest.

And so much I find both in our own and foreign story, that dukes, earls, and marquisses were at first not hereditary, not empty and vain titles, but names of trust and office, and with the office ceasing; as induces me to be of opinion, that every worthy man in Parliament—for the word baron imports no more—might for the public good be thought a fit peer and judge of the king, without regard had to petty caveats and circumstances, the chief impediment in high affairs, and ever stood upon most by circumstantial men. Whence doubtless our ancestors who were not ignorant with what rights either nature or ancient constitution had endowed them, when oaths both at coronation and renewed in parliament would not serve, thought it no way illegal to depose and put to death their tyrannous kings. Insomuch that the Parliament drew up a charge against Richard the Second, and the Commons requested to have judgment decreed against him, that the realm might not be endangered. And Peter Martyr, a divine of foremost rank, on the third of Judges approves their doings. Sir Thomas Smith also, a Protestant and a statesman, in his Commonwealth of England, putting the question, "whether it be lawful to rise against a tyrant;" answers, "that the vulgar judge of it according to the event and the learned according to the purpose of them that do it."

But far before those days, Gildas, the most ancient of all our historians, speaking of those times wherein the Roman empire decaying, quitted and relinquished what right they had by conquest to this island, and resigned it all into the people's hands, testifies that the people thus reinvested with their own original right, about the year 446, both elected them kings, whom they thought best, the first Christian British kings that ever reigned here since the Romans, and by the same right, when they apprehended cause, usually deposed and put them to death. This is the most fundamental and ancient tenure that any King of England can produce or pretend to; in comparison of which, all other titles and pleas are but of yesterday. If any object, that Gildas condemns the Britons for so doing, the answer is as ready; that he condemns them no more for so doing than he did before for choosing such; for, saith he, "They anointed them kings not of God, but such as were more bloody than the rest." Next, he condemns them not at all for deposing or putting them to death, but for doing it over hastily, without trial or well examining the cause, and for electing others worse in their room.

Thus we have here both domestic and most ancient examples, that the people of Britain have deposed and put to death their kings in those primitive Christian times. And to couple reason with example, if the Church in all ages, primitive, Romish, or Protestant, held it ever no less their duty than the power of their keys, though without express warrant of Scripture, to bring indifferently both king and peasant under the utmost rigour of their canons and censures ecclesiastical, even to the smiting him with a final excommunion if he persist impenitent; what hinders but that the temporal law both may and ought, though without a special text or precedent, extend with like indifference the civil sword, to the cutting off, without exemption, him that capitally offends, seeing that justice and religion are from the same God, and works of justice ofttimes more acceptable? Yet because that some lately, with the tongues and arguments of malignant backsliders, have written that the proceedings now in Parliament against the king are without precedent from any Protestant state or kingdom, the examples which follow shall be all Protestant, and chiefly Presbyterian.

In the year 1546, the Duke of Saxony, Landgrave of Hesse, and the whole Protestant league, raised open war against Charles the Fifth, their emperor, sent him a defiance, renounced all faith and allegiance toward him, and debated long in council whether they should give him so much as the title of Cæsar. Let all men judge what this wanted of deposing or of killing, but the power to do it.

In the year 1559, the Scots Protestants claiming promise of their queen-regent for liberty of conscience, she answering that promises were not to be claimed of princes beyond what was commodious for them to grant, told her to her face in the Parliament then at Stirling, that if it were so, they renounced their obedience; and soon after betook them to arms. Certainly, when allegiance is renounced, that very hour the king or queen is in effect deposed.

In the year 1564, John Knox, a most famous divine, and the Reformer of Scotland to the Presbyterian discipline, at a General Assembly maintained openly, in a dispute against Lethington, the Secretary of State, that subjects might and ought to execute God's judgments upon their king; that the fact of Jehu and others against their king, having the ground of God's ordinary command to put such and such offenders to death, was not extraordinary, but to be imitated of all that preferred the honour of God to the affection of flesh and wicked princes; that kings, if they offend, have no privilege to be exempted from the punishments of law more than any other subject: so that if the king be a murderer, adulterer, or idolater, he should suffer, not as a king, but as an offender; and this position he repeats again and again before them. Answerable was the opinion of John Craig, another learned divine, and that laws made by the tyranny of princes or the negligence of people their posterity might abrogate, and reform all things according to the original institution of commonwealths. And Knox being commanded by the nobility to write to Calvin and other learned men for their judgments in that question, refused, alleging, that both himself was fully resolved in conscience, and had heard their judgments, and had the same opinion under handwriting of many the most godly and most learned that he knew in Europe; that if he should move the question to them again, what should he do but show his own forgetfulness or inconstancy? All this is far more largely in the ecclesiastical history of Scotland (l. iv.) with many other passages to this effect all the book over, set out with diligence by Scotsmen of best repute among them at the beginning of these troubles; as if they laboured to inform us what we were to do, and what they intended upon the like occasion.

And to let the world know, that the whole Church and Protestant state of Scotland in those purest times of Reformation were of the same belief, three years after, they met in the field Mary, their lawful and hereditary queen, took her prisoner, yielding before fight, kept her in prison, and the same year deposed her.

And four years after that, the Scots, in justification of their deposing Queen Mary, sent ambassadors to Queen Elizabeth, and in a written declaration alleged, that they had used towards her more lenity than she deserved; that their ancestors had heretofore punished their kings by death or banishment; that the Scots were a free nation, made king whom they freely chose, and with the same freedom unkinged him if they saw cause, by right of ancient laws and ceremonies yet remaining, and old customs yet among the highlanders in choosing the head of their clans or families; all which, with many other arguments, bore witness, that regal power was nothing else but a mutual covenant or stipulation between King and People. These were Scotchmen and Presbyterians: but what measure then have they lately offered, to think such liberty less beseeming us than themselves, presuming to put him upon us for a master whom their law scarce allows to be their own equal? If now then we hear them in another strain than heretofore in the purest times of their Church, we may be confident it is the voice of faction speaking in them, not of truth and reformation, which no less in England than in Scotland, by the mouths of those faithful witnesses commonly called Puritans and Nonconformists, spake as clearly for the putting down, yea, the utmost punishing of kings, as in their several treatises may be read; even from the first reign of Elizabeth to these times. Insomuch that one of them, whose name was Gibson, foretold King James he should be rooted out, and conclude his race, if he persisted to uphold bishops. And that very inscription, stamped upon the first coins at his coronation, a naked sword in a hand with these words, "*Si mereor in me*," "Against me, if I deserve," not only manifested the judgment of that state, but seemed also to presage the sentence of divine justice in this event upon his son.

In the year 1581, the States of Holland, in a general assembly at the Hague, abjured all obedience and subjection to Philip, King of Spain; and in a declaration justify their so doing; for that by his tyrannous government, against faith so many times given and broken, he had lost his right to all the Belgic provinces; that therefore they deposed him, and declared it lawful to choose another in his stead. From that time to this, no state or kingdom in the world hath equally prospered: but let them remember not to look with an evil and prejudicial eye upon their neighbours, walking by the same rule.

But what need these examples to Presbyterians, I mean to those who now of late would seem so much to abhor deposing, whenas they to all Christendom have given the latest and the liveliest example of doing it themselves? I question not the lawfulness of raising war against a tyrant in defence of religion, or civil liberty; for no Protestant Church, from the first Waldenses of Lyons and Languedoc to this day, but done it round, and maintained it lawful. But this I doubt not to affirm, that the Presbyterians, who now so much condemn deposing, were the men themselves that deposed the king, and cannot, with all their shifting and relapsing, wash off the guiltiness from their own hands. For they themselves, by these their late doings, have made it guiltiness, and turned their own warrantable actions into rebellion.

There is nothing that so actually makes a King of England, as rightful possession and supremacy in all causes both civil and ecclesiastical: and nothing that so actually makes a subject of England as those two oaths of allegiance and supremacy observed without equivocating or any mental reservation. Out of doubt then, when the king shall command things already constituted in Church or State, obedience is the true essence of a subject, either to do, if it be lawful, or if he hold the thing unlawful, to submit to that penalty which the law imposes, so long as he intends to remain a subject. Therefore when the people, or any part of them, shall rise against the king and his authority, executing the law in anything established, civil or ecclesiastical, I do not say it is rebellion, if the thing commanded though established be unlawful, and that they sought first all due means of redress (and no man is further bound to law); but I say it is an absolute renouncing both of supremacy and allegiance, which, in one word, is an actual and total deposing of the king, and the setting up of another supreme authority over them.

And whether the Presbyterians have not done all this and much more, they will not put me, I suppose, to reckon up a seven years' story, fresh in the memory of all men. Have they not utterly broke the oath of allegiance, rejecting the king's command and authority sent them from any part of the kingdom, whether in things lawful or unlawful? Have they not abjured the oath of supremacy, by setting up the Parliament without the king, supreme to all their obedience; and though their vow and covenant bound them in general to the Parliament, yet sometimes adhering to the lesser part of Lords and Commons that remained faithful, as they term it, and even of them, one while to the Commons without the Lords, another while to the Lords without the Commons? Have they not still declared their meaning, whatever their oath were, to hold them only for supreme whom they found at any time most yielding to what they petitioned? Both these oaths which were the straitest bond of an English subject in reference to the king, being thus broke and made void, it follows undeniably, that the king from that time was by them in fact absolutely deposed, and they no longer in reality to be thought his subjects, notwithstanding their fine clause in the Covenant to preserve his person, crown, and dignity, set there by some dodging casuist with more craft than sincerity, to mitigate the matter in case of ill success, and not taken, I suppose, by any honest man, but as a condition subordinate to every the least particle, that might more concern religion, liberty, or the public peace.

To prove it yet more plainly, that they are the men who have deposed the king, I thus argue. We know that king and subject are relatives, and relatives have no longer being than in the relation; the relation between king and subject can be no other than regal authority and subjection. Hence I infer, past their defending, that if the subject, who is one relative, take away the relation, of force he takes away also the other relative; but the Presbyterians, who were one relative, that is to say, subjects, have for this seven years taken away the relation, that is to say, the king's authority, and their subjection to it; therefore the Presbyterians for these seven years have removed and extinguished the other relative, that is to say, the king; or, to speak more in brief, have deposed him; not only by depriving him the execution of his authority, but by conferring it upon others.

If then their oaths of subjection broken, new supremacy obeyed, new oaths and covenant taken, notwithstanding frivolous evasions, have in plain terms unkinged the king, much more than hath their seven years' war; not deposed him only, but outlawed him, and defied him as an alien, a rebel to law, and enemy to the state; it must needs be clear to any man not averse fromre ason, that hostility and subjection are two direct and positive contraries, and can no more in one subject stand together in respect of the same king, than one person at the same time can be in two remote places. Against whom therefore the subject is in act of hostility, we may be confident, that to him he is in no subjection: and in whom hostility takes place of subjection, for they can by no means consist together, to him the king can be not only no king, but an enemy.

So that from hence we shall not need dispute, whether they have deposed him, or what they have defaulted towards him as no king, but show manifestly how much they have done towards the killing him. Have they not levied all these wars against him, whether offensive or defensive—for defence in war equally offends, and most prudently beforehand—and given commission to slay, where they knew his person could not be exempt from danger? And if chance or flight had not saved him, how often had they killed him, directing their artillery, without blame or prohibition, to the very place where they saw him stand? Have they not sequestered him, judged or unjudged, and converted his revenue to other uses, detaining from him, as a grand delinquent, all means of livelihood, so that for them long since he might have perished or have starved? Have they not hunted and pursued him round about the kingdom with sword and fire? Have they not formerly denied to treat with him, and their now recanting ministers preached against him, as a reprobate incurable, an enemy to God and his Church, marked for destruction, and therefore not to be treated with? Have they not besieged him, and to their power forbid him water and fire, save what they shot against him to the hazard of his life? Yet while they thus assaulted and endangered it with hostile deeds, they swore in words to defend it, with his crown and dignity; not in order, as it seems now, to a firm and lasting peace, or to his repentance after all this blood; but simply, without regard, without remorse, or any comparable value of all the miseries and calamities suffered by the poor people, or to suffer hereafter, through his obstinacy or impenitence.

No understanding man can be ignorant, that covenants are ever made according to the present state of persons and of things; and have ever the more general laws of nature and of reason included in them, though not expressed. If I make a voluntary covenant, as with a man to do him good, and he prove afterward a monster to me, I should conceive a disobligement. If I covenant not to hurt an enemy, in favour of him and forbearance and hope of his amendment, and he, after that, shall do me tenfold injury and mischief to what he had done when I so covenanted, and still be plotting what may tend to my destruction, I question not but that his after-actions release me; nor know I covenant so sacred, that withholds me from demanding justice on him.

Howbeit, had not their distrust in a good cause, and the fast and loose of our prevaricating divines, oversrwayed, it had been doubtless better not to have inserted in a Covenant unnecessary obligations, and words, not works, of supererogating allegiance to their enemy; no way advantageous to themselves, had the king prevailed, as to their cost many would have felt, but full of snare and distraction to our friends; useful only, as we now find, to our adversaries, who under such a latitude and shelter of ambiguous interpretation have ever since been plotting and contriving new opportunities to trouble all again. How much better had it been, and more becoming an undaunted virtue, to have declared openly and boldly whom and what power the people were to hold supreme, as on the like occasion Protestants have done before, and many conscientious men now in these times have more than once besought the Parliament to do, that they might go on upon a sure foundation, and not with a riddling Covenant in their mouths, seeming to swear counter, almost in the same breath, allegiance and no allegiance; which doubtless had drawn off all the minds of sincere men from siding with them, had they not discerned their actions far more deposing him than their words upholding him; which words, made now the subject of cavillous interpretations, stood ever in the Covenant, by judgment of the more discerning sort, an evidence of their fear, not of their fidelity.

What I should return to speak on, of those attempts for which the king himself hath often charged the Presbyterians of seeking his life, whenas, in the due estimation of things, they might without a fallacy be said to have done the deed outright? Who knows not, that the king is a name of dignity and office, not of person? Who therefore kills a king, must kill him while he is a king. Then they certainly who by deposing him have long since taken from him the life of a king, his office and his dignity, they in the truest sense may be said to have killed the king: not only by their deposing and waging war against him, which besides the danger to his personal life, set him in the furthest opposite point from any vital function of a king, but by their holding him in prison, vanquished and yielded into their absolute and despotic power, which brought him to the lowest degradement and incapacity of the regal name. I say not by whose matchless valour, next under God, lest the story of their ingratitude thereupon carry me from the purpose in hand, which is to convince them that they, which I repeat again, were the men who in the truest sense killed the king, not only as is proved before; but by depressing him, their king, far below the rank of a subject to the condition of a captive, without intention to restore him, as the chancellor of Scotland in a speech told him plainly at Newcastle, unless he granted fully all their demands, which they knew he never meant.

Nor did they treat, or think of treating, with him, till their hatred to the army that delivered them, not their love or duty to the king, joined them secretly with men sentenced so oft for reprobates in their own mouths, by whose subtle inspiring they grew mad upon a most tardy and improper treaty. Whereas if the whole bent of their actions had not been against the king himself, but only against his evil counsellors, as they feigned and published, wherefore did they not restore him all that while to the true life of a king, his office, crown, and dignity, when he was in their power and they themselves his nearest counsellors? The truth, therefore, is, both that they would not, and that indeed they could not without their own certain destruction, having reduced him to such a final pass as was the very death and burial of all that in him was regal, and from whence never King of England yet revived, but by the new reinforcement of his own party which was a kind of resurrection to him.

Thus having quite extinguished all that could be in him of a king, and from a total privation clad him over, like another specifical thing, with forms and habitudes destructive to the former, they left in his person, dead as to law and all the civil right either of king or subject, the life only of a prisoner, a captive and a malefactor. Whom the equal and impartial hand of justice finding was no more to spare than another ordinary man, not only made obnoxious to the doom of law, by a charge more than once drawn up against him, and his own confession to the first article at Newport, but summoned and arraigned in the sight of God and his people, cursed and devoted to perdition worse than any Ahab or Antiochus, with exhortation to curse all those in the name of God that made not war against him, as bitterly as Meroz was to be cursed that went not out against a Canaanitish king, almost in all the sermons, prayers, and fulminations, that have been uttered this seven years by those cloven tongues of falsehood and dissension who now, to the stirring up of new discord, acquit him, and against their own discipline, which they boast to be the throne and sceptre of Christ, absolve him, unconfound him; though unconverted, unrepentant, insensible of all their precious saints and martyrs whose blood they have so often laid upon his head, and now again, with a new sovereign anointment, can wash it all off, as if it were as vile and no more to be reckoned for than the blood of so many dogs in a time of pestilence: giving the most opprobrious lie to all the acted zeal that for these many years hath filled their bellies and fed them fat upon the foolish people. Ministers of sedition, not of the Gospel, who, while they saw it manifestly tend to civil war and bloodshed, never ceased exasperating the People against him; and now that they see it likely to breed new commotion, cease not to incite others against the People that have saved them from him, as if sedition were their only aim, whether against him or for him.

But God, as we have cause to trust, will put other thoughts into the people, and turn them from giving ear or heed to these mercenary noisemakers, of whose fury and false prophecies we have enough experience; and from the murmurs of new discord will incline them to hearken rather with erected minds to the voice of our supreme magistracy, calling us to liberty, and the flourishing deeds of a reformed commonwealth; with this hope, that as God was heretofore angry with the Jews who rejected him and his form of government to choose a king, so that he will bless us, and be propitious to us who reject a king to make Him only our leader, and supreme governor, in the conformity, as near as may be, of his own ancient government. If we have at least but so much worth in us to entertain the sense of our future happiness, and the courage to receive what God vouchsafes us; wherein we have the honour to precede other nations, who are now labouring to be our followers.

For as to this question in hand, what the people by their just right may do in change of government, or of governor, we see it cleared sufficiently, besides other ample authority, even from the mouths of princes themselves. And surely they that shall boast, as we do, to be a free nation, and not have in themselves the power to remove or to abolish any governor, supreme or subordinate, with the government itself, upon urgent causes, may please their fancy with a ridiculous and painted freedom, fit to cozen babies; but then are indeed under tyranny and servitude, as wanting that power which is the root and source of all liberty, to dispose and economise in the land which God hath given them, as masters of family in their own house and free inheritance. Without which natural and essential power of a free nation, though bearing high their heads, they can in due esteem be thought no better than slaves and vassals born in the tenure and occupation of another inheriting lord, whose government, though not illegal, or intolerable, hangs over them as a lordly scourge, not as a free government; and therefore to be abrogated.

How much more justly then may they fling off tyranny, or tyrants, who being once deposed can be no more than private men, as subject to the reach of justice and arraignment as any other transgressors? And certainly if men, not to speak of heathen, both wise and religious, have done justice upon tyrants what way they could soonest, how much more mild and humane then is it, to give them fair and open trial; to teach lawless kings, and all who so much adore them, that not mortal man or his imperious will, but Justice, is the only true sovereign and supreme Majesty upon earth? Let men cease therefore, out of faction and hyprocrisy, to make outcries and horrid things of things so just and honourable, though perhaps till now no Protestant state or kingdom can be alleged to have openly put to death their king, which lately some have written, and imputed to their great glory; much mistaking the matter. It is not, neither ought to be, the glory of a Protestant state never to have put their king to death; it is the glory of a Protestant king never to have deserved death. And if the Parliament and military council do what they do without precedent, if it appear their duty, it argues the more wisdom, virtue and magnanimity, that they know themselves able to be a precedent to others; who perhaps in future ages, if they prove not too degenerate, will look up with honour, and aspire towards these exemplary and matchless deeds of their ancestors, as to the highest top of their civil glory and emulation; which heretofore, in the pursuance of fame and foreign dominion, spent itself vaingloriously abroad; but henceforth may learn a better fortitude, to dare execute highest justice on them that shall by force of arms endeavour the oppressing and bereaving of Religion and their Liberty at home. That no unbridled potentate or tyrant, but to his sorrow, for the future may presume such high and irresponsible licence over mankind, to havoc and turn upside down whole kingdoms of men, as though they were no more in respect of his perverse will than a nation of pismires.

As for the party called Presbyterian, of whom I believe very many to be good and faithful Christians, though misled by some of turbulent spirit, I wish them, earnestly and calmly not to fall off from their first principles, nor to affect rigour and superiority over men not under them; not to compel unforcible things, in religion especially, which, if not voluntary, becomes a sin; not to assist the clamour and malicious drifts of men whom they themselves have judged to be the worst of men, the obdurate enemies of God and his Church: nor to dart against the actions of their brethren, for want of other argument, those wrested laws and Scriptures thrown by prelates and malignants against their own sides, which though they hurt not otherwise, yet taken up by them to the condemnation of their own doings, give scandal to all men, and discover in themselves either extreme passion or apostacy. Let them not oppose their best friends and associates, who molest them not at all, infringe not the least of their liberties, unless they call it their liberty to bind other men's consciences, but are still seeking to live at peace with them and brotherly accord. Let them beware an old and perfect enemy, who, though he hope by sowing discord to make them his instruments, yet cannot forbear a minute the open threatening of his destined revenge upon them, when they have served his purposes. Let them fear, therefore, if they be wise, rather what they have done already, than what remains to do, and be warned in time that they put no confidence in princes whom they have provoked, lest they be added to the examples of those that miserably have tasted the event.

Stories can inform them how Christiern the Second, King of Denmark, not much above a hundred years past, driven out by his subjects, and received again upon new oaths and conditions, broke through them all to his most bloody revenge; slaying his chief opposers, when he saw his time, both them and their children, invited to a feast for that purpose; how Maximilian dealt with those of Bruges, though by mediation of the German princes reconciled to them by solemn and public writings drawn and sealed; how the massacre at Paris was the effect of that credulous peace, which the French Protestants made with Charles IX. their king: and that the main visible cause, which to this day hath saved the Netherlands from utter ruin, was their final not believing the perfidious cruelty, which, as a constant maxim of state, hath been used by the Spanish kings on their subjects that have taken arms, and after trusted them; as no latter age but can testify, heretofore in Belgia itself, and this very year in Naples. And to conclude with one past exception, though far more ancient, David, whose sanctified prudence might be alone sufficient, not to warrant us only, but to instruct us, when once he had taken arms never after that trusted Saul, though with tears and much relenting he twice promised not to hurt him. These instances, few of many, might admonish them, both English and Scotch, not to let their own ends, and the driving on of a faction, betray them blindly into the snare of those enemies whose revenge looks on them as the men who first begun, fomented, and carried on, beyond the cure of any sound or safe accommodation, all the evil which hath since unavoidably befallen them and their king.

I have something also to the divines, though brief to what were needful: not to be disturbers of the civil affairs, being in hands better able and more belonging to manage them; but to study harder, and to attend the office of good pastors, knowing that he whose flock is least among them hath a dreadful charge not performed by mounting twice into the chair with a formal preachment huddled up at the odd hours of a whole lazy week, but by incessant pains and watching, in season and out of season, from house to house, over the souls of whom they have to feed. Which if they ever well considered, how little leisure would they find, to be the most pragmatical sidesmen of every popular tumult and sedition, and all this while are to learn what the true end and reason is of the Gospel which they teach; and what a world it differs from the censorious and supercilious droling over conscience. It would be good also they lived so as might persuade the people they hated covetousness, which, worse than heresy, is idolatry; hated pluralities, and all kind of simony; left rambling from benefice to benefice, like ravenous wolves seeking where they may devour the biggest. Of which if some, well and warmly seated from the beginning, be not guilty, it were good they held not conversation with such as are. Let them be sorry that, being called to assemble about reforming the Church, they fell to progging and soliciting the Parliament, though they had renounced the name of priests, for a new settling of their tithes and oblations, and double-lined themselves with spiritual places of commodity beyond the possible discharge of their duty. Let them assemble in consistory with their elders and deacons, according to ancient ecclesiastical rule, to the preserving of Church discipline, each in his several charge, and not a pack of clergymen by themselves to bellycheer in their presumptuous Sion, or to promote designs, abuse and gull the simple laity, and stir up tumult, as the prelates did, for the maintenance of their pride and avarice.

These things if they observe, and wait with patience, no doubt but all things will go well without their importunities or exclamations; and the printed letters, which they sent subscribed with the ostentation of great characters and little moment, would be more considerable than now they are. But if they be the ministers of Mammon instead of Christ, and scandalise his Church with the filthy love of gain, aspiring also to sit the closest and the heaviest of all tyrants upon the conscience, and fall notoriously into the same sins whereof so lately and so loud they accused the prelates; as God rooted out those wicked ones immediately before, so will he root out them, their imitators; and, to vindicate his own glory and religion, will uncover their hypocrisy to the open world, and visit upon their own heads that "Curse ye Meroz," the very motto of their pulpits, wherewith so frequently, not as Meroz, but more like atheists, they have blasphemed the vengeance of God, and traduced the zeal of his people.

And that they be not what they go for, true ministers of the Protestant doctrine, taught by those abroad, famous and religious men, who first reformed the Church, or by those no less zealous who withstood corruption and the bishops here at home, branded with the name of Puritans and Nonconformists, we shall abound with testimonies to make appear: that men may yet more fully know the difference between Protestant divines, and these pulpit-firebrands. "Such is the state of-things at this day, that men neither can, nor will, nor indeed, ought to endure longer the domination of you princes." "Neither is Cæsar to make war as head of Christendom, protector of the Church, defender of the faith; these titles being false and windy, and most kings being the greatest enemies to religion." What hinders then, but that we may depose or punish them? These also are recited by Cochlæus in his Miscellanies to be the words of Luther, or some other eminent divine, then in Germany, when the Protestants there entered into solemn covenant at Smalcaldia: "Ut ora iis obturem," &c. "That I may stop their mouths, the pope and emperor are not born, but elected; and may also be deposed, as hath been often done." If Luther, or whoever else, thought so, he could not stay there; for the right of birth or succession can be no privilege in nature to let a tyrant sit irremovable over a nation freeborn, without transforming that nation from the nature and condition of men born free, into natural, hereditary, and successive slaves. Therefore he saith further: "To displace and throw down this exactor, this Phalaris, this Nero, is a work pleasing to God;" namely, for being such a one: which is a moral reason. Shall then so slight a consideration as his hap to be not elective simply, but by birth, which was a mere accident, overthrow that which is moral, and make unpleasing to God that which otherwise had so well pleased him? Certainly not: for if the matter be rightly argued, election, much rather than chance, binds a man to content himself with what he suffers by his own bad election. Though indeed neither one nor the other binds any man, much less any people, to a necessary sufferance of those wrongs and evils which they have ability and strength enough given them to remove.

"When kings reign perfidiously, and against the rule of Christ, they may, according to the Word of God, be deposed." "I know not how it comes to pass that kings reign by succession, unless it be with consent of the whole people." "But when by suffrage and consent of the whole people, or the better part of them, a tyrant is deposed or put to death, God is the chief leader in that action." "Now that we are so lukewarm in upholding public justice, we endure the vices of tyrants to reign now-a-days with impunity; justly therefore by them we are trod underfoot, and shall at length with them be punished.' Yet ways are not wanting by which tyrants may be removed, but there wants public justice." "Beware, ye tyrants! for now the Gospel of Jesus Christ, spreading far and wide, will renew the lives of many to love innocence and justice; which if ye also shall do, ye shall be honoured. But if ye shall go on to rage, and do violence, ye shall be trampled on by all men." "When the Roman empire, or any other, shall begin to oppress religion, and we negligently suffer it, we are as much guilty of religion so violated, as the oppressors themselves." [Zwinglius.]

"Now-a-days monarchs pretend always in their titles to be kings by the grace of God; but how many of them to this end only pretend it, that they may reign without control! For to what purpose is the grace of God mentioned in the title of kings, but that they may acknowledge no superior? In the meanwhile God, whose name they use to support themselves, they willingly would tread under their feet. It is therefore a mere cheat, when they boast to reign by the grace of God." "Earthly princes depose themselves, while they rise against God; yea, they are unworthy to be numbered among men: rather it behoves us to spit upon their heads than to obey them." [Calvin.]

"If a sovereign prince endeavour by arms to defend transgressors, to subvert those things which are taught in the Word of God, they, who are in authority under him, ought first to dissuade him; if they prevail not, and that he now bears himself not as a prince but as an enemy, and seeks to violate privileges and rights granted to inferior magistrates or commonalties, it is the part of pious magistrates, imploring first the assistance of God, rather to try all ways and means than to betray the flock of Christ to such an enemy of God: for they also are to this end ordained, that they may defend the people of God and maintain those things which are good and just. For to have supreme power lessens not the evil committed by that power, but makes it the less tolerable by how much the more generally hurtful. Then certainly the less tolerable, the more unpardonably to be punished." [Brucer.] Of Peter Martyr we have spoke before. "They whose part is to set up magistrates. may restrain them also from outrageous deeds, or pull them down; but all magistrates are set up either by Parliament or by electors, or by other magistrates; they, therefore, who exalted them may lawfully degrade and punish them." [Paræus.]

Of the Scots divines I need not mention others than the famousest among them, Knox, and his fellow-labourers in the reformation of Scotland; whose large treatise on this subject defends the same opinion. To cite them sufficiently, were to insert their whole books, written purposely on this argument. "Knox's Appeal," and "To the Reader," where he promises in a postscript that the book which he intended to set forth, called "The Second Blast of the Trumpet," should maintain more at large, that the same men most justly may depose and punish him whom unadvisedly they have elected, notwithstanding birth, succession, or any oath of allegiance. Among our own divines, Cartwright and Fenner, two of the learnedest, may in reason satisfy us what was held by the rest. Fenner, in his book of Theology, maintaining, that they who have power, that is to say, a Parliament, may either by fair means or by force depose a tyrant, whom he defines to be him that wilfully breaks all or the principal conditions made between him and the commonwealth. And Cartwright, in a prefixed epistle, testifies his approbation of the whole book.

"Kings have their authority of the people, who may upon occasion reassume it to themselves." "The people may kill wicked princes, as monsters and cruel beasts." [Gilby.] "When kings or rulers become blasphemers of God, oppressors and murderers of their subjects, they ought no more to be accounted kings, or lawful magistrates, but as private men to be examined, accused, and condemned and punished by the law of God; and being convicted and punished by that law, it is not man's but God's doing." "By the civil laws, a fool or idiot born, and so proved, shall lose the lands and inheritance whereto he is born, because he is not able to use them aright: and especially ought in no case be suffered to have the government of a whole nation; but there is no such evil can come to the commonwealth by fools and idiots as doth by the rage and fury of ungodly rulers; such, therefore, being without God, ought to have no authority over God's people, who by his Word requireth the contrary." "No person is exempt by any law of God from this punishment: be he king, queen, or emperor, he must die the death; for God hath not placed them above others to transgress his laws as they list, but to be subject to them as well as others; and if they be subject to his laws, then to the punishment also, so much the more as their example is more dangerous." "When magistrates cease to do their duty, the people are, as it were, without magistrates, yea, worse, and then God giveth the sword into the people's hand, and he himself is become immediately their head." "If princes do right, and keep promise with you, then do you owe to them all humble obedience; if not, ye are discharged, and your study ought to be in this case how ye may depose and punish according to the law such rebels against God, and oppressors of their country." [Goodman.]

This Goodman was a minister of the English church at Geneva, as Dudley Fenner was at Middleburgh, or some other place in that country. These were the pastors of those saints and confessors, who, flying from the bloody persecution of Queen Mary, gathered up at length their scattered members into many congregations; whereof some in Upper, some in Lower Germany, part of them settled at Geneva; where this author having preached on this subject, to the great liking of certain learned and godly men who heard him, was by them sundry times and with much instance required to write more fully on that point. Who thereupon took it in hand, and conferring with the best learned in those parts (among whom Calvin was then living in the same city), with their special approbation he published this treatise, aiming principally, as is testified by Whittingham in the Preface, that his brethren of England, the Protestants, might be persuaded in the truth of that doctrine concerning obedience to magistrates.

These were the true Protestant divines of England, our fathers in the faith we hold; this was their sense, who for so many years labouring under prelacy, through all storms and persecutions kept religion from extinguishing; and delivered it pure to us, till there arose a covetous and ambitious generation of divines (for divines they call themselves), who, feigning on a sudden to be new converts and proselytes from episcopacy under which they had long temporised, opened their mouths at length in show against pluralities and prelacy, but with intent to swallow them down both; gorging themselves like harpies on those simonious places and preferments of their outed predecessors, as the quarry for which they hunted, not to plurality only but to multiplicity, for possessing which they had accused them, their brethren, and aspiring under another title to the same authority and usurpation over the consciences of all men.

Of this faction, divers reverend and learned divines, as they are styled in the phylactery of their own title-page, pleading the lawfulness of defensive arms against the king, in a treatise called "Scripture and Reason," seem in words to disclaim utterly the deposing of a king; but both the Scripture, and the reasons which they use, draw consequences after them which, without their bidding, conclude it lawful. For if by Scripture, and by that especially to the Romans, which they most insist upon, kings, doing that which is contrary to St. Paul's definition of a magistrate, may be resisted, they may altogether with as much force of consequence be deposed or punished. And if by Reason the unjust authority of kings "may be forfeited in part, and his power be reassumed in part, either by the Parliament or people, for the case in hazard and the present necessity," as they affirm, p. 34, there can no Scripture be alleged, no imaginable reason given, —that necessity continuing as it may always, and they in all prudence and their duty may take upon them to foresee it,—why in such a case they may not finally amerce him with the loss of his kingdom of whose amendment they have no hope. And if one wicked action persisted in against religion, laws, and liberties, may warrant us to thus much in part, why may not forty times as many tyrannies, by him committed, warrant us to proceed on restraining him, till the restraint become total? For the ways of justice are exactest proportion; if for one trespass of a king it require so much remedy or satisfaction, then for twenty more as heinous crimes, it requires of him twenty-fold; and so proportionably, till it come to what is utmost among men. If in these proceedings against their king they may not finish, by the usual course of justice, what they have begun, they could not lawfully begin at all. For this golden rule of justice and morality, as well as of arithmetic, out of three terms which they admit, will as certainly and unavoidably bring out the fourth as any problem that ever Euclid or Apollonius made good by demonstration.

And if the Parliament, being undeposable but by themselves, as is affirmed, p. 37, 38, might for his whole life, if they saw cause, take all power, authority, and the sword out of his hand, which in effect is to unmagistrate him, why might they not, being then themselves the sole magistrates in force, proceed to punish him, who, being lawfully deprived of all things that define a magistrate can be now no magistrate to be degraded lower, but an offender to be punished. Lastly, whom they may defy and meet in battle, why may they not as well prosecute by justice? For lawful war is but the execution of justice against them who refuse law. Among whom if it be lawful (as they deny not, p. 19, 20), to slay the king himself coming in front at his own peril, wherefore may not justice do that intendedly, which the chance of a defensive war might without blame have done casually, nay, purposely, if there it find him among the rest? They ask, p. 19, "By what rule of conscience or God a state is bound to sacrifice religion, laws, and liberties, rather than a prince defending such as subvert them should come in hazard of his life." And I ask by what conscience, or divinity, or law, or reason, a state is bound to leave all these sacred concernments under a perpetual hazard and extremity of danger, rather than cut off a wicked prince who sits plotting day and night to subvert them.

They tell us that the law of nature justifies any man to defend himself, even against the king in person: let them show us then why the same law may not justify much more a state or whole people to do justice upon him against whom each private man may lawfully defend himself; seeing all kind of justice done is a defence to good men, as well as a punishment to bad; and justice done upon a tyrant is no more but the necessary self-defence of a whole commonwealth. To war upon a king that his instruments may be brought to condign punishment, and thereafter to punish them, the instruments, and not to spare only but to defend and honour him, the author, is the strangest piece of justice to be called Christian, and the strangest piece of Reason to be called human, that by men of reverence and learning, as their style imports them, ever yet was vented. They maintain in the third and fourth section, that a judge or inferior magistrate is anointed of God, is his minister, hath the sword in his hand, is to be obeyed by St. Peter's rule as well as the supreme, and without difference anywhere expressed: and yet will have us fight against the supreme till he remove and punish the inferior magistrate, for such were greatest delinquents; whereas by Scripture and by Reason there can no more authority be shown to resist the one than the other; and altogether as much to punish or depose the supreme himself, as to make war upon him till he punish or deliver up his inferior magistrates, whom in the same terms we are commanded to obey, and not to resist.

Thus while they, in a cautious line or two here and there stuffed in, are only verbal against the pulling down or punishing of tyrants, all the Scripture and the reason which they bring, is in every leaf direct and rational, to infer it altogether as lawful as to resist them. And yet in all their sermons, as hath by others been well noted, they went much further. For divines, if we observe them, have their postures and their motions no less expertly, and with no less variety, than they that practice feats in the Artillery-ground. Sometimes they seem furiously to march on, and presently march counter; by and by they stand, and then retreat; or if need be, can face about, or wheel in a whole body, with that cunning and dexterity as is almost unperceivable, to wind themselves by shifting ground into places of more advantage. And Providence only must be the drum, Providence the word of command, that calls them from above, but always to some larger benefice, or acts them into such or such figures and promotions. At their turns and doublings no men readier, to the right, or to the left; for it is their turns which they serve chiefly; herein only singular, that with them there is no certain hand right or left but as their own commodity thinks best to call it. But if there come a truth to be defended which to them and their interest of this world seems not so profitable, straight these nimble motionists can find not even legs to stand upon; and are no more of use to reformation thoroughly performed and not superficially, or to the advancement of Truth—which among mortal men is always in her progress—than if on a sudden they were struck maim and crippled. Which the better to conceal, or the more to countenance by a general conformity to their own limping, they would have Scripture, they would have Reason also, made to halt with them for company; and would put us off with impotent conclusions, lame and shorter than the premisses.

In this posture they seem to stand with great zeal and confidence on the wall of Sion; but like Jebusites, not like Israelites, or Levites: blind also as well as lame, they discern not David from Adonibezec: but cry him up for the Lord's anointed, whose thumbs and great toes not long before they had cut off upon their pulpit cushions. Therefore he who is our only King, the Root of David, and whose kingdom is eternal righteousness, with all those that war under him, whose happiness and final hopes are laid up in that only just and rightful kingdom which we pray incessantly may come soon, and in so praying wish hasty ruin and destruction to all tyrants, even he our immortal King, and all that love him, must of necessity have in abomination these blind and lame defenders of Jerusalem, as the soul of David hated them, and forbid them entrance into God's house and his own. But as to those before them, which I cited first, and with an easy search, for many more might be added, as they there stand, without more in number, being the best and chief of Protestant divines, we may follow them for faithful guides, and without doubting may receive them as witnesses abundant of what we here affirm concerning tyrants. And indeed I find it generally the clear and positive determination of them all, not prelatical, or of this late faction subprelatical, who have written on this argument, that to do justice on a lawless king is to a private man unlawful; to an inferior magistrate lawful: or if they were divided in opinion, yet greater than these here alleged, or of more authority in the Church, there can be none produced.

If any one shall go about, by bringing other testimonies to disable these, or by bringing these against themselves in other cited passages of their books, he will not only fail to make good that false and impudent assertion of those mutinous ministers, that the deposing and punishing of a king or tyrant, "is against the constant judgment of all Protestant divines," it being quite the contrary; but will prove rather what perhaps he intended not, that the judgment of divines, if it be so various and inconstant to itself, is not considerable, or to be esteemed at all. Ere which be yielded, as I hope it never will, these ignorant assertors in their own art will have proved themselves more and more, not to be Protestant divines, whose constant judgment in this point they have so audaciously belied, but rather to be a pack of hungry church-wolves, who in the steps of Simon Magus their father, following the hot scent of double livings and pluralities, advowsons, donatives, inductions, and augmentations, though uncalled to the flock of Christ, but by the mere suggestion of their bellies—

like those priests of Bel whose pranks Daniel found out—have got possession, or rather seized upon the pulpit, as the stronghold and fortress of their sedition and rebellion against the Civil Magistrate. Whose friendly and victorious hand having rescued them from the bishops, their insulting lords, fed them plenteously both in public and in private, raised them to be high and rich, of poor and base; only suffered not their covetousness and fierce ambition—which as the pit that sent out their fellow-locusts hath been ever bottomless and boundless—to interpose in all things, and over all persons, their impetuous ignorance and importunity?

FREEDOM IN CHURCH AND STATE.

> "To know
> Both Spiritual Power and Civil, what each means,
> What severs each, thou hast learned, which few have done;
> The bounds of either sword to thee we owe:
> Therefore on thy firm hand Religion bows
> In peace, and reckons thee her eldest son."
> —*Milton's Sonnet to Sir Henry Vane the Younger.*

A TREATISE OF CIVIL POWER IN ECCLESIASTICAL CAUSES;

Showing that it is not lawful for any Power on Earth to Compel in Matters of Religion.

To the Parliament of the Commonwealth of England, with the Dominions thereof.

I HAVE prepared, supreme Council, against the much-expected time of your sitting, this treatise; which, though to all Christian magistrates equally belonging, and therefore to have been written in the common language of Christendom, natural duty and affection hath confined, and dedicated first to my own nation; and in a season wherein the timely reading thereof, to the easier accomplishment of your great work, may save you much labour and interruption: of two parts usually proposed, Civil and Ecclesiastical, recommending Civil only to your proper care; Ecclesiastical, to them only from whom it takes both that name and nature.

Yet not for this cause only do I require or trust to find acceptance, but in a twofold respect besides. First, as bringing clear evidence of Scripture, and Protestant maxims, to the Parliament of England, who in all their late acts, upon occasion, have professed to assert only the true Protestant Christian Religion, as it is contained in the Holy Scriptures. Next, in regard that your power being but for a time, and having in yourselves a Christian liberty of your own, which at one time or other may be oppressed, thereof truly sensible, it will concern you while you are in power so to regard other men's Consciences as you would your own should be regarded in the power of others; and to consider that any law against Conscience is alike in force against any conscience, and so may one way or other justly redound upon yourselves.

One advantage I make no doubt of, that I shall write to many eminent persons of your number already perfect and resolved in this important article of Christianity. Some of whom I remember to have heard often for several years, at a Council next in authority to your own, so well joining Religion with Civil Prudence, and yet so well distinguishing the different power of either; and this not only voting, but frequently reasoning why it should be so, that if any there present had been before of an opinion contrary he might doubtless have departed thence a convert in that point, and have confessed that then both Commonwealth and Religion will at length, if ever, flourish in Christendom when either they who govern discern between Civil and Religious or they only who so discern shall be admitted to govern. Till then, nothing but troubles, persecutions, commotions can be expected; the inward decay of true Religion among ourselves, and the utter overthrow at last by a common enemy.

Of Civil Liberty I have written heretofore by the appointment, and not without the approbation, of civil power: of Christian Liberty I write now, which others long since having done with all freedom under heathen emperors, I should do wrong to suspect that I now shall with less under Christian governors, and such especially as profess openly their defence of Christian liberty. Although I write this, not otherwise appointed or induced, than by an inward persuasion of the Christian duty which I may usefully discharge herein to the common Lord and Master of us all, and the certain hope of His approbation, first and chiefest to be sought: in the hand of whose providence I remain, praying all success and good event on your public councils to the defence of true Religion and our Civil Rights.

JOHN MILTON.

A TREATISE OF CIVIL POWER IN ECCLESIASTICAL CAUSES.

Two things there be, which have been ever found working much mischief to the Church of God and the advancement of truth: Force on one side restraining, and Hire on the other side corrupting, the teachers thereof. Few ages have been since the ascension of our Saviour, wherein the one of these two, or both together, have not prevailed. It can be at no time, therefore, unseasonable to speak of these things; since by them the Church is either in continual detriment and oppression, or in continual danger. The former shall be at this time my argument; the latter as I shall find God disposing me, and opportunity inviting. What I argue shall be drawn from the Scripture only; and therein from true fundamental principles of the Gospel, to all knowing Christians undeniable. And if the governors of this Commonwealth, since the rooting out of prelates, have made least use of force in Religion and most have favoured Christian liberty of any in this island before them since the first preaching of the Gospel, for which we are not to forget our thanks to God, and their due praise; they may, I doubt not, in this treatise find that which not only will confirm them to defend still the Christian Liberty which we enjoy, but will incite them also to enlarge it, if in aught they yet straiten it. To them who perhaps hereafter, less experienced in Religion, may come to govern or give us laws, this or other such, if they please, may be a timely instruction: however, to the truth it will be at all times no unneedful testimony, at least some discharge of that general duty which no Christian, but according to what he hath received, knows is required of him, if he have aught more conducing to the advancement of Religion than what is usually endeavoured, freely to impart it.

It will require no great labour of exposition to unfold what is here meant by matters of Religion; being as soon apprehended as defined, such things as belong chiefly to the knowledge and service of God, and are either above the reach and light of nature without revelation from above, and therefore liable to be variously understood by human reason, or such things as are enjoined or forbidden by divine precept, which else by the light of reason would seem indifferent to be done or not done, and so likewise must needs appear to every man as the precept is understood. Whence I here mean by Conscience or Religion that full persuasion whereby we are assured that our belief and practice, as far as we are able to apprehend and probably make appear, is according to the will of God and his Holy Spirit within us, which we ought to follow much rather than any law of man, as not only his Word everywhere bids us, but the very dictate of reason tells us, Acts iv. 19: "Whether it be right in the sight of God, to hearken to you more than to God, judge ye." That for belief or practice in Religion according to this conscientious persuasion, no man ought to be punished or molested by any outward force on earth whatsoever, I distrust not, through God's implored assistance, to make plain by these following arguments.

First, it cannot be denied,—being the main foundation of our Protestant Religion,—that we of these ages, having no other divine rule or authority from without us warrantable to one another as a common ground but the Holy Scripture, and no other within us but the illumination of the Holy Spirit so interpreting that Scripture as warrantable only to ourselves and to such whose consciences we can so persuade, can have no other ground in matters of Religion but only from the Scriptures. And these being not possible to be understood without this divine illumination, which no man can know at all times to be in himself much less to be at any time for certain in any other, it follows clearly, that no man or body of men in these times can be the infallible judges or determiners in matters of Religion to any other men's consciences but their own. And therefore those Bereans are commended, Acts xvii. 11, who after the preaching even of St. Paul, "searched the Scriptures daily, whether those things were so." Nor did they more than what God himself in many places commands us by the same Apostle, to search, to try, to judge of these things ourselves: and gives us reason also, Gal. vi. 4, 5: "Let every man prove his own work, and then shall he have rejoicing in himself alone, and not in another: for every man shall bear his own burden."

If then we count it so ignorant and irreligious in the papist, to think himself discharged in God's account believing only as the Church believes, how much greater condemnation will it be to the Protestant, his condemner, to think himself justified believing only as the State believes? With good cause, therefore, it is the general consent of all sound Protestant writers, that neither traditions, councils, nor canons of any visible Church, much less edicts of any magistrate or civil session, but the Scripture only can be the final judge or rule in matters of Religion, and that only in the Conscience of every Christian to himself. Which protestation made by the first public Reformers of our Religion against the imperial edicts of Charles the Fifth, imposing Church traditions without Scripture, gave first beginning to the name of Protestant. And with that name hath ever been received this doctrine, which prefers the Scripture before the Church, and acknowledges none but the Scripture sole interpreter of itself to the conscience. For if the Church be not sufficient to be implicitly believed, as we hold it is not, what can there else be named of more authority than the Church but the Conscience, than which God only is greater? 1 John iii. 20. But if any man shall pretend that the Scripture judges to his conscience for other men, he makes himself greater not only than the Church but also than the Scripture, than the consciences of other men. A presumption too high for any mortal, since every true Christian able to give a reason of his faith hath the Word of God before him, the promised Holy Spirit, and the mind of Christ within him, 1 Cor. ii. 16; a much better and safer guide of conscience, which, as far as concerns himself he may far more certainly know than any outward rule imposed upon him by others, whom he inwardly neither knows nor can know; at least knows nothing of them more sure than this one thing, that they cannot be his judges in Religion; 1 Cor. ii. 15: "The spiritual man judgeth all things, but he himself is judged of no man."

Chiefly for this cause do all true Protestants account the pope Antichrist, for that he assumes to himself this Infallibility over both the Conscience and the Scripture; "sitting in the temple of God," as it were opposite to God, "and exalting himself above all that is called God, or is worshipped," 2 Thess. ii. 4.; that is to say, not only above all judges and magistrates, who though they be called gods, are far beneath infallible; but also above God himself, by giving law both to the Scripture, to the Conscience, and to the Spirit itself of God within us, whenas we find, James iv. 12, "There is one lawgiver, who is able to save and to destroy: Who art thou that judgest another?"

That Christ is the only lawgiver of his Church, and that it is here meant in religious matters, no well-grounded Christian will deny. Thus also St. Paul, Rom. xiv. 4, "Who art thou that judgest the servant of another? to his own lord he standeth or falleth: but he shall stand; for God is able to make him stand." As therefore of one beyond expression bold and presumptuous, both these Apostles demand, "Who art thou" that presumest to impose other law or judgment in Religion than the only lawgiver and judge Christ, who only can save and destroy, gives to the Conscience? And the forecited place to the Thessalonians, by compared effects, resolves us, that be he or they who or wherever they be or can be, they are of far less authority than the Church, whom in these things as Protestants they receive not, and yet no less Antichrist in this main point of Antichristianism, no less a pope or popedom than he at Rome, if not much more, by setting up supreme interpreters of Scripture—either those doctors whom they follow, or, which is far worse, themselves—as a civil papacy, assuming unaccountable supremacy to themselves not in civil only but in ecclesiastical causes. Seeing then that in matters of Religion, as hath been proved, none can judge or determine here on earth, no, not Church governors themselves, against the consciences of other believers, my inference is, or rather not mine but our Saviour's own, that in those matters they neither can command nor use constraint, lest they run rashly on a pernicious consequence, forewarned in that parable, Matt. xiii. from ver. 29 to 31: "Lest while ye gather up the tares, ye root up also the wheat with them. Let both grow together until the harvest: and in the time of harvest I will say to the reapers, Gather ye together first the tares," &c. Whereby he declares, that this work neither his own ministers nor any else can discerningly enough or judgingly perform without his own immediate direction, in his own fit season; and that they ought till then not to attempt it. Which is further confirmed, 2 Cor. i. 24, "Not that we have dominion over your faith, but are helpers of your joy." If Apostles had no dominion or constraining power over faith or conscience, much less have ordinary ministers: 1 Pet. v. 2, 3, "Feed the flock of God, &c., not by constraint, neither as being lords over God's heritage."

But some will object, that this overthrows all Church Discipline, all censure of errors, if no man can determine. My answer is, that what they hear is plain Scripture, which forbids not Church sentence or determining, but as it ends in violence upon the conscience unconvinced. Let whoso will interpret or determine, so it be according to true Church Discipline which is exercised on them only who have willingly joined themselves in that Covenant of Union, and proceeds only to a separation from the rest; proceeds never to any corporal enforcement, or forfeiture of money, which in all spiritual things are the two arms of Antichrist, not of the True Church; the one being an Inquisition, the other no better than a temporal Indulgence of sin for money, whether by the Church exacted or by the magistrate; both the one and the other a temporal satisfaction for what Christ hath satisfied eternally: a popish commuting of penalty, corporal for spiritual; a satisfaction to man, especially to the magistrate, for what and to whom we owe none. These and more are the injustices of force and fining in religion, besides what I most insist on, the violation of God's express commandment in the Gospel, as hath been shown.

Thus then, if Church Governors cannot use force in Religion, though but for this reason, because they cannot infallibly determine to the Conscience without convincement, much less have Civil Magistrates authority to use force where they can much less judge; unless they mean only to be the civil executioners of them who have no civil power to give them such commission, no, nor yet ecclesiastical, to any force or violence in Religion. To sum up all in brief, if we must believe as the Magistrate appoints, why not rather as the Church? If not as either without convincement, how can force be lawful?

But some are ready to cry out, What shall then be done to blasphemy? Them I would first exhort not thus to terrify and pose the people with a Greek word; but to teach them better what it is, being a most usual and common word in that language to signify any slander, any malicious or evil speaking, whether against God or man or anything to good belonging. Blasphemy or evil speaking against God maliciously, is far from Conscience in religion, according to that of Mark ix. 39, "There is none who doth a powerful work in my name, and can lightly speak evil of me." If this suffice not, I refer them to that prudent and well deliberated act, August 9, 1650, where the Parliament defines Blasphemy against God, as far as it is a crime belonging to civil judicature, *plenius ac melius Chrysippo et Crantore;* in plain English, more warily, more judiciously, more orthodoxally than twice their number of divines have done in many a prolix volume: although in all likelihood they whose whole study and profession these things are, should be most intelligent and authentic therein, as they are for the most part; yet neither they nor these unerring always, or infallible.

But we shall not carry it thus; another Greek apparition stands in our way,—Heresy and Heretic, in like manner also railed at to the people as in a tongue unknown. They should first interpret to them that Heresy, by what it signifies in that language, is no word of evil note, meaning only the choice or following of any opinion, good or bad, in Religion, or any other learning, and thus not only in heathen authors, but in the New Testament itself, without censure or blame: Acts xv. 5, "Certain of the heresy of the Pharisees which believed;" and xxvi. 5, "After the exactest heresy of our religion I lived a Pharisee." In which sense Presbyterian or Independent may without reproach be called a Heresy. Where it is mentioned with blame, it seems to differ little from Schism: 1 Cor. xi. 18, 19, "I hear that there be schisms among you," &c., "for there must also heresies be among you," &c. Though some, who write of Heresy after their own heads, would make it far worse than Schism; whenas on the contrary, Schism signifies division, and in the worst sense; Heresy, choice only of one opinion before another, which may be without discord. In apostolic times, therefore, ere the Scripture was written, heresy was a doctrine maintained against the doctrine by them delivered; which in these times can be no otherwise defined than a doctrine maintained against the light which we now only have of the Scripture.

Seeing, therefore, that no man, no synod, no session of men, though called the Church, can judge definitely the sense of Scripture to another man's Conscience, which is well known to be a general maxim of the Protestant Religion; it follows plainly, that he who holds in Religion that belief or those opinions which to his Conscience and utmost understanding appear with most evidence or probability in the Scripture, though to others he seem erroneous, can no more be justly censured for a heretic than his censurers; who do but the same thing themselves while they censure him for so doing. For ask them, or any Protestant, which hath most authority, the Church or the Scripture? They will answer, doubtless, that the Scripture: and what hath most authority that no doubt but they will confess is to be followed. He then who to his best apprehension follows the Scripture, though against any point of doctrine by the whole Church received, is not the heretic; but he who follows the Church against his conscience and persuasion grounded on the Scripture. To make this yet more undeniable, I shall only borrow a plain simile, the same which our own writers, when they would demonstrate plainest that we rightly prefer the Scripture before the Church, use frequently against the papist in this manner. As the Samaritans believed Christ, first for the woman's word, but next and much rather for his own, so we the Scripture: first on the Church's word, but afterwards and much more for its own, as the Word of God; yea, the Church itself we believe then for the Scripture. The inference of itself follows: If by the Protestant doctrine we believe the Scripture, not for the Church's saying, but for its own, as the Word of God, then ought we to believe what in our Conscience we apprehend the Scripture to say, though the visible Church with all her doctors gainsay. And being taught to believe them only for the Scripture, they who so do are not heretics, but the best Protestants: and by their opinions, whatever they be, can hurt no Protestant, whose rule is not to receive them but from the Scripture: which to interpret convincingly to his own conscience, none is able but himself, guided by the Holy Spirit; and not so guided, none than he to himself can be a worse deceiver. To Protestants, therefore, whose common rule and touchstone is the Scripture, nothing can with more conscience, more equity, nothing more protestantly can be permitted, than a free and lawful debate at all times by writing, conference, or disputation of what opinion soever disputable by Scripture: concluding that no man in Religion is properly a heretic at this day but he who maintains traditions or opinions not probable by Scripture, who, for aught I know, is the papist only, he the only heretic who counts all heretics but himself.

Such as these, indeed, were capitally punished by the law of Moses, as the only true heretics, idolaters, plain and open deserters of God and his known Law. But in the Gospel such are punished by excommunion only: Tit. iii. 10, "An heretic, after the first and second admonition, reject." But they who think not this heavy enough, and understand not that dreadful awe and spiritual efficacy which the Apostle hath expressed so highly to be in Church Discipline, 2 Cor. x., of which anon, and think weakly that the Church of God cannot long subsist but in a bodily fear, for want of other proof will needs rest that place of St. Paul, Rom. xiii., to set up Civil Inquisition, and give power to the magistrate both of Civil Judgment and punishment in causes Ecclesiastical. But let us see with what strength of argument. "Let every soul be subject to the higher powers." First, how prove they that the Apostle means other powers than such as they to whom he writes were then under, who meddled not at all in ecclesiastical causes, unless as tyrants and persecutors? And from them, I hope, they will not derive either the right of magistrates to judge in spiritual things, or the duty of such our obedience.

How prove they next that he entitles them here to spiritual causes from whom he withheld as much as in him lay the judging of civil? 1 Cor. vi. 1, &c. If he himself appealed to Cæsar, it was to judge his innocence not his religion. "For rulers are not a terror to good works, but to the evil:" then they are not a terror to Conscience, which is the rule or judge of good works grounded on the Scripture. But Heresy, they say, is reckoned among evil works, Gal. v. 20, as if all evil works were to be punished by the magistrate; whereof this place, their own citation, reckons up besides heresy a sufficient number to confute them; "uncleanness, wantonness, enmity, strife, emulations, animosities, contentions, envyings;" all which are far more manifest to be judged by him than heresy, as they define it; and yet I suppose they will not subject these evil works, nor many more suchlike, to his cognizance and punishment. " Wilt thou then not be afraid of the power? Do that which is good, and thou shalt have praise of the same." This shows that religious matters are not here meant; wherein from the power here spoken of they could have no praise. " For he is the minister of God to thee for good : " true ; but in that office, and to that end, and by those means, which in this place must be clearly found, if from this place they intend to argue. And how for thy good, by forcing, oppressing, and ensnaring thy conscience?

Many are the Ministers of God, and their offices no less different than many; none more different than State and Church Government. Who seeks to govern both, must needs be worse than any lord prelate, or church pluralist : for he in his own faculty and profession, the other not in his own, and for the most part not thoroughly understood, makes himself supreme lord or pope of the Church, as far as his civil jurisdiction stretches, and all the ministers of God therein, his ministers or his curates rather, in the function only not in the government, while he himself assumes to rule by civil power things to be ruled only by spiritual. Whenas this very chapter, verse 6, appointing him his peculiar office, which requires utmost attendance, forbids him this worse than church plurality from that full and weighty charge wherein alone he is the minister of God, attending continually on this very thing.

To little purpose will they here instance Moses, who did all by immediate divine direction; no, nor yet Asa, Jehoshaphat, or Josiah, who both might, when they pleased, receive answer from God, and had a commonwealth by him delivered them, incorporated with a national Church, exercised more in bodily than in spiritual worship: so as that the Church might be called a Commonwealth, and the whole Commonwealth a Church. Nothing of which can be said of Christianity, delivered without the help of magistrates, yea, in the midst of their opposition; how little then with any reference to them or mention of them, save only of our obedience to their civil laws as they countenance good and deter evil, which is the proper work of the magistrate, following in the same verse, and shows distinctly wherein he is the minister of God, "a revenger to execute wrath on him that doth evil."

But we must first know who it is that doth evil. The heretic, they say, among the first. Let it be known then certainly who is a heretic; and that he who holds opinions in Religion professedly from tradition or his own inventions, and not from Scripture but rather against it, is the only heretic. And yet though such, not always punishable by the magistrate, unless he do evil against a civil law properly so called, hath been already proved without need of repetition: "But if thou do that which is evil, be afraid." To do by Scripture and the Gospel, according to Conscience, is not to do evil. If we thereof ought not to be afraid, he ought not by his judging to give cause: causes therefore of religion are not here meant. "For he beareth not the sword in vain:" Yes, altogether in vain if it smite he knows not what; if that for heresy, which not the Church itself, much less he, can determine absolutely to be so— if truth for error, being himself so often fallible—he bears the sword not in vain only, but unjustly and to evil. "Be subject not only for wrath, but for conscience sake:" How for conscience sake, against conscience? By all these reasons it appears plainly, that the Apostle in this place gives no judgment or coercive power to magistrates, neither to those then, nor these now, in matters of Religion; and exhorts us no otherwise than he exhorted those Romans.

It hath now twice befallen me to assert, through God's assistance, this most wrested and vexed place of Scripture: heretofore against Salmasius, and regal tyranny over the State; now against Erastus, and state tyranny over the Church. If from such uncertain, or rather such improbable grounds as these, they endue magistracy with spiritual judgment, they may as well invest him in the same spiritual kind with power of utmost punishment, excommunication; and then turn spiritual into corporal, as no worse authors did than Chrysostom, Jerome, and Austin, whom Erasmus and others in their notes on the New Testament have cited, to interpret that cutting off which St. Paul wished to them who had brought back the Galatians to circumcision, no less than the amercement of their whole virility. And Grotius adds, that this concising punishment of circumcisers became a penal law thereupon among the Visigoths: a dangerous example of beginning in the spirit to end so in the flesh; whereas that cutting off much likelier seems meant a cutting off from the Church, not unusually so termed in Scripture, and a zealous imprecation, not a command. But I have mentioned this passage to show how absurd they often prove who have not learned to distinguish rightly between Civil power and Ecclesiastical. How many persecutions, then, imprisonments, banishments, penalties, and stripes; how much bloodshed have the Forcers of Conscience to answer for, and Protestants rather than Papists! For the Papist, judging by his principles, punishes them who believe not as the Church believes, though against the Scripture; but the Protestant, teaching every one to believe the Scripture, though against the Church, counts heretical and persecutes against his own principles them who in any particular so believe as he in general teaches them; them who most honour and believe divine Scripture, but not against it any human interpretation, though universal; them who interpret Scripture only to themselves, which by his own position none but they to themselves can interpret: them who use the Scripture no otherwise by his own doctrine to their edification than he himself uses it to their punishing. And so whom his Doctrine acknowledges a true believer, his Discipline persecutes as a heretic. The Papist exacts our belief as to the Church due above Scripture; and by the Church, which is the whole people of God, understands the Pope, the General Councils, prelatical only, and the surnamed Fathers. But the forcing Protestant, though he deny such belief to any Church whatsoever, yet takes it to himself and his teachers of far less authority than to be called the Church and above Scripture believed: which renders his practice both contrary to his belief, and far worse than that belief which he condemns in the Papist. By all which, well considered, the more he professes to be a true Protestant, the more he hath to answer for his persecuting than a Papist. No Protestant therefore, of what sect soever, following Scripture only, which is the common sect wherein they all agree, and the granted rule of every man's conscience to himself, ought by the common doctrine of Protestants to be forced or molested for religion.

But as for popery and idolatry, why they also may not hence plead to be tolerated, I have much less to say. Their religion the more considered, the less can be acknowledged a religion, but a Roman principality rather, endeavouring to keep up her old universal dominion under a new name, and mere shadow of a catholic religion; being indeed more rightly named a catholic heresy against the Scripture, supported mainly by a civil, and, except in Rome, by a foreign, power: justly therefore to be suspected, not tolerated, by the magistrate of another country.

Besides, of an implicit faith which they profess, the conscience also becomes implicit, and so by voluntary servitude to man's law, forfeits her Christian liberty. Who then can plead for such a conscience as, being implicitly enthralled to man instead of God, almost becomes no conscience, as the will not free becomes no will? Nevertheless, if they ought not to be tolerated, it is for just reason of State more than of Religion; which they who force, though professing to be Protestants, deserve as little to be tolerated themselves, being no less guilty of popery in the most popish point. Lastly, for idolatry, who knows it not to be evidently against all Scripture, both of the Old and New Testament, and therefore a true heresy, or rather an impiety, wherein a right conscience can have nought to do; and the works thereof so manifest, that a magistrate can hardly err in prohibiting and quite removing at least the public and scandalous use thereof?

From the riddance of these objections, I proceed yet to another reason why it is unlawful for the Civil Magistrate to use force in matters of Religion; which is, because to judge in those things though we should grant him able, which is proved he is not, yet as a Civil Magistrate he hath no right. Christ hath a government of his own, sufficient of itself to all his ends and purposes in governing his Church, but much different from that of the Civil Magistrate; and the difference in this very thing principally consists, that it governs not by outward force. And that for two reasons: First, Because it deals only with the inward man and his actions, which are all spiritual and to outward force not liable. Secondly, To show us the divine excellence of his spiritual kingdom, able, without worldly force, to subdue all the powers and kingdoms of this world, which are upheld by outward force only. That the inward man is nothing else but the inward part of man, his understanding and his will; and that his actions thence proceeding, yet not simply thence but from the work of divine grace upon them, are the whole matter of Religion under the Gospel, will appear plainly by considering what that Religion is; whence we shall perceive yet more plainly that it cannot be forced. What Evangelic Religion is, is told in two words,— Faith and Charity, or Belief and Practice. That both these flow, either, the one from the understanding, the other from the will, or both jointly from both, once indeed naturally free, but now only as they are regenerate and wrought on by divine grace, is in part evident to common sense and principles unquestioned, the rest by Scripture. Concerning our belief, Matt. xvi. 17, "Flesh and blood hath not revealed it unto thee, but my Father which is in heaven;" concerning our practice, as it is religious, and not merely civil, Gal. v. 22, 23, and other places, declare it to be the fruit of the spirit only. Nay, our whole practical duty in Religion is contained in Charity, or the Love of God and our Neighbour, no way to be forced, yet the fulfilling of the whole law; that is to say, our whole practice in religion. If then both our Belief and Practice, which comprehend our whole Religion, flow from faculties of the inward man, free and unconstrainable of themselves by nature, and our practice not only from faculties endued with freedom, but from Love and Charity besides incapable of force, and all these things by transgression lost but renewed and regenerated in us by the power and gift of God alone; how can such Religion as this admit of force from man, or force be any way applied to such religion, especially under the free offer of grace in the Gospel, but it must forthwith frustrate and make of no effect both the Religion and the Gospel? And that to compel outward profession, which they will say perhaps ought to be compelled though inward religion cannot, is to compel hypocrisy, not to advance religion, shall yet, though of itself clear enough, be ere the conclusion further manifest.

The other reason why Christ rejects outward force in the government of his Church, is, as I said before, to show us the divine excellence of his spiritual kingdom, able without worldly force to subdue all the powers and kingdoms of this world, which are upheld by outward force only. By which to uphold Religion,—otherwise than to defend the religious from outward violence,—is no service to Christ or his kingdom, but rather a disparagement, and degrades it from a divine and spiritual kingdom, to a kingdom of this world: which he denies it to be, because it needs not force to confirm it: John xviii. 36, "If my kingdom were of this world, then would my servants fight, that I should not be delivered to the Jews." This proves the kingdom of Christ not governed by outward force, as being none of this world, whose kingdoms are maintained all by force only; and yet disproves not that a Christian Commonwealth may defend itself against outward force, in the cause of Religion as well as in any other: though Christ himself coming purposely to die for us, would not be so defended. 1 Cor. i. 27 : "God hath chosen the weak things of the world to confound the things which are mighty." Then surely he hath not chosen the Force of this world to subdue Conscience, and conscientious men, who in this world are counted weakest; but rather Conscience, as being weakest, to subdue and regulate Force, his adversary, not his aid or instrument in governing the Church: 2 Cor. x. 3, 4, 5, 6, "For though we walk in the flesh, we do not war after the flesh: for the weapons of our warfare are not carnal, but mighty through God to the pulling down of strongholds, casting down imaginations, and every high thing that exalts itself against the knowledge of God, and bringing into captivity every thought to the obedience of Christ : and having in a readiness to avenge all disobedience." It is evident by the first and second verses of this chapter, and the Apostle here speaks of that spiritual power by which Christ governs his Church, how all-sufficient it is, how powerful to reach the conscience and the inward man with whom it chiefly deals, and whom no power else can deal with. In comparison of which, as it is here thus magnificently described, how ineffectual and weak is outward force with all her boisterous tools, to the shame of those Christians, and especially those churchmen, who to the exercising of Church Discipline, never cease calling on the Civil Magistrate to interpose his fleshly force! An argument that all true ministerial and spiritual power is dead within them who think the Gospel, which both began and spread over the whole world for above three hundred years, under heathen and persecuting emperors, cannot stand or continue, supported by the same divine presence and protection, to the world's end, much easier under the defensive favour only of a Christian magistrate, unless it be enacted and settled, as they call it, by the State, a statute or a State Religion ; and understand not that the Church itself cannot, much less the State, settle or impose one tittle of Religion upon our obedience implicit, but can only recommend or propound it to our free and conscientious examination. Unless they mean to set the State higher than the Church in religion, and with a gross contradiction give to the State in their settling petition that command of our implicit belief which they deny in their settled confession both to the State and to the Church.

Let them cease then to importune and interrupt the Magistrate from attending to his own charge in civil and moral things,—the settling of things just, things honest, the defence of things religious, settled by the Churches within themselves, and the repressing of their contraries, determinable by the common light of nature; which is not to constrain or to repress Religion probable by Scripture, but the violaters and persecutors thereof: of all which things he hath enough and more than enough to do, left yet undone, for which the land groans, and justice goes to wrack the while. Let him also forbear force where he hath no right to judge—for the conscience is not his province—lest a worse woe arrive him for worse offending than was denounced by our Saviour, Matt. xxiii. 23, against the Pharisees: Ye have forced the conscience, which was not to be forced; but judgment and mercy ye have not executed; this ye should have done, and the other let alone. And since it is the counsel and set purpose of God in the Gospel, by spiritual means which are counted weak to overcome all power which resists him; let them not go about to do that by worldly strength which he hath decreed to do by those means which the world counts weakness, lest they be again obnoxious to that saying, which in another place is also written of the Pharisees, Luke vii. 30, that they frustrated the counsel of God.

The main plea is, and urged with much vehemence to their imitation, that the kings of Judah, as I touched before, and especially Josiah, both judged and used force in religion: 2 Chron. xxxiv. 33, "He made all that were present in Israel to serve the Lord their God:" an argument, if it be well weighed, worse than that used by the false prophet Shemaia to the high priest, that in imitation of Jehoiada, he ought to put Jeremiah in the stocks, Jer. xxix. 24, 26, &c.; for which he received his due denouncement from God. But to this besides I return a threefold answer.

First, That the state of Religion under the Gospel is far differing from what it was under the Law. Then was the state of rigour, childhood, bondage, and works, to all which force was not unbefitting. Now is the state of grace, manhood, freedom, and faith, to all which belongs willingness and reason, not force: the Law was then written on tables of stone, and to be performed according to the letter, willingly or unwillingly. The Gospel, our new covenant, upon the heart of every believer, to be interpreted only by the sense of charity and inward persuasion. The law had no distinct government or governors of Church and Commonwealth, but the priests and Levites judged in all causes, not ecclesiastical only, but Civil, Deut. xvii. 8, &c.; which under the Gospel is forbidden to all Church ministers, as a thing which Christ their Master in his ministry disclaimed, Luke xii. 14, as a thing beneath them, 1 Cor. vi. 4, and by many other statutes, as to them who have a peculiar and far-differing government of their own. If not, why different the governors? Why not Church ministers in State affairs, as well as State ministers in Church affairs? If Church and State shall be made one flesh again, as under the Law, let it be withal considered, that God, who then joined them, hath now severed them. That which, he so ordaining, was then a lawful conjunction, to such on either side as join again what he hath severed would be nothing now but their own presumptuous fornication.

Secondly, the kings of Judah, and those magistrates under the Law, might have recourse, as I said before, to divine inspiration; which our magistrates under the Gospel have not, more than to the same Spirit which those whom they force have ofttimes in greater measure than themselves: and so, instead of forcing the Christian, they force the Holy Ghost; and, against that wise forewarning of Gamaliel, fight against God.

Thirdly, those kings and magistrates used force in such things only as were undoubtedly known and forbidden in the Law of Moses, idolatry and direct apostacy from that national and strict enjoined worship of God; whereof the corporal punishment was by himself expressly set down. But magistrates under the Gospel, our free, elective, and rational worship, are most commonly busiest to force those things which in the Gospel are either left free, nay, sometimes abolished when by them compelled, or else controverted equally by writers on both sides, and sometimes with odds on that side which is against them. By which means they either punish that which they ought to favour and protect, or that with corporal punishment and of their own inventing which not they but the Church had received command to chastise with a spiritual rod only.

Yet some are so eager in their zeal of forcing, that they refuse not to descend at length to the utmost shift of that parabolical proof, Luke xiv. 16, &c., "Compel them to come in:" therefore Magistrates may compel in Religion. As if a parable were to be strained through every word or phrase, and not expounded by the general scope thereof; which is no other here than the earnest expression of God's displeasure on those recusant Jews, and his purpose to prefer the Gentiles on any terms before them, expressed here by the word compel. But how compels he? Doubtless no other way than he draws, without which no man can come to him, John vi. 44; and that is by the inward persuasive motions of his Spirit, and by his ministers; not by the outward compulsions of a magistrate or his officers.

The true people of Christ, as is foretold, Psalm cx. 3, "are a willing people in the day of his power;" then much more now when he rules all things by outward weakness, that both his inward power and their sincerity may the more appear. "God loveth a cheerful giver:" then certainly is not pleased with an uncheerful worshipper: as the very words declare of his evangelical invitation, Isa. lv. 1, "Ho, every one that thirsteth, come." John vii. 37, "If any man thirsteth." Rev. iii. 18, "I counsel thee." And xxii. 17, "Whosoever will, let him take the water of life freely." And in that grand commission of preaching, to invite all nations, Mark xvi. 16, as the reward of them who come, so the penalty of them who come not, is only spiritual.

But they bring now some reason with their force, which must not pass unanswered, that the Church of Thyatira was blamed, Rev. ii. 20, for suffering the false "prophetess to teach and to seduce." I answer, That seducement is to be hindered by fit and proper means ordained in Church Discipline, by instant and powerful demonstration to the contrary; by opposing truth to error, no unequal match; truth the strong to error the weak, though sly and shifting. Force is no honest confutation, but uneffectual, and for the most part unsuccessful; ofttimes fatal to them who use it. Sound doctrine, diligently and duly taught, is of herself both sufficient, and of herself (if some secret judgment of God hinder not) always prevalent against seducers. This the Thyatirans had neglected, suffering, against Church Discipline, that woman to teach and seduce among them. Civil Force they had not then in their power, being the Christian part only of that city, and then especially under one of those ten great persecutions, whereof this, the second, was raised by Domitian: force therefore in these matters could not be required of them who were under force themselves.

I have shown that the Civil Power neither hath right, nor can do right, by forcing religious things. I will now show the wrong it doth by violating the fundamental privilege of the Gospel, the new birthright of every true believer, Christian Liberty: 2 Cor. iii. 17, "Where the Spirit of the Lord is, there is Liberty." Gal. iv. 26, "Jerusalem which is above is free; which is the mother of us all." And verse 31, "We are not children of the Bondwoman, but of the Free." It will be sufficient in this place to say no more of Christian Liberty, than that it sets us free not only from the bondage of those ceremonies, but also from the forcible imposition of those circumstances, place and time, in the worship of God, which though by him commanded in the old law, yet in respect of that verity and freedom which is evangelical, St. Paul comprehends—both kinds alike, that is to say, both ceremony and circumstance—under one and the same contemptuous name of "weak and beggarly rudiments," Gal. iv. 3, 9, 10; Col. ii. 8 with 16, conformable to what our Saviour Himself taught, John iv. 21, 23, "Neither in this mountain, nor yet at Jerusalem. In spirit and in truth; for the Father seeketh such to worship him." That is to say, not only sincere of heart, for such he sought ever; but also, as the words here chiefly import, not compelled to place, and by the same reason, not to any set time. As his Apostle by the same Spirit hath taught us, Rom. xiv. 6, &c., "One man esteemeth one day above another," &c.; Gal. iv. 10, "Ye observe days and months," &c.; Col. ii. 16. These and other such places in Scripture, the best and learnedest reformed writers have thought evident enough to instruct us in our freedom not only from ceremonies but from those circumstances also, though imposed with a confident persuasion of morality in them, which they hold impossible to be in place or time.

By what warrant then our opinions and practices herein are of late turned quite against all other Protestants, and that which is to them orthodoxal to us becomes scandalous and punishable by statute, I wish were once again considered, if we mean not to proclaim a schism in this point from the best and most reformed Churches abroad. They who would seem more knowing, confess that these things are indifferent, but for that very cause by the magistrate may be commanded. As if God of his special grace in the Gospel had to this end freed us from his own commandments in these things, that our freedom should subject us to a more grievous yoke, the commandments of men. As well may the magistrate call that common or unclean which God hath cleansed, forbidden to St. Peter, Acts x. 15; as well may he loosen that which God hath straitened or straiten that which God hath loosened, as he may enjoy those things in Religion which God hath left free, and lay on that yoke which God hath taken off. For he hath not only given us this gift as a special privilege and excellence of the free Gospel above the servile Law, but strictly also hath commanded us to keep it and enjoy it: Gal. v. 13, "You are called to Liberty." 1 Cor. vii. 23, "Be not made the servants of men." Gal. v. 14, "Stand fast therefore in the Liberty wherewith Christ hath made us free: and be not entangled again with the yoke of bondage."

Neither is this a mere command, but for the most part in these forecited places, accompanied with the very weightiest and inmost reasons of Christian religion: Rom. xiv. 9, 10, "For to this end Christ both died, and rose, and revived, that he might be Lord both of the dead and living. But why dost thou judge thy brother?" &c. How presumest thou to be his lord, to be whose only Lord, at least in these things, Christ both died, and rose, and lived again? "We shall all stand before the judgment-seat of Christ." Why then dost thou not only judge, but persecute in these things for which we are to be accountable to the tribunal of Christ only, our Lord and lawgiver? 1 Cor. vii. 23, "Ye are bought with a price: be not made the servants of men." Some trivial price belike and for some frivolous pretences paid, in their opinion, if—bought and by him redeemed, who is God, from what was once the service of God—we shall be enthralled again and forced by men to what now is but the service of men: Gal. iv. 31, with v. 1, "We are not children of the bondwoman, &c.; stand fast therefore," &c. Col. ii. 8, "Beware lest any man spoil you, &c., after the rudiments of the world, and not after Christ." Solid reasons whereof are continued through the whole chapter. Ver. 10, "Ye are complete in him, which is the head of all principality and power:" not completed therefore or made the more religious by those ordinances of civil power from which Christ their head hath discharged us; "blotting out the handwriting of ordinances that was against us, which was contrary to us; and took it out of the way, nailing it to his cross," ver. 14. Blotting out ordinances written by God himself, much more those so boldly written over again by men; ordinances which were against us, that is, against our frailty, much more those which are against our conscience. "Let no man therefore judge you in respect of," &c., ver. 16; Gal. iv. 3, &c. "Even so we, when we were children, were in bondage under the rudiments of the world : but when the fulness of time was come, God sent forth his Son, &c., to redeem them that were under the law, that we might receive the adoption of sons, &c. Wherefore thou art no more a servant, but a son, &c. But now, &c., how turn ye again to the weak and beggarly rudiments, whereunto ye desire again to be in bondage? Ye observe days," &c. Hence it plainly appears, that if we be not free, we are not sons, but still servants unadopted; and if we turn again to those weak and beggarly rudiments, we are not free; yea, though willingly, and with a misguided conscience, we desire to be in bondage to them; how much more then if unwillingly and against our conscience? Ill was our condition changed from legal to evangelical, and small advantage gotten by the Gospel, if for the spirit of adoption to freedom promised us, we receive again the spirit of bondage to fear; if our fear, which was then servile towards God only, must be now servile in religion towards men. Strange also and preposterous fear, if when and wherein it hath attained by the redemption of our Saviour to be filial only towards God, it must be now servile towards the magistrate, who, by subjecting us to his punishment in these things, brings back into religion that law of terror and satisfaction belonging now only to civil crimes; and thereby in effect abolishes the Gospel, by establishing again the Law to a far worse yoke of servitude upon us than before. It will therefore not misbecome the meanest Christian to put in mind Christian magistrates, and so much the more freely by how much the more they desire to be thought Christian,—for they will be thereby, as they ought to be in these things, the more our brethren and the less our lords,—that they meddle not rashly with Christian Liberty, the birthright and outward testimony of our adoption; lest while they little think it, nay, think they do God service, they themselves, like the sons of that bondwoman, be found persecuting them who are freeborn of the Spirit, and by a sacrilege of not the least aggravation, bereaving them of that sacred Liberty which our Saviour with his own blood purchased for them.

A fourth reason why the Magistrate ought not to use Force in Religion, I bring from the consideration of all those ends which he can likely pretend to the interposing of his force therein. And those hardly can be other than first the glory of God; next, either the spiritual good of them whom he forces, or the temporal punishment of their scandal to others. As for the promoting of God's glory, none, I think, will say that His glory ought to be promoted in religious things by unwarrantable means, much less by means contrary to what He hath commanded. That outward force is such, and that God's glory in the whole administration of the Gospel according to his own will and counsel ought to be fulfilled by weakness—at least so refuted, not by force; or if by force, inward and spiritual, not outward and corporeal—is already proved at large. That outward force cannot tend to the good of him who is forced in Religion, is unquestionable. For in Religion whatever we do under the Gospel, we ought to be thereof persuaded without scruple; and are justified by the faith we have, not by the work we do: Rom. xiv. 5, "Let every man be fully persuaded in his own mind." The other reason, which follows necessarily, is obvious, Gal. ii. 16, and in many other places of St. Paul, as the groundwork and foundation of the whole Gospel, that we are "justified by the faith of Christ, and not by the works of the law." If not by the works of God's law, how then by the injunctions of man's law? Surely Force cannot work persuasion, which is Faith; cannot therefore justify nor pacify the Conscience. And that which justifies not in the Gospel, condemns; is not only not good, but sinful to do: Rom. xiv. 23, "Whatsoever is not of faith, is sin." It concerns the Magistrate, then, to take heed how he forces in Religion conscientious men, lest, by compelling them to do that whereof they cannot be persuaded, that wherein they cannot find themselves justified, but by their own consciences condemned, instead of aiming at their spiritual good, he force them to do evil; and while he thinks himself Asa, Josiah, Nehemiah, he be found Jeroboam, who caused Israel to sin; and thereby draw upon his own head all those sins and shipwrecks of implicit faith and conformity which he hath forced, and all the wounds given to those little ones, whom to offend he will find worse one day than that violent drowning mentioned Matt. xviii. 6.

Lastly, as a preface to force, it is the usual pretence, that although tender consciences shall be tolerated, yet scandals thereby given shall not be unpunished. Profane and licentious men shall not be encouraged to neglect the performance of religious and holy duties by colour of any law giving liberty to tender consciences. By which contrivance, the way lies ready open to them hereafter who may be so minded to take away by little and little that Liberty which Christ and his Gospel, not any magistrate, hath right to give: though this kind of his giving be but to give with one hand and take away with the other, which is a deluding not a giving. As for scandals, if any man be offended at the conscientious liberty of another, it is a taken scandal not a given. To heal one conscience, we must not wound another. And men must be exhorted to beware of scandals in Christian liberty not forced by the magistrate; lest while he goes about to take away the scandal, which is uncertain whether given or taken, he take away our Liberty, which is the certain and the sacred gift of God, neither to be touched by him nor to be parted with by us. None more cautious of giving scandal than St. Paul. Yet while he made himself "servant to all," that he "might gain the more," he made himself so of his own accord, was not made so by outward force, testifying at the same time that he "was free from all men," 1 Cor. ix. 19; and thereafter exhorts us also, Gal. v. 13, "Ye were called to liberty, &c., but by love serve one another:" then not by force. As for that fear lest profane and licentious men should be encouraged to omit the performance of religious and holy duties, how can that care belong to the civil magistrate, especially to his force? For if profane and licentious persons must not neglect the performance of religious and holy duties, it implies that such duties they can perform; which no Protestant will affirm. They who mean the outward performance, may so explain it; and it will then appear yet more plainly, that such performance of religious and holy duties, especially by profane and licentious persons, is a dishonouring rather than a worshipping of God; and not only by him not required, but detested: Prov. xxi. 27, "The sacrifice of the wicked is an abomination; how much more when he bringeth it with a wicked mind?" To compel, therefore, the profane to things holy, in his profaneness, is all one under the Gospel as to have compelled the unclean to sacrifice in his uncleanness under the Law. And I add withal, that to compel the licentious in his licentiousness, and the conscientious against his conscience, comes all to one; tends not to the honour of God, but to the multiplying and the aggravating of sin to them both. We read not that Christ ever exercised force but once, and that was to drive profane ones out of his temple, not to force them in. And if their being there was an offence, we find by many other Scriptures that their praying there was an abomination. And yet to the Jewish law that nation, as a servant, was obliged; but to the Gospel each person is left voluntary, called only as a son, by the preaching of the Word; not to be driven in by edicts and force of arms. For if by the Apostle, Rom. xii. 1, we are "beseeched as brethren by the mercies of God to present our bodies a living sacrifice, holy, acceptable to God, which is our reasonable service," or worship, then is no man to be forced by the compulsive laws of men to present his body a dead sacrifice; and so under the Gospel most unholy and unacceptable, because it is his unreasonable service, that is to say, not only unwilling but unconscionable.

But if profane and licentious persons may not omit the performance of holy duties, why may they not partake of holy things? Why are they prohibited the Lord's Supper, since both the one and the other action may be outward; and outward performance of duty may attain at least an outward participation of benefit? The Church denying them that communion of grace and thanksgiving, as it justly doth, why doth the Magistrate compel them to the union of performing that which they neither truly can, being themselves unholy, and to do seemingly is both hateful to God, and perhaps no less dangerous to perform holy duties irreligiously than to receive holy signs or sacraments unworthily? All profane and licentious men, so known, can be considered but either so without the Church as never yet within it, or departed thence of their own accord, or excommunicate. If never yet within the Church, whom the Apostle, and so, consequently, the Church have nought to do to judge, as he professes, 1 Cor. v. 12, then by what authority doth the Magistrate judge, or, which is worse, compel, in relation to the Church? If departed of his own accord, like that lost sheep, Luke xv. 4, &c., the true Church, either with her own or any borrowed force worries him not in again, but rather in all charitable manner sends after him; and if she find him, lays him gently on her shoulders, bears him, yea, bears his burdens, his errors, his infirmities any way tolerable, "so fulfilling the law of Christ," Gal. vi. 2. If excommunicate, whom the Church hath bid go out in whose name doth the Magistrate compel to go in? The Church, indeed, hinders none from hearing in her public congregation, for the doors are open to all: nor excommunicates to destruction; but, as much as in her lies, to a final saving. Her meaning, therefore, must needs be, that as her driving out brings on no outward penalty, so no outward force of penalty of an improper and only a destructive power should drive in again her infectious sheep, therefore sent out because infectious, and not driven in but with the danger not only of the whole and sound but also of his own utter perishing, since Force neither instructs in Religion, nor begets repentance or amendment or life, but, on the contrary, hardness of heart, formality, hypocrisy, and, as I said before, every way increase of sin; more and more alienates the mind from a violent Religion expelling out and compelling in, and reduces it to a condition like that which the Britons complain of in our story, driven to and fro between the Picts and the sea. If, after excommunion, he be found intractable, incurable, and will not hear the Church, he becomes as one never yet within her pale, "a heathen or a publican," Matt. xviii. 17, not further to be judged, no, not by the Magistrate, unless for civil causes; but left to the final sentence of that Judge, whose coming shall be in flames of fire; that Maranatha, 1 Cor. xvi. 22, than which, to him so left, nothing can be more dreadful, and ofttimes to him particularly nothing more speedy, that is to say, The Lord cometh: in the meanwhile delivered up to Satan, 1 Cor. v. 5, 1 Tim. i. 20, that is, from the fold of Christ and kingdom of grace to the world again, which is the kingdom of Satan; and as he was received "from darkness to light, and from the power of Satan to God," Acts xxvi. 18, so now delivered up again from light to darkness, and from God to the power of Satan; yet so as is in both places manifested, to the intent of saving him, brought sooner to contrition by spiritual than by any corporal severity. But grant it belonging any way to the magistrate, that profane and licentious persons omit not the performance of holy duties which in them were odious to God even under the Law, much more now under the Gospel; yet ought his care both as a magistrate and a Christian, to be much more that Conscience be not inwardly violated, than that licence in these things be made outwardly conformable: since his part is undoubtedly as a Christian, which puts him upon this office much more than as a Magistrate, in all respects to have more care of the conscientious than of the profane; and not for their sakes to take away (while they pretend to give) or to diminish the rightful liberty of religious consciences.

On these four scriptural reasons, as on a firm square, this Truth, the right of Christian and Evangelic Liberty, will stand immovable against all those pretended consequences of licence and confusion, which for the most part men most licentious and confused themselves, or such as whose severity would be wiser than divine wisdom, are ever aptest to object against the ways of God. As if God without them, when he gave us this Liberty, knew not of the worst which these men in their arrogance pretend will follow. Yet knowing all their worst, he gave us this liberty as by him judged best. As to those Magistrates who think it their work to settle Religion, and those Ministers or others, who so oft call upon them to do so, I trust, that having well considered what hath been here argued, neither they will continue in that intention, nor these in that expectation from them; when they shall find that the settlement of Religion belongs only to each particular Church by persuasive and spiritual means within itself, and that the defence only of the Church belongs to the magistrate. Had he once learned not further to concern himself with Church affairs, half his labour might be spared, and the commonwealth better tended.

To which end, that which I premised in the beginning, and in due place treated of more at large, I desire now, concluding, that they would consider seriously what Religion is; and they will find it to be, in sum, both our belief and our practice depending upon God only. That there can be no place then left for the Magistrate or his force in the settlement of Religion, by appointing either what we shall believe in divine things, or practise in religious,—neither of which things are in the power of man either to perform himself or to enable others,—I persuade me in the Christian ingenuity of all religious men the more they examine seriously the more they will find clearly to be true; and find how false and deviseable that common saying is, which is so much relied upon, that the Christian magistrate is *Custos utriusque*

Tabulæ, Keeper of both Tables; unless is meant by keeper the defender only. Neither can that maxim be maintained by any proof or argument, which hath not in this discourse first or last been refuted. For the two Tables, or Ten Commandments, teach our duty to God and our Neighbour from the Love of both; give magistrates no authority to force either. They seek that from the judicial law, though on false grounds, especially in the first Table, as I have shown; and both in first and second execute that authority for the most part, not according to God's judicial laws, but their own. As for civil crimes and of the outward man,—which all are not, no, not of those against the second Table, as that of coveting,—in them what power they have they had from the beginning, long before Moses or the two Tables were in being. And whether they be not now as little in being to be kept by any Christian, as they are two legal Tables, remains yet as undecided, as it is sure they never were yet delivered to the keeping of any Christian Magistrate. But of these things, perhaps, more some other time. What may serve the present hath been above discoursed sufficiently out of the Scriptures: and to those produced, might be added testimonies, examples, experiences, of all succeeding ages to these times, asserting this doctrine. But having herein the Scripture so copious and so plain, we have all that can be properly called true strength and nerve; the rest would be but pomp and encumbrance. Pomp and ostentation of reading is admired among the vulgar; but doubtless, in matters of Religion, he is learnedest who is plainest. The brevity I use, not exceeding a small manual, will not therefore, I suppose, be thought the less considerable, unless with them, perhaps, who think that great books only can determine great matters. I rather choose the common rule, not to make much ado where less may serve; which in controversies, and those especially of Religion, would make them less tedious, and by consequence read oftener by many more and with more benefit.

THE READY AND EASY WAY

TO ESTABLISH

A FREE COMMONWEALTH,

AND THE EXCELLENCE THEREOF,

COMPARED WITH THE INCONVENIENCES AND DANGERS OF READMITTING KINGSHIP IN THIS NATION.

[*First published in 1660.*]

" Et nos
Consilium dedimus Syllæ, demus Populo nunc."

ALTHOUGH, since the writing of this treatise, the face of things hath had some change, writs for new elections have been recalled, and the members at first chosen re-admitted from exclusion; yet not a little rejoicing to hear declared the resolution of those who are in power, tending to the establishment of a Free Commonwealth, and to remove, if it be possible, this noxious humour of returning to bondage, instilled of late by some deceivers, and nourished from bad principles and false apprehensions among too many of the people, I thought best not to suppress what I had written, hoping that it may now be of much more use and concernment to be freely published, in the midst of our elections to a free Parliament, or their sitting to consider freely of the government whom it behoves to have all things represented to them that may direct their judgment therein. And I never read of any state, scarce of any tyrant, grown so incurable, as to refuse counsel from any in a time of public deliberation, much less to be offended. If their absolute determination be to enthral us, before so long a Lent of servitude they may permit us a little shroving-time first, wherein to speak freely and to take our leaves of Liberty. And because in the former edition, through haste, many faults escaped, and many books were suddenly dispersed ere the note to mend them could be sent, I took the opportunity from this occasion to revise and somewhat to enlarge the whole discourse, especially that part which argues for a Perpetual Senate. The treatise thus revised and enlarged is as follows :

The Parliament of England, assisted by a great number of the people who appeared and stuck to them faithfulest in defence of Religion and their Civil Liberties, judging kingship by long experience a government unnecessary, burdensome, and dangerous, justly and magnanimously abolished it, turning regal bondage into a Free Commonwealth, to the admiration and terror of our emulous neighbours. They took themselves not bound by the light of Nature or Religion to any former covenant from which the king himself, by many forfeitures of a latter date or discovery and our own longer consideration thereon, had more and more unbound us both to himself and his posterity; as hath been ever the justice and the prudence of all wise nations that have ejected tyranny. They covenanted "to preserve the king's person and authority, in the preservation of the true religion, and our liberties;" not in his endeavouring to bring in upon our consciences a popish religion; upon our liberties, thraldom; upon our lives, destruction, by his occasioning, if not complotting, as was after discovered, the Irish massacre; his fomenting and arming the rebellion; his covert leaguing with the rebels against us; his refusing, more than seven times, propositions most just and necessary to the true religion and our liberties, tendered him by the Parliament both of England and Scotland. They made not their covenant concerning him with no difference between a king and a God; or promised him, as Job did to the Almighty, "to trust in him though he slay us." They understood that the solemn engagement wherein we all foreswore kingship, was no more a breach of the covenant, than the covenant was of the protestation before, but a faithful and prudent going on both in words well weighed, and in the true sense of the covenant "without respect of persons," when we could not serve two contrary masters, God and the King, or the king and that more supreme law sworn in the first place to maintain our safety and our liberty. They knew the people of England to be a free people, themselves the representers of that freedom; and although many were excluded, and as many fled, so they pretended, from tumults to Oxford, yet they were left a sufficient number to act in Parliament, therefore not bound by any statute of preceding parliaments, but by the Law of Nature only. Which is the only law of laws truly and properly to all mankind fundamental; the beginning and the end of all government; to which no parliament or people that will thoroughly reform but may and must have recourse, as they had, and must yet have in Church Reformation (if they thoroughly intend it) to evangelic rules, not to ecclesiastical canons, though never so ancient, so ratified and established in the land by statutes which for the most part are mere positive laws, neither natural nor moral, and so by any parliament for just and serious considerations, without scruple to be at any time repealed.

If others of their number in these things were under force,—they were not, but under free conscience :—if others were excluded by a power which they could not resist, they were not therefore to leave the helm of government in no hands, to discontinue their care of the public peace and safety, to desert the people in anarchy and confusion, no more than when so many of their members left them as made up in outward formality a more legal parliament of three estates against them. The best affected also and best principled of the people stood not numbering or computing on which side were most voices in Parliament, but on which side appeared to them most reason, most safety, when the House divided upon main matters. What was well mentioned and advised, they examined not whether fear or persuasion carried it in the vote, neither did they measure votes and counsels by the intentions of them that voted; knowing that intentions either are but guessed at, or not soon enough known, and although good, can neither make the deed such, nor prevent the consequence from being bad. Suppose bad intentions otherwise well done; what was well done was by them who so thought, not the less obeyed or followed in the State; since in the Church, who had not rather follow Iscariot or Simon the magician, though to covetous ends preaching, than Saul, though in the uprightness of his heart persecuting the Gospel?

Safer they, therefore, judged what they thought the better counsels, though carried on by some perhaps to bad ends, than the worst by others, though endeavoured with best intentions. And yet they were not to learn that a greater number might be corrupt within the walls of a Parliament, as well as of a City. Whereof in matters of nearest concernment all men will be judges; nor easily permit that the odds of voices in their greatest Council shall more endanger them by corrupt or credulous votes, than the odds of enemies by open assaults; judging that most voices ought not always to prevail where main matters are in question. If others hence will pretend to disturb all counsels, what is that to them who pretend not, but are in real danger, not they only so judging, but a great, though not the greatest number of their chosen patriots, who might be more in weight than the others in numbers; there being in number little virtue, but by weight and measure wisdom working all things. And the dangers on either side they seriously thus weighed?

From the treaty, short fruits of long labours, and seven years' war; security for twenty years, if we can hold it; Reformation in the Church for three years: then put to shift again with our vanquished master. His justice, his honour, his conscience declared quite contrary to ours; which would have furnished him with many such evasions as in a book entitled "An Inquisition for Blood," soon after were not concealed. Bishops not totally removed, but left, as it were, in ambush, a reserve, with ordination in their sole power; their lands already sold, not to be alienated, but rented, and the sale of them called "sacrilege." Delinquents, few of many brought to condign punishment; accessories punished, the chief author, above pardon, though, after utmost resistance, vanquished, not to give, but to receive, laws; yet besought, treated with, and to be thanked for his gracious concessions, to be honoured, worshipped, glorified.

If this we swore to do, with what righteousness in the sight of God, with what assurance that we bring not by such an oath the whole sea of blood-guiltiness upon our heads? If on the other side we prefer a Free Government, though for the present not obtained, yet all those suggested fears and difficulties, as the event will prove, easily overcome, we remain finally secure from the exasperated regal power, and out of snares; shall retain the best part of our Liberty, which is our Religion, and the civil part will be from these who defer us much more easily recovered, being neither so subtle nor so awful as a king reinthroned. Nor were their actions less both at home and abroad than might become the hopes of a glorious rising Commonwealth: nor were the expressions both of army and people, whether in their public declarations or several writings, other than such as testified a spirit in this nation, no less noble and well-fitted to the liberty of a commonwealth, than in the ancient Greeks or Romans. Nor was the heroic cause unsuccessfully defended to all Christendom against the tongue of a famous and thought invincible adversary; nor the constancy and fortitude that so nobly vindicated our liberty, our victory at once against two the most prevailing usurpers over mankind, superstition and tyranny, unpraised or uncelebrated in a written monument, likely to outlive detraction as it hath hitherto convinced or silenced not a few of our detractors, especially in parts abroad.

After our Liberty and Religion thus prosperously fought for, gained, and many years possessed, except in those unhappy interruptions which God hath removed; now that nothing remains, but in all reason the certain hopes of a speedy and immediate settlement for ever in a firm and free Commonwealth,—for this extolled and magnified nation, regardless both of honour won, or deliverances vouchsafed from heaven, to fall back, or rather to creep back so poorly as it seems the multitude would, to their once abjured and detested thraldom of kingship ; to be ourselves the slanderers of our own just and religious deeds, though done by some to covetous and ambitious ends yet not therefore to be stained with their infamy, or they to asperse the integrity of others ; and yet these now by revolting from the conscience of deeds well done both in Church and State, to throw away and forsake, or rather to betray, a just and noble cause for the mixture of bad men who have ill-managed and abused it (which had our fathers done heretofore, and on the same pretence deserted true religion, what had long ere this become of our Gospel, and all Protestant Reformation so much intermixed with the avarice and ambition of some reformers ?) and by thus relapsing, to verify all the bitter predictions of our triumphing enemies, who will now think they wisely discerned and justly censured both us and all our actions as rash, rebellious, hypocritical, and impious ;—not only argues a strange, degenerate contagion suddenly spread among us, fitted and prepared for new slavery, but will render us a scorn and derision to all our neighbours. And what will they at best say of us, and of the whole English name, but scoffingly, as of that foolish builder mentioned by our Saviour, who began to build a tower, and was not able to finish it :—Where is this goodly tower of a Commonwealth, which the English boasted they would build to overshadow kings, and be another Rome in the west ? The foundation indeed they laid gallantly, but fell into a worse confusion, not of tongues, but of factions, than those at the tower of Babel ; and have left no memorial of their work behind them remaining but in the common laughter of Europe! Which must needs redound the more to our shame, if we but look on our neighbours the United Provinces, to us inferior in all outward advantages ; who notwithstanding, in the midst of greater difficulties, courageously, wisely, constantly went through with the same work, and are settled in all the happy enjoyments of a potent and flourishing republic to this day.

Besides this, if we return to kingship, and soon repent (as undoubtedly we shall, when we begin to find the old encroachment coming on by little and little upon our consciences, which must necessarily proceed from king and bishop united inseparably in one interest), we may be forced perhaps to fight over again all that we have fought, and spend over again all that we have spent, but are never like to attain thus far as we are now advanced to the recovery of our freedom, never to have it in possession as we now have it, never to be vouchsafed hereafter the like mercies and signal assistances from Heaven in our cause, if by our ingrateful backsliding we make these fruitless ; flying now to regal concessions from his divine condescensions and gracious answers to our once importuning prayers against the tyranny which we then groaned under ; making vain and viler than dirt the blood of so many thousand faithful and valiant Englishmen, who left us in this liberty, bought with their lives ; losing by a strange after-game of folly all the battles we have won, together with all Scotland as to our conquest hereby lost, which never any of our kings could conquer ; all the treasure we have spent, not that corruptible treasure only, but that far more precious of all our late miraculous deliverances ; treading back again with lost labour all our happy steps in the progress of Reformation, and most pitifully depriving ourselves the instant fruition of that free government which we have so dearly purchased, a Free Commonwealth, not only held by wisest men in all ages the noblest, the manliest, the equallest, the justest government, the most agreeable to all due liberty and proportioned equality, both human, civil, and Christian, most cherishing to virtue and true religion, but also (I may say it with greatest probability) plainly commended or rather enjoined by our Saviour himself to all Christians, not without remarkable disallowance and the brand of Gentilism upon kingship.

God in much displeasure gave a king to the Israelites, and imputed it a sin to them that they sought one ; but Christ apparently forbids his disciples to admit of any such heathenish government. "The kings of the Gentiles," saith he, "exercise lordship over them," and they that "exercise authority upon them are called benefactors : but ye shall not be so ; but he that is greatest among you, let him be as the younger ; and he that is chief, as he that serveth." The occasion of these his words was the ambitious desire of Zebedee's two sons to be exalted above their brethren in his kingdom, which they thought was to be ere long upon earth. That he speaks of civil government, is manifest by the former part of the comparison, which infers the other part to be always in the same kind. And what government comes nearer to this precept of Christ, than a Free Commonwealth ; wherein they who are the greatest are perpetual servants and drudges to the public at their own cost and charges, neglect their own affairs, yet are not elevated above their brethren ; live soberly in their families, walk the street as other men, may be spoken to freely, familiarly, friendly, without adoration ? Whereas a king must be adored like a demigod, with a dissolute and haughty court about him, of vast expense and luxury, masks and revels, to the debauching of our prime gentry both male and female, not in their pastimes only, but in earnest, by the loose employments of court-service, which will be then thought honourable. There will be a queen of no less charge; in most likelihood outlandish and a papist, besides a queen-mother such already; together with both their Courts and numerous train. Then a royal issue, and ere long severally their sumptuous Courts, to the multiplying of a servile crew, not of servants only but of nobility and gentry bred up then to the hopes not of public but of Court-offices, to be stewards, chamberlains, ushers, grooms even of the close-stool. And the lower their minds debased with Court-opinions contrary to all virtue and reformation, the haughtier will be their pride and profuseness. We may well remember this not long since at home; nor need but look at present into the French court, where enticements and preferments daily draw away and pervert the Protestant nobility.

As to the burden of expense, to our cost we shall soon know it, for any good to us, deserving to be termed no better than the vast and lavish price of our subjection and their debauchery, which we are now so greedily cheapening and would so fain be paying most inconsiderately to a single person who, for anything wherein the public really needs him, will have little else to do but to bestow the eating and drinking of excessive dainties, to set a pompous face upon the superficial actings of State, to pageant himself up and down in progress among the perpetual bowings and cringings of an abject people on either side deifying and adoring him for nothing done that can deserve it. For what can he more than another man who, even in the expression of a late court-poet, sits only like a great cipher set to no purpose before a long row of other significant figures. Nay, it is well and happy for the people if their king be but a cipher, being ofttimes a mischief, a pest, a scourge of the nation and, which is worse, not to be removed, not to be controlled, much less accused or brought to punishment, without the danger of a common ruin, without the shaking and almost subversion of the whole land. Whereas in a Free Commonwealth, any governor or chief counsellor offending may be removed and punished without the least commotion.

Certainly then that people must needs be mad or strangely infatuated that build the chief hope of their common happiness or safety on a single person; who, if he happen to be good, can do no more than another man; if to be bad, hath in his hands to do more evil without check than millions of other men. The happiness of a nation must needs be firmest and certainest in full and free Council of their own electing, where no single person, but Reason only, sways. And what madness is it for them who might manage nobly their own affairs themselves, sluggishly and weakly to devolve all on

a single person, and, more like boys under age than men, to commit
all to his patronage and disposal who neither can perform what he
undertakes, and yet for undertaking it, though royally paid, will not
be their servant, but their lord.   How unmanly must it needs be to
count such a one the breath of our nostrils, to hang all our felicity
on him, all our safety, our well-being, for which if we were aught else
but sluggards or babies we need depend on none but God and our
own counsels, our own active virtue and industry !   Go to the ant,
thou sluggard, saith Solomon ; consider her ways, and be wise ;
which having no prince, ruler, or lord, provides her meat in the
summer, and gathers her food in the harvest.   Which evidently
shows us that they who think the nation undone without a king,
though they look grave or haughty, have not so much true spirit and
understanding in them as a pismire.   Neither are these diligent
creatures hence concluded to live in lawless anarchy, or that commended ; but are set the examples to imprudent and ungoverned men
of a frugal and self-governing democracy or commonwealth, safer and
more thriving in the joint providence and counsel of many industrious
equals than under the single domination of one imperious lord.

It may be well wondered that any nation styling themselves free
can suffer any man to pretend hereditary right over them as their
lord ; whenas, by acknowledging that right, they conclude themselves
his servants and his vassals, and so renounce their own freedom.
Which how a people, and their leaders especially, can do, who have
fought so gloriously for liberty ; how they can change their noble
words and actions, heretofore so becoming the majesty of a free
people, into the base necessity of court flatteries and prostrations, is
not only strange and admirable but lamentable to think on.   That a
nation should be so valorous and courageous to win their liberty in
the field, and when they have won it, should be so heartless and
unwise in their counsels as not to know how to use it, value it, what
to do with it, or with themselves, but after ten or twelve years' prosperous war and contestation with tyranny, basely and besottedly to
run their necks again into the yoke which they have broken, and
prostrate all the fruits of their victory for nought at the feet of the
vanquished,—besides our loss of glory, and such an example as kings
or tyrants never yet had the like to boast of,—will be an ignominy if
it befall us that never yet befell any nation possessed of their liberty.
Worthy indeed themselves, whatsoever they be, to be for ever slaves :
but that part of the nation which consents not with them, as I persuade me of a great number, far worthier than by their means to be
brought into the same bondage.

Considering these things so plain, so rational, I cannot but yet further admire on the other side how any man who hath the true principles of justice and religion in him can presume or take upon him to be a king and lord over his brethren whom he cannot but know, whether as men or Christians, to be for the most part every way equal or superior to himself; how he can display with such vanity and ostentation his regal splendour so supereminently above other mortal men; or, being a Christian, can assume such extraordinary honour and worship to himself, while the kingdom of Christ, our common king and lord, is hid to this world, and such gentilish imitation forbid in express words by himself to all his disciples. All Protestants hold that Christ in his Church hath left no vicegerent of his power; but himself, without deputy, is the only head thereof, governing it from heaven. How then can any Christian man derive his kingship from Christ, but with worse usurpation than the pope his headship over the Church, since Christ not only hath not left the least shadow of a command for any such vicegerence from him in the State, as the pope pretends for his in the Church, but hath expressly declared that such regal dominion is from the gentiles, not from him, and hath strictly charged us not to imitate them therein?

I doubt not but all ingenuous and knowing men will easily agree with me, that a Free Commonwealth without Single Person or House of Lords is by far the best government, if it can be had; but we have all this while, say they, been expecting it, and cannot yet attain it. It is true, indeed, when Monarchy was dissolved, the form of a Commonwealth should have forthwith been framed, and the practice thereof immediately begun, that the people might have soon been satisfied and delighted with the decent order, ease and benefit thereof. We had been then by this time firmly rooted, past fear of commotions or mutations, and now flourishing; this care of timely settling a new government instead of the old, too much neglected, hath been our mischief. Yet the cause thereof may be ascribed with most reason to the frequent disturbances, interruptions, and dissolutions, which the Parliament hath had, partly from the impatient or disaffected people, partly from some ambitious leaders in the army, much contrary, I believe, to the mind and approbation of the army itself, and their other commanders, once undeceived or in their own power.

Now is the opportunity, now the very season, wherein we may obtain a Free Commonwealth, and establish it for ever in the land, without difficulty or much delay. Writs are sent out for elections, and, which is worth observing, in the name, not of any king, but of the keepers of our liberty, to summon a free parliament; which then only will indeed be free, and deserve the true honour of that supreme title, if they preserve us a free people. Which never Parliament was more free to do, being now called, not, as heretofore, by the summons of a king, but by the voice of liberty. And if the people, laying aside prejudice and impatience, will seriously and calmly now consider their own good, both religious and civil, their own liberty and the only means thereof, as shall be here laid down before them, and will elect their knights and burgesses able men, and according to the just and necessary qualifications—which, for aught I hear, remain yet in force unrepealed, as they were formerly decreed in Parliament—men not addicted to a Single Person or House of Lords, the work is done; at least the foundation firmly laid of a Free Commonwealth, and good part also erected of the main structure.

For the ground and basis of every just and free government—since men have smarted so oft for committing all to one person—is a General Council of ablest men, chosen by the People to consult of public affairs from time to time for the common good. In this Grand Council must the sovereignty, not transferred but delegated only and as it were deposited, reside; with this caution, they must have the forces by sea and land committed to them for preservation of the common peace and liberty; must raise and manage the public revenue, at least with some inspectors deputed for satisfaction of the people how it is employed; must make or propose, as more expressly shall be said anon, civil laws; treat of commerce, peace or war with foreign nations; and, for the carrying on some particular affairs with more secrecy and expedition, must elect, as they have already out of their own number and others, a Council of State.

And, although it may seem strange at first hearing, by reason that men's minds are prepossessed with the notion of Successive Parliaments, I affirm, that the Grand or General Council, being well chosen, should be Perpetual. For so their business is or may be, and ofttimes urgent; the opportunity of affairs gained or lost in a moment. The day of Council cannot be set as the day of a festival, but must be ready always to prevent or answer all occasions. By this continuance they will become every way skilfullest, best provided of intelligence from abroad, best acquainted with the people at home, and the people with them. The ship of the commonwealth is always under sail; they sit at the stern, and if they steer well, what need is there to change them, it being rather dangerous? Add to this, that the Grand Council is both foundation and main pillar of the whole State; and to move pillars and foundations, not faulty, cannot be safe for the building.

I see not, therefore, how we can be advantaged by successive and transitory parliaments; but that they are much likelier continually to unsettle rather than to settle a free government, to breed commotions, changes, novelties, and uncertainties, to bring neglect upon present affairs and opportunities, while all minds are in suspense with expectation of a new assembly, and the assembly, for a good space, taken up with the new settling of itself. After which, if they find no great work to do, they will make it, by altering or repealing former acts, or making and multiplying new, that they may seem to see what their predecessors saw not, and not to have assembled for nothing; till all law be lost in the multitude of clashing statutes. But if the ambition of such as think themselves injured, that they also partake not of the government, and are impatient till they be chosen, cannot brook the perpetuity of others chosen before them; or if it be feared, that long continuance of power may corrupt sincerest men, the known expedient is, and by some lately propounded, that annually (or if the space be longer, so much perhaps the better) the third part of senators may go out according to the precedence of their election, and the like number be chosen in their places, to prevent their settling of too absolute a power, if it should be perpetual: and this they call "partial rotation."

But I could wish, that this wheel, or partial wheel in State, if it be possible, might be avoided, as having too much affinity with the wheel of Fortune. For it appears not how this can be done, without danger and mischance of putting out a great number of the best and ablest: in whose stead new elections may bring in as many raw, unexperienced, and otherwise affected, to the weakening and much altering for the worse of public transactions. Neither do I think a Perpetual Senate especially chosen or entrusted by the people much in this land to be feared, where the well-affected either in a standing army or in a settled militia have their arms in their own hands. Safest therefore to me it seems, and of least hazard or interruption to affairs, that none of the Grand Council be moved, unless by death, or just conviction of some crime: for what can be expected firm or steadfast from a floating foundation? However, I forejudge not any probable expedient, any temperament that can be found in things of this nature, so disputable on either side.

Yet lest this which I affirm be thought my single opinion, I shall add sufficient testimony. Kingship itself is therefore counted the more safe and durable because the king, and for the most part his council, is not changed during life. But a Commonwealth is held immortal, and therein firmest, safest, and most above fortune; for the death of a king causeth ofttimes many dangerous alterations; but the death now and then of a senator is not felt, the main body of them still continuing permanent in greatest and noblest commonwealths and as it were eternal. Therefore among the Jews, the supreme council of seventy, called the Sanhedrim, founded by Moses, in Athens that of Areopagus, in Sparta that of the Ancients, in Rome the Senate, consisted of members chosen for term of life; and by that means remained as it were still the same to generations. In Venice they change indeed oftener than every year some particular Council of State, as that of Six, or such other: but the true Senate, which upholds and sustains the government, is the whole aristocracy immovable. So in the United Provinces, the States General, which are indeed but a Council of State deputed by the whole union, are not usually the same persons for above three or six years; but the States of every city, in whom the sovereignty hath been placed time out of mind, are a standing Senate, without succession, and accounted chiefly in that regard the main prop of their liberty. And why they should be so in every well-ordered commonwealth, they who write of policy give these reasons: That to make the Senate successive, not only impairs the dignity and lustre of the Senate, but weakens the whole Commonwealth, and brings it into manifest danger; while by this means the secrets of state are frequently divulged, and matters of greatest consequence committed to inexpert and novice counsellors, utterly to seek in the full and intimate knowledge of affairs past.

I know not, therefore, what should be peculiar in England, to make successive parliaments thought safest, or convenient here more than in other nations, unless it be the fickleness which is attributed to us as we are islanders. But good education and acquisite wisdom ought to correct the fluxible fault, if any such be, of our watery situation. It will be objected, that in those places where they had Perpetual Senates, they had also popular remedies against their growing too imperious: as in Athens, besides Areopagus, another senate of four or five hundred; in Sparta, the Ephori; in Rome, the Tribunes of the People.

But the event tells us, that these remedies either little availed the people, or brought them to such a licentious and unbridled democracy, as in fine ruined themselves with their own excessive power. So that the main reason urged why popular assemblies are to be trusted with the people's liberty, rather than a senate of principal men, because great men will be still endeavouring to enlarge their power, but the common sort will be contented to maintain their own liberty, is by experience found false; none being more immoderate and ambitious to amplify their power than such popularities. Which were seen in the People of Rome, who, at first contented to have their tribunes, at length contended with the senate that one consul, then both, soon after, that the censors and prætors also, should be created plebeian, and the whole empire put into their hands; adoring lastly those who most were adverse to the senate, till Marius, by fulfilling their inordinate desires, quite lost them all the power for which they had so long been striving, and left them under the tyranny of Sylla. The balance therefore must be exactly so set, as to preserve and keep up due authority on either side, as well in the Senate as in the People. And this annual rotation of a Senate to consist of three hundred, as is lately propounded, requires also another popular assembly upward of a thousand, with an answerable rotation. Which, besides that it will be liable to all those inconveniences found in the aforesaid remedies, cannot but be troublesome and chargeable, both in their motion and their session, to the whole land; unwieldy with their own bulk; unable in so great a number to mature their consultations as they ought, if any be allotted them, and that they meet not from so many parts remote to sit a whole year lieger in one place, only now and then to hold up a forest of fingers, or to convey each man his bean or ballot into the box without reason shown or common deliberation; incontinent of secrets, if any be imparted to them; emulous and always jarring with the other senate. The much better way doubtless will be, in this wavering condition of our affairs, to defer the changing or circumscribing of our Senate, more than may be done with ease, till the Commonwealth be thoroughly settled in peace and safety, and they themselves give us the occasion.

Military men hold it dangerous to change the form of battle in view of an enemy: neither did the people of Rome bandy with their Senate, while any of the Tarquins lived, the enemies of their liberty; nor sought, by creating tribunes, to defend themselves against the fear of their patricians, till, sixteen years after the expulsion of their kings, and in full security of their state, they had or thought they had just cause given them by the Senate. Another way will be, to well qualify and refine elections: not committing all to the noise and shouting of a rude multitude, but permitting only those of them who are rightly qualified to nominate as many as they will; and out of that number others of a better breeding, to choose a less number more judiciously; till after a third or fourth sifting and refining of exactest choice, they only be left chosen who are the due number, and seem by most voices the worthiest.

To make the people fittest to choose, and the chosen fittest to govern, will be to mend our corrupt and faulty education, to teach the people faith, not without virtue, temperance, modesty, sobriety, parsimony, justice; not to admire wealth or honour; to hate turbulence and ambition; to place every one his private welfare and happiness in the public peace, liberty, and safety. They shall not then need to be much mistrustful of their chosen patriots in the Grand Council; who will be then rightly called the true keepers of our liberty, though the most of their business will be in foreign affairs. But to prevent all mistrust, the people then will have their several ordinary Assemblies (which will henceforth quite annihilate the odious power and name of Committees) in the chief towns of every county, without the trouble, charge, or time lost of summoning and assembling from far in so great a number, and so long residing from their own houses or removing of their families, to do as much at home in their several shires, entire or subdivided, toward the securing of their liberty, as a numerous Assembly of them all formed and convened on purpose with the wariest rotation. Whereof I shall speak more ere the end of this discourse; for it may be referred to time, so we be still going on by degrees to perfection. The people well weighing and performing these things, I suppose would have no cause to fear, though the Parliament, abolishing that name, as originally signifying but the parley of our lords and commons with the Norman king when he pleased to call them, should, with certain limitations of their power, sit perpetual if their ends be faithful and for a free commonwealth, under the name of a Grand or General Council.

Till this be done, I am in doubt whether our State will be ever certainly and throughly settled; never likely till then to see an end of our troubles and continual changes, or at least never the true settlement and assurance of our liberty. The Grand Council being thus firmly constituted to perpetuity, and still, upon the death or default of any member, supplied and kept in full number, there can be no cause alleged why peace, justice, plentiful trade, and all prosperity should not thereupon ensue throughout the whole land, with as much assurance as can be of human things, that they shall so continue—if God favour us, and our wilful sins provoke him not—even to the coming of our true and rightful, and only to be expected King, only worthy, as he is our only Saviour, the Messiah, the Christ, the only heir of his eternal Father, the only by him anointed and ordained since the work of our redemption finished, universal Lord of mankind.

The way propounded is plain, easy, and open before us; without intricacies, without the introducement of new or absolute forms or terms, or exotic models; ideas that would effect nothing but with a number of new injunctions to manacle the native liberty of mankind; turning all virtue into prescription, servitude, and necessity, to the great impairing and frustrating of Christian liberty. I say again, this way lies free and smooth before us; is not tangled with inconveniences; invents no new incumbrances; requires no perilous, no injurious alteration or circumscription of men's lands and properties; secure, that in this commonwealth, Temporal and Spiritual lords removed, no man or number of men can attain to such wealth or vast possession, as will need the hedge of an agrarian law—never successful, but the cause rather of sedition, save only where it began seasonably with first possession—to confine them from endangering our public liberty.

To conclude, it can have no considerable objection made against it, that it is not practicable; lest it be said hereafter, that we gave up our liberty for want of a ready way or distinct form proposed of a Free Commonwealth. And this facility we shall have above our next neighbouring commonwealth, if we can keep us from the fond conceit of something like a duke of Venice, put lately into many men's heads, by some one or other subtly driving on under that notion his own ambitious ends to lurch a crown, that our liberty shall not be hampered or hovered over by any engagement to such a potent family as the house of Nassau, of whom to stand in perpetual doubt and suspicion; but we shall live the clearest and absolutest free nation in the world.

On the contrary, if there be a king, which the inconsiderate multitude are now so mad upon, mark how far short we are like to come of all those happinesses which in a Free State we shall immediately be possessed of. First, the Grand Council, which, as I showed before, should sit perpetually—unless their leisure give them now and then some intermissions or vacations, easily manageable by the Council of State left sitting—shall be called, by the king's good will and utmost endeavour, as seldom as may be. For it is only the king's right, he will say, to call a Parliament; and this he will do most commonly about his own affairs rather than the kingdom's, as will appear plainly so soon as they are called. For what will their business then be, and the chief expense of their time, but an endless tugging between Petition of Right, and Royal Prerogative, especially about the negative voice, militia, or subsidies, demanded and ofttimes extorted without reasonable cause appearing to the Commons, who are the only true representatives of the people and their liberty, but will be then mingled with a Court-faction. Besides which, within their own walls the sincere part of them who stand faithful to the people will again have to deal with two troublesome counter-working adversaries from without, mere creatures of the king, spiritual, and the greater part, as is likeliest, of temporal lords, nothing concerned with the people's liberty.

If these prevail not in what they please, though never so much against the people's interest, the Parliament shall be soon dissolved, or sit and do nothing; not suffered to remedy the least grievance, or enact aught advantageous to the people.

Next, the Council of State shall not be chosen by the Parliament, but by the king, still his own creatures, courtiers, and favourers; who will be sure in all their counsels to set their master's grandeur and absolute power, in what they are able, far above the people's liberty. I deny not but that there may be such a king who may regard the common good before his own, may have no vicious favourite, may hearken only to the wisest and incorruptest of his Parliament. But this rarely happens in a monarchy not elective: and it behoves not a wise nation to commit the sum of their wellbeing, the whole state of their safety, to fortune. What need they? And how absurd would it be, whenas they themselves, to whom his chief virtue will be but to hearken, may with much better management and dispatch, with much more commendation of their own worth and magnanimity, govern without a master? Can the folly be paralleled, to adore and be slaves of a single person for doing that which it is ten thousand to one whether he can or will do, and we without him might do more easily, more effectually, more laudably ourselves? Shall we never grow old enough to be wise, to make seasonable use of gravest authorities, experiences, examples? Is it such an unspeakable joy to serve, such felicity to wear a yoke?. to clink our shackles, locked on by pretended law of subjection, more intolerable and hopeless to be ever shaken off than those which are knocked on by illegal injury and violence?

Aristotle, our chief instructor in the Universities, lest this doctrine be thought sectarian as the Royalist would have it thought, tells us in the third of his Politics, that certain men at first, for the matchless excellence of their virtue above others, or some great public benefit, were created kings by the people in small cities and territories, and in the scarcity of others to be found like them; but when they abused their power, and governments grew larger, and the number of prudent men increased, that then the people, soon deposing their tyrants, betook them, in all civilest places, to the form of a Free Commonwealth. And why should we thus disparage and prejudicate our own nation, as to fear a scarcity of able and worthy men united in counsel to govern us, if we will but use diligence and impartiality to find them out and choose them; rather yoking ourselves to a single person, the natural adversary and oppressor of liberty, though good, yet far easier corruptible by the excess of his single power and exaltation, or at best not comparably sufficient to bear the weight of government, nor equally disposed to make us happy in the enjoyment of our liberty under him?

But admit that monarchy of itself may be convenient to some nations; yet to us who have thrown it out, received back again it cannot but prove pernicious. For kings to come, never forgetting their former ejection, will be sure to fortify and arm themselves sufficiently for the future against all such attempts hereafter from the people; who shall be then so narrowly watched and kept so low, that though they would never so fain and at the same rate of their blood and treasure, they never shall be able to regain what they now have purchased and may enjoy, or to free themselves from any yoke imposed upon them. Nor will they dare to go about it; utterly disheartened for the future, if these their highest attempts prove unsuccessful. Which will be the triumph of all tyrants hereafter over any people that shall resist oppression; and their song will then be, to others, How sped the rebellious English? to our posterity, How sped the rebels, your fathers?

This is not my conjecture, but drawn from God s known denouncement against the gentilising Israelites, who, though they were governed in a commonwealth of God's own ordaining, he only their king, they his peculiar people, yet affecting rather to resemble heathen, but pretending the misgovernment of Samuel's sons, no more a reason to dislike their commonwealth than the violence of Eli's sons was imputable to that priesthood or religion, clamoured for a king. They had their longing, but with this testimony of God's wrath: "Ye shall cry out in that day, because of your king whom ye shall have chosen, and the Lord will not hear you in that day." Us if he shall hear now, how much less will he hear when we cry hereafter, who once delivered by him from a king, and not without wondrous acts of his providence, insensible and unworthy of those high mercies, are returning precipitantly, if he withhold us not, back to the captivity from whence he freed us.

Yet neither shall we obtain or buy at an easy rate this new gilded yoke which thus transports us. A new royal revenue must be found, a new episcopal; for those are individual: both which being wholly dissipated, or bought by private persons, or assigned for service done, and especially to the army, cannot be recovered without general detriment and confusion to men's estates or a heavy imposition on all men's purses; benefit to none but to the worst and ignoblest sort of men, whose hope is to be either the ministers of court riot and excess, or the gainers by it. But not to speak more of losses and extraordinary levies on our estates, what will then be the revenges and offences remembered and returned, not only by the chief person, but by all his adherents; accounts and reparations that will be required, suits, indictments, inquiries, discoveries, complaints, informations, who knows against whom or how many, though perhaps neuters, if not to utmost infliction, yet to imprisonment, fines, banishment, or molestation? if not these, yet disfavour, discountenance, disregard, and contempt on all but the known royalist, or whom he favours, will be plenteous.

Nor let the new royalised Presbyterians persuade themselves that their old doings, though now recanted, will be forgotten, whatever conditions be contrived or trusted on. Will they not believe this, nor remember the pacification, how it was kept to the Scots; how other solemn promises many a time to us? Let them but now read the diabolical forerunning libels, the faces, the gestures, that now appear foremost and briskest in all public places, as the harbingers of those that are in expectation to reign over us. Let them but hear the insolencies, the menaces, the insultings, of our newly animated common enemies, crept lately out of their holes, their hell I might say by the language of their infernal pamphlets, the spew of every drunkard, every ribald, nameless, yet not for want of licence but for very shame of their own vile persons not daring to name themselves, while they traduce others by name, and give us to foresee that they intend to second their wicked words, if ever they have power, with more wicked deeds.

Let our zealous backsliders forethink now with themselves how their necks yoked with these tigers of Bacchus, these new fanatics of not the preaching but the sweating-tub, inspired with nothing holier than the venereal pox, can draw one way under monarchy to the establishing of Church Discipline with these new disgorged atheisms. Yet shall they not have the honour to yoke with these, but shall be yoked under them; these shall plough on their backs. And do they among them who are so forward to bring in the single person, think to be by him trusted or long regarded? So trusted they shall be, and so regarded, as by kings are wont reconciled enemies; neglected, and soon after discarded, if not persecuted for old traitors; the first inciters, beginners, and more than to the third part actors, of all that followed.

It will be found also, that there must be then, as necessarily as now—for the contrary part will be still feared—a standing army; which for certain shall not be this, but of the fiercest cavaliers, of no less expense, and perhaps again under Rupert. But let this army be sure they shall be soon disbanded, and likeliest without arrear or pay; and being disbanded, not be sure but they may as soon be questioned for being in arms against their king. The same let them fear who have contributed money, which will amount to no small number, that must then take their turn to be made delinquents and compounders. They who past reason and recovery are devoted to kingship perhaps will answer, that a greater part by far of the nation will have it so; the rest therefore must yield.

Not so much to convince these, which I little hope, as to confirm them who yield not, I reply, that this greatest part have both in reason and the trial of just battle, lost the right of their election what the government shall be. Of them who have not lost that right, whether they for kingship be the greater number who can certainly determine? Suppose they be, yet of freedom they partake all alike, one main end of government, which if the greater part value not, but will degenerately forego, is it just or reasonable that most voices against the main end of government should enslave the less number that would be free? More just it is, doubtless, if it come to force, that a less number compel a greater to retain—which can be no wrong to them—their liberty, than that a greater number, for the pleasure of their baseness, compel a less most injuriously to be their fellow-slaves. They who seek nothing but their own just liberty, have always right to win it and to keep it whenever they have power, be the voices never so numerous that oppose it. And how much we above others are concerned to defend it from kingship, and from them who in pursuance thereof so perniciously would betray us and themselves to most certain misery and thraldom, will be needless to repeat.

Having thus far shown with what ease we may now obtain a Free Commonwealth, and by it, with as much ease, all the freedom, peace, justice, plenty, that we can desire; on the other side, the difficulties, troubles, uncertainties, nay, rather impossibilities, to enjoy these things constantly under a Monarch; I will now proceed to show more particularly wherein our freedom and flourishing condition will be more ample and secure to us under a free commonwealth, than under kingship.

The whole freedom of man consists either in spiritual or civil liberty. As for spiritual, who can be at rest, who can enjoy anything in this world with contentment, who hath not liberty to serve God and to save his own soul according to the best light which God hath planted in him to that purpose by the reading of his revealed will and the guidance of his Holy Spirit? That this is best pleasing to God, and that the whole Protestant Church allows no supreme judge or rule in matters of religion, but the Scriptures, and these to be interpreted by the Scriptures themselves, which necessarily infers Liberty of Conscience, I have heretofore proved at large in another treatise; and might yet further, by the public declarations, confessions, and admonitions of whole Churches and States, obvious in all histories since the Reformation.

This Liberty of Conscience, which above all other things ought to be to all men dearest and most precious, no government more inclinable not to favour only, but to protect, than a Free Commonwealth; as being most magnanimous, most fearless, and confident of its own fair proceedings. Whereas kingship, though looking big, yet indeed most pusillanimous, full of fears, full of jealousies, startled at every umbrage, as it hath been observed of old to have ever suspected most and mistrusted them who were in most esteem for virtue and generosity of mind, so it is now known to have most in doubt and suspicion them who are most reputed to be religious. Queen Elizabeth, though herself accounted so good a Protestant, so moderate, so confident of her subjects' love, would never give way so much as to Presbyterian Reformation in this land, though once and again besought, as Camden relates; but imprisoned and persecuted the very proposers thereof, alleging it as her mind and maxim unalterable, that such Reformation would diminish regal authority.

What Liberty of Conscience can we then expect of others, far worse principled from the cradle, trained up and governed by Popish and Spanish counsels, and on such depending hitherto for subsistence? Especially what can this last Parliament expect, who having revived lately and published the Covenant, have re-engaged themselves, never to readmit episcopacy? Which no son of Charles returning but will most certainly bring back with him, if he regard the last and strictest charge of his father, "to persevere in, not the doctrine only, but government of the Church of England, not to neglect the speedy and effectual suppressing of errors and schisms;" among which he accounted Presbytery one of the chief.

Or if, notwithstanding that charge of his father, he submit to the Covenant, how will he keep faith to us, with disobedience to him; or regard that faith given, which must be founded on the breach of that last and solemnest paternal charge, and the reluctance, I may say the antipathy, which is in all kings, against Presbyterian and Independent discipline? For they hear the Gospel speaking much of Liberty; a word which monarchy and her bishops both fear and hate, but a Free Commonwealth both favours and promotes; and not the word only, but the thing itself. But let our governors beware in time, lest their hard measure to Liberty of Conscience be found the rock whereon they shipwreck themselves, as others have now done before them in the course wherein God was directing their steerage to a Free Commonwealth; and the abandoning of all those whom they call sectaries, for the detected falsehood and ambition of some, be a wilful rejection of their own chief strength and interest in the freedom of all Protestant Religion, under what abusive name soever calumniated.

The other part of our freedom consists in the Civil Rights and advancements of every person according to his merit: the enjoyment of those never more certain, and the access to these never more open, than in a Free Commonwealth. Both which, in my opinion, may be best and soonest obtained, if every county in the land were made a kind of subordinate commonalty or commonwealth, and one chief town or more, according as the shire is in circuit, made cities, if they be not so called already; where the nobility and chief gentry, from a proportionable compass of territory annexed to each city, may build houses or palaces befitting their quality, may bear part in the government, make their own judicial laws, or use those that are, and execute them by their own elected judicatures and judges without appeal, in all things of Civil Government between Man and Man. So they shall have justice in their own hands, law executed fully and finally in their own counties and precincts, long wished and spoken of, but never yet obtained. They shall have none then to blame but themselves, if it be not well administered; and fewer laws to expect or fear from the supreme authority. Or to those that shall be made, of any great concernment to public liberty, they may, without much trouble in these commonalties, or in more general assemblies called to their cities from the whole territory on such occasion, declare and publish their assent or dissent by deputies, within a time limited, sent to the Grand Council; yet so as this their judgment declared shall submit to the greater number of other counties or commonalties, and not avail them to any exemption of themselves, or refusal of agreement with the rest, as it may in any of the United Provinces, being sovereign within itself ofttimes to the great disadvantage of that Union.

In these employments they may, much better than they do now, exercise and fit themselves till their lot fall to be chosen into the Grand Council, according as their worth and merit shall be taken notice of by the people. As for controversies that shall happen between men of several counties, they may repair, as they do now, to the capital city, or any other more commodious, indifferent place, and equal judges. And this I find to have been practised in the old Athenian commonwealth, reputed the first and ancientest place of civility in all Greece, that they had in their several cities a peculiar, in Athens a common government, and their right, as it befell them, to the administration of both.

They should have here also Schools and Academies at their own choice, wherein their children may be bred up in their own sight to all learning and noble education; not in grammar only, but in all liberal arts and exercises. This would soon spread much more knowledge and civility, yea, religion, through all parts of the land, by communicating the natural heat of government and culture more distributively to all extreme parts, which now lie numb and neglected; would soon make the whole nation more industrious, more ingenious at home, more potent, more honourable abroad. To this a Free Commonwealth will easily assent; nay, the Parliament hath had already some such thing in design; for of all governments a Commonwealth aims most to make the people flourishing, virtuous, noble, and high-spirited. Monarchs will never permit; whose aim is to make the people wealthy indeed perhaps, and well fleeced for their own shearing and the supply of regal prodigality, but otherwise softest, basest, viciousest, servilest, easiest to be kept under, and not only in fleece but in mind also sheepishest. And will have all the benches of judicature annexed to the throne, as a gift of royal grace that we have justice done us; whenas nothing can be more essential to the freedom of a people than to have the administration of justice and all public ornaments in their own election, and within their own bounds, without long travelling or depending upon remote places to obtain their right, or any civil accomplishment, so it be not supreme, but subordinate to the general power and union of the whole Republic.

In which happy firmness, as in the particular above-mentioned, we shall also far exceed the United Provinces, by having not as they, to the retarding and distracting ofttimes of their counsels on urgentest occasions, many sovereignties united in one Commonwealth, but many commonwealths under one united and intrusted Sovereignty. And when we have our forces by sea and land, either of a faithful army or a settled militia, in our own hands, to the firm establishing of a free commonwealth, public accounts under our own inspection, general laws and taxes, with their causes in our own domestic suffrages, judicial laws, offices, and ornaments at home in our own ordering and administration, all distinction of lords and commoners that may any way divide or sever the public interest removed; what can a Perpetual Senate have then, wherein to grow corrupt, wherein to encroach upon us, or usurp? Or if they do, wherein to be formidable? Yet if all this avail not to remove the fear or envy of a perpetual sitting, it may be easily provided, to change a third part of them yearly, or every two or three years, as was above mentioned: or that it be at those times in the people's choice, whether they will change them, or renew their power, as they shall find cause.

I have no more to say at present. Few words will save us, well considered; few and easy things, now seasonably done. But if the people be so affected as to prostitute Religion and Liberty to the vain and groundless apprehension that nothing but kingship can restore trade, not remembering the frequent plagues and pestilences that then wasted this city, such as through God's mercy we never have felt since; and that trade flourishes nowhere more than in the Free Commonwealths of Italy, Germany, and the Low Countries, before their eyes at this day; yet if trade be grown so craving and importunate through the profuse living of tradesmen that nothing can support it but the luxurious expenses of a nation upon trifles or superfluities; so as if the people generally should betake themselves to frugality, it might prove a dangerous matter, lest tradesmen should mutiny for want of trading; and that therefore we must forego and set to sale religion, liberty, honour, safety, all concernments divine or human, to keep up trading; if, lastly, after all this light among us, the same reason shall pass for current, to put our necks again under kingship, as was made use of by the Jews to return back to Egypt and to the worship of their idol queen, because they falsely imagined that they then lived in more plenty and prosperity; our condition is not sound, but rotten, both in religion and all civil prudence, and will bring us soon, the way we are marching, to those calamities which attend always and unavoidably on luxury, all national judgments under foreign and domestic slavery: so far we shall be from mending our condition by monarchising our government, whatever new conceit now possesses us.

However, with all hazard I have ventured what I thought my duty to speak in season, and to forewarn my country in time; wherein I doubt not but there be many wise men in all places and degrees, but am sorry the effects of wisdom are so little seen among us. Many circumstances and particulars I could have added in those things whereof I have spoken; but a few main matters now put speedily in execution will suffice to recover us and set all right. And there will want at no time who are good at circumstances; but men who set their minds on main matters and sufficiently urge them, in these most difficult times I find not many.

What I have spoken, is the language of that which is not called amiss "The good old Cause:" if it seem strange to any, it will not seem more strange, I hope, than convincing to backsliders. Thus much I should perhaps have said, though I was sure I should have spoken only to trees and stones; and had none to cry to, but with the prophet, "O earth, earth, earth!" to tell the very soil itself what her perverse inhabitants are deaf to. Nay, though what I have spoke should happen—which thou suffer not, who didst create mankind free, nor thou next, who didst redeem us from being servants of men!—to be the last words of our expiring liberty. But I trust I shall have spoken persuasion to abundance of sensible and ingenious men,—to some, perhaps, whom God may raise from these stones to become children of reviving liberty, and may reclaim, though they seem now choosing them a captain back for Egypt, to bethink themselves a little, and consider whither they are rushing; to exhort this torrent also of the people, not to be so impetuous, but to keep their due channel; and at length recovering and uniting their better resolutions, now that they see already how open and unbounded the insolence and rage is of our common enemies, to stay these ruinous proceedings, justly and timely fearing to what a precipice of destruction the deluge of this epidemic madness would hurry us, through the general defection of a misguided and abused multitude.

THE END.

www.ingramcontent.com/pod-product-compliance
Lightning Source LLC
Chambersburg PA
CBHW022143300426
44115CB00006B/319